ALL ■ IN ■ ONE

Sun Certified Solaris 8 System Administrator

EXAM GUIDE

ALL ▪ IN ▪ ONE

Sun Certified Solaris 8 System Administrator

Paul Watters

McGraw-Hill / Osborne

New York • Chicago • San Francisco • Lisbon
London • Madrid • Mexico City • Milan • New Delhi
San Juan • Seoul • Singapore • Sydney • Toronto

McGraw-Hill/Osborne
2600 Tenth Street
Berkeley, California 94710
U.S.A.

To arrange bulk purchase discounts for sales promotions, premiums, or fund-raisers, please contact McGraw-Hill/Osborne at the above address. For information on translations or book distributors outside the U.S.A., please see the International Contact Information page immediately following the index of this book.

Sun Certified Solaris 8 System Administrator All-in-One Exam Guide

1234567890 DOC DOC 0198765432

Book p/n 0-07-212655-8 and CD p/n 0-07-212656-6
parts of

ISBN 0-07-212657-4

Publisher
Brandon A. Nordin

Vice President & Associate Publisher
Scott Rogers

Editorial Director
Gareth Hancock

Acquisitions Editor
Michael Sprague

Project Manager
Jenn Tust

Acquisitions Coordinators
Paulina Pobocha
Alex Corona

Technical Editor
Tim Gibbs

Cover Design
Greg Scott

Compositor and Indexer
MacAllister Publishing Services, LLC

DEDICATION

This book is dedicated to my nephews, Joshua Lloyd and Vincenzo.
You guys are the coolest.

ACKNOWLEDGMENTS

I would like to acknowledge the professionalism and support of the team at McGraw-Hill/Osborne . Michael Sprague and Gareth Hancock have worked very hard to ensure that this certification title arrived on the market in a timely fashion, but also with a strict commitment to quality. Paulina Pobocha and Alexander Corona provided valuable insight and feedback on each chapter, while Andy Stone (MacAllister Publishing Services, LLC) politely but thoroughly corrected every typo and error in the manuscript. The technical editor, Dr. Tim Gibbs, was tough but fair, as always. Thanks Tim!

To everyone at my agency, Studio B, thanks for your past and continued support. To Neil Salkind and Vicki Harding, my agents, thanks for your wisdom and pragmatic advice. To Kristen Pickens and Stacey Barone, thanks for going in to bat for me! Many thanks to Craig Wiley, who can shoot a dud contract at 100 paces. To Sherry and David Rogelberg, thanks for making it all happen.

To Keith Watson and Ravi Iyer, at Sun Microsystems, thanks for your continued support of my publishing efforts.

Finally, thanks to my family, especially my wife Maya, for always being there, through good times and tough times.

ABOUT THE AUTHOR

Paul A. Watters recently completed his PhD in computer science at Macquarie University. He also has degrees from the University of Cambridge, the University of Tasmania and the University of Newcastle. He has worked in both commercial and R&D organizations, designing systems and software on the Solaris platform. His commercial interests are focused on Java and e-commerce, while his research areas include neural networks, artificial intelligence and natural language processing. He is a columnist for the trade journal Inside Solaris, and has previously written *Solaris 8: The Complete Reference* and *Solaris Administration: A Beginner's Guide*, both published by McGraw-Hill/Osborne. Watters is Managing Director of Cassowary Computing Pty Ltd, and lives with his wife Maya in Sydney, Australia.

BRIEF CONTENTS

CONTENTS

INTRODUCTION

Putting your skills to the test in a certification exam is not an easy task. In the field, you can use your trusty man pages or AnswerBook to look up command options, recall procedures, or ask a colleague for advice. During a certification exam, it's just you, the computer and the exam questions. Even the most experienced and qualified system administrators rightly feel nervous heading into exams! After all, certification exams exist to sort sheep from goats, novices from experts, and by achieving certification, you'll be recognized as an industry professional with up-to-date skills. This will make your resume infinitely more marketable to recruiters and potential employers.

There are several largely unwritten rules about certification exams which it pays to know, especially when taking either of the exams covered in this book. Firstly, remember that the certification exam is going to test your knowledge of the Solaris product *as released by Sun*. Thus, there's not much point reviewing material about non-Sun software for the exams, even if it forms an integral part of your daily sysadmin routine. For example, while you may be asked to interpret a Bourne shell script in the exam, you won't be asked to analyze a Perl script, even though you might use Perl more often "in real life". Secondly, it pays to memorize pesky and seemingly trivial command options for all of the common commands—many a test candidate has been stumped trying to recall a largely unused parameter for a command that they use regularly. Having said that, certification exams do not deliberately try and mislead you, and by examining the table of contents for this book, you'll see that many of the topics are familiar. Thirdly, it pays to practice: use the review questions in the book after reading each chapter to see if you can accurately recall material appropriately, and use the testing tool provided on the CD-ROM to put your skills to the test in real time. Only by simulating actual exam conditions will you truly be able to evaluate your readiness to attempt a certification exam.

PART I

Sun Certified System Administrator for Solaris 8

Taking the Administrator's Exam

The following objectives will be met upon completing this chapter's material:

- What are the Solaris operating environment and the SunOS operating system
- The different types of Solaris certification exams available
- The optional Solaris courses available through Sun Educational Services
- An overview of the exam's target material
- A description of the certification process
- Exam tips and tricks

What Is Solaris?

Solaris is an enterprise-level operating environment that encompasses the multi-process, multi-user Sun Operating System (SunOS). It is a network operating system that runs on Intel-based PC systems as well as systems built around the SPARC and UltraSPARC central processing unit (CPU) architecture. These systems can have up to 64 CPUs operating concurrently in the E10000 server system. Thus, when administrators speak of "Sun," they could be referring to SPARC-based computer systems or the Solaris operating environment.

You might be wondering what Solaris can do, where it came from, and why you should (or shouldn't) use it. Some administrators may be concerned about the use of proprietary hardware, or the often-reported statistic that 80 percent of the world's computers run a Microsoft operating system. Since the average Solaris system can support graphic user interface (GUI) logins for hundreds of users, making comparisons with single-user operating systems like some versions of Microsoft Windows is quite mean-ingless. Different scenarios may well justify the expense of purchasing an E10000 in some organizations, but if you just need domain support and/or centralized filesystem management, then Microsoft Windows might be more appropriate.

Solaris is the dominant UNIX-like operating system on the market today. Sun sys-tems are the hardware of choice for high-availability applications, such as database sys-tems and Web servers, and for computationally intensive tasks, such as modeling and simulation. They are widely deployed in commercial and research and development (R&D) organizations. They also integrate well into heterogeneous networks, composed of Linux and Microsoft Windows systems, particularly as reliable fileservers. For exam-ple, the Network File System (NFS) and the Network Information System (NIS) support Linux clients, while Microsoft Windows clients are supported with Server Message Block (SMB) networking and Samba-based primary domain control. Since Solaris operates largely on a client/server model, clients from multiple operating systems are usually supported.

Sun recently released Solaris 8, which is the latest in a long line of releases that have delivered increased functionality and reliability at each stage. Recent innovations in Solaris include support for 64-bit kernels, high-availability "full moon" clustering, and the adoption of the Common Desktop Environment (CDE), which is the standard, X11-based desktop deployed by most UNIX vendors in recent years.

The benefits of using Solaris over other operating systems typically become apparent in a symmetric multiprocessing (SMP) and/or multi-user environment. Although Microsoft Windows does support multiple CPU support, Solaris supports up to 64 CPUs operating concurrently, with an almost linear scaling of performance. Some other operating systems appear to devote most of the processing capacity of a second, third, or fourth CPU to scheduling rather than operations. In addition, Solaris is particularly suited to supporting hundreds of interactive users on a single system; that is, every user can be "logged in," using a desktop that is being executed on a central server. Although Microsoft Windows features great products like pcAnywhere, which allow users to run a desktop remotely, these products typically only allow a single user to run a session at any one time. Few hard constraints are placed on Solaris systems in terms of support for concurrently logged-in users. This is one major reason why Solaris systems are favored at the enterprise level.

Often, I hear administrators saying that Linux does all of this and more. It's true that Linux has SMP support, and it's also true that Linux is a multi-user system. However, you have to consider the investment that a company makes in both hardware and soft-ware to really understand the main benefits of Solaris as a platform. Solaris is 100 per-cent owned and managed by Sun Microsystems. Linux is developed by Linus Torvalds, and commercial support is provided by a number of different vendors, including Red Hat (**http://www.redhat.com/**) and SuSE (**http://www.suse.com/**). However, although you can pay support fees to these organizations, just like you can pay them to Sun, they do not "own" the source code to the operating system they support, while Sun does. In this sense, Solaris has more in common with Microsoft Windows. It is a proprietary platform that is 100 percent owned and supported by its managing organization.

However, Sun does support the notion that operating system software should be free for educational purposes and developers. This is why they have binary and source license programs for Solaris, where users can receive several CDs full of Solaris software for around U.S.$75 or download them for free. This is not an evaluation version; this is the same version of the software that an enterprise system user will be installing and using on their E10000. Taking advantage of the "free" Solaris program has lured many administrators away from the uncertainties of Linux to the advantages of a Sun-supported and developed product.

Sun has also begun attracting Linux administrators because of its support of the Intel platform for Solaris. Several releases of Solaris for Intel have been made now, and Sun is committed to supporting the platform in the future. Indeed, Microsoft Windows administrators who have shied away from using UNIX in the past because of concerns over proprietary hardware can now install Solaris on their favorite PC. In addition, Solaris fully supports dual-booting on these platforms, meaning that a boot manager like LILO or BootMagic can be used to launch Solaris and/or Microsoft Windows and/or Linux from the same system.

Another feather in Sun's cap has been the specification and development of the Java programming language, which has rapidly grown to capture around 10 percent of the world marketplace in software engineering. This is a phenomenal rise, since Java has only been released in full production for around five years. The basic idea behind Java is that the choice of operating systems should be a separate issue from software design and implementation. That is, good object-oriented development principles should not be sacrificed because a particular language is not available in a standard format on a particular platform. Thus, Java aims to compile and execute on any platform. Binaries generated on Microsoft Windows' development system, for example, can be shipped across to a Solaris deployment server without having to be recompiled, thanks to the cross-platform bytecode developed by Sun. Java also incorporates cross-platform networking and GUI development methods, meaning that a network-monitoring tool written on Solaris should execute exactly the same on a Microsoft Windows or Linux system. This means that the choice of deployment platform can be governed by performance studies and objective testing, rather than irrational and subjective arguments about which operating system is "the best."

In summary, Solaris shares some key features with other operating systems, but it excels in the support of SMP systems, cross-platform OS and developer support, and Sun's capability to control its operating system, but make it available free of charge to educational users and developers. The adoption of the Intel hardware platform is one key attraction for existing Microsoft Windows and Linux administrators.

Another recent advantage is the acquisition of Star Division's StarOffice suite. This product is competitive with Microsoft's Office suite, however, it is completely free for commercial and non-commercial use. It provides an integrated environment for word processing, spreadsheets, presentations, and database applications. It is available in several different European languages. This means that SPARC system users can share data seamlessly with users on the Microsoft Windows and Linux platforms, as Star Office is available on all three.

Solaris, SunOS, and UNIX

The SunOS operating system is a variant of the UNIX operating system, which was originally produced at Bell Laboratories in 1969 by Ken Thompson in an era when mainframes were dominant, and smaller, leaner systems (such as the DEC PDP-7) were a novelty. Most kernels during the 1960s were written using assembly language or machine (binary) code, so the development of a high-level language for writing kernels (the C language) was one of the founding ideas of UNIX. This level of abstraction from hardware meant that kernels could be ported to other hardware platforms without having to be completely rewritten. The tradition of writing kernels in C continues today, with the Linux kernel, for example, being written in C. Obviously, a kernel alone is not a complete operating environment, so many additional applications, such as the visual editor (vi), were later added to what UNIX users would recognize as the suite of standard UNIX tools. In later years, tools such as the Practical Extraction and Reporting Language (Perl) and the GNU GCC compiler would be added to this toolkit.

Two main variants of UNIX systems exist: the commercial version (System V, produced by AT&T) and the Berkeley (BSD) distribution. The split occurred after universities (such as the University of California) were granted source licenses for the UNIX operating system, which they then used as the basis for further development and innovation. After realizing that UNIX may well have some valuable intellectual property, AT&T restricted the terms of the license and began charging fees. The Berkeley group responded by completely rewriting the operating system so that it contained no proprietary code and contained key innovations such as virtual memory and fast filesystems. However, as the two codebases further diverged, some differences in coding style and command options led to many shell scripts being unportable from one system to the next without major revisions. Although the BSD products are still available in the forms of NetBSD and FreeBSD, most commercial UNIX systems are based on AT&T UNIX.

The one exception to this rule is Solaris, which began life as a BSD-style UNIX, but it has slowly migrated to the System V standard. This is because some of the founding fathers at Sun, including Bill Joy, were instrumental in the development of the BSD distribution. It is also one of the reasons that Sun garnered more support in the early years, since they were perceived to be more in touch with their developers, and since their platform growth was essentially developer-driven. In later years, Sun has attempted to make Solaris more compatible with other UNIX systems, adopting the Common Desktop Environment (CDE) over its OpenWindows product, and working towards a Common Open Software Environment (COSE) with IBM, HP, and other enterprise market players.

Sun Microsystems distinguished itself early on as providing a complete end-to-end service for their Solaris systems, based on the high-end SPARC CPU architecture that was specifically designed to work with Solaris. Other hardware innovations included the development of the OpenBoot monitor and integrated power management, which far exceeds the capabilities of a PC Basic Input/Output System (BIOS). In addition, early versions of Solaris introduced SMP support, implemented the Network File System (NFS), and the OpenWindows graphical user environment, which was based on the X11 graphics system. More recently, Solaris has led the way for the UNIX industry by complying with relevant standards (such as UNIX 95 and UNIX 98) as well as improving NFS, developing high-availability and clustering solutions, and enhanced volume management. In addition, the introduction of 64-bit kernels, Java, JumpStart installations, and the integration of Kerberos authentication into its security architecture have greatly benefited Solaris users and administrators. Solaris now features a number of standard tools, such as package, patch, and storage management, which are supported by a Portable Operating System Interface for UNIX (POSIX)-compliant development environment.

Solaris Certification Exams

Now that we've examined what Solaris is, we'll look at the certification process for Solaris. The two exams we will cover in this book are

- Sun Certified System Administrator for the Solaris 8 Operating Environment Part I (310-011)

- Sun Certified System Administrator for the Solaris 8 Operating Environment Part II (310-011)

These exams were also available for Solaris 7 and previous releases. The exams will be referred to as Sysadmin I and Sysadmin II throughout this book. It's important to note that passing both Sysadmin I and Sysadmin II is required for full certification.

Booking a test can be done in several ways. You must contact Sun Educational Services through one of the following ways and purchase a voucher:

- Snail: UBRM12-175, 500 Eldorado Blvd., Broomfield, CO 80021

- Phone: (800) 422-8020 or (303) 464-4097

- Fax: (303) 464-4490

- WWW: **http://suned.sun.com/USA/certification/**

Once you have a voucher for the test you want to take, you need to contact a Prometric Test Center at a location that is convenient to you. You can register online with Prometric at **http://www.2test.com/**. Once you have attended the center and taken both Sysadmin Part I and Sysadmin Part II, you'll be certified immediately if you have passed both exams. Of course, you don't need to take them on the same day; it makes sense to attempt Sysadmin I and pass it before attempting Sysadmin II. Since Sysadmin I is a prerequisite for Sysadmin II, you won't be able to book a sitting for Sysadmin II until your Sysadmin I results are certified.

The current costs for attempting Sysadmin I and Sysadmin II are $150 each. Sysadmin I has 57 questions, comprising multiple choice, free response, and drag and drop types. You will need a score of at least 66 percent to pass the test, and you will only have 90 minutes in which to complete it. Sysadmin II has 61 questions, comprising multiple choice, free response, and drag and drop types. You will need a score of at least 70 percent to pass the test, and you will only have 90 minutes in which to complete it.

Solaris Exam Preparation Courses

Three preparation courses are available for Solaris certification:

- Fundamentals of Solaris 8 Operating Environment for System Administrators (SA-118)

- Solaris 8 System Administration I (SA-238)

- Solaris 8 System Administration II (SA-288)

Let's examine what material is covered in each exam.

Fundamentals of Solaris 8 Operating Environment for System Administrators (SA-118)

If you're completely new to Solaris, you may benefit from taking one or more of the exams that does not lead to a specific certification test. The Fundamentals of Solaris 8 Operating Environment for System Administrators (SA-118) is one such course. It is designed to endow up-and-coming administrators with basic UNIX skills, including the following:

- Navigating the hierarchical filesystem
- Setting file permissions
- Using the vi visual editor
- Using UNIX shells
- Understanding Solaris network facilities

After completing the course, students should feel confident performing the following tasks:

- Changing settings in configuration files
- Creating new directories
- Creating new text files and edit existing files using vi
- Identifying and sending signals to user processes
- Moving around mounted filesystems
- Setting permissions on existing files
- Using a shell to execute commands
- Using the Common Desktop Environment (CDE)

Solaris 8 System Administration I (SA-238)

The SA-238 course aims to build a set of core skills required to administer standalone Solaris systems. Typically, these core skills are what is required to install and run a single Solaris system, including

- The management of disks, filesystems, and partitions
- Backup and restore techniques

- User and group administration

- Hardware device configuration

- Process management and operations

The course lasts for five days and costs $2,495. After completing the course, newly skilled sysadmins should feel confident performing the following tasks:

- Adding users and groups to a system

- Adding new packages

- Backing up a system and recovering a lost filesystem

- Changing a system's run-level (init state)

- Configuring hardware devices

- Controlling user and system processes

- Managing system printing

- Mounting filesystems

- Patching existing packages

- Recovering damaged filesystems using fsck

- Reviewing disk layout using format

- Securing a system

- Setting up system-wide shell configurations

- Shutting down a system

- Understanding client-server architectures

- Understanding the root filesystem and the UNIX directory structure

- Using eeprom to set boot parameters

- Using file permissions to implement file security

The course consists of 17 different modules, including the following topics:

- Module 1: Introduction to Solaris 8 Operating Environment Administration

- Module 2: Adding Users

- Module 3: System Security

- Module 4: The Directory Hierarchy

- Module 5: Device Configuration
- Module 6: Disks, Slices, and Format
- Module 7: Solaris ufs File Systems
- Module 8: Mounting File Systems
- Module 9: Maintaining File Systems
- Module 10: Scheduled Process Control
- Module 11: The Print Service
- Module 12: The Boot PROM
- Module 13: System Initialization of the Boot Process
- Module 14: Installing the Solaris 8 Operating Environment on a Standalone System
- Module 15: Installation of Software Packages
- Module 16: Administration of Software Patches
- Module 17: Backup and Recovery

Solaris 8 System Administration II (SA-288)

The SA-288 course aims to build a set of core skills required to administer networked Solaris systems. Typically, these are the skills required to install and run multiple Solaris systems and Solaris networks. The course lasts for five days and costs $2,495. After completing the course, newly skilled network admins should feel confident performing the following tasks:

- Centralizing home directory access using the automounter
- Configuring the major naming services
- Installation of multiple Solaris client systems using JumpStart
- Installation of Solaris server systems
- Managing systems remotely
- Sharing disks using the Network File System (NFS) protocol
- Using the system log facility
- Using the admintool
- Volume management

The course consists of 13 different modules, including the following topics:

- Module 1: The Solaris 8 Network Environment
- Module 2: Network Models
- Module 3: Solaris Syslog
- Module 4: Introduction to Virtual Disk Management
- Module 5: Introduction to Swap Space and Pseudo File Systems
- Module 6: Configuring the NFS Environment
- Module 7: CacheFS File Systems
- Module 8: Using Automount
- Module 9: Naming Services Overview
- Module 10: NIS Configuration
- Module 11: Solstice AdminSuite
- Module 12: JumpStart
- Module 13: System Administration Workshop

What's on the Exam?

The topics covered in the Sysadmin I exam map those covered in the SA-238 course. These topics include

- Adding users and groups
- Securing a Solaris system
- Understanding directory structures
- Configuring devices
- Using the format command
- Understanding UFS filesystems
- Mounting filesystems
- Filesystem housekeeping
- Scheduling processes
- Managing printing
- Using the OpenBoot PROM monitor

- Understanding run levels
- Switching init states
- Installing Solaris
- Adding and removing packages
- Backing up and recovering a system

The topics covered in the Sysadmin I exam map those covered in the SA-238 course. These topics include

- Understanding the basics of Solaris networking
- Reviewing the OSI networking model and its application to the TCP/IP suite of network protocols
- Logging system events using the syslog facility
- Managing virtual disks and other storage systems (including swap space and pseudo-filesystems)
- Installing and configuring NFS, and sharing disks across the network
- Understanding the caching filesystem (CacheFS)
- Centralizing home directories using the automounter
- Setting up naming services like DNS and NIS
- Using AdminSuite
- Automating installations with JumpStart

Exam Tips and Tricks

A comprehensive strategy is required to ensure success in passing the Solaris certification exams. This strategy should be based around at least some of the following components:

- Taking the preparatory courses
- Practicing your skills on a Solaris system and/or network
- Reading books on Solaris (including this book)
- Reading man pages
- Practicing the questions in this book
- Signing up for a simulated exam service

Without a study plan, even experienced Solaris system administrators may fail the certification exam. This is because the exams are based on the "official" Sun information on many system administration issues, which may differ substantially from what is used in the field. For example, many sites don't use the Internet super daemon inetd to provide remote access facilities and other network services: they often use more secure alternatives. However, alternative methods will not be covered in the exam, so we rarely mention them in the text.

Taking at least some of the preparatory courses ensures that you will be familiar with most of the material that is found on the certification exams. This material is prepared by Sun Educational Services, the same group who develop the exams. Thus, a certain degree of overlap should be anticipated between course materials and exam contents. However, it should be noted that not all of the course material will be examined, and that some process-based questions can only be effectively answered by practical experience using and administering Solaris systems.

This is why it is critical that, as a prospective Solaris administrator, you gain access to a Solaris as a user, and preferably as an administrator. Even supervised administrative access, with a senior staff member or colleague assisting you, will give you the experience and perspective you need to be able to answer questions on operational issues. You cannot expect to pass the exams if you've never used a Solaris system in real life.

You should also read widely on Solaris. This includes companion volumes such as *Solaris 8: The Complete Reference* and *Solaris Administration: A Beginner's Guide*, both published by Osborne/McGraw-Hill. These books cover some common material with this book, but cover some topics in more depth, and contain longer and more detailed examples.

Reading man pages is an essential review process for memorizing command options. This is because some exam questions may not just pertain to the Solaris command set, but also to the multitude of options available for each command. You should consult the man pages when you're using commands to ensure that you're using the most appropriate options for a specific command. However, if you'd like to consult man pages offline, *UNIX In A Nutshell*, published by O'Reilly, contains many annotated man pages. Note that these are not Solaris-specific, and some options may not work on Solaris 8.

It's important to attempt the questions contained in this book as if you were taking the exam. Sitting for two to three hours under exam conditions will help you to develop strategies for best answering the questions contained in the test. In addition to the practice questions contained in this book, it may be useful for you to purchase a subscription to one of the online certification practice tests, offered at the following sites:

- http://networkessentials.com/certified/sca/

- http://www.inlink.com/~hoechstj/solaris/

- http://www.solariscert.com/

- http://www.solarisprep.com/

- http://www.sunguru.com/

- http://www.learnsolaris.com/

One excellent way to determine whether your skills are up to speed is to join the comp.unix.solaris Usenet forum and see whether you can answer some of the more "frequently asked questions" there.

The Web also offers some great sites. You can learn more about Solaris from the Sun Microsystems home page for Solaris (**http://www.sun.com**). (Some key documents within the Sun site for Solaris include the following:

- Solaris overview (**http://www.sun.com/software/solaris/ds/ds-sol8oe/**)

- Solaris downloads (**http://www.sun.com/software/solaris/downloads.html**)

- Solaris support (**http://www.sun.com/software/solaris/support.html**)

- Solaris education (**http://www.sun.com/software/solaris/education.html**)

- Solaris clustering (**http://www.sun.com/software/fullmoon/**)

- Solaris Intel platform (**http://www.sun.com/software/intel**)

Possibly the most important link on the Sun site is the documentation at **http://docs.sun.com**). (Here you can interactively search or browse all of the Sun documentation and/or download entire manuals in PDF format. These manuals include the following:

- 64-bit developer's guide

- Binary compatibility guide

- CDE transition guide

- CDE user guide

- Device drivers guide

- Internationalization guide

- JumpStart guide

- Mail server guide

- Naming services guide
- NFS administration guide
- NIS+ guide
- OpenWindows user guide
- Power management user guide
- Source compatibility guide
- SPARC assembly language guide
- STREAMS guide
- SunShield security guide
- System administration guides
- TCP/IP guide
- Troubleshooting guides
- WebNFS developer's guide

Two FAQs for Solaris are available at **http://www.wins.uva.nl/pub/solaris/solaris2/** and **http://sun.pmbc.com/faq/** for Solaris SPARC and Solaris Intel respectively. If you prefer a mailing list format to Usenet, then you should definitely join the Sun Manager's List at **ftp://ftp.cs.toronto.edu/pub/jdd/sun-managers/faq**.

Summary

In this chapter, we've examined the structure and components of Solaris certification tests, the courses available from Sun Educational Services that prepare students for taking the tests, and a comprehensive strategy for ensuring success in the tests. This strategy recommends a mix of private study, practical experience, and exam practice to ensure success.

System Concepts

The following objectives will be met upon completing this chapter's material:

- Understanding the role of the kernel, shell, and filesystem
- Reviewing commonly used Solaris shells
- Investigating the distinction between a multi-user system and a multi-tasking system
- Exploring the role of clients and servers
- Defining hosts, hostnames, networks, and IP addresses

Understanding what makes Solaris different to other operating systems is critical to appreciating why it is the environment of choice for high-availability, client-server environments. In this chapter, we review the terms used to describe Solaris systems and their major components, as well as the networking terminology associated with Solaris networks. This will ensure that later chapters can be understood within a specific context, since some generic terms may have a specific meaning in Solaris, but not in other operating systems. For example, although the term "host" may be used generically to identify any system attached to a network, it may be used more specifically in Solaris such as when referring to multi-homed hosts, for instance.

The Kernel

Operating systems are the building blocks of computer systems and provide the interface between user applications and computer hardware. Solaris is a multi-user, multi-tasking operating system, developed and sold by Sun Microsystems (**http://www.sun.com/**), and is one implementation of the UNIX operating system that draws on both the

System V (AT&T) and Berkeley (BSD) systems. It has risen from little more than a research project to become the dominant UNIX operating system in the international marketplace today. Solaris 8 is the latest in a long line of operating environment releases that are based around the SunOS operating system, which is currently in version 5.8. Solaris is commonly found in large corporations and educational institutions that require concurrent, multi-user access on individual hosts and between hosts connected via the Internet.

Many desktop computer users have never heard of the word Sun in the context of computing, nor are they usually familiar with the term Solaris as an operating environment. However, almost every time that an Internet user sends an e-mail message, or opens a file from a networked server running Sun's Network File System (NFS) product, Solaris is transparently supporting many of today's existing Internet applications. In the enterprise computing industry, Sun is synonymous with highly available, highly reliable performance hardware, while Solaris is often the operating environment of choice to support database servers and application servers. Sun's hardware solutions are based around the SPARC and UltraSPARC integrated circuit technologies, which currently support up to 128 processors in a single-server system (the E10000 StarFire configuration).

It is hard to define what UNIX is, because different vendors have historically introduced different features to arrive at the entities that most users would think of as UNIX. However, it is easy enough to list the fundamental characteristics that are common to all UNIX and UNIX-like systems:

- They have a kernel, written in the C programming language, which mainly manages input/output processing, rather than being a complete operating system. The kernel has the ultimate responsibility for allocating system resources to complete various tasks.

- They have a hierarchical filesystem, which begins with a "root" directory, and from which the "branches" of all other directories (and filesystems) are mounted.

- System hardware devices are represented logically on the filesystem as special files (such as /dev/pty for pseudo-terminals).

- They are process-based, with all services and user shells being represented a single identifying number (the process ID or PID).

- They share a set of command-line utilities that can be used for various text and numeric processing, such as troff, col, cat, head, tbl, and so on.

- User processes can be spawned from a shell, such as the Bourne shell, which interactively execute application programs.

- Multiple processes can be executed concurrently by a single user and sent into the background by using the "&" operator.

- Multiple users can execute commands concurrently by logging in from pseudo-terminals.

Note that a graphical user interface (GUI) is not necessarily a defining feature of UNIX, unlike other desktop operating systems that place a lot of stock in "look and feel," even though most UNIX systems support X11 graphics and the Common Desktop Environment (CDE). Solaris also supports the GNOME desktop, which was primarily developed for Linux. The reasons for the distinction between user interface and back-end processing are largely historical and relate to the UNIX design philosophy, as we will see later in this chapter. The layering of the various components of a UNIX system is shown in Figure 2-1.

Broadly speaking, a UNIX system is layered according to applications, which are invoked through user shells that are managed by a kernel, which in turn, uses filesystems to create a persistence storage mechanism. Since the kernel provides the interface between shells and the filesystem (and by extension, between applications and the filesystem), it is considered the central part of UNIX technology.

Solaris kernels can trace their origins to both the System V and BSD variants of UNIX, while Microsoft NT is based on the VMS kernel originally developed for the high-end VAX systems. Most kernels during the 1960s were written using assembly language or machine (binary) code, so the development of a high-level language for writing kernels (the C language) was one of the founding ideas of UNIX. This level of abstraction from hardware meant that kernels could be ported to other hardware platforms without

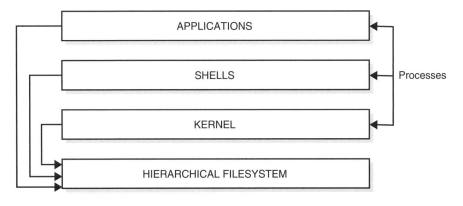

Figure 2-1   Components of a UNIX system

having to be completely rewritten. The tradition of writing kernels in C continues today, with the Linux kernel, for example, being written in C. Obviously, a kernel alone is not a complete operating environment, so many additional applications, such as the visual editor (vi), were later added to what UNIX users would recognize as the suite of standard UNIX tools.

All UNIX systems have a kernel, which is the central logical processor that provides an interface between the system hardware and the system services and user shells that directly enable applications. For example, support for network interfaces is provided in the form a kernel module and a device file that logically represents the physical device. Services are defined in the services database, and network daemons provide the final layer for supporting applications that use the network to transmit data. Since UNIX kernels are typically written in the C programming language, many system-level applications and daemons are also written in C.

Of course, UNIX systems share some common characteristics with other operating systems, including the use of a hierarchical filesystem, in which special files called directories are used to logically arrange related files. But UNIX has some distinctive features as well; explicit permissions to read, execute, and modify files on the UNIX filesystem can be granted to specific users or groups of users, making it easy to share work and collaborate with other users on the system.

Since UNIX was created by active developers, rather than operating system gurus, there was always a strong focus on creating an operating system that suited programmers' needs. A *Bell System Technical Journal* article in 1978 lists the key guiding principles of UNIX development:

- Create small, self-contained programs that perform a single task. When a new task needs to be solved, either create a new program that performs it or combine tools from the toolset that already exist to arrive at a solution. This is a similar orientation to the current trend towards encapsulation and independent component building (such as Enterprise Java Beans) where complicated systems are built from smaller, interacting, but logically-independent modules.

- Programs should accept data from standard input and write to standard input. Thus, programs can be "chained" to process each other's output sequentially. Interactive input should be avoided in favor of command-line options that specify a program's actions to be performed. Presentation should be separated from what a program is trying to achieve. These ideas are consistent with the concept of piping, which is still fundamental to the operation of user shells. For example, the output of the ls command to list all files in a directory can be "piped" using the | symbol to a program such as grep to perform pattern matching. The number of pipes on a single command line instruction is not limited.

- Creating a new operating system or program should be undertaken on a scale of weeks not years. The creative spirit that leads to cohesive design and implementation should be exploited. If software doesn't work, then don't be afraid to built something better. This process of iterative revisions of programs has resurfaced in recent years with the rise of object-oriented development.

- Make the best use of all the tools available, rather than asking for more help. The motivation behind UNIX is to construct an operating system that supports the kinds of toolsets that are required for successful development.

This is not intended to be an exhaustive list of the kernel-oriented characteristics that define UNIX, but these features are central to understanding the importance that UNIX developers often ascribe to the operating system. It is designed to be a programmer-friendly system.

The Shell

A key Solaris concept is the functional separation between the user interface and the operating system. This distinction means that a user can access a Solaris system by using either a terminal-based character user interface (CUI) or a high-resolution graphical user interface (GUI), without modifying the underlying operating system.

If so much attention has been paid to GUI environments, why are CUI environments still important to Solaris? Are they just a historical hangover that Windows has managed to overcome? Or are they simply the tools of choice for long-haired network administrators who have never used a mouse? In fact, mastering the Solaris command line is one of the effective tools available under any UNIX environment, and the good news is, it's not that difficult to learn. Using the command line (or shell) has the following advantages over GUI environments:

- The shell is essential for programming repetitive tasks, which can only be performed laboriously through a GUI. An example would be searching a filesystem for all document files that have changed each day, and making a copying of all these files (with the extension .doc) to a backup directory (with the extension .bak).

- The shell can be used to search for, modify, edit, and replace Solaris configuration files, which are typically storied in text format. This is much like the approach taken with Windows .ini configuration files, which were text-based. However, versions of Windows after Windows 95 used the Registry to store configuration information in a binary format, making it impossible to manually edit. All Solaris configuration files (including the startup scripts described in Chapters 2 and 3) are text-based.

- The shell has a number of built-in commands that typically mirror those provided in the C programming language. This means it is possible to write small programs as shell statements that are executed as sequential steps, without having to use a compiler (just like MS-DOS batch files are interpreted without requiring a compiler).

- The shell can be used to launch applications that use a CUI, which is especially useful for logging in to a remote system, and the shell can use all the commands that the administrator uses on the console. In the era of global information systems, this is very useful. Although Windows applications like Symantec's pcAnywhere can be used for remote access to the Windows desktop, they don't easily support multi-user access (or multi-user access where one user requires a CUI and another a GUI).

- The shell can be used to execute commands for which no equivalent GUI application exists. Although many operations could conceivably be performed using a GUI, it is usually easier to write a shell script than to create a completely new GUI application. Some commonly used shells include Bourne shell, C shell, Cornell shell, and Bourne again shell.

Many applications in Solaris, Linux, and Windows are now available through a GUI interface. If you feel more comfortable using GUI interfaces, there is little reason to stop using them if you can find the tools to perform all of the tasks you need to undertake regularly, such as monitoring resource usage, setting process alarms and diagnostics, and/or remote access. However, if you want to make the most of Solaris and competently administer the system, you will need to become familiar with the shell and command-line utilities.

The Filesystem

UNIX also features a hierarchical filesystem, which makes it easy to logically separate related files into directories, which are themselves special files. Although MS-DOS and similar operating systems feature a hierarchical filesystem that offers simple file access permissions (such as read-only), UNIX has a complete user-based file access permission system. Like process management, each file on the system is "owned" by a specific user, and by default, only that user can perform operations on that file. Privileged users can perform all operations on all files on the filesystem. Interestingly, a special file permission allows unprivileged users to execute certain commands and applications with super-user privileges (setuid).

The following filesystem types are supported by the kernel:

- **cachefs**   The CacheFS cached filesystem

- **hsfs**   The High Sierra file system

- **nfs**   The Network File System (NFS)

- **pcfs**   The MS-DOS filesystem

- **tmpfs**   A filesystem that uses memory

- **ufs**   The standard UNIX filesystem

The default local filesystem type is contained in the /etc/default/fs file, while the default remote filesystem type is contained in the /etc/default/fstypes file.

Commonly Used Shells

In keeping with the philosophy that different administrators have different needs and styles, several different shells are available under Solaris that you can choose from:

- **Bourne shell (sh)**   The original UNIX shell that is used to write all system scripts by convention

- **C shell (Csh)**   Has a command syntax similar to the C programming language

- **Cornell Shell (Tcsh)**   Has improved terminal handling compared to the original C Shell

- **Bourne Again Shell (Bash)**   Is an open source, much improved version of the Bourne shell

Multi-user Versus Multi-tasking

Operating systems like MS-DOS are single-user, single-task systems; they are designed to be used by a single user who wants to execute a single program from the shell. However, with advances in CPU technology, even the humble MS-DOS shell has expanded to allow multi-tasking, allowing more than one application to execute concurrently. This approach has been extended even further with Microsoft Windows to allow several applications to be executed concurrently in a GUI environment. In addition, Microsoft

Windows has support for multiple users, although it is generally only possible for a single user to initiate a "console" session, limiting its concurrency.

UNIX provides the best of both worlds, since it is designed from the ground up to permit multiple users to initiate multiple shells, which in turn can execute multiple applications. In addition, Solaris supports lightweight processes, such as threads, which allow the traditional concept of multi-tasking to be generalized to execute multiple threads within a single process. Solaris also supports symmetric multi-processing, meaning that the physical execution of processes, threads, and user applications may occur on one of many different supported processors.

Client-Server Networks

Although PC operating systems were designed in response to the waning of client-server systems, Solaris and other UNIX systems are firmly designed as client-server systems. Although a PC is designed to run many high-powered applications using the local CPU, a client-server network is designed around the concept of multiple "thin" clients accessing data and executing applications on a "fat" centralized server, or a number of servers that are dedicated to one particular purpose. For example, a typical Solaris network might consist of hundreds of Sun Ray thin client systems, which are supported on the front-line by several E450 departmental servers as well as a set of rack-mounted 420R systems that run database, Web server, and development systems.

The client-server topology is also reflected in the structure of UNIX services. Client applications running on client systems are designed to connect through to server applications running on server systems. Sun was instrumental in initiating key distributed computing technologies, such as the Remote Procedure Call (RPC) technology used in the Network File System (NFS) protocol. In addition, the Remote Method Invocation (RMI) technology developed as part of the Java networking and distributed computing APIs allows objects to be passed around the network as seamlessly as RPC.

Networking Terminology

A Solaris network consists of a number of different hosts that are interconnected using a switch or a hub. Solaris networks connect to each other by using routers, which can be dedicated hardware systems, or by using Solaris itself, with systems that have more than one network interface. Each host on a Solaris network is identified by a unique hostname. These hostnames often reflect the function of the host in question. For example, a set of four Web servers may have the hostnames www1, www2, www3, and www4 respectively.

Every host and network that is connected to the Internet uses the Internet Protocol (IP) to support higher-level protocols such as TCP and UDP. Every interface of every host on the Internet has a unique IP address, which is based on the network IP address block assigned to the local network. Networks are addressable by using an appropriate netmask that corresponds to a Class A (255.0.0.0), Class B (255.255.0.0), or Class C (255.255.255.0) network respectively.

Solaris supports multiple Ethernet interfaces that can be installed on a single machine. These are usually designated by files like

```
/etc/hostname.hmen
```

or for older machines

```
/etc/hostname.len
```

where *n* is the interface number, and le and hme are interface types.

Interface files contain a single IP address, with the primary network interface being designated with an interface number of zero. Thus, the primary interface of a machine called server would be defined by the file /etc/server.hme0, which might contain the IP address 203.17.64.28.

A secondary network interface, connected to a different subnet, might be defined in the file /etc/server.hme1. In this case, the file might contain the IP address 10.17.65.28. This setup is commonly used in organizations that have a provision for a failure of the primary network interface or that enables load balancing of server requests across multiple subnets (such as for an intranet Web server processing HTTP requests).

A system with a second network interface can either act as a router or as a multi-homed host. Hostnames and IP addresses are locally administered through a naming service, which is usually the Domain Name Service (DNS) for companies connected to the Internet and the Network Information Service (NIS/NIS+) for companies with large internal networks that require administrative functions beyond what DNS provides, including centralized authentication.

It is also worth mentioning at this point that it is quite possible to assign different IP addresses to the same network interface. This can be useful for hosting virtual domains that require their own IP address, rather than relying on application-level support for multi-homing (such as when using the Apache Web server). Simply create a new /etc/hostname.hmeX:Y file for each IP address required, where X represents the physical device interface and Y represents the virtual interface number.

The subnet mask used by each of these interfaces must also be defined in /etc/net-masks. This is particularly important if the interfaces lie on different subnets or if they serve different network classes. In addition, it might also be appropriate to assign a fully qualified domain name to each of the interfaces, although this will depend on the purpose to which each interface is assigned.

Summary

In this chapter, we examined some basic system concepts, such as the client-server system, as well as basic networking terms, such as IP addresses and hostnames. Understanding these concepts is necessary to make best use of the Solaris operating environment.

Questions

1. Which of the following best describes Solaris?
   A. Single-user, single-process
   B. Single-user, multi-process
   C. Multi-user, single-process
   D. Multi-user, multi-process

2. What is the main responsibility of the kernel?
   A. Allocating system resources to complete assigned tasks
   B. Displaying graphics using X11
   C. Managing applications
   D. Choosing the appropriate shell

3. What sort of native filesystem does Solaris support?
   A. A flat filesystem, which begins with a C:\ directory
   B. A hierarchical filesystem, which begins with a root directory
   C. A flat filesystem, which begins with a root directory
   D. A hierarchical filesystem, which begins with a C:\ directory

4. How are hardware devices logically represented on Solaris hosts?
   A. Special files
   B. Database entries

PART I

   C. Device plug-ins

   D. Control panel

5. How are processes distinguished in Solaris?

   A. Process names

   B. Command names

   C. Process IDs

   D. Session variables

6. Which of the following filesystems is NOT supported by Solaris?

   A. High-Sierra

   B. Joliet

   C. UFS

   D. MS-DOS

7. Which of the following subnets matches with a Class B network?

   A. 255.0.0.0

   B. 255.255.0.0

   C. 0.255.255.255

   D. 255.255.255.255

8. Which would the file /etc/hostname.hme0 contain?

   A. Hostname of interface hme0

   B. IP address of interface hme0

   C. Netmask of interface hme0

   D. Ethernet address of interface hme0

Answers

1. D
2. A
3. B
4. A
5. C
6. B
7. B
8. B

The OpenBoot PROM

The following objectives will be met upon completing this chapter's material:

- Analyze host setup details using OpenBoot commands
- Change the default boot device
- Test system hardware
- Create device aliases using nvalias
- Remove custom devices using nvunalias
- Diagnose and troubleshoot booting problems
- Halt a hung system

The OpenBoot PROM Monitor

One of the main hardware differences between SPARC systems which run Solaris and PC systems which run Linux or Microsoft Windows is that SPARC systems have an Open Boot PROM monitor program, which can be used to modify firmware settings prior to booting. It is based on the Forth programming language, and can be used to run Forth programs which perform the following functions:

- Booting the system, by using the boot command
- Performing diagnostics on hardware devices by using the diag command
- Testing network connectivity by using the watch-net command

The OpenBoot monitor has two prompts from which commands can be issued: the ok prompt, and the > prompt. In order to switch from the > prompt to the ok prompt, you simply need to type **n**:

```
> n
ok
```

Commands are typically issued from the ok prompt. These commands include boot, which boots a system from the default system boot device, or from an optional device specified at the prompt. Thus, if a system is at run level 0, and needs to be booted, the boot command with no options specified will boot the system:

```
ok boot
SPARCstation 20, Type 5 Keyboard
ROM Rev. 2.4, 256 MB memory installed, Serial #456543
Ethernet address 5:2:12:c:ee:5a HostID 456543
Rebooting with command:
Boot device:
/iommu@f,e0000000/sbus@f,e0001000/espdma@f,400000/esp@f,8...
SunOS Release 5.8 Version Generic 32-bit
Copyright (c) 1983-2000 by Sun Microsystems, Inc.
configuring IPv4 interfaces: hme0.
Hostname: winston
The system is coming up. Please wait.
checking ufs filesystems
/dev/rdsk/c0t0d0s1: is clean.
NIS domainname is Cassowary.Net.
starting rpc services: rpcbind keyserv ypbind done.
Setting netmask of hme0 to 255.255.255.0
Setting default IPv4 interface for multicast: add net 224.0/
4: gateway winston
syslog service starting.
Print services started.
volume management starting.
The system is ready.
winston console login:
```

Alternatively, if you have modified your hardware configuration since the last boot, and you want the new devices to be recognized, you should always reboot using the command

```
ok boot -r
```

This is equivalent to performing a reconfiguration boot using the following command sequence in a shell as the superuser:

```
# touch /reconfigure; sync; init 6
```

So far, we've looked at automatic booting. However, sometimes it is desirable to perform a manual boot, using the command boot -a, where parameters at each stage of the booting process can be specified. These parameters include the

- Path to the kernel that you wish to boot
- Path to the kernel's modules directory
- Path to the system file
- Type of the root filesystem
- Name of the root device

For example, if we wished to use a different kernel, such as an experimental kernel, we would enter the following parameters during a manual boot:

```
Rebooting with command: boot -a
Boot device: /pci@1f,0/pci@1,2/ide@1/disk@0,1:a File and args: -a
Enter filename [kernel/sparcv9/unix]: kernel/experimental/unix
Enter default directory for modules [/platform/SUNW,Sparc-20/kernel
/platform/sun4m/kernel /kernel /usr/kernel]:
Name of system file [etc/system]:
SunOS Release 5.8 Version Generic 64-bit
Copyright (c) 1983-2000 by Sun Microsystems, Inc.
root filesystem type [ufs]:
Enter physical name of root device
[/pci@1f,0/pci@1,2/ide@1/disk@0,1:a]:
```

To accept the default parameters, simply press enter when prompted. Thus, to only change the path to the experimental kernel, we would enter **kernel/experimental/unix** at the **Enter filename** prompt.

Analyzing System Configuration

To view the OpenBoot release information for your firmware, and the system configuration, use the command:

```
ok banner
SPARCstation 20, Type 5 Keyboard
ROM Rev. 2.4, 256 MB memory installed, Serial #456543
Ethernet address 5:2:12:c:ee:5a HostID 456543
```

Here, we can see the system is a SPARCstation 20, with a standard keyboard, and that the OpenBoot release level is 2.4. There are 256M RAM installed on the system, which has a hostid of 456543. Finally, the ethernet address of the primary ethernet device is 5:2:12:c:ee:5a.

Changing the Default Boot Device

To boot from the default boot device (usually the primary hard drive), you would type

```
ok boot
```

However, it is also possible to boot using the CDROM by using the command

```
ok boot cdrom
```

The system may be booted from a host on the network by using the command

```
ok boot net
```

Alternatively, if you have a boot floppy, the following command may be used:

```
ok boot floppy
```

As many early Solaris distributions were made on magnetic tape, it's also possible to boot using a tape drive with the following command:

```
ok boot tape
```

Instead of specifying a different boot device each time you want to reboot, it is possible to set an environment variable within the OpenBoot monitor, so that a specific device is booted by default. For example, to set the default boot device to be the primary hard disk, you would use the following command:

```
ok setenv boot-device disk
boot-device = disk
```

To verify that the boot device has been set correctly to disk, the following command can be used:

```
ok printenv boot-device
boot-device disk disk
```

To reset the system to use the new settings, you simply use the reset command:

```
ok reset
```

To set the default boot device to be the primary network device, you would use the following command:

```
ok setenv boot-device net
boot-device = net
```

This configuration is commonly used for diskless clients, such as Sun Rays, which use RARP and NFS to boot across the network. To verify that the boot device has been set correctly to net, the following command can be used:

```
ok printenv boot-device
boot-device net disk
```

To set the default boot device to be the primary CD-ROM device, you would use the following command:

```
ok setenv boot-device cdrom
boot-device = cdrom
```

To verify that the boot device has been set correctly to cdrom, the following command can be used:

```
ok printenv boot-device
boot-device cdrom disk
```

To set the default boot device to be the primary floppy drive, you would use the following command:

```
ok setenv boot-device floppy
boot-device = floppy
```

To verify that the boot device has been set correctly to floppy, the following command can be used:

```
ok printenv boot-device
boot-device floppy disk
```

To set the default boot device to be the primary tape drive, you would use the following command:

```
ok setenv boot-device tape
boot-device = tape
```

To verify that the boot device has been set correctly to tape, the following command can be used:

```
ok printenv boot-device
boot-device tape disk
```

Testing System Hardware

The test command is used to test specific hardware devices, such as the loopback network device. This device could be tested by using the command:

```
ok test net
Internal Loopback test - (OK)
External Loopback test - (OK)
```

This indicates that the loopback device is operating correctly. Alternatively, the watch-clock command is used to test the clock device.

```
ok watch-clock
Watching the 'seconds' register of the real time clock chip.
 It should be ticking once a second.
 Type any key to stop.
1
2
3
```

These results can be cross-checked against a reliable timing device for accuracy.

If the system is meant to boot across the network, but a boot attempt does not succeed, it is possible to test network connectivity using the watch-net program. This determines whether or not the system's primary network interface is able to read packets from the network which it is connected to. The output from watch-net program looks like

```
Internal Loopback test - succeeded
External Loopback test - succeeded
Looking for Ethernet packets.
'.' is a good packet. 'X' is a bad packet.
Type any key to stop
......X.........XXXX.........XX............
```

In this case, a number of packets are marked as bad, even though the system has been connected successfully to the network.

In addition to the watch-net command, the OpenBoot monitor can perform a number of other diagnostic tests. For example, all the SCSI devices attached to the system can be detected by using the probe-scsi command. The probe-scsi command displays all the SCSI devices attached to the system. The output of probe-scsi looks like this:

```
ok probe-scsi all
Target 1
Unit 0 Disk SUN0104 Copyright (C) 1995 Sun Microsystems All rights
reserved
Target 1
Unit 0 Disk SUN0207 Copyright (C) 1995 Sun Microsystems All rights
reserved
```

Here, we can see that two SCSI disks have been detected. If any other disks or SCSI devices were attached to the chain, they have not been detected, indicating a misconfiguration or hardware error.

Creating and Removing Device Aliases

The OpenBoot monitor is able to store certain environment variables in nonvolatile RAM (NVRAM), so that they can be used from boot to boot, by using the nvalias command. For example, to set the network device to use RARP for booting, we would use the following command:

```
ok nvalias net /pci@1f,4000/network@1,1:rarp
```

This means that booting using the net device, as shown in the following example, would use the /pci@1f,4000/network@1,1 device to boot the system across the network:

```
ok boot net
```

However, if we wanted to use the Dynamic Host Configuration Protocol (DHCP) to retrieve the host's IP address when booting, instead of using RARP, we would use the following command:

```
ok boot net:dhcp
```

To remove the alias from NVRAM, you simply use the nvunalias command:

```
ok nvunalias net
```

This would restore the default value of net.

Troubleshooting Booting Problems

If a system fails to start correctly in multi-user mode, it's likely that one of the scripts being run in /etc/rc2.d is the cause. In order to prevent the system from going multiuser, it is possible to boot directly into single-user mode from the ok prompt:

```
INIT: SINGLE USER MODE
Type Ctrl-d to proceed with normal startup,
(or give root password for system maintenance):
```

At this point, the root password can be entered, and the user will be given a root shell. However, not all filesystems will be mounted, although individual scripts can then be checked individually for misbehaving applications.

If the system will not boot into single-user mode, then the solution is more complicated, since the default boot device cannot be used. For example, if an invalid entry has been in the /etc/passwd file for the root user, then the system will not boot into single or multiuser mode. To recover the installed system, the host needs to be booted from the installation CD-ROM into singleuser mode. At this point, the default root filesystem can be mounted on a separate mount point, the /etc/passwd file edited, and the system rebooted with the default boot device. This sequence of steps is shown below, assuming that /etc is located on /dev/dsk/c0t0d0s1:

```
ok boot cdrom
...
INIT: SINGLE USER MODE
Type Ctrl-d to proceed with normal startup,
(or give root password for system maintenance):
# mkdir /temp
# mount /dev/dsk/c0t0d0s1 /temp
# vi /temp/etc/passwd
# sync; init 6
```

Halting a Hung System

If a system is hung, and commands cannot be entered into a shell on the console, then the key combination STOP+a can be used to halt the system, and access the OpenBoot PROM monitor. If the system is halted and rebooted in this way, all data which has not been written to disk will be lost, unless the go command is used to resume the system's normal operation. An alternative method of accessing a system if the console is locked is to telnet to the system as an unprivileged user, use the su command to obtain superuser status, and kill whatever process is hanging the system. Normal operation can then be resumed.

Summary

The OpenBoot PROM monitor is one of the outstanding features of the SPARC architecture. It allows a wide range of system parameters to be configured using a high-level programming language, which is independent of the installed operating system. A wide range of diagnostic and testing applications are included with OpenBoot.

Questions

1. How can the default boot device be set to CD-ROM from the OpenBoot PROM monitor?
   - A. setenv boot-device cdrom
   - B. set boot-device cdrom
   - C. set boot cdrom
   - D. setenv bootdevice cdrom

2. How can the default boot device be set to disk from the OpenBoot PROM monitor?
   - A. setenv boot-device disk
   - B. set boot-device disk
   - C. set boot disk
   - D. setenv bootdevice disk

3. How can the default boot device be set to net from the OpenBoot PROM monitor?
   - A. setenv boot-device net
   - B. set boot-device net
   - C. set boot net
   - D. setenv bootdevice net

4. How can the default boot device be set to tape from the OpenBoot PROM monitor?
   - A. setenv boot-device tape
   - B. set boot-device tape
   - C. set boot tape
   - D. setenv bootdevice tape

5. How can the default boot device be set to floppy from the OpenBoot PROM monitor?
   - A. setenv boot-device floppy
   - B. set boot-device floppy
   - C. set boot floppy
   - D. setenv bootdevice floppy

6. How can a reconfiguration boot be performed from the OpenBoot PROM monitor?
   - A. reboot -configure
   - B. boot -configure

    C. boot -reconfigure

    D. boot -r

7. How can a manual boot be performed from the OpenBoot PROM monitor?

    A. boot -manual

    B. boot -man

    C. boot -a

    D. boot -m

8. How can the system clock be tested from the OpenBoot PROM monitor?

    A. watch-time

    B. watch-clock

    C. test-clock

    D. test-time

9. How can the network connection be tested from the OpenBoot PROM monitor?

    A. watch-network

    B. watch-net

    C. test-net

    D. test-network

Answers

1. A

2. A

3. A

4. A

5. A

6. D

7. C

8. B

9. B

Installing Solaris 8 on a Single Host

The following objectives will be met upon completing this chapter's material:

- Reviewing which software packages and CD-ROMs make up the Solaris 8 distribution
- Understanding hardware configurations that are supported by Solaris 8
- Learning about system pre-installation tasks
- Installing Solaris 8 using the Web Start Wizard

Solaris runs best on the Scalable Processor ARChitecture (SPARC), which is managed by the SPARC architecture group **(http://www.sparc.org/).** Although vendor-specific hardware is often viewed as a disadvantage by some administrators, the performance of Sun workstations is legendary—the low central processing unit (CPU) speeds of older systems are not reflective of the high-throughput input/output (I/O) performance achieved by the Sun workstation bus. In this chapter, the reader will be walked through the installation and basic configuration of Solaris for Sun SPARC.

Solaris 8 Distribution

The Solaris operating environment is typically not available in your local computer store; it must be obtained directly from Sun or through an authorized reseller. The good news is that if your Sparc system has eight CPUs or less, you may now obtain a Solaris license free of charge by applying directly to Sun. The catch is that you must pay for postage and handling, which Sun calculates to be U.S. $75 per package. This is an increase of the previous shipping and handling charges associated with previous editions of the "free" Solaris program. However, the new package has a number of value-added extras, including the Oracle database server. It is also possible to obtain the source code to Solaris **(http://www.sun.com/software/solaris/source/).** This is now ending at the end of June 2001.

The free Solaris license program is targeted at home users who want to take advantage of the stability of the Solaris platform for using Star Office and other productivity applications. It is also aimed at Solaris developers who want to deploy on the Solaris platform. More information is available from **http://www.sun.com/software/solaris/binaries/.**

The Solaris 8 media pack comes with several CDs, including the following:

- The Web Start Installation CD, which is used to install the Solaris operating environment.

- Two Solaris Software CDs, which contain all of the standard Solaris packages.

- The Solaris documentation CDs, which contain all of the Solaris documentation in Answer Book format.

- A languages CD, which contains local customizations for nine different languages.

- The Star Office 5.2 productivity suite.

- The Forte for Java integrated development environment.

- The iPlanet software suite, which provides a Web server, directory server, certificate manager, sun screen firewall, and an application server.

- The Oracle database server.

- A supplemental software CD, including support for OpenGL, Java 3D, and advanced networking support including SunATM, SunFDDI, and Sun Gigabit-Ethernet.

- A GNU software CD, which includes Perl, the GNU compiler suite (GCC), and many other commonly used GNU packages.

Four primary configurations have been developed for Solaris SPARC, and they are shown along with their approximate installed size in Table 4-1.

Supported Hardware

Sun has developed a wide range of hardware systems over the past few years, much of which is still supported by Solaris 8. These systems are based on the Scalable Processor ARChitecture (SPARC), which is managed by a SPARC member organization **(http://www.sparc.org/).** In addition to Sun Microsystems, Fujitsu **(http://www.fujitsu.com/)**

Table 4-I   Sizes of Different Solaris Installations

Distribution	Approximate Size
Entire distribution plus OEM support	2.4G
Entire distribution without OEM support	2.3G
Developer system support	1.9G
End user system support	1.6G

and T.Sqware (http://www.tsqware.com/) also build SPARC-compliant CPU systems. System vendors who sell systems based on SPARC CPUs include Amdahl Corporation (http://www.amdahl.com/), Tatung (http://www.tatung.com/), Tadpole (http://www.tadpole.com/) and Toshiba (http://www.toshiba.com/). Vendors of system boards and peripherals for SPARC CPU-based systems include Hitachi (http://www.hitachi.com/), Seagate (http://www.seagate.com/), and Kingston Technology (http://www.kingston.com/). Although media critics and competitors often paint SPARC systems from Sun as standalone, vendor-specific traps for the unwary, the reality is that a large number of hardware vendors also support the SPARC platform. It should also be noted that software vendors, such as Red Hat, also support SPARC versions of Linux, meaning that Solaris is not the only operating systems that powers the SPARC platform. The SPARC standards can be downloaded free-of-charge from **http://www.sparc.org/standards.html.**

Often, administrators of Linux and Microsoft Windows systems, who are used to PC hardware, are incredulous to discover that some supported systems (such as the SPARC-classic) have CPUs that run at sub-100 MHz. This must seem a very slow CPU speed in the age of Intel CPUs and their clones reaching the 1 GHz mark. However, CPU speed is only one component that contributes to the overall performance of a system; SPARC systems are renowned for their high-speed buses and very fast I/O performance. In addition, many SPARC systems were designed for continuous operation. It is not unheard of for systems to have several years of uptime, compared to several days for other operating systems. The many impressive features of the Solaris operating systems were developed with the SPARC hardware platform as a target, and these systems naturally have the best performance.

However, Sun has not ignored hardware developments and emerging standards. In recent years, they have created the Ultra series of workstations and servers, which feature a PCI bus and compatibility with Super VGA (SVGA) multi-sync monitors commonly sold with PC systems. Of course, SPARC systems have always supported the SCSI standard, and all SCSI devices will work with Solaris. At the same time, Sun has proceeded with innovations, such as the 64-CPU Enterprise 10000 system, which can operate as a single system with massively parallel computational capabilities or it can be logically partitioned to act as up to 64 different systems. Imagine being able to control an entire ASP, with no apparent "shared hosting" to the client, which was actually being serviced by a single physical system. Although the upfront cost of an E10000 far exceeds that required for 64 systems running Linux or Microsoft Windows, only one administrator is required to manage an E10000, while 64 different systems might require more than one administrator.

Supported SPARC Platforms

The following SPARC systems are supported under Solaris 8:

- SPARCclassic
- SPARCstation LX
- SPARCstation 4
- SPARCstation 5
- SPARCstation 10
- SPARCstation 20
- Ultra 1 (including Creator and Creator 3D models)
- Enterprise 1
- Ultra 2 (including Creator and Creator 3D models)
- Ultra 5
- Ultra 10
- Ultra 30
- Ultra 60
- Ultra 450
- Blade 100
- Blade 1000
- Enterprise 2
- Enterprise 150
- Enterprise 250
- Enterprise 450
- Enterprise 3000

- Enterprise 3500

- Enterprise 4000

- Enterprise 4500

- Enterprise 5000

- Enterprise 5500

- Enterprise 6000

- Enterprise 10000

- SPARCserver 1000

- SPARCcenter 2000

Some popular systems are no longer supported, such as the SPARCstation 1 and SPARCstation 2. Often, these can be upgraded with a firmware or CPU change to be compatible with Solaris 8. In addition, a minimum of 64M RAM is required to install Solaris 8. The installer will not let you proceed unless it can detect this amount of physical RAM, so be sure to check that your system meets the basic requirements before attempting to install Solaris 8.

Device Nomenclature

Some of the most challenging aspects of understanding Solaris hardware are the device names and references used by Solaris to manage devices. Solaris uses a very specific set of naming conventions to associate physical devices with instance names on the operating system. In addition, devices can also be referred to by their device name, which is associated with a device file created in the /dev directory after configuration. For example, a hard disk may have the physical device name/pci@1f,0/pci@1,1/ide@3/dad@0,0, which is associated with the device file /dev/dsk/c0t0d0.

The benefit of the complex Solaris device names and physical device references is that it is easy to interpret the characteristics of each device by looking at its name. For the disk example given previously, we can see that the IDE hard drive is located on a PCI bus at target 0. When we view the amount of free disk space on the system, for example, it is easy to identify slices on the same disk by looking at the device name:

```
bash-2.03# df -k
Filesystem            kbytes     used     avail   capacity   Mounted on
/proc                      0        0         0        0%    /proc
/dev/dsk/c0t0d0s0    1982988   615991   1307508       33%    /
fd                         0        0         0        0%    /dev/fd
/dev/dsk/c0t0d0s     1487119   357511   1070124       26%    /usr
swap                  182040      416    181624        1%    /tmp
```

Here we can see that /dev/dsk/c0t0d0s0 and /dev/dsk/c0t0d0s3 are slice 0 and slice 3 of the disk /dev/dsk/c0t0d0. If you're ever unsure of which physical disk is associated with a specific disk device name, then the format command will tell you:

```
bash-2.03# format
Searching for disks...done
AVAILABLE DISK SELECTIONS:
0. c1t3d0 <SUN2.1G cyl 2733 alt 2 hd 19 sec 80>
       /pci@1f,0/pci@1/scsi@1/sd@3,0
```

Here we can see that physical device /pci@1f,0/pci@1/scsi@1/sd@3,0 is matched with the disk device /dev/dsk/c1t3d0. In addition, a list of mappings between physical devices to instance names is always kept in the /etc/path_to_inst file:

```
"/sbus@1f,0" 0 "sbus"
"/sbus@1f,0/sbusmem@2,0" 2 "sbusmem"
"/sbus@1f,0/sbusmem@3,0" 3 "sbusmem"
"/sbus@1f,0/sbusmem@0,0" 0 "sbusmem"
"/sbus@1f,0/sbusmem@1,0" 1 "sbusmem"
"/sbus@1f,0/SUNW,fas@2,8800000" 1 "fas"
"/sbus@1f,0/SUNW,fas@2,8800000/ses@f,0" 1 "ses"
"/sbus@1f,0/SUNW,fas@2,8800000/sd@1,0" 16 "sd"
"/sbus@1f,0/SUNW,fas@2,8800000/sd@0,0" 15 "sd"
"/sbus@1f,0/SUNW,fas@2,8800000/sd@3,0" 18 "sd"
"/sbus@1f,0/SUNW,fas@2,8800000/sd@2,0" 17 "sd"
"/sbus@1f,0/SUNW,fas@2,8800000/sd@5,0" 20 "sd"
"/sbus@1f,0/SUNW,fas@2,8800000/sd@4,0" 19 "sd"
"/sbus@1f,0/SUNW,fas@2,8800000/sd@6,0" 21 "sd"
"/sbus@1f,0/SUNW,fas@2,8800000/sd@9,0" 23 "sd"
"/sbus@1f,0/SUNW,fas@2,8800000/sd@8,0" 22 "sd"
"/sbus@1f,0/SUNW,fas@2,8800000/sd@a,0" 24 "sd"
"/sbus@1f,0/SUNW,fas@2,8800000/st@1,0" 8 "st"
"/sbus@1f,0/SUNW,fas@2,8800000/st@0,0" 7 "st"
"/sbus@1f,0/SUNW,fas@2,8800000/sd@c,0" 26 "sd"
"/sbus@1f,0/SUNW,fas@2,8800000/st@3,0" 10 "st"
"/sbus@1f,0/SUNW,fas@2,8800000/sd@b,0" 25 "sd"
"/sbus@1f,0/SUNW,fas@2,8800000/st@2,0" 9 "st"
"/sbus@1f,0/SUNW,fas@2,8800000/sd@e,0" 28 "sd"
"/sbus@1f,0/SUNW,fas@2,8800000/st@5,0" 12 "st"
"/sbus@1f,0/SUNW,fas@2,8800000/sd@d,0" 27 "sd"
"/sbus@1f,0/SUNW,fas@2,8800000/st@4,0" 11 "st"
"/sbus@1f,0/SUNW,fas@2,8800000/sd@f,0" 29 "sd"
"/sbus@1f,0/SUNW,fas@2,8800000/st@6,0" 13 "st"
"/sbus@1f,0/SUNW,CS4231@d,c000000" 0 "audiocs"
"/sbus@1f,0/dma@0,81000" 0 "dma"
"/sbus@1f,0/dma@0,81000/esp@0,80000" 0 "esp"
"/sbus@1f,0/dma@0,81000/esp@0,80000/sd@0,0" 30 "sd"
"/sbus@1f,0/dma@0,81000/esp@0,80000/sd@1,0" 31 "sd"
"/sbus@1f,0/dma@0,81000/esp@0,80000/sd@2,0" 32 "sd"
"/sbus@1f,0/dma@0,81000/esp@0,80000/sd@3,0" 33 "sd"
"/sbus@1f,0/dma@0,81000/esp@0,80000/sd@4,0" 34 "sd"
```

```
"/sbus@1f,0/dma@0,81000/esp@0,80000/sd@5,0"  35  "sd"
"/sbus@1f,0/dma@0,81000/esp@0,80000/sd@6,0"  36  "sd"
"/sbus@1f,0/dma@0,81000/esp@0,80000/st@0,0"  14  "st"
"/sbus@1f,0/dma@0,81000/esp@0,80000/st@1,0"  15  "st"
"/sbus@1f,0/dma@0,81000/esp@0,80000/st@2,0"  16  "st"
"/sbus@1f,0/dma@0,81000/esp@0,80000/st@3,0"  17  "st"
"/sbus@1f,0/dma@0,81000/esp@0,80000/st@4,0"  18  "st"
"/sbus@1f,0/dma@0,81000/esp@0,80000/st@5,0"  19  "st"
"/sbus@1f,0/dma@0,81000/esp@0,80000/st@6,0"  20  "st"
"/sbus@1f,0/sbusmem@f,0"  15  "sbusmem"
"/sbus@1f,0/sbusmem@d,0"  13  "sbusmem"
"/sbus@1f,0/sbusmem@e,0"  14  "sbusmem"
"/sbus@1f,0/cgthree@1,0"  0  "cgthree"
"/sbus@1f,0/SUNW,hme@e,8c00000"  0  "hme"
"/sbus@1f,0/zs@f,1000000"  1  "zs"
"/sbus@1f,0/zs@f,1100000"  0  "zs"
"/sbus@1f,0/SUNW,bpp@e,c800000"  0  "bpp"
"/sbus@1f,0/lebuffer@0,40000"  0  "lebuffer"
"/sbus@1f,0/lebuffer@0,40000/le@0,60000"  0  "le"
"/sbus@1f,0/SUNW,hme@2,8c00000"  1  "hme"
"/sbus@1f,0/SUNW,fdtwo@f,1400000"  0  "fd"
"/options"  0  "options"
"/pseudo"  0  "pseudo"
```

Here we can see entries for the network interface /sbus@1f,0/SUNW,hme@2,
|8c00000 as well as the floppy disk /sbus@1f,0/SUNW,fdtwo@f,1400000 and
the SBUS sbus@1f,0.

Pre-Installation Tasks

Before installing your system, you will require the following information from your
network administrator:

- *Hostname* (such as www) This is the name that you want to give your host to
  identify it uniquely on the local area network.

- *IP address* (such as 204.58.32.46) The IP address is used by the transport layer to
  locate a specific host on the worldwide Internet.

- *Domain name* (such as paulwatters.com) The domain name is the organization to
  which your host belongs. All hosts on the Internet must belong to a domain.

- *DNS server* (such as ns) The DNS server maps IP addresses to domain names, and
  domain names to IP addresses.

- *Subnet mask* (such as 255.255.255.0) This mask is used to locate hosts that form
  part of the same subnet on the local area network.

You will also need to decide which language you will want to use when installing Solaris. The following languages are supported for performing the installation process:

- English
- French
- German
- Italian
- Japanese
- Korean
- Simplified Chinese
- Spanish
- Swedish
- Traditional Chinese

If the system has never had Solaris installed, you can simply insert the CD-ROM into its caddy and/or CD-ROM drive, and the Web Start installer will start. Alternatively, once the system has started booting, you can press the STOP+a keys, and when you get the OK prompt, you can simply type the following:

```
ok boot cdrom
```

You will then see output similar to the following:

```
Boot device: /sbus/espdma@e,8400000/esp@e,8800000/sd@6,0:f File
and args:
SunOS Release 5.8 Version Generic 32-bit
Copyright 1983-2000 Sun Microsystems, Inc. All rights reserved.
Configuring /dev and /devices
Using RPC Bootparams for network configuration information.
Solaris Web Start 3.0 installer
English has been selected as the language in which to perform the
install.
Starting the Web Start 3.0 Solaris installer
Solaris installer is searching the system's hard disks for a
location to place the Solaris installer software.
Your system appears to be upgradeable.
Do you want to do a Initial Install or Upgrade?
1) Initial Install
2) Upgrade
3) Please Enter 1 or 2 >
```

If the following message appears in the boot messages, then you may elect to perform an upgrade of the existing Solaris installation. However, most administrators would backup their existing software, perform a fresh install, and then restore their data and applications once their system is operational. In this case, we will choose to perform an Initial Install, which will overwrite the existing operating system.

After you enter 1 and hit Enter, you will see a message like this:

```
The default root disk is /dev/dsk/c0t0d0.
The Solaris installer needs to format
/dev/dsk/c0t0d0 to install Solaris.
WARNING: ALL INFORMATION ON THE DISK WILL BE ERASED!
Do you want to format /dev/dsk/c0t0d0? [y,n,?,q]
```

Formatting the hard drive will overwrite all existing data on the drive. You must ensure that, if you had previously installed an operating system on the target drive (c0t0d0), you have backed up all the data you will need in the future. This includes both user directories and application installations.

After answering y, the following screen will appear:

```
NOTE: The swap size cannot be changed during filesystem layout.
Enter a swap slice size between 384MB and 2027MB, default = 512MB
[?]
```

Just hit the Enter key to accept the default on 512M if your system has 256M physical RAM, as the sample system has. However, as a general rule, you should only allocate twice the amount of physical RAM as swap space; otherwise, system performance will be impaired. The swap partition should be placed at the beginning of the drive, as the following message indicates, so that other slices are not dependent on its physical location:

```
The Installer prefers that the swap slice is at the beginning of
the disk. This will allow the most flexible filesystem partition-
ing later in the installation.
Can the swap slice start at the beginning of the disk [y,n,?,q]
```

After answering y to this question, you will see be asked to confirm the formatting settings:

```
You have selected the following to be used by the Solaris
installer:
Disk Slice : /dev/dsk/c0t0d0
Size : 1024 MB
Start Cyl. : 0
WARNING: ALL INFORMATION ON THE DISK WILL BE ERASED!
Is this OK [y,n,?,q]
```

If you answer y, then the disk will be formatted, and a mini-root filesystem will be copied to the disk, after which the system will be rebooted, and the Web Start wizard installation process can begin:

```
The Solaris installer will use disk slice, /dev/dsk/c0t0d0s1.
After files are copied, the system will automatically reboot, and
installation will continue.
Please Wait...
Copying mini-root to local disk....done.
Copying platform specific files....done.
Preparing to reboot and continue installation.
Rebooting to continue the installation.
Syncing file systems... 41 done
rebooting...
Resetting ...
SPARCstation 20 (1 X 390Z50), Keyboard Present
ROM Rev. 2.4, 256 MB memory installed, Serial #456543
Ethernet address 5:2:12:c:ee:5a HostID 456543
Rebooting with command: boot
/sbus@1f,0/espdma@e,8400000/esp@e,8800000/sd@0,0:b
Boot device: /sbus@1f,0/espdma@e,8400000/esp@e,8800000/sd@0,0:b
File and args:
SunOS Release 5.8 Version Generic 32-bit
Copyright 1983-2000 Sun Microsystems, Inc. All rights reserved.
Configuring /dev and /devices
Using RPC Bootparams for network configuration information.
```

Web Start Installation

Using the Web Start wizard is the easiest way to install and configure Solaris. Although it is possible to use the Solaris Interactive installer supplied with previous Solaris versions, the Web Start wizard allows users to install entire distributions or groups of packages and automatically size, layout, and create slices on the filesystem. It also configures the boot disk and other disks that are installed locally. However, if you want to install individual packages or change the size of the swap file, then you will not be able to use the Web Start wizard.

Network

The first section of the wizard involves setting up the network. The Network Connectivity screen gives users the option to select a networked or non-networked system. If you don't need to install network support, you will still need a unique hostname, and this must then be entered. Network users will have to enter a hostname, but must firstly identify how their system obtains IP support. One possibility is that the system will use the Dynamic Host Configuration Protocol (DHCP), which is useful when IP addresses are becoming scarce on a Class C network. DHCP allows individual systems to be allocated only for the period during which they are up. Thus, if a client machine is only operated between 9 a.m. and 5 p.m. every day, it is only "leased" an IP address for that period of time. When an IP address is not leased to a specific host, it can be reused by another host. Solaris DHCP servers can service Solaris clients as well as Microsoft Windows and Linux clients. Chapter 17 provides more information about DHCP services under Solaris.

Next, you need to indicate whether IP version 6 (IPv6) needs to be supported by this system. The decision to use or not to use DHCP will depend on whether your network is part of the mbone, the IPv6-enabled version of the Internet. As proposed in RFC 2471, IPv6 will replace IPv4 in the years to come, as it provides for many more IP addresses than IPv4. Once IPv6 is adopted worldwide, there will be less reliance on stopgap measures like DHCP. However, IPv6 also incorporates a number of innovations above and beyond the addition of more IP addresses for the Internet. Enhanced security provided by authenticating header information, for example, will reduce the risk of IP spoofing and denial of service attacks succeeding. Since IPv6 support does not interfere with existing IPv4 support, most administrators will want to support it.

Finally, you need to enter the IP address assigned to this system by the network administrator. It is important not to use an IP address that is currently being used by another host, since packets may be misrouted. You will also need to enter the netmask for the system, which will be 255.0.0.0 (Class A), 255.255.0.0 (Class B), or 255.255.255.0 (Class C). If you're not sure, ask your network administrator.

Name Service

A name service allows your system to find other hosts on the Internet or on the local area network. Solaris supports several different naming servers, including the Network Information Service (NIS/NIS+), the Domain Name Service (DNS), or file-based name resolution. NIS/NIS+ is used to manage large domains by creating maps of hosts, services, and resources that are shared between hosts and can be centrally managed. The domain name service, on the other hand, only stores maps of IP addresses and host-names. Solaris supports the concurrent operation of different naming services, so it's possible to select NIS/NIS+ at this point and set up DNS manually later. However, since most hosts are now connected to the Internet, it may be more appropriate to install DNS first and install NIS/NIS+ after installation.

If you select DNS or NIS/NIS+, you will be asked to enter a domain name for the local system. This should be the fully qualified domain name (such as paulwatters.com). If you selected DNS, then you will either need to search the local subnet for a DNS server or enter the IP address of the primary DNS server that is authoritative for your domain. You may also enter up to two secondary DNS servers that have records of your domain. This is can be a useful backup if your primary DNS server goes down.

It is also possible that, when searching for hosts with a hostname rather than a fully qualified domain name, you would want to search multiple local domains. For example, the host **www.finance.paulwatters.com** belongs to the finance.paulwatters. com domain. However, your users may want to locate other hosts within the broader paulwatters.com domain by using the simple hostname, in which case, you can add the paulwatters.com domain to a list of domains to be searched for hosts.

Date and Time

The next section requires that you enter your time zone, as specified by geographic region, the number of hours beyond or before Greenwich Mean Time (GMT), or by timezone file. Using the geographic region is the easiest method, although if you already know the GMT offset and/or the name of the time zone file, you may enter that instead. Next, you are required to enter the current time and date with a four-digit year, a month, day, hour, and minute.

Root Password

The most important stage of the installation procedure occurs next, the selection of the root password. The root user has the same powers as the root user on Linux or the Administrator account on Windows NT. If an intruder gains root access, he or she is free to roam the system, deleting or stealing data, removing or adding user accounts, or installing trojan horses that transparently modify the way that your system operates.

One way to protect against an authorized user gaining root access is to use a difficult-to-guess root password. This makes it difficult for a cracker to use a password-cracking program to guess your password. The optimal password is a completely random string of alphanumeric and punctuation characters. Some applications, which will be discussed in Chapter 15, can be used to generate passwords that are easy to remember, but which contain almost random combinations of characters.

In addition, the root password should never be written down, unless it is locked in the company safe or told to anyone who doesn't need to know it. If users require levels of access that are typically privileged (such as mounting CD-ROMs), it is better to use the sudo utility to limit the access of each user to specific applications for execution as a super-user, rather than giving out the root password to everyone who asks for it.

The root password must be entered twice just in case you should happen to make a typographical error, as the characters that you type are masked on the screen.

Power Management

Do you want your system to switch off automatically after 30 minutes of inactivity? If you can honestly answer yes to this question (such as, you have a workstation that does not run services), then you should enable power management, as it can save costly power bills. However, if you're administering a server, then you'll definitely want to turn power management off.

Proxy Server

A proxy server acts as a buffer between hosts on a local network and the rest of the Internet. A proxy server passes connections back and forth between local hosts and any other host on the Internet. It usually acts in conjunction with a firewall to block access to internal systems, thereby protecting sensitive data. One of the most popular firewalls is squid, which also acts as a caching server.

To enable access to the Internet through a proxy server, you need to enter the hostname of the proxy server and the port on which the proxy operates.

Kiosk

After all of the configuration settings have been entered, the following message will be seen on the screen:

```
Please wait while the system is configured with your settings...
```

The installation Kiosk will then appear on the screen. The Kiosk is primarily used to select the type of installation that you want to perform. To begin the software selection process, you need to eject the Web Start CD-ROM and insert the Software (1) CD-ROM. Next, you have the option of installing all Solaris software using the default options or customizing your selection before copying the files from the CD-ROM. Obviously, if you have a lot of disk space and a fast system, you may prefer to install the entire distribution and delete packages after installation that you no longer require. This is definitely the fastest method. Alternatively, you can elect to perform a customized installation.

You are then presented with a screen of all the available software groups. Here you may select or deselect individual package groups or package clusters, depending on your requirements. For example, you may decide to install the Netscape Navigator software, but not install the NIS/NIS+ server for Solaris. After choosing the packages that you want to install, you are then required to enter your locale based on geographic region (the U.S. entry is selected by default). You may also elect to install third-party software during the Solaris installation process. This is particularly useful if you have a standard operating environment that consists of using the Oracle database server in conjunction with the Solaris operating environment, for example. You would need to insert the product CD-ROM at this point so that it can be identified.

After selecting your software, you will need to layout the disks. This involves defining disk slices that will store the different kinds of data on your system. The fastest configuration option involves selecting the boot disk and allowing the installer to automatically layout the partitions according to the software selection that you have chosen. For example, you may want to expand the size of the /var partition to allow for large print jobs to be spooled or Web servers logs to be recorded.

Finally, you will be asked to confirm your software selections and proceed with installation. All of the packages will then be installed to your system. A progress bar displayed on the screen indicates which packages have been installed at any particular point and how many remain to be installed. After you have installed all of the software, you will have to reboot the system. After restarting, your system should boot directly into Solaris unless you have a dual-booting system, in which case you will need to select the Solaris boot partition from the Solaris boot manager.

After installation, the system will reboot and display a status message when starting up, which is printed on the console. A sample console display during booting will look something like this:

```
ok boot
Resetting ...
SPARCstation 20 (1 X 390Z50), Keyboard Present
ROM Rev. 2.4, 256 MB memory installed, Serial #456543
Ethernet address 5:2:12:c:ee:5a HostID 456543
Boot device: /iommu/sbus/espdma@f,400000/esp@f,800000/sd@1,0
File and args:
SunOS Release 5.8 Version generic [UNIX(R) System V Release 4.0]
Copyright (c) 1983-2000, Sun Microsystems, Inc.
configuring network interfaces: le0.
Hostname: server
The system is coming up. Please wait.
add net default: gateway 204.58.62.33
NIS domainname is paulwatters.net
starting rpc services: rpcbind keyserv ypbind done.
Setting netmask of le0 to 255.255.255.0
Setting default interface for multicast: add net 224.0.0.0: gate-
way emu
syslog service starting.
Print services started.
volume management starting.
The system is ready.
emu console login:
```

By default, the CDE login screen is then displayed.

Summary

In this chapter, we've examined the contents of the Solaris 8 distribution and outlined the major kinds of SPARC hardware that support this platform. In addition, we reviewed the key pre-installation tasks that must be undertaken prior to beginning a Web Start installation, which is also covered in detail.

Questions

1. Which of the following Solaris 8 installation types requires the greatest amount of disk space?
   A. Entire Distribution without OEM Support
   B. Entire Distribution plus OEM Support
   C. Developer System
   D. End User System

2. The acronym SPARC stands for which of the following names?
   A. Super Processor ARChitecture
   B. Super Processor Adaptable Recurrent Computation
   C. Scalable Processor ARChitecture
   D. Special ARChitecture

3. What are the main advantages of the SPARC architecture? (Choose two.)
   A. High-speed bus
   B. Fastest available CPU speeds
   C. Fast I/O performance
   D. Compatibility with Intel CPUs

4. Which of the following SPARC systems is supported under Solaris 8? (Choose two.)
   A. SPARCclassic
   B. SPARCstation LX
   C. SPARCstation 1
   D. SPARCstation 2

5. What is the minimum amount of RAM required to run Solaris 8?
   A. 16M
   B. 32M
   C. 64M
   D. 128M

6. Which is a valid physical device for /pci@1f,0/pci@1,1/ide@3/dad@0,0?
   A. /dev/dsk/c0t0d0
   B. /dev/dsk/c0t0d1
   C. /dev/dsk/c1t0d0
   D. /dev/dsk/c0t1d0

7. What is a hostname?
   A. A network name that identifies a group of hosts
   B. A special username that has super-user privileges
   C. A unique name that is associated with a system
   D. A network name that identifies an entire network

8. What is an IP address?
   A. A network address that identifies a group of hosts
   B. A number that is used to locate hosts on the same local subnet
   C. A unique name that is associated with a system
   D. A network number that identifies a single host

9. What is a domain name?
   A. An IP address that identifies a group of hosts
   B. A number that is used to locate hosts on the same local subnet
   C. A unique name that is associated with a system
   D. A network name that identifies a group of hosts

10. What is a subnet mask?
    A. An IP address that identifies a group of hosts
    B. A number that is used to locate hosts on the same local subnet
    C. A unique name that is associated with a system
    D. A network name that identifies a group of hosts

11. What is a root password?
    A. An authentication token for the super-user
    B. A hacking tool used to crack low-level accounts
    C. A password that cannot be used to gain indirect access to the nobody account
    D. A network name that identifies a group of hosts

12. What is DHCP?

    A. A protocol for permanently assigning IP addresses to hosts

    B. A protocol for leasing IP addresses to hosts

    C. A method for invoking super-user privileges

    D. A protocol for identifying a group of hosts

Answers

1. A

2. C

3. A, C

4. A, B

5. C

6. A

7. C

8. D

9. D

10. B

11. A

12. B

Software Package Administration

The following objectives will be met upon completing this chapter's material:

- Printing a list of all files contained within a Solaris package using the CLI
- Printing a list of all files contained within a Solaris package using the admintool
- Installing a Solaris package using the CLI
- Uninstalling a Solaris package using the CLI
- Installing a Solaris package using the admintool GUI
- Uninstalling a Solaris package using the admintool GUI

All Solaris software that is installed as part of the operating environment comes packaged in an archive known as a package. Solaris packages provide an easy way to bring together application binaries, configuration files, and documentation for distribution to other systems. In addition to the Solaris packaging system, Solaris also supports standard UNIX archiving and compression tools, such as tar (tape archive) and compress. In this chapter, we examine how to manage packages by using the standard Solaris packaging tools. Operations reviewed include installing packages, displaying information about packages, and removing packages using both the CLI and admintool graphic user interface (GUI).

Printing Package Information Using the CLI

Packages are text files that contain an archive of binary applications, configuration files, documentation, or even source code. All files in the Solaris operating environment are now supplied as part of a package, meaning that it is easy to group files associated with different applications. If files are installed without packaging, then it becomes difficult over the years for administrators to remember which files were installed with particular applications. Packaging makes it easy to recognize application dependencies, since all files required by a specific application can be included within the archive. For example, we can use the pkgchk (or pkginfo) command to examine the package properties of a file that has already been installed:

```
bash-2.03# pkgchk -l -p /usr/bin/mkdir
Pathname: /usr/bin/mkdir
Type: regular file
Expected mode: 0555
Expected owner: bin
Expected group: bin
Expected file size (bytes): 9876
Expected sum(1) of contents: 38188
Expected last modification: Oct 06 05:47:55 PM 1998
Referenced by the following packages:
        SUNWcsu
Current status: installed
```

Another advantage of using packages is the standard installation interface provided to install Solaris packages. This means that all of Solaris is installed using the same application (pkgadd or the admintool), rather than each application having its own installation program. This reduces coding time and makes it easier for administrators to install software because only a single interface, with standard options such as over-writing existing files, needs to be learned. Table 5-1 summarizes the various commands that are used to create, install, and remove packages.

In this chapter, we will examine how to install new packages, display information about downloaded packages, and remove packages that have previously been installed on the system.

At any time, we can examine which packages have been installed on a system by using the pkginfo command:

```
bash-2.03# pkginfo
application GNU1stdc         libstdc++
application GNUmake           make
system      NCRos86r         NCR Platform Support, OS Functionality
                             (Root)
system      SFWaalib         ASCII Art Library
```

Table 5-1   Solaris Packaging Commands

Command	Description
pkgproto	Creates a prototype file that specifies the files contained in a package.
pkgmk	Creates a package directory.
pkgadd	Installs a package from a package file.
pkgtrans	Converts package directory into a file.
pkgrm	Uninstalls a package.
pkgchk	Verifies that a package is valid.
pkginfo	Prints the contents of a package

```
system      SFWaconf      GNU autoconf
system      SFWamake      GNU automake
system      SFWbison      GNU bison
system      SFWemacs      GNU Emacs
system      SFWflex       GNU flex
system      SFWfvwm       fvwm virtual window manager
system      SFWgcc        GNU compilers
system      SFWgdb        GNU source-level debugger
system      SFWgimp       GNU Image Manipulation Program
system      SFWglib       GLIB - Library of useful routines for
                          C programming
system      SFWgm4        GNU m4
system      SFWgmake      GNU make
system      SFWgs         GNU Ghostscript
system      SFWgsfot      GNU Ghostscript Other Fonts
system      SFWgsfst      GNU Ghostscript Standard Fonts
system      SFWgtk        GTK - The GIMP Toolkit
system      SFWjpg        The Independent JPEG Groups JPEG
                          software
system      SFWlxrun      lxrun
system      SFWmpage      mpage - print multiple pages per sheet
system      SFWmpeg       The MPEG Library
system      SFWncur       ncurses library
system      SFWolvwm      OPEN LOOK Virtual Window Manager
system      SFWpng        PNG reference library
```

This system has quite a few packages installed in both the system and application categories, including lxrun, the application that allows Linux binaries to be executed on Solaris Intel, and the Gimp, a graphics manipulation program. Very few restrictions exist on the kinds of files and applications that can be installed by using packages.

Printing Package Information Using admintool

Viewing information about installed packages is made easy by using the admintool GUI interface (/usr/bin/admintool). Figure 5-1 shows the view provided of all the installed software packages after selecting Browse, Software from the admintool

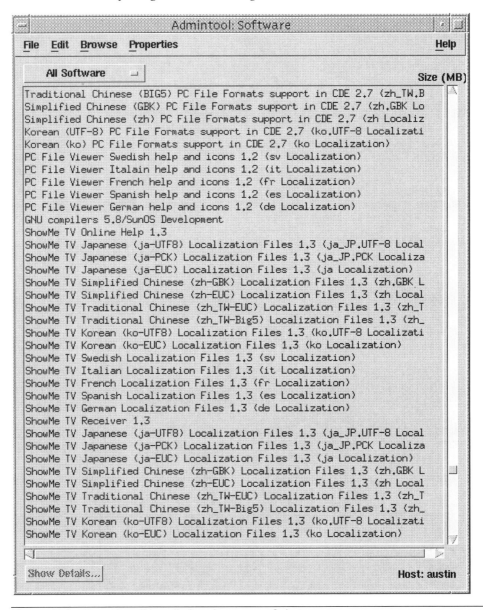

Figure 5-1 Browsing all installed packages on a Solaris system

menubar. We can see that many different packages have already been installed on the system, including PC File Viewer help in Swedish, Italian, French, and German, as well as support files for the ShowTV multimedia software suite.

It is also possible to display only files that have been installed as System packages, by deselecting All Software from the software selection dropdown menu and selecting System Software, as shown in Figure 5-2. We can see that several key System packages have

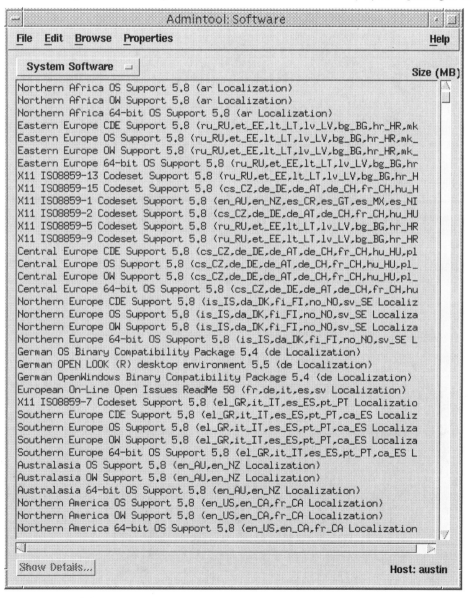

```
Admintool: Software

File   Edit   Browse   Properties                                    Help

  System Software  ⌐                                            Size (MB)

Northern Africa OS Support 5.8 (ar Localization)
Northern Africa OW Support 5.8 (ar Localization)
Northern Africa 64-bit OS Support 5.8 (ar Localization)
Eastern Europe CDE Support 5.8 (ru_RU,et_EE,lt_LT,lv_LV,bg_BG,hr_HR,mk
Eastern Europe OS Support 5.8 (ru_RU,et_EE,lt_LT,lv_LV,bg_BG,hr_HR,mk_
Eastern Europe OW Support 5.8 (ru_RU,et_EE,lt_LT,lv_LV,bg_BG,hr_HR,mk_
Eastern Europe 64-bit OS Support 5.8 (ru_RU,et_EE,lt_LT,lv_LV,bg_BG,hr
X11 ISO8859-13 Codeset Support 5.8 (ru_RU,et_EE,lt_LT,lv_LV,bg_BG,hr_H
X11 ISO8859-15 Codeset Support 5.8 (cs_CZ,de_DE,de_AT,de_CH,fr_CH,hu_H
X11 ISO8859-1 Codeset Support 5.8 (en_AU,en_NZ,es_CR,es_GT,es_MX,es_NI
X11 ISO8859-2 Codeset Support 5.8 (cs_CZ,de_DE,de_AT,de_CH,fr_CH,hu_HU
X11 ISO8859-5 Codeset Support 5.8 (ru_RU,et_EE,lt_LT,lv_LV,bg_BG,hr_HR
X11 ISO8859-9 Codeset Support 5.8 (ru_RU,et_EE,lt_LT,lv_LV,bg_BG,hr_HR
Central Europe CDE Support 5.8 (cs_CZ,de_DE,de_AT,de_CH,fr_CH,hu_HU,pl
Central Europe OS Support 5.8 (cs_CZ,de_DE,de_AT,de_CH,fr_CH,hu_HU,pl_
Central Europe OW Support 5.8 (cs_CZ,de_DE,de_AT,de_CH,fr_CH,hu_HU,pl_
Central Europe 64-bit OS Support 5.8 (cs_CZ,de_DE,de_AT,de_CH,fr_CH,hu
Northern Europe CDE Support 5.8 (is_IS,da_DK,fi_FI,no_NO,sv_SE Localiz
Northern Europe OS Support 5.8 (is_IS,da_DK,fi_FI,no_NO,sv_SE Localiza
Northern Europe OW Support 5.8 (is_IS,da_DK,fi_FI,no_NO,sv_SE Localiza
Northern Europe 64-bit OS Support 5.8 (is_IS,da_DK,fi_FI,no_NO,sv_SE L
German OS Binary Compatibility Package 5.4 (de Localization)
German OPEN LOOK (R) desktop environment 5.5 (de Localization)
German OpenWindows Binary Compatibility Package 5.4 (de Localization)
European On-Line Open Issues ReadMe 58 (fr,de,it,es,sv Localization)
X11 ISO8859-7 Codeset Support 5.8 (el_GR,it_IT,es_ES,pt_PT Localizatio
Southern Europe CDE Support 5.8 (el_GR,it_IT,es_ES,pt_PT,ca_ES Localiz
Southern Europe OS Support 5.8 (el_GR,it_IT,es_ES,pt_PT,ca_ES Localiza
Southern Europe OW Support 5.8 (el_GR,it_IT,es_ES,pt_PT,ca_ES Localiza
Southern Europe 64-bit OS Support 5.8 (el_GR,it_IT,es_ES,pt_PT,ca_ES L
Australasia OS Support 5.8 (en_AU,en_NZ Localization)
Australasia OW Support 5.8 (en_AU,en_NZ Localization)
Australasia 64-bit OS Support 5.8 (en_AU,en_NZ Localization)
Northern America OS Support 5.8 (en_US,en_CA,fr_CA Localization)
Northern America OW Support 5.8 (en_US,en_CA,fr_CA Localization)
Northern America 64-bit OS Support 5.8 (en_US,en_CA,fr_CA Localization

  Show Details...                                          Host: austin
```

Figure 5-2   Browsing all installed System packages on a Solaris system

been installed, including operating system (OS), Common Desktop Environment (CDE), Open Windows (OW), and 64 bit architecture support for Eastern European, Central European, Southern European, and German locales.

It is also possible to display only files that have been installed as Application packages by deselecting System Software from the software selection dropdown menu and selecting Application Software, as shown in Figure 5-3. We can see that several key

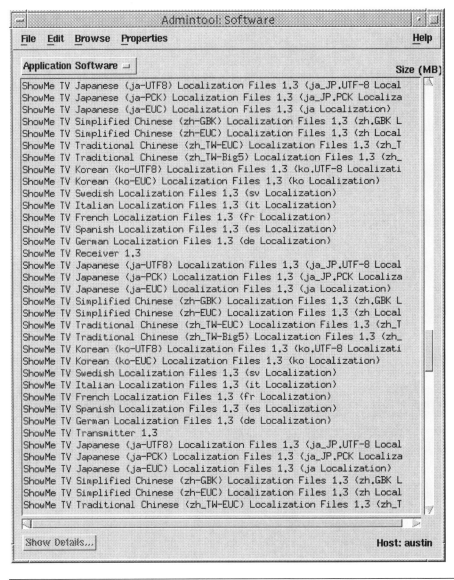

Figure 5-3 Browsing all installed Application packages on a Solaris system

Application packages have been installed, including many support packages for the ShowTV multimedia software suite.

Installing a Solaris Package Using the CLI

The best way to learn about adding packages is to use an example. In this section, we downloaded a package from **www.sunfreeware.com** called gpw-6.94-sol8-intel-local.gz, which is Van Vleck's random password creation application. Let's look more closely at the package name to determine what software this package contains:

- The .gz extension means that the package file has been compressed using gzip after it was created. Other possible extensions include .Z, which indicates compression with the compress program, while a .z extension would suggest compression by the pack program.

- The local string indicates that the package contents will be installed under the directory /usr/local. Other typical installation targets include the /opt directory, where optional packages from the Solaris distribution are also installed.

- The intel string states that the package is intended for use on Solaris Intel and not Solaris Sparc.

- The 6.94 string indicates the current software revision level.

- The gpw string states the application's name.

To actually use the package file, we first need to decompress it by using the gzip command:

```
bash-2.03# gzip -d gpw-6.94-sol8-intel-local
```

Next, we can examine the contents of the file by using the head command:

```
bash-2.03# head gpw-6.94-sol8-intel-local
# PaCkAgE DaTaStReAm
TVVgpw 1 150
# end of header
NAME=gwp
ARCH=intel
VERSION=6.94
CATEGORY=application
VENDOR=Tom Van Vleck
EMAIL=steve@smc.vnet.net
```

This kind of header exists for all Solaris packages and makes it easy to understand which platform a package is designed for, who the vendor was, and who to contact for more information. Now that we have a package, we can begin the installation process by using the pkgadd command. In order to install the gpw-6.94-sol8-intel-local package, we use the following command:

```
bash-2.03# pkgadd -d gpw-6.94-sol8-intel-local
```

We would then see the following output:

```
The following packages are available:
  1  TVVgpw       gwp
                  (sparc) 6.94

Select package(s) you wish to process (or 'all' to process
all packages). (default: all) [?,??,q]:  all
```

Pressing ENTER at this point will allow you to proceed with the installation:

```
Processing package instance <TVVgpw> from </tmp/gpw-6.94-sol8-
intel-local>

gwp
(sparc) 6.94
Tom Van Vleck
Using </usr/local> as the package base directory.
## Processing package information.
## Processing system information.
   2 package pathnames are already properly installed.
## Verifying disk space requirements.
## Checking for conflicts with packages already installed.
## Checking for setuid/setgid programs.

Installing gwp as <TVVgpw>

## Installing part 1 of 1.
/usr/local/bin/gpw
/usr/local/doc/gpw/README.gpw
[ verifying class <none> ]

Installation of <TVVgpw> was successful.
```

After processing package and system information, and checking that the required amount of disk space is available, the pkgadd command copies only two files from the archive to the local filesystem: /usr/local/bin/gpw and /usr/local/doc/gpw/README.gpw.

Uninstalling a Solaris Package Using the CLI

Once a package has been installed on the system, it can easily be removed by using the pkgrm command. For example, if we wanted to remove the gpw program, after being installed in the /usr/local directory, we would use the command:

```
bash-2.03# pkgrm TVVgpw

The following package is currently installed:
   TVVgpw          gwp
                   (sparc) 6.94

Do you want to remove this package? Y

## Removing installed package instance <TVVgpw>
## Verifying package dependencies.
## Processing package information.
## Removing pathnames in class <none>
/usr/local/doc/gpw/README.gpw
/usr/local/doc/gpw
/usr/local/doc <shared pathname not removed>
/usr/local/bin/gpw
/usr/local/bin <shared pathname not removed>
## Updating system information.

Removal of <TVVgpw> was successful.
```

The pkgrm command also operates in an interactive mode, where multiple packages can be removed using the same interface:

```
bash-2.03# pkgrm

The following packages are available:
  1  GNUlstdc       libstdc++
                    (i86pc) 2.8.1.1
  2  GNUmake        make
                    (i86pc) 3.77
  3  NCRos86r       NCR Platform Support, OS Functionality (Root)
                    (i386) 1.1.0,REV=1998.08.07.12.41
  4  SFWaalib       ASCII Art Library
                    (i386) 1.2,REV=1999.11.25.13.32
  5  SFWaconf       GNU autoconf
                    (i386) 2.13,REV=1999.11.25.13.32
  6  SFWamake       GNU automake
                    (i386) 1.4,REV=1999.11.25.13.32
  7  SFWbison       GNU bison
                    (i386) 1.28,REV=1999.11.25.13.32
  8  SFWemacs       GNU Emacs
                    (i386) 20.4,REV=1999.11.25.13.32
```

```
 9   SFWflex          GNU flex
                      (i386) 2.5.4,REV=1999.11.25.13.32
10   SFWfvwm          fvwm virtual window manager
                      (i386) 2.2.2,REV=1999.11.25.13.32

... 288 more menu choices to follow;
<RETURN> for more choices, <CTRL-D> to stop display:
```

At this point, the number of the package that you want to remove can be entered.

Installing a Solaris Package Using admintool

The package format is very flexible and is independent of the interface used to install specific packages. This means that although administrators from a Linux background may prefer to use the pkgadd command, administrators from a Windows background might find the package administration features of the admintool easier to use. As shown in Figure 5-4, the admintool provides an easy-to-use interface for installing packages, where the following options may be selected from drop-down boxes:

- Check for existing files.
- Check for existing packages.
- Check for existing partial installations.
- Allow setuid/setgid files to be installed.
- Allow setuid/setgid scripts to be run.
- Check that installation dependencies have been met.
- Check that removal dependencies have been met.
- Check for correct run level.
- Check for sufficient space.
- Display copyrights.
- Run the installation interactively.

The admintool also allows the administrator to specify an installation source, so that packages may be installed directly from a CD-ROM, as shown in Figure 5-5.

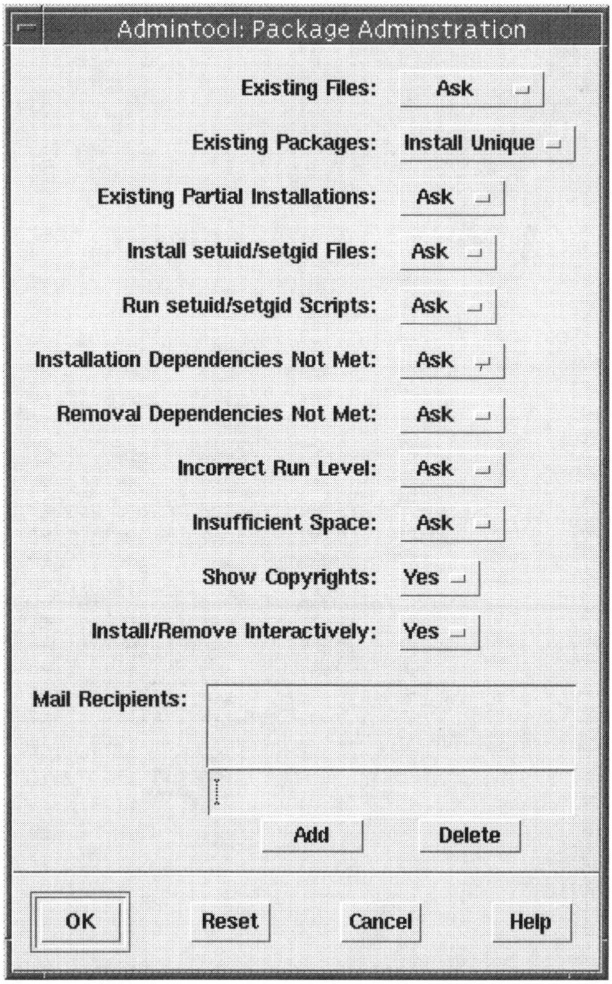

```
┌─────────────────────────────────────────────┐
│ ─    Admintool: Package Adminstration        │
├─────────────────────────────────────────────┤
│                                               │
│              Existing Files:   Ask      ⌐     │
│                                               │
│          Existing Packages:   Install Unique ⌐│
│                                               │
│   Existing Partial Installations:  Ask   ⌐    │
│                                               │
│      Install setuid/setgid Files:  Ask   ⌐    │
│                                               │
│      Run setuid/setgid Scripts:  Ask   ⌐      │
│                                               │
│  Installation Dependencies Not Met:  Ask  ⌐   │
│                                               │
│   Removal Dependencies Not Met:  Ask   ⌐      │
│                                               │
│            Incorrect Run Level:  Ask   ⌐      │
│                                               │
│           Insufficient Space:  Ask   ⌐        │
│                                               │
│            Show Copyrights:  Yes  ⌐           │
│                                               │
│   Install/Remove Interactively:  Yes  ⌐       │
│                                               │
│  Mail Recipients: ┌─────────────────────────┐ │
│                   │                         │ │
│                   │                         │ │
│                   │                         │ │
│                   ├─────────────────────────┤ │
│                   │                         │ │
│                   └─────────────────────────┘ │
│                   ┌──────┐     ┌────────┐     │
│                   │ Add  │     │ Delete │     │
│                   └──────┘     └────────┘     │
├─────────────────────────────────────────────┤
│ ┌──────┐   ┌───────┐   ┌────────┐  ┌──────┐   │
│ │  OK  │   │ Reset │   │ Cancel │  │ Help │   │
│ └──────┘   └───────┘   └────────┘  └──────┘   │
└─────────────────────────────────────────────┘
```

Figure 5-4   The admintool interface for adding packages

Once a valid CD-ROM directory containing packages has been selected, the Add Software interface is displayed, as shown in Figure 5-6. The left-hand pane shows all of the full titles for the packages that have been located in the specified directory. The right-hand pane shows the description of the last selected software package. For example, the package SUNWcesh is the Sun Management Center Simplified Chinese help package, which is distributed by Sun Microsystems Inc., and is less than 1M when installed.

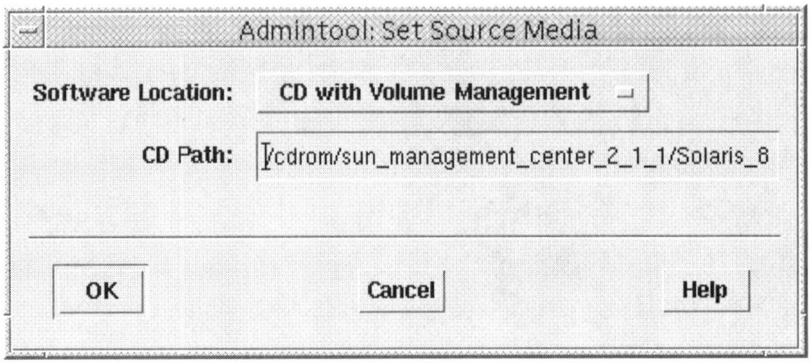

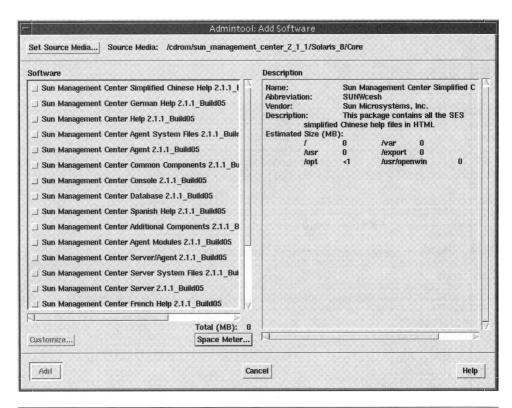

Figure 5-5   The admintool interface for selecting the package installation source

Figure 5-6   Adding packages from the CD-ROM using the admintool interface

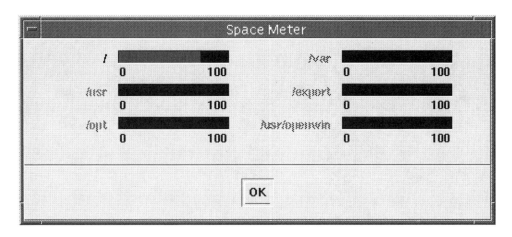

Figure 5-7   Checking available disk space using the Space Meter

You should always verify that you have sufficient space available in the indicated partitions by checking the Space Meter, as shown in Figure 5-7. Here we can see that more than enough space is available to install the required files for the SUNWcesh package.

After checking the boxes associated with every package that you want to install, you can then proceed with installation by clicking the Add button. A separate installation window then appears, as shown in Figure 5-8. In this example, the SUNWescon software package is being installed (this is the Sun Management Center console package). After setting the installation target directory (/opt), the package and system information is processed. After disk space requirements have been verified, any conflicts with existing packages are identified. Next, all setuid and setgid applications are identified, and assent must be granted to install any setuid or setgid files that are found in the package. Finally, the files are installed into their appropriate target directories.

Packages may also be installed from a special package spooling directory (/var/spool/pkg) using the admintool or any directory that contains a valid package file, as shown in Figure 5-9.

Once a valid spooling directory containing packages has been selected, the Add Software interface is displayed, as shown in Figure 5-10. The left-hand pane shows all of the full titles for the packages that have been located in the specified directory. The right-hand pane shows the description of the last selected software package. The only package shown is SUNWcesh, the Sun Management Center Simplified Chinese help package, which is distributed by Sun Microsystems Inc., and is less than 1M when

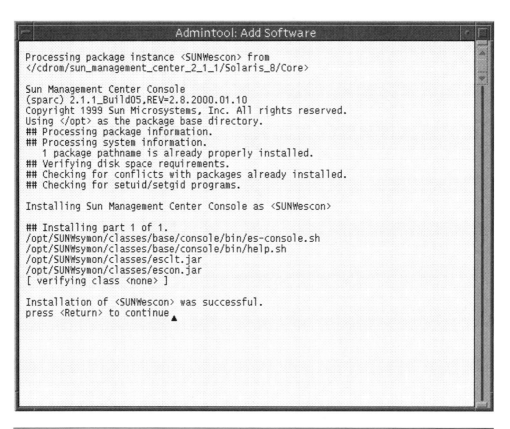

Figure 5-8 Package installation phase during admintool installation

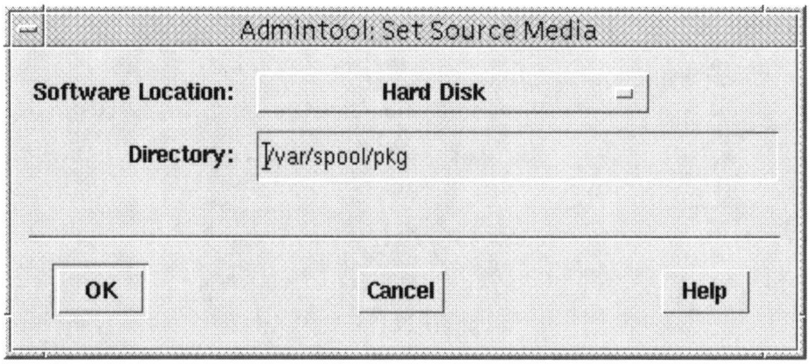

Figure 5-9 The admintool interface for selecting the package installation source

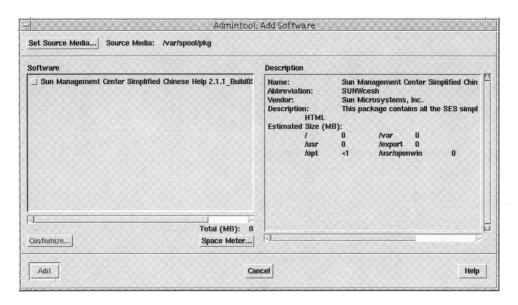

Figure 5-10   Adding packages from the spooling directory using the admintool interface

installed. After checking the boxes associated with the SUNWcesh package, you can then proceed with installation by clicking the Add button. A separate installation window then appears, and the software is installed.

Uninstalling a Solaris Package Using Admintool

Once a package has been installed on the system, it can easily be removed by using the admintool. Simply select Browse, Software; highlight the package that you want to remove; and then click Edit, Delete. A popup window then appears, as shown in Figure 5-11, asking for confirmation of the deletion instruction.

Once you've clicked OK, a separate window will open, showing the output of the package removal:

```
The following package is currently installed:
    SUNWdesmt       ShowMe TV German Localization Files
                    (sparc) 1.1,REV=1999.04.30
```

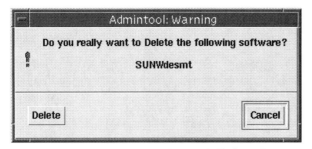

Figure 5-11   Confirming the deletion instruction

```
Do you want to remove this package? y

## Removing installed package instance <SUNWdesmt>
## Verifying package dependencies.
## Processing package information.
## Removing pathnames in class <none>
/opt/SUNWsmtv/lib/locale/de/share/showmetv-defaults
/opt/SUNWsmtv/lib/locale/de/share
/opt/SUNWsmtv/lib/locale/de/help/xdh_saveFile.html
/opt/SUNWsmtv/lib/locale/de/help/xdh_printItem.html
/opt/SUNWsmtv/lib/locale/de/help/xdh_openFile.html
/opt/SUNWsmtv/lib/locale/de/help/xdh_historyDialog.html
/opt/SUNWsmtv/lib/locale/de/help/xdh_findText.html
/opt/SUNWsmtv/lib/locale/de/help/xdh_entry.html
/opt/SUNWsmtv/lib/locale/de/help/watchtimer.html
/opt/SUNWsmtv/lib/locale/de/help/videosettings.html
/opt/SUNWsmtv/lib/locale/de/help/undelete.html
/opt/SUNWsmtv/lib/locale/de/help/transmitterproperties.html
/opt/SUNWsmtv/lib/locale/de/help/transmitter.html
/opt/SUNWsmtv/lib/locale/de/help/statistics.html
/opt/SUNWsmtv/lib/locale/de/help/showcards.html
/opt/SUNWsmtv/lib/locale/de/help/recordtimer.html
/opt/SUNWsmtv/lib/locale/de/help/record.html
/opt/SUNWsmtv/lib/locale/de/help/receiver.html
/opt/SUNWsmtv/lib/locale/de/help/properties.html
/opt/SUNWsmtv/lib/locale/de/help/programinfo.html
/opt/SUNWsmtv/lib/locale/de/help/printsnap.html
/opt/SUNWsmtv/lib/locale/de/help/printformat.html
/opt/SUNWsmtv/lib/locale/de/help/print.html
/opt/SUNWsmtv/lib/locale/de/help/preview.html
/opt/SUNWsmtv/lib/locale/de/help/preferences.html
/opt/SUNWsmtv/lib/locale/de/help/open.html
/opt/SUNWsmtv/lib/locale/de/help/new.html
/opt/SUNWsmtv/lib/locale/de/help/mail.html
/opt/SUNWsmtv/lib/locale/de/help/import.html
```

```
/opt/SUNWsmtv/lib/locale/de/help/group.html
/opt/SUNWsmtv/lib/locale/de/help/findres.html
/opt/SUNWsmtv/lib/locale/de/help/filewindow.html
/opt/SUNWsmtv/lib/locale/de/help/exportcards.html
/opt/SUNWsmtv/lib/locale/de/help/broadcast.html
/opt/SUNWsmtv/lib/locale/de/help/addrbook.html
/opt/SUNWsmtv/lib/locale/de/help/addfields.html
/opt/SUNWsmtv/lib/locale/de/help
/opt/SUNWsmtv/lib/locale/de/LC_MESSAGES/splitmov.cat
/opt/SUNWsmtv/lib/locale/de/LC_MESSAGES/showmetvt.cat
/opt/SUNWsmtv/lib/locale/de/LC_MESSAGES/showmetvh.cat
/opt/SUNWsmtv/lib/locale/de/LC_MESSAGES/showmetvd.cat
/opt/SUNWsmtv/lib/locale/de/LC_MESSAGES/showmetvab.cat
/opt/SUNWsmtv/lib/locale/de/LC_MESSAGES/showmetv.cat
/opt/SUNWsmtv/lib/locale/de/LC_MESSAGES/pic.cat
/opt/SUNWsmtv/lib/locale/de/LC_MESSAGES/mpext.cat
/opt/SUNWsmtv/lib/locale/de/LC_MESSAGES/libvid.cat
/opt/SUNWsmtv/lib/locale/de/LC_MESSAGES/libvcr.cat
/opt/SUNWsmtv/lib/locale/de/LC_MESSAGES/libtv.cat
/opt/SUNWsmtv/lib/locale/de/LC_MESSAGES/libsunsolxt.cat
/opt/SUNWsmtv/lib/locale/de/LC_MESSAGES/libsunsol.cat
/opt/SUNWsmtv/lib/locale/de/LC_MESSAGES/libsnmp.cat
/opt/SUNWsmtv/lib/locale/de/LC_MESSAGES/librtp.cat
/opt/SUNWsmtv/lib/locale/de/LC_MESSAGES/libregserv.cat
/opt/SUNWsmtv/lib/locale/de/LC_MESSAGES/libpdb.cat
/opt/SUNWsmtv/lib/locale/de/LC_MESSAGES/libh261.cat
/opt/SUNWsmtv/lib/locale/de/LC_MESSAGES/libavdata.cat
/opt/SUNWsmtv/lib/locale/de/LC_MESSAGES/libaud.cat
/opt/SUNWsmtv/lib/locale/de/LC_MESSAGES/libab.cat
/opt/SUNWsmtv/lib/locale/de/LC_MESSAGES/h261vis.cat
/opt/SUNWsmtv/lib/locale/de/LC_MESSAGES/devthr.cat
/opt/SUNWsmtv/lib/locale/de/LC_MESSAGES
/opt/SUNWsmtv/lib/locale/de
/opt/SUNWsmtv/lib/locale <shared pathname not removed>
/opt/SUNWsmtv/lib <shared pathname not removed>
/opt/SUNWsmtv/app-defaults/de/showmetvh
/opt/SUNWsmtv/app-defaults/de/help.mesgs
/opt/SUNWsmtv/app-defaults/de
/opt/SUNWsmtv/app-defaults <shared pathname not removed>
/opt/SUNWsmtv <shared pathname not removed>
## Updating system information.

Removal of <SUNWdesmt> was successful.
press <Return> to continue
```

Summary

In this chapter, we've examined how to retrieve descriptions of installed Solaris packages using the admintool GUI and the shell GUI. In addition, we've also learned how to install new packages and remove unwanted packages by using the same methods. All of the software supplied with Solaris (including system patches available from **www.sunsolve.com**) is now packaged using the package format, and many sites will build software from the source, create a package from these binaries, and install a package, rather than copying files to the system directories manually. This makes it easier to manage dependencies and to understand how files are related to one another.

Questions

1. Which of the following media can be used to install packages using admintool? (Choose two.)
   A. CD-ROM
   B. Floppy disk
   C. Network drive
   D. Hard drive

2. Which of the following commands is used to install packages using the CLI?
   A. pkgchk
   B. pkgadd
   C. pkgrm
   D. pkgmk

3. Which of the following commands is used to verify packages using the CLI?
   A. pkgchk
   B. pkgadd
   C. pkgrm
   D. pkgmk

4. Which of the following commands is used to remove packages using the CLI?
   A. pkgchk
   B. pkgadd
   C. pkgrm
   D. pkgmk

5. Which types of packages can be installed on Solaris? (Choose two.)
   A. Utility Package
   B. System Package
   C. Application Package
   D. Network Package

6. What is the sequence in which operations are performed during a pkgadd?
   A. Processing package information, processing system information, verifying disk space requirements, checking for conflicts with packages already installed, checking for setuid/setgid programs
   B. Processing package information, processing system information, verifying disk space requirements, checking for setuid/setgid programs, checking for conflicts with packages already installed
   C. Checking for setuid/setgid programs, processing package information, processing system information, verifying disk space requirements, checking for conflicts with packages already installed
   D. Checking for setuid/setgid programs, processing system information, verifying disk space requirements, checking for conflicts with packages already installed, processing package information

7. Which options can be set for package installation using admintool? (Choose two.)
   A. Limit the number of packages that can be installed.
   B. Automatically upgrade packages through the Internet.
   C. Check for existing files.
   D. Allow setuid/setgid files to be installed.

8. How can available disk space be checked within admintool?
   A. The df command
   B. Space meter
   C. Space wizard
   D. Progress meter

Answers

1. A, D

2. B

3. A

4. C

5. A, B

6. A

7. C, D

8. B

Maintaining Patches

The following objectives will be met upon completing this chapter's material:

- Understanding where to download patches
- Reviewing currently installed patches
- Adding new patches
- Removing currently installed patches

Patches are binary code modifications that affect the way that Sun-supplied software operates. They can be released by Sun because of previously identified bugs that have now been fixed, or because a security exploit has been discovered in a piece of software, and a simple workaround is inadequate to prevent the intrusion or disruption of normal system activity. For example, many of the older Solaris daemons suffered from buffer overflow vulnerabilities until recently, and now the fixed boundaries on an array are deliberately overwritten by a rogue client to crash the system. Many of the system daemons, such as Web servers, may be crashed because memory is overwritten with arbitrary values outside the declared size of an array. Without appropriate bounds checking, passing a GET request to a Web server of 1,025 bytes when the array size is 1,024 would clearly result in unpredictable behavior, as the C language does not prevent a program from doing this. Because Solaris daemons are typically written in C, a number have been fixed in recent years to prevent this problem from occurring (but you may be surprised at just how often new weaknesses are exposed). The Sendmail, Internet Mail Access Protocol (IMAP), and Post Office Protocol (POP) daemons for Solaris have all experienced buffer overflow vulnerabilities in the past, which have required the urgent installation of security patches.

For early Solaris 8 installations out of the box, two critical problems were typically identified, both associated with gaining root access via buffer overflow:

- The Common Desktop Environment-based (CDE) Calendar Manager service might be vulnerable to a buffer overflow attack, as identified in CVE 1999-0320 and 1999-0696. The Calendar Manager is used to manage appointments and other date/time-based functions.

- The remote administration daemon (sadmind) might be vulnerable to a buffer overflow attack, as described in CVE 1999-0977. The remote administration daemon is used to manage system administration activities across a number of different hosts.

The CVE number matches the descriptions of each security issue from the Common Vulnerabilities and Exposures database (**http://cve.mitre.org**). Each identified vulnerability contains a hyperlink back to the CVE database, so that information displayed about every issue is updated directly from the source. New patches and bug fixes are also listed.

Understanding Patches

To find information about current patches, sysadmins are directed to the **www. sunsolve.com** site. Here details about current patches for each operating system release can be found. Two basic types of patches are available from SunSolve: single patches and jumbo patches. Single patches have a single patch number associated with them, are generally aimed at resolving a single outstanding issue, and usually insert, delete, or update data in a small number of files. Single patches are also targeted at resolving specific security issues. Each patch is associated with an internal bug number from Sun's bug database. For example, patch number 108435-01 aims to fix BugId 4318566, involving a shared library issue with the 64-bit C++ compiler.

In contrast, a jumbo patch consists of many single patches that have been bundled together, on the basis of operating system release levels, to ensure that the most common issues for a particular platform are resolved by the installation of the jumbo patch. It's standard practice to install the current jumbo patch for Solaris 8 after it's been installed from scratch, or if the system has been upgraded from Solaris 7, for example.

Some of the latest patches released for Solaris 8 include the following:

- 110322-01: Patch for /usr/lib/netsvc/yp/ypbind
- 110853-01: Patch for Sun-Fire-880

- 110856-01: Patch for /etc/inet/services
- 110888-01: Patch for figgs
- 110894-01: Patch for country name
- 110927-01: Patch for SUNW_PKGLIST
- 111078-01: Patch for Solaris Resource Manager
- 111295-01: Patch for /usr/bin/sparcv7/pstack and /usr/bin/sparcv9/pstack
- 111297-01: Patch for /usr/lib/libsendfile.so.1
- 111337-01: Patch for /usr/sbin/ocfserv
- 111400-01: Patch for KCMS Configure tool
- 111402-01: Patch for crontab
- 111431-01: Patch for /usr/lib/libldap.so.4
- 111439-01: Patch for /kernel/fs/tmpfs
- 111473-01: Patch for PCI Host Adapter
- 111562-01: Patch for /usr/lib/librt.so.1
- 111564-01: Patch for SunPCi 2.2.1
- 111570-01: Patch for uucp
- 111588-01: Patch for /kernel/drv/wc
- 111606-01: Patch for /usr/sbin/in.ftpd
- 111624-01: Patch for /usr/sbin/inetd
- 111648-01: Patch for env3test, cpupmtest, ifbtest, and rsctest
- 111656-01: Patch for socal and sf drivers
- 111762-01: Patch for Expert3D and SunVTS

One of the most useful guides to the currently available patches for Solaris 8 is the SunSolve Patch Report (**ftp://sunsolve.sun.com/pub/patches/Solaris8.PatchReport**). This report provides a quick reference to all newly released patches for the platform, as well as updates on previous patches that have now been modified. A list of suggested patches for the platform is also contained in the report, while recommended security patches are listed separately. Finally, a list of obsolete patches is provided. Some of the currently listed security patches available include the following:

- 108528-09: Patch for kernel update
- 108869-06: Patch for snmpdx/mibiisa/libssasnmp/snmplib

- 108875-09: Patch for c2audit
- 108968-05: Patch for vol/vold/rmmount
- 108975-04: Patch for /usr/bin/rmformat and /usr/sbin/format
- 108985-03: Patch for /usr/sbin/in.rshd
- 108991-13: Patch for /usr/lib/libc.so.1
- 109091-04: Patch for /usr/lib/fs/ufs/ufsrestore
- 109134-19: Patch for WBEM
- 109234-04: Patch for Apache and NCA
- 109279-13: Patch for /kernel/drv/ip
- 109320-03: Patch for LP
- 109322-07: Patch for libnsl
- 109326-05: Patch for libresolv.so.2 and in.named
- 109354-09: Patch for dtsession
- 109783-01: Patch for /usr/lib/nfs/nfsd
- 109805-03: Patch for pam_krb5.so.1
- 109887-08: Patch for smartcard
- 109888-05: Patch for platform drivers
- 109892-03: Patch for /kernel/drv/ecpp driver
- 109894-01: Patch for /kernel/drv/sparcv9/bpp driver
- 109896-04: Patch for USB driver
- 109951-01: Patch for jserver buffer overflow

Figure 6-1 shows the main screen on SunSolve that lists all of the available jumbo patches and recommended clusters for Solaris 8.

Verifying Installed Patches

To determine which patches are currently installed on your system, you need to use the showrev command as follows:

```
# showrev -p
Patch: 107430-01 Obsoletes:   Requires:   Incompatibles:   Packages: SUNWwsr
Patch: 108029-01 Obsoletes:   Requires:   Incompatibles:   Packages: SUNWwsr
```

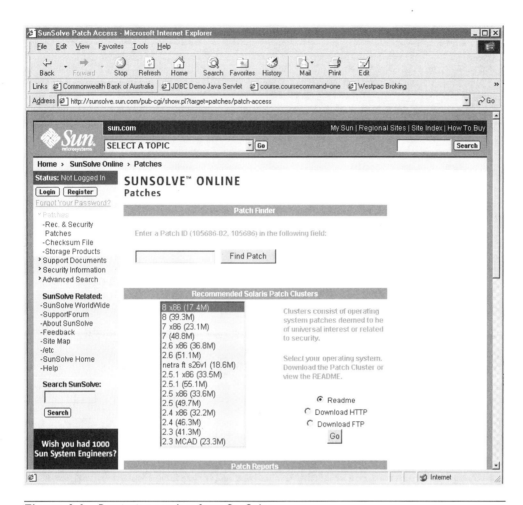

Figure 6-1 Retrieving patches from SunSolve

```
Patch: 107437-03 Obsoletes:  Requires:  Incompatibles:  Packages: SUNWtiu8
Patch: 107316-01 Obsoletes:  Requires:  Incompatibles:  Packages: SUNWploc
Patch: 107453-01 Obsoletes:  Requires:  Incompatibles:  Packages: SUNWkvm,
SUNWcar
Patch: 106541-06 Obsoletes: 106976-01, 107029-01, 107030-01, 107334-01
Requires:
   Incompatibles:  Packages: SUNWkvm, SUNWcsu, SUNWcsr, SUNWcsl, SUNWcar,
SUNWesu, SUNWarc, SUNWatfsr, SUNWcpr, SUNWdpl, SUNWhea, SUNWtoo, SUNWpcmci,
SUNWtnfc, SUNWvolr
Patch: 106541-10 Obsoletes: 106832-03, 106976-01, 107029-01, 107030-01,
107334-01, 107031-01, 107117-05, 107899-01 Requires: 107544-02
Incompatibles:  Packages:
```

```
SUNWkvm, SUNWcsu, SUNWcsr, SUNWcsl, SUNWcar, SUNWesu, SUNWarc, SUNWatfsr,
SUNWscpu, SUNWcpr, SUNWdpl, SUNWhea, SUNWipc, SUNWtoo, SUNWpcmci,
SUNWpcmcu, SUNWtnfc, SUNWvolr
Patch: 106541-15 Obsoletes: 106832-03, 106976-01, 107029-01, 107030-01,
107334-01, 107031-01, 107117-05, 107899-01, 108752-01, 107147-08, 109104-04
Requires: 107544-02 Incompatibles:  Packages: SUNWkvm, SUNWcsu, SUNWcsr,
SUNWcsl, SUNWcar, SUNWesu, SUNWarc, SUNWatfsr, SUNWscpu, SUNWcpr, SUNWdpl,
SUNWhea, SUNWipc, SUNWtoo, SUNWnisu, SUNWpcmci, SUNWpcmcu, SUNWtnfc,
SUNWvolu, SUNWvolr
```

From the example shown here, we can see that showrev reports several different properties of each patch installed:

- The patch number
- Whether the patch obsoletes a previously released patch (or patches) and which version numbers
- Whether the current patch depends on any pre-requisite patches (and their version numbers)
- Whether the patch is incompatible with any other patches
- Which standard Solaris packages are affected by installation of the patch

From one of the examples above (106541-15), we can see that it obsoletes a large number of other patches, including 106832-03, 106976-01, 107029-01, 107030-01, 107334-01, 107031-01, 107117-05, 107899-01, 108752-01, 107147-08, and 109104-04. In addition, it depends on patch 107544-02 and is compatible with all other known patches. Finally, it affects a large number of different packages, including SUNWkvm, SUNWcsu, SUNWcsr, SUNWcsl, SUNWcar, SUNWesu, SUNWarc, SUNWatfsr, SUNWscpu, SUNWcpr, SUNWdpl, SUNWhea, SUNWipc, SUNWtoo, SUNWnisu, SUNWpcmci, SUNWpcmcu, SUNWtnfc, SUNWvolu, and SUNWvolr.

Installing Patches

To install single patches, you simply need to use the patchadd command:

```
# patchadd /patches/106541-15
```

/patches is the directory where your patches are downloaded, and 106541-15 is the name of the patch filename (it should be the same as the patch number).

To add a large number of patches from the same directory, the following command could be used:

```
# patchadd /patches/106541-15 106541-10 107453-01
```

106541-15, 106541-10, and 107453-01 are the patches to be installed. After the patches have been successfully installed, they can be verified by using the showrev command. For example, to check that patch 106541-15 has been successfully installed, the following command could be used:

```
# showrev -p | grep 106541-15
```

Backing out Patches

Patches can be easily removed by using the patchrm command. For example, to remove the patch 106541-15, the following command would be used:

```
# patchrm 106541-15
```

If the patch was previously installed, it would now be removed. However, if the patch was not previously installed, the following error message would be displayed:

```
Checking installed packages and patches...
Patch 106541-15 has not been applied to this system.
patchrm is terminating.
```

Summary

In this chapter, we have examined how to download and install system patches, which are responsible for rectifying bugs in system software. In addition, high-priority security bugs were also reviewed, and their potential effects outlined. Finally, we examined how to remove patches when they have been obsoleted by newer releases.

Questions

1. Which of the following is a valid patch number?
   A. A07430-01
   B. 107430-01
   C. 107430-0X
   D. 107430-X1

2. Which command is used to review installed patches?
   A. showrev
   B. patchview
   C. showpatch
   D. patchreview

3. Which command is used to apply a patch?
   A. patchapply
   B. addpatch
   C. patchadd
   D. applypatch

4. Which command is used to delete a patch?
   A. patchrm
   B. deletepatch
   C. patchdelete
   D. rmpatch

Answers

1. B

2. A

3. C

4. A

The Boot Process

The following objectives will be met upon completing this chapter's material:

- Understanding each of the Solaris run levels
- Learning about the various boot phases during system startup
- Exploring the role of the /sbin/init application
- Creating startup scripts in /etc/init.d to enable system services

Switching Run-Levels

In terms of system startup, Solaris has some similarities to Microsoft Windows and Linux. Although it doesn't have an AUTOEXEC.BAT or CONFIG.SYS file, Solaris does have a number of script files that are executed in a specific order to start services, just like Linux. These scripts are typically created in the /etc/init.d directory as Bourne shell scripts and are then symbolically linked into the run-level directories. Just like Microsoft Windows has safe modes, Solaris supports a number of different modes of operation, from restricted single-user modes to full multi-user run levels. The complete set of run levels, with their respective run control script directories, is displayed in Table 7-1.

Each run level is associated with a run-level script, as shown in Table 7-2. The run-level script is responsible for the orderly execution of all run-level scripts within a specific run-level directory. The script name matches the run level and directory name.

When a Solaris system starts, the init process is spawned, which is responsible for managing processes and the transitions between run levels. You can actually switch manually between run levels yourself by using the init command. To halt the operating system (run level 6), you can simply type the following command:

```
bash-2.03# init 6
```

Table 7-1   Solaris Run Levels and Their Functions

Run Level	Description	User Status	Run Control Script Directory
0	Hardware maintenance mode	Console access	/etc/rc0.d
1	Administrative state; only root filesystem is available	Single user	/etc/rc1.d
2	First multi-user state; NFS resources unavailable	Multi-user	/etc/rc2.d
3	NFS resources available	Multi-user	/etc/rc3.d
4	User-defined state	Not specified	N/A
5	Power down firmware state	Console access	/etc/rc5.d
6	Operating system halted for reboot	Single user	/etc/rc6.d
S	Administrative tasks and repair of corrupted filesystems	Console access	/etc/rcS.d

Table 7-2   Solaris Run-Level Scripts

Run Level	Run Control Script
0	/etc/rc0
1	/etc/rc1
2	/etc/rc2
3	/etc/rc3
4	N/A
5	/etc/rc5
6	/etc/rc6
S	/etc/rcS

Every Solaris init state (such as init state 6) has its own run-level script directory (such as /etc/rc6.d). This contains a set of symbolic links (like shortcuts in Microsoft Windows) that are associated with the service startup files in the /etc/init.d directory. Each linked script starts with a letter S (start) or the letter K (kill) and are used to start or kill processes respectively. When a system is booted, processes are started. When a system is shutdown, processes are killed. The start and kill links are typically made to the same script file, which interprets two parameters: *start* and *stop*. The scripts are executed in numerical order, so a script like /etc/rc3.d/ S20dhcp is executed before /etc/rc3.d/ S21sshd. If you're curious about which kind of scripts are started or killed in Solaris during startup and shutdown, Table 7-3 shows the startup scripts in /etc/rc2.d, while Table 7-4 shows the kill scripts found in /etc/rc0.d. It's important to realize that these will change from system to system.

Table 7-3   Typical Multi-user Startup Scripts under Solaris 8

Script	Description
S05RMTMPFILES	Removes temporary files in the /tmp directory.
S20sysetup	Establishes system setup requirements, and checks /var/crash to determine whether the system is recovering from a crash.
S21perf	Enables system accounting using /usr/lib/sa/sadc and /var/adm/sa/sa.
S30sysid.net	Executes /usr/sbin/sysidnet, /usr/sbin/sysidconfig, and /sbin/ifconfig, which are responsible for configuring network services.
S69inet	Initiates second phase of TCP/IP configuration, following on from the basic services established during single-user mode (rcS). Setting up the IP routing (if /etc/defaultrouter exists), performing TCP/IP-parameter tuning (using ndd), and setting the NIS domain-name (if required) are all performed here.
S70uucp	Initializes the UNIX-to-UNIX copy program (UUCP) by removing locks and other unnecessary files.
S71sysid.sys	Executes /usr/sbin/sysidsys and /usr/sbin/sysidroot.
S72autoinstall	Script to execute JumpStart installation if appropriate.
S72inetsvc	Final network configuration using /usr/sbin/ifconfig after NIS/NIS+ has been initialized. Also initializes the Internet Domain Name Service (DNS) if appropriate.
S80PRESERVE	Preserves editing files by executing /usr/lib/expreserve.
S91leoconfig	Configuration for ZX graphics cards (if installed).
S92rtvc-config	Configuration for SunVideo cards (if installed).
S92volmgt	Starts volume management for removeable media using /usr/sbin/vold.

Table 7-4   Typical Single-user Kill Scripts under Solaris 8

Script	Description
K00ANNOUNCE	Announces that "system services are now being stopped."
K10dtlogin	Initializes tasks for the Common Desktop Environment (CDE), including killing the dtlogin process.
K20lp	Stops printing services using /usr/lib/lpshut.
K22acct	Terminates process accounting using /usr/lib/acct/shutacct.
K42audit	Kills the auditing daemon (/usr/sbin/audit).
K47asppp	Stops the asynchronous PPP daemon (/usr/sbin/aspppd).
K50utmpd	Kills the utmp daemon (/usr/lib/utmpd).
K55syslog	Terminates the system logging service (/usr/sbin/syslogd).
K57sendmail	Halts the sendmail mail service (/usr/lib/sendmail).
K66nfs.server	Kills all processes required for the NFS server (/usr/lib/nfs/nfsd).
K69autofs	Stops the automounter (/usr/sbin/automount).
K70cron	Terminates the cron daemon (/usr/bin/cron).
K75nfs.client	Disables client NFS.
K76nscd	Kills the name service cache daemon (/usr/sbin/nscd).
K85rpc	Disables remote procedure call (rpc) services (/usr/sbin/rpcbind).

Understanding Booting

Booting the kernel is a straightforward process once the operating system has been successfully installed. The Solaris kernel can be identified by the pathname /platform/ PLATFORM_NAME/kernel/unix where PLATFORM_NAME is the name of the current architecture. For example, sun4u systems boot with the kernel /platform/sun4u/ kernel/. Kernels can be alternatively booted from a CD-ROM drive or through a network connection (by using the **boot cdrom** and **boot net** commands from the Open-Boot PROM monitor respectively).

When a SPARC system is powered on, the system executes a series of basic hardware tests before attempting to boot the kernel. These Power-On Self-Tests (POSTs) ensure that your system hardware is operating correctly. If the POST tests fail, you will not be able to boot the system.

Once the POST tests are complete, the system will attempt to boot the default kernel using the path specified in the firmware. Alternatively, if you want to boot a different kernel, you can press STOP+a, enter **boot kernel/name**, and boot the kernel specified by kernel/name. For example, to boot a kernel called newunix, you would use the command **boot kernel/newunix**.

To examine the default boot devices and the default values used by your system for booting the kernel, simply use the **/usr/sbin/eeprom** command:

```
bash-2.03$ /usr/sbin/eeprom
tpe-link-test?=true
scsi-initiator-id=7
keyboard-click?=false
keymap: data not available.
ttyb-rts-dtr-off=false
ttyb-ignore-cd=true
ttya-rts-dtr-off=false
ttya-ignore-cd=true
ttyb-mode=9600,8,n,1,-
ttya-mode=9600,8,n,1,-
pcia-probe-list=1,2,3,4
pcib-probe-list=1,2,3
mfg-mode=off
diag-level=max
#power-cycles=50
system-board-serial#: data not available.
system-board-date: data not available.
fcode-debug?=false
output-device=screen
input-device=keyboard
load-base=16384
boot-command=boot
auto-boot?=true
watchdog-reboot?=false
diag-file: data not available.
diag-device=net
boot-file: data not available.
boot-device=disk net
local-mac-address?=false
ansi-terminal?=true
screen-#columns=80
screen-#rows=34
silent-mode?=false
use-nvramrc?=false
nvramrc: data not available.
security-mode=none
security-password: data not available.
security-#badlogins=0
oem-logo: data not available.
oem-logo?=false
oem-banner: data not available.
oem-banner?=false
```

```
hardware-revision: data not available.
last-hardware-update: data not available.
diag-switch?=false
```

You can also change the values of the boot device and boot command from within Solaris by using the **eeprom** command, rather than having to reboot, jump into the OpenBoot monitor, and set the values directly.

Systems either boot from a UFS filesystem (whether on the local hard disk or a local CD-ROM drive) or across the network. Two applications facilitate these different boot types; ufsboot is responsible for booting kernels from disk devices, while inetboot is responsible for booting kernels using a network device. Although servers typically boot themselves using ufsboot, diskless clients must use inetboot.

The ufsboot application reads the bootblock on the active partition of the boot device, while inetboot performs a broadcast on the local subnet, searching for a trivial FTP (TFTP) server. Once located, the kernel is downloaded using NFS and booted.

The init Process

After the kernel is loaded into memory, the /sbin/init process is initialized, and the system is bought up to the default init state, which is determined by the initdefault value contained in /etc/inittab, which controls the behavior of the init process. Each entry has the form

```
identifier:runlevel:action:command
```

where identifier is a unique, two-character identifier, runlevel specifies the run level to be entered, action specifies the process characteristics of the command to be executed, and command is the name of the program to be run. The program can be an application or a script file. The run level must be one of s, a, b, c, 1, 2, 3, 4, 5, or 6. Alternatively, if the process is to be executed by all run levels, no run level should be specified. The action field should only contain one of the following standard process actions:

- respawn
- wait
- once
- boot
- bootwait
- powerfail

- powerwait

- off

- ondemand

- initdefault

- sysinit

The following is a standard inittab file:

```
ap:sysinit:/sbin/autopush -f /etc/iu.ap
ap:sysinit:/sbin/soconfig -f /etc/sock2path
fs:sysinit:/sbin/rcS sysinit               >/dev/msglog 2<>/dev/msglog
</dev/console
is:3:initdefault:
p3:s1234:powerfail:/usr/sbin/shutdown -y -i5 -g0 >/dev/msglog
2<>/dev/msglog
sS:s:wait:/sbin/rcS                        >/dev/msglog
2<>/dev/msglog </dev/console
s0:0:wait:/sbin/rc0                        >/dev/msglog
2<>/dev/msglog </dev/console
s1:1:respawn:/sbin/rc1                     >/dev/msglog
2<>/dev/msglog </dev/console
s2:23:wait:/sbin/rc2                       >/dev/msglog
2<>/dev/msglog </dev/console
s3:3:wait:/sbin/rc3                        >/dev/msglog
2<>/dev/msglog </dev/console
s5:5:wait:/sbin/rc5                        >/dev/msglog
2<>/dev/msglog </dev/console
s6:6:wait:/sbin/rc6                        >/dev/msglog
2<>/dev/msglog </dev/console
fw:0:wait:/sbin/uadmin 2 0                 >/dev/msglog
2<>/dev/msglog </dev/console
of:5:wait:/sbin/uadmin 2 6                 >/dev/msglog
2<>/dev/msglog </dev/console
rb:6:wait:/sbin/uadmin 2 1                 >/dev/msglog
2<>/dev/msglog </dev/console
sc:234:respawn:/usr/lib/saf/sac -t 300
co:234:respawn:/usr/lib/saf/ttymon -g -h -p "'uname -n' console
login: " -T sun -d /dev/console -l console -m ldterm,ttcompat
```

Writing Startup Scripts

The generic form of a startup and shutdown script is shown in the following section. A startup file for the daemon someprogram is created in /etc/init.d, which is then symbolically linked to a K (kill) and S (start) script in one of the /etc/rc directories. For example, to start someprogram in run level two, we would create a symbolic link between /etc/init.d/someprogram and /etc/rc2.d/S99someprogram, where 99 indicates the relative precedence of the execution of all scripts in the /etc/rc2.d directory. Lower-numbered scripts are executed before higher-numbered scripts.

If the script is passed the parameter *start* (from a S script), then it checks that the daemon to be executed exists on the filesystem. If it exists, the daemon is executed. If the script is passed the parameter *stop* (from a K script), then it checks that the daemon to be executed exists on the filesystem. If it exists, the daemon is killed by using the **pkill** command.

```
#!/bin/sh

#
# Start/stop process for some program
#

case "$1" in
'start')
        if [ -x /path/to/daemon/name ]
        then
                /path/to/daemon/name
        ;;
'stop')

        if [ -x /path/to/daemon/name ]
        then
                pkill -9 name
        fi
        ;;
*)
        echo "Usage: /etc/init.d/someprogram { start | stop }"
        ;;
esac
```

Summary

In this chapter, we've examined how Solaris systems boot, how they initialize processes using the init process spawner and the /etc/inittab file, and how to create startup files to initialize and kill system daemons at various run levels.

Questions

1. What is the purpose of run level 0?
   A. First multi-user state
   B. Administrative state
   C. Hardware maintenance state
   D. Power down firmware

2. What is the purpose of run level 1?
   A. First multi-user state
   B. Administrative state
   C. Hardware maintenance state
   D. Power down firmware

3. What is the purpose of run level 2?
   A. First multi-user state
   B. Administrative state
   C. Hardware maintenance state
   D. Power down firmware

4. What is the purpose of run level 5?
   A. First multi-user state
   B. Administrative state
   C. Hardware maintenance state
   D. Power down firmware

5. What user access is granted at run level 0?
   A. Console access
   B. Single-user access
   C. Multi-user access
   D. Not specified

6. What user access is granted at run level 1?
   A. Console access
   B. Single-user access
   C. Multi-user access
   D. Not specified

7. What user access is granted at run level 2?
   A. Console access
   B. Single-user access
   C. Multi-user access
   D. Not specified

8. What user access is granted at run level 4?
   A. Console access
   B. Single-user access
   C. Multi-user access
   D. Not specified

Answers

1. C

2. B

3. A

4. D

5. A

6. B

7. C

8. D

Changing System States

The following objectives will be met upon completing this chapter's material:

- Understanding why a system should be halted
- Knowing all the commands that can be used to modify the run level of a system
- Knowing all the commands that can be used to shut down a system

Understanding System Halts

A Solaris system is designed to stay up continuously with as few disruptions to service through rebooting as possible. This design is facilitated by a number of key high-availability and redundancy features in Solaris, including the following:

- Dual power supplies, in which a secondary supply can continue to power the system if the primary power supply fails.

- The mirroring of disk data, which enables the system to generally continue to operate, even in the face of multiple disk failure.

- Hot-swappable disks, which enable one to remove and replace a faulty disk while the system is still online. The new disk can be formatted and used immediately, especially when DiskSuite is used.

- The use of domains on E10000 systems, where maintenance performed on one virtual host can be performed while a second domain acts in its place.

However, a number of situations can occur when a super-user must halt a Solaris system:

- Performing a reconfiguration boot
- Powering down the system

Let's look at these operations in detail.

Performing a Reconfiguration Boot

Performing a reconfiguration boot involves updating the hardware configuration for the system. If new hardware is added to the system, other than a disk, the system must be brought down to the hardware maintenance state (level 0) before the new device can be inserted. In addition, the system must be notified of a reconfiguration reboot by either booting from the OpenBoot PROM monitor with the command boot -r or by creating an empty file called /reconfigure before changing to run level 0. This can be achieved by using the command touch /reconfigure.

Powering down the System

Powering down the system is always performed when the system needs to be moved. A Solaris system should never be physically relocated while it is up, or even while it is powered on. In this case, the system should be brought to run level 0 and powered down with the command power-off. Once the system has been relocated, the appropriate power-on switch can be activated to start the system and boot into the default run level.

Performing System Halts and Shutdowns

A number of different commands are available to shut down and halt a system, and which one should be used depends on the specific situation at hand. For example, some commands cycle through a series of shutdown scripts that ensure that key applications and services, such as databases, are cleanly shut down. Other commands are designed to ensure that a system is powered down as rapidly as possible. For example, if a storm strikes out the main power system, and you're only left with a few minutes of battery backup, it might be wise to perform a rapid powerdown to protect equipment from further damage. We'll investigate the following commands: init, shutdown, poweroff, halt, and reboot.

/sbin/init

In addition to being the process spawner, init can be used to switch run levels at any time. For example, to perform hardware maintenance, the following command would be used:

```
# init 0
```

To enter the administrative state, the following command would be used:

```
# init 1
```

To enter the first multi-user state, the following command would be used:

```
# init 2
```

To enter the second multi-user state, the following command would be used:

```
# init 3
```

To enter a user-defined state, the following command would be used:

```
# init 4
```

To power down the system, the following command would be used:

```
# init 5
```

To halt the operating system, the following command would be used:

```
# init 6
```

To enter the administrative state with all of the filesystems available, the following command would be used:

```
# init S
```

Before using init in this way, it's often advisable to precede its execution with a call to sync. The sync command renews the disk superblock, which ensures that all outstanding data operations are flushed, and the filesystem is stable before shutting down.

/usr/sbin/shutdown

The shutdown command is used to change a system's state, performing a function similar to init, as described previously. However, shutdown has several advantages over init:

- A grace period can be specified, so that the system can be shut down at some time in the future, rather than immediately.

- A confirmation message requires that the super-user confirm the shutdown before it proceeds. If an automated shutdown is to be executed at some time in the future, the confirmation message can be avoided by using the -y option.

- Only init states that 0, 1, 5, 6, and S can be reached using shutdown.

For example, to shut down the system to run level 5 so that the system can be moved, the following command would be used, giving 60 seconds notice:

```
bash-2.03# shutdown -i 5 -g 60 "System will be powered off for
maintenance. LOGOUT NOW."
```

This will print the following messages at 60 and 30 seconds respectively:

```
Shutdown started.    Thu Jun   21  12:00:00 EST  2001
Broadcast Message from root (pts/1) on cassowary Thu Jun    21
12:00:00 EST  2001...
         The system will be shut down in 1 minute
System will be powered off for maintenance. LOGOUT NOW.
Shutdown started.    Thu Jun   21  12:00:30 EST  2001
Broadcast Message from root (pts/1) on cassowary Thu Jun    21
12:30:00 EST  2001...
         The system will be shut down in 30 seconds
System will be powered off for maintenance. LOGOUT NOW.
```

Once the countdown has been completed, the following message will appear:

```
Do you want to continue? (y or n):
```

If you type y, the shutdown will proceed. If you type n, the shutdown will be cancelled, and the system will remain at the current run level.

/usr/sbin/halt

The halt command is used to rapidly shut down the system to the level of the Open-Boot PROM monitor without cycling through any intermediate run levels and without executing the kill scripts specified for those run levels. This ensures that a very fast shutdown can be achieved when emergency situations dictate that the system cannot remain live, even with the risk of data loss. For example, if a system is under a denial of service attack, and the decision is made to pull the plug on the service, halt will do so much faster than init or shutdown. The central processing unit (CPU) is halted as quickly as possible, no matter what the run level.

The halt command has several options. The -l flag can be used to prevent the recording of the system halt in the system log, which it normally attempts before halting the

CPU, while the -n option prevents the refreshing of the superblock, which is performed by default, in order to protect the mounted filesystems. The most extreme option is -q, which does not attempt any kind of fancy actions before halting.

/usr/sbin/poweroff

The poweroff command is used to rapidly shut down the system and switch off power (such as switching to run level 5) without cycling through any intermediate run levels or executing the kill scripts specified for those run levels. This ensures that a very fast shutdown can be achieved when emergency situations dictate that the system cannot remain live, even with the risk of data loss. For example, if a system is under a denial of service attack, and the decision is made to pull the plug on the service, halt will do so much faster than init or shutdown. The CPU is halted as quickly as possible, no matter what the run level.

The poweroff command has several options. The -l flag can be used to prevent the recording of the system halt in the system log, which it normally attempts before halt-ing the CPU, while the -n option prevents the refreshing of the superblock, which is performed by default, in order to protect the mounted filesystems. The most extreme option is -q, which does not attempt any kind of fancy actions before shutting down.

/usr/sbin/reboot

The reboot command is used to reboot the system from the current run level to the default run level and it prevents the system from changing to any other run level. The reboot command has several options: The -l flag can be used to prevent the recording of the system halt in the system log, which it normally attempts before halting the CPU. The -n option prevents the refreshing of the superblock, which is performed by default, to protect the mounted filesystems. The most extreme option is -q, which does not attempt any kind of fancy actions before shutting down.

In addition, reboot accepts the standard parameters passed to the boot command if they are preceded by two dashes and are placed after the reboot parameters described previously on the command line.

For example, to perform a configuration reboot without recording an entry in the system log, the following command could be used:

```
bash-2.03# reboot -l -- -r
```

Summary

In this chapter, we have examined several different ways to shut down a Solaris system. Shutdowns typically either cycle through a series of kill scripts associated with the current run level before shutting down or rapidly bring the system down to avoid damage (or save time).

Questions

1. Which command would be used to shut down the system for hardware maintenance?
   A. init 0
   B. init 1
   C. init 2
   D. init 3

2. Which command would be used to enter the administrative state?
   A. init 0
   B. init 1
   C. init 2
   D. init 3

3. Which command would be used to enter the first multi-user state?
   A. init 0
   B. init 1
   C. init 2
   D. init 3

4. Which command would be used to enter the second multi-user state?
   A. init 0
   B. init 1
   C. init 2
   D. init 3

5. Which command would be used to enter the user-defined state?
   A. init 4
   B. init 5
   C. init 6
   D. init S

6. Which command would be used to power down the system?
   A. init 4
   B. init 5
   C. init 6
   D. init S

7. Which command would be used to halt the operating system?
   A. init 4
   B. init 5
   C. init 6
   D. init S

8. Which command would be used to enter the administrative state with all of the filesystems available?
   A. init 4
   B. init 5
   C. init 6
   D. init S

Answers

1. A

2. B

3. C

4. D

5. A

6. B

7. C

8. D

System Security

The following objectives will be met upon completing this chapter's material:

- Understanding user credentials
- Understanding group credentials
- Exploring the power of the super-user
- Securing files and directories by setting permissions
- Monitoring active users
- Reviewing the role of the password files in system security

Security is a central concern to system administrators of all network operating systems, since all services may potentially have inherent flaws or weaknesses revealed through undetected bugs or design errors, which may compromise a networked system. Solaris is no exception, and new Solaris administrators will find themselves revisiting similar issues that they may have encountered with other operating systems. For example, Linux, Microsoft Windows, and Solaris all run database systems that have daemons that listen for connections coming through the Internet. These servers may be shipped with default user accounts that have well-known passwords that are not inactivated by local administrators after configuration and administration. Consequently, exploits involving such services are broadcast on Usenet newsgroups, cracking mailing lists, and Web sites. Alternatively, some security issues are specific to Solaris. Username and password sniffing while a remote user is using telnet to spawn a local shell is unique to Solaris and other UNIX systems, since PC-based products that provide remote access (such as Symantec's pcAnywhere product) encrypt the exchange of authentication credentials by default.

In this chapter, we will focus on laying the groundwork for an understanding of the vulnerabilities of the Solaris operating system, as well as the techniques used by Solaris managers to reduce the risk of a successful attack by a rogue user. Our starting point will be the single host, which can be secured from both internal and externals threats by strict administration of user accounts and groups, and their corresponding entries within standard password and shadowed password files. In addition, it is critical to maintain access to various files and directories by setting user and group ownerships on those files. Once a user and group have been assigned ownership of a file or directory, they are free to determine which other users (if any) are able to read or write to that file, or, if it is a directory, whether any files can be created underneath that directory. An exception to user and group-based access control is the special super-user account (the root user), who has global read, write, and create access on all files on a Solaris system. This includes normal files as well as directories and device files. Finally, we'll examine how to keep tabs on all active users on a Solaris system, so that their behavior and activities can be monitored to ensure that only authorized activities are being conducted at all times.

Checking User and Group Identification

The concept of the user is central to Solaris. All processes and files on a Solaris system are "owned" by a particular user and are assigned to a specific user group. No data or activities on the system may exist without a valid user or group. Managing users and groups as a Solaris administrator can be a challenging activity. You will be responsible for assigning all of the privileges granted or denied to a user or group of users, and many of these permissions carry great risk. For example, a user with an inappropriate privilege level may execute commands as the super-user, causing damage to your system.

It is possible to determine which user is currently logged in from a terminal session by using the id command:

```
bash-2.03$ id
uid=1001(pwatters) gid=10(staff)
```

The output shows that the currently logged-in user is pwatters, with UID = 1001. In addition, the current group of pwatters is staff, with GID = 10. It is possible for the user and group credentials to change during a single terminal session. For example, if the su facility is used to effectively become the super-user, then the UID and GID associated with the current terminal session will also change:

```
bash-2.03$ su root
Password:
# id
uid=0(root) gid=1(other)
```

Here, the root user (UID = 0) belonging to the group other (GID = 1) has spawned a new shell with full super-user privileges.

You can obtain a list of all groups that a user belongs to by using the **groups** command. For example, to view all of the groups that the root users belongs to, we use the following command:

```
bash-2.03# groups root
other root bin sys adm uucp mail tty lp nuucp daemon
```

The Super-user Account

We've just examined how to use the su facility to invoke super-user privileges from an unprivileged account. The user with UID = 0 (typically root) has unlimited powers to act on a Solaris system. The root user can perform the following potentially dangerous functions:

- Add, delete, or modify all other user accounts
- Read and write all files, and create new ones
- Add or delete devices to the system
- Install new system software
- Read everyone's e-mail
- Snoop network traffic for usernames and passwords of other systems on the local area network
- Modify all system logs to remove all traces of super-user access
- Pretend to be an unprivileged user, and access his or her accounts on other systems where login access is only authenticated against a username

These powers combine to make the root account sound rather sinister; however, many of these activities are legitimate, necessary system administration routines that are undertaken daily. For example, network traffic can be snooped to determine where network outages are occurring, and copying user files to backup tapes every night is generally in everyone's interest. However, if an intruder gains root access, he or she is free to roam the system, deleting or stealing data, removing or adding user accounts, or installing trojan horses that transparently modify the way that your system operates.

One way to protect against an authorized user gaining root access is to use a difficult-to-guess root password. This makes it difficult for a cracker to use a password-cracking program to guess your password to be successful. The optimal password is a completely random string of alphanumeric and punctuation characters.

In addition, the root password should never be written down, unless it is locked in the company safe, or told to anyone who doesn't need to know it. Indeed, most day-to-day operations should be carried out by unprivileged users, with sysadmins using the su facility to gain root access when needed. The root password must usually be entered twice, just in case you should happen to make a typographical error, as the characters that you type are masked on the screen.

File and Directory Ownership

One of the most confusing issues for novice users of Solaris is understanding the Solaris file access permissions system. The basic approach to setting and interpreting relative file permissions is using a set of symbolic codes to represent users and permission types. However, even advanced users may find it difficult to understand the octal permission codes that are used to set absolute permissions. When combined with a default permission mask set in the user's shell (the umask), octal permission codes are more powerful than symbolic permission codes. In this section, we only review relative file permissions using symbolic codes.

Symbolic Permission Codes

The Solaris UFS filesystem permits three basic kinds of file access: the ability to read (r), write (w), and to execute (x) a file or directory. These permissions can be granted exclusively or non-exclusively on individual files, or on a group of files specified by a wildcard (*). These permissions can be set by using the chmod command in combination with a "+" operator. Permissions can be easily removed with the chmod command by using the "-" operator.

For example, to set the read permissions (for the current users) on the file /usr/local/lib/libproxy.a, we would use the command

```
bash-2.03$ chmod +r /usr/local/lib/libproxy.a
```

Alternatively, to set read permissions for all users on the file /usr/local/lib/libproxy.a, we would use the command

```
bash-2.03$ chmod a+r /usr/local/lib/libproxy.a
```

To remove read permissions on the file /usr/local/lib/libproxy.a for all users who are not members of the current user's default group, we would use the command

```
bash-2.03$ chmod o-r /usr/local/lib/libproxy.a
```

This does not remove the group and user read permissions that were set previously. Similarly, execute and write permissions can be set. For example, to set execute permissions on the /usr/local/bin/gcc files for each class of user (current user, group, and world), we would use the commands

```
bash-2.03$ chmod u+x /usr/local/bin/gcc; chmod g+x
/usr/local/bin/gcc; chmod o+x /usr/local/bin/gcc
```

To explicitly remove write permissions on the /usr/local/bin/gcc files for each class of user (current user, group, and world), we would use the commands

```
bash-2.03$ chmod u-w /usr/local/bin/gcc; chmod g-w
/usr/local/bin/gcc; chmod o-w /usr/local/bin/gcc
```

The rationale behind using read and write permissions should be clear. Permitting read access on a file allows an identified user to access the text of a file by reading it byte by byte, while write access permits the user to modify or delete any file on which the write permission is granted, regardless of who originally created the file. Thus, individual users can create files that are readable and writeable by any other user on the system.

The permission to execute a file must be granted on scripts (such as shell scripts or Perl scripts) in order for them to be executed, while compiled and linked applications must also have the execute bit set on a specific application. The executable permission must also be granted on the special files that represent directories on the filesystem if the directory's contents are to be accessed by a specific class of user.

The different options available for granting file access permissions can sometimes lead to interesting but confusing scenarios. For example, permissions can be set to allow a group to delete a file, but not to execute it. More usefully, a group might be given execute permission on an application, but be unable to write over it. In addition, setting file permissions using relative permission strings (rather than absolute octal permission codes) means that permissions set by a previous change of permission command (chmod) are not revoked by any subsequent chmod commands.

However, the permissions themselves are only half the story. Unlike single-user filesystems, permissions on Solaris are associated with different file owners (all files and processes on a Solaris system are owned by a specific user). In addition, groups of users can be granted read, write, and execute permissions on a file or set of files stored in a directory. Alternatively, file permissions can be granted on a system-wide basis, effectively granting file access without respect to file ownership. Since filesystems can be exported using NFS and/or Samba, it's bad practice to grant system-wide read, write, and execute permissions on any file, unless every user needs access to that file. For example, all users need to read the password database (/etc/passwd), but only the root user should have read access to the shadow password database (/etc/shadow). Blindly exporting all files with world read, write, or execute permissions on a NFS-shared volume is inviting trouble!

The three filesystem categories of ownership are defined by three permission setting categories: the user (u) who owns the file, the group members (g), who have access to the file, and all other users (o) on the system. The group specified by g can be the user's primary group (as defined in /etc/passwd) or a secondary group that the file has been assigned to (defined in /etc/group).

It is important to remember that there are ultimately few secrets on a Solaris filesystem. The root user has full access at all times (read, write, and execute) on all files on the filesystem. Even if a user removes all permissions on a file, the rule of root is absolute. If the contents of a file really need to be hidden, it is best to encrypt a file's contents using pretty good privacy (PGP), crypt, or similar. A root user can also change the ownership of a file. Thus, a user's files do not absolutely belong to a specific user. The chown command can only be used by the super-user for this purpose.

Policies regarding default file permissions need to be set selectively in different environments. For example, in a production Web server system that processes credit card data, access should be denied by default to all users except those that are required to conduct online transactions (such as the apache user for the Apache Web server). On a system which supports team-based development, obviously permissions will need to be set that allow the exchange of data between team partners, but which prevent the access to development files by others. Very few Solaris systems would allow a default world-writeable policy on any filesystem, except for the temporary swap (/tmp) filesystem.

It is possible to enforce system-wide permissions by using a default umask, which sets the read, write, and execute permissions on all new files created by a specific user. If a user wants to use a umask other than the default system-wide setting, this can be achieved by setting it on the command-line when required or in the user's shell start-up file (such as .kshrc for Korn shell).

We start our examination of Solaris file permissions by examining how to create files, set permissions, change ownerships, group memberships, and how to use the ls command to examine existing file permissions. All of these commands can be used by non-privileged users, except for the chown command.

The ls command is the main directory and file permission listing program used in Solaris. When displaying a long listing, it prints file access permissions, user and group ownerships, file size and creation date, and the filename. For example, for the password file /etc/passwd, the output from ls would look like

```
bash-2.03# ls -l /etc/passwd
-r--r--r--   1 root     other              256 Sep  18 00:40 passwd
```

This directory entry can be read from left to right in the following way:

- The password file is not a directory, indicated by the first "-."

- The password file has read-only permissions for the owner "r--" (but not execute or write permissions).

- The password file has read-only permissions for group members "r--."

- The password file has read-only permissions for other staff "r--."

- The password file is owned by the root user.

- The password file has other group permissions.

- The password file size is 256 kilobytes.

- The password file was created on September eighteenth at 00:40 A.M.

- The name of the password file is passwd.

The permissions string shown changes depending on the permissions that have been set by the owner. For example, if the password file had execute and write permissions for the root user, then the permissions string would read -rwxr--r--, rather than just -r--r--r--. Each of the permissions can be set using symbolic or octal permissions codes by using the chmod command.

We've seen how a normal file looks under ls, but let's compare this with a directory entry, which is a special kind of file that is usually created by the mkdir command:

```
bash-2.03# mkdir samples
```

We can check the permissions of the directory entry by using the ls command:

```
bash-2.03# ls -l
total 8
drwxrwxr-x   2 root     other              512 Sep  5 13:41 samples
```

The directory entry for the directory samples can be read from left to right in the following way:

- The directory entry is a special file denoted by a leading d.

- The directory entry has read, write, and execute permissions for the owner rwx.

- The directory entry has read, write and execute permissions for group members rwx.

- The directory entry has read and execute permissions for other staff r-x.

- The directory entry is owned by the root user.

- The directory entry has other group permissions.

- The directory entry size is 512 kilobytes.

- The directory entry was created on September fifth at 1:41 P.M.

- The name of the directory is samples.

For a directory to be accessible to a particular class of user, the executable bit must be set using the chmod command.

Monitoring User Activity

System access can be monitored interactively using a number of measures. For example, syslog entries can be automatically viewed in real-time by using the command

```
bash-2.03$ tail -f /var/adm/messages
```

However, most administrators want to interactively view what remote users are doing on a system at any one time. We will examine two methods here for viewing remote user activity. The command **who** displays who is currently logged into the system. The output of who displays the username, connecting line, date of login, idle time, process id, and a comment. An example output is as follows:

```
bash-2.03$ who
root        console       Nov 22 12:39
pwatters    pts/0         Nov 19 21:05      (client.site.com)
```

This command can be automated to update the list of active users. An alternative to who is the **w** command, which displays a more detailed summary of the current activity on the system, including the current process name for each user. The header output from w shows the current time, the uptime of the current system, and the number of users actively logged into the system. The average system load is also displayed as a series of three numbers at the end of the w header, indicating the average number of jobs in the run queue for the first, fifth and fifteenth minutes prior to the command being executed. In addition to the output generated by who, the w command displays the current foreground process for each user, which is usually a shell. For example, the

following command shows that the root user has an active shelltool running under
Open Windows, while the user pwatters is running the Cornell shell:

```
7:15pm  up 1 day(s),  5:11,  2 users,  load average: 1.00, 1.00,
1.01
User     tty             login@ idle   JCPU   PCPU  what
root     console     Thu12pm 3days     6      6
/usr/openwin/bin/shelltool
pwatters  pts/12      Thu11am  8:45         9
/usr/local/bin/tcsh
```

The w and who commands are very useful tools for getting an overview of current
usage patterns on any Solaris system. A final useful command is **last**, which displays
historical usage patterns for the current system in a sequential format:

```
bash-2.03# last
pwatters  pts/4     hp          Wed Apr 11 19:00    still logged in
root      console   :0          Tue Apr 10 20:11    still logged in
pwatters  pts/2     nec         Tue Apr 10 19:17 - 19:24  (00:06)
pwatters  pts/6     austin      Tue Apr 10 15:53 - 15:53  (00:00)
root      console   :0          Tue Apr 10 14:24 - 16:25  (02:01)
reboot    system boot           Tue Apr 10 14:04
pwatters  pts/5     hp          Thu Apr  5 21:38 - 21:40  (00:01)
pwatters  pts/5     hp          Thu Apr  5 21:22 - 21:37  (00:15)
pwatters  pts/5     10.64.18    Thu Apr  5 19:30 - 20:00  (00:30)
pwatters  pts/5     hp          Thu Apr  5 19:18 - 19:29  (00:11)
root      console   :0          Thu Apr  5 19:17 - 22:05 (4+02:48)
reboot    system boot           Thu Apr  5 19:14
pwatters  pts/5     hp          Tue Apr  3 16:14 - 18:26  (02:11)
pwatters  pts/5     hp          Tue Apr  3 08:48 - 10:35  (01:47)
root      console   :0          Tue Apr  3 08:45 - 22:01  (13:15)
reboot    system boot           Tue Apr  3 08:43
root      console   :0          Fri Mar 30 18:54 - 19:27  (00:32)
reboot    system boot           Fri Mar 30 18:46
pwatters  pts/6     hp          Tue Mar 27 20:46 - 21:51  (01:04)
root      console   :0          Tue Mar 27 19:50 - 21:51  (02:01)
reboot    system boot           Tue Mar 27 19:48
root      console   :0          Mon Mar 26 17:43 - 17:47  (00:04)
```

The /etc/passwd and /etc/shadow Password Files

All Solaris users have a username and password associated with their account, except
when a user account has been explicitly locked (designated *LK*) or when a system
account has been specified not to have a password at all (NP). Many early exploits of
Solaris systems were associated with default passwords used on some system accounts,

and the most common method of gaining unauthorized access to a Solaris system remains password cracking and/or guessing. In this section, we examine the password database (/etc/passwd) and its more secure counterpart, the shadow database (/etc/shadow). We'll also examine strategies for making passwords safer.

The standard password database is stored in the file /etc/passwd and looks like this:

```
bash-2.03 # cat /etc/passwd
root:x:0:1:Super-User:/:/sbin/sh
daemon:x:1:1:/:
bin:x:2:2:/usr/bin:
sys:x:3:3:/:
adm:x:4:4:Admin:/var/adm:
lp:x:71:8:Line Printer Admin:/usr/spool/lp:
uucp:x:5:5:uucp Admin:/usr/lib/uucp:
nuucp:x:9:9:uucp Admin:/var/spool/uucppublic:/usr/lib/uucp/uucico
listen:x:37:4:Network Admin:/usr/net/nls:
nobody:x:60001:60001:Nobody:/:
noaccess:x:60002:60002:No Access User:/:
nobody4:x:65534:65534:SunOS 4.x Nobody:/:
security:x:1898:600:Security User:/security:/bin/ksh
pwatters:x:1001:10:/staff/pwatters:/bin/sh
```

These fields have the following meaning:

- **username field**   Has a maximum of eight characters

- **encrypted password field**   In a system using shadow passwords is crossed with an x

- **user ID field**   Contains the numeric and unique UID

- **primary group ID field**   Contains the numeric GID

- **user comment**   Contains a description of the user

- **path to the user's home directory**

- **user's default shell**

In older versions of Solaris, the encrypted password field would have contained an encrypted password string like X14oLaiYg7bO2. However, this presented a security problem, as the login program required all users to have read access to the password file:

```
bash-2.03# ls -l /etc/passwd
-rw-r--r--   1 root     sys          605 Jul 24 11:04 /etc/passwd
```

Thus, any user with the lowest form privilege would be able to access the encrypted password field for the root user and attempt to gain root access by guessing the password. A number of programs were specifically developed for this purpose, such as "crack," which takes a standard Solaris password file and uses a dictionary and some clever lexical rules to guess passwords. Once a root password has been obtained, a rogue user may perform any operation on a Solaris system, including formatting hard disks, installing trojan horses, and launching attacks on other systems.

The cryptographic algorithm used by Solaris is not easy to crack. Indeed, a brute-force guess of a password composed of a completely random set of characters would take many central processing unit (CPU) years to compute. The task would be made even more difficult (if not impossible) if the root password was changed weekly, again with a random set of characters. However, the reality is that most users enter passwords that are easily guessed from a dictionary, or from some knowledge about the user. Raise your hand if you've entered a spouse's, parent's, child's, or pet's name as a password! Or a password like root, sun, windows, linux, and so on. Since we are constantly required to use PINs and passwords, people choose passwords that are easy to remember. However, easily remembered passwords are also the easiest to crack.

Solaris has reduced the chances of a rogue user obtaining the password file in the first place by implementing a shadow password facility. This creates a file called /etc/shadow, which is similar to the password file (/etc/passwd), but is only readable by root and contains the encrypted password fields for each UID. Thus, if a rogue user cannot obtain the encrypted password entries, it is impossible to use them as the basis for a crack attack. A shadow password file corresponding to the password file shown above looks like the following:

```
bash-2.03# cat /etc/shadow
root:YTS88sd7fSS:10528:::
daemon:NP:6445:::
bin:NP:6445:::
sys:NP:6445:::
adm:NP:6445:::
lp:NP:6445:::
uucp:NP:6445:::
nuucp:NP:6445:::
listen:*LK*::::
nobody:NP:6445:::
noaccess:NP:6445:::
nobody4:NP:6445:::
security:*LK*::::
pwatters:hY72er3Ascc::::
```

If a system is correctly installed, the /etc/passwd file should be readable by all users, but contain no passwords. Conversely, the /etc/shadow file should only be readable by root and should contain the encrypted password strings traditionally stored in /etc/passwd.

Summary

In this chapter, we have focused on understanding system security from a single host perspective. It is particularly important to secure local systems as well as those connected to the Internet, as local users could also attempt to gain unauthorized access to data if file permissions have been incorrectly set. To this extent, it is important that administrators regularly monitor the activities of users by using the commands reviewed in this chapter.

Questions

1. Which of the following files do not need to be owned by a user?
   A. Directories
   B. Device files
   C. Metadevices
   D. None of the above

2. Which of the following printouts represents a possible output from the id command?
   A. gid = 1001(scott) uid = 100(tiger)
   B. uid = 1001(scott) gid = 100(tiger)
   C. uid = 1001(scott) gid = −100(tiger)
   D. None of the above

3. What is the UID of the super-user?
   A. 0
   B. 1
   C. 100
   D. 666

4. Name one restriction placed on the root account?
   A. The root user cannot read other users' e-mail.
   B. The root user cannot delete a user's account without his or her permission.
   C. The root user cannot rlogin to another system as root without a credential.
   D. The root user cannot modify disk partition sizes.

5. Name the default permissions mask set in the user's shell?
   A. mask
   B. omask

    C. chmod

    D. umask

6. How could read, write, and execute permissions be set on a file called /etc/passwd for all users?

    A. chmod a+rwx /etc/passwd

    B. chmod o+rwx /etc/passwd

    C. chmod u+rwx /etc/passwd

    D. chmod u-rwx /etc/passwd

7. How could read, write, and execute permissions be removed from a file called /etc/passwd for all users who do not belong to the owner's group?

    A. chmod a+rwx /etc/passwd

    B. chmod o+rwx /etc/passwd

    C. chmod u+rwx /etc/passwd

    D. chmod u-rwx /etc/passwd

8. Which command displays the username, connecting line, date of login, idle time, process ID, and a comment for all logged-in users?

    A. who

    B. w

    C. which

    D. show

Answers

1. D

2. B

3. A

4. C

5. D

6. A

7. D

8. A

Managing Users

The following objectives will be met upon completing this chapter's material:

- Understanding the concepts of users and groups
- Discovering Solaris password management facilities
- Learning how to create users and groups using the Command Line Interface (CLI)
- Reviewing the management of users and groups using the admintool graphical user interface (GUI)

The concept of the user is central to Solaris. All processes and files on a Solaris system are "owned" by a particular user and are assigned to a specific user group. No data or activities on the system may exist without a valid user or group. Managing users and groups as a Solaris administrator can be a challenging activity. You will be responsible for assigning all of the privileges granted or denied to a user or group of users, and many of these permissions carry great risk. For example, a user with an inappropriate privilege level may execute commands as the super-user, causing damage to your system.

In this chapter, we will learn how to add users to the system, and how to add and modify groups. In addition, the contents and structure of key user databases, including the password, shadow password, and group files, are examined in detail. Finally, we introduce the admintool, which is a GUI-based user administration tool designed to make user management easier under Solaris.

Users

All users on a Solaris system have a number of unique identifiers and characteristics that can be used to distinguish individual users from each other and also to logically group related users. Most physical users of a Solaris system will have a unique "login" assigned to them, which is identified by a username with a maximum of eight characters. Once a user account is created, it can be used for the following purposes:

- Spawning a shell
- Executing applications interactively
- Scheduling applications to run on specific times and dates
- Access database applications and other system services

In addition to user accounts, Solaris also uses a number of system accounts (such as root, daemon, bin, sys, lp, adm, and uucp) to perform various kind of routine maintenance, including

- Allocation of system resources to perform specific tasks
- Running a mail server
- Running a Web server
- Process management

Users can access a Solaris system by accessing the console or through a remote terminal, in either graphical or text mode. In each case, a set of authentication credentials is presented to the system, including the username and password. When entered, a user's password is compared to an encrypted string stored in the password database (/etc/passwd) or the shadow password database (/etc/shadow). Once the string entered by the user has been encrypted, it is matched against the already encrypted entry in the password database. If a match is made, authentication occurs, and the user may spawn a shell. A Solaris username can have a maximum of eight characters, as can a Solaris password. Since the security of a Solaris system relies heavily on the difficulty of guessing passwords, user policies should be developed to either recommend or enforce the use of passwords containing random or semi-random character strings.

User Characteristics

A number of other user characteristics are associated with each user, in addition to a username and password. These features include

- The user ID (UID), which is a unique integer that begins with the root user (UID = 1), and other UIDs are typically (but not necessarily) allocated sequentially. Some systems will reserve all UIDs below 1023 for system accounts (such as the apache user for managing the Apache Web server), while those UIDs 1024 and above are designated for ordinary users. The UID of 0 designates the super-user account, which is typically called root.

- A flexible mechanism for distinguishing different classes of users, known as groups. Groups are not just sets of related users. The Solaris filesystem allows for group-designated read, write, and execute file access for groups, in addition to permissions granted to the individual user, and to all users. Every UID is associated with a primary group ID (GID); however, UIDs may also be associated with more than one secondary group.

- A home directory, which is the default file storage location for all files created by a particular user. If the automounter is used, then home directories may be exported using NFS on /home. When a user spawns a login shell, the current working directory will always be the home directory.

- A login shell, which can be used to issue commands interactively or to write simple programs. A number of different shells are available under Solaris, including the Bourne shell (sh), C shell (csh), the Bourne again shell (bash), and the Cornell shell (tcsh). The choice of shell depends largely on personal preference, user experience with C-like programming constructs, and terminal handling.

- A comment, which is typically the user's full name, such as Paul Watters. However, system accounts may use names that describe their purpose (for example, the command **Web Server** might be associated with the apache user).

Adding Users

Adding a user to a Solaris system is easy; however, the root user is the only one who can perform this operation. Two options are available: the first option is to edit the /etc/passwd file directly, incrementing the UID, adding the appropriate GID, adding a home directory (and remembering to physically create it on the filesystem), inserting a comment, and choosing a login name. In addition, a passwd for the user must be set using the passwd command.

Does this sound difficult? If so, then you should consider using the automated useradd command, which will do all of the hard work for you, as long as you supply the correct information. The useradd command has the following format:

```
bash# useradd -u uid -g gid -d home_directory -s path_to_shell
-c comment login_name
```

Let's add a user to our system and examine the results:

```
bash-2.03# useradd -u 1004 -g 10 -d /opt/www -s /bin/sh -c "Web
User" www
```

Here we are adding a Web User called www with the UID 1004, the GID 10, the home directory /opt/www, and the Bourne shell as the login shell. At the end of the useradd script, an appropriate line should appear in the /etc/passwd file:

```
bash-2.03# grep www /etc/passwd
www:x:1004:10:Web User:/opt/www:/bin/sh
```

However, the useradd command may fail under the following conditions:

- The UID that you specified has already been taken by another user. UIDs may be recycled, as long as precautions are taken to ensure that a previous owner of the UID no longer owns files on the filesystem.

- The GID that you specified does not exist. You can verify its entry in the groups database (/etc/group).

- The comment contains special characters like double quotes (""), exclamation marks (!), or slashes (/).

- The shell that you specified does not exist. Check that the shell actually exists in the path specified, and that the shell has an entry in the shells database (/etc/shells).

Modifying User Attributes

Once you have created a user account, it is possible to change any of its characteristics by directly editing the password database (/etc/passwd) or by using the usermod command. For example, if we wanted to modify the UID of the www account from 1004 to 1005, we would use the command:

```
bash-2.03# usermod -u 1005 www
```

Again, we can verify that the change has been made correctly by examining the entry for www in the password database:

```
bash-2.03# grep www /etc/passwd
www:x:1005:10:Web User:/opt/www:/bin/sh
```

Remember that if you change a UID or GID, you must manually update the existing directory and file ownerships manually by using the chmod, chgrp, and chown commands where appropriate.

Once a user account has been created, the next step is to set a password, which can be performed by the passwd command:

```
bash-2.03# passwd user
```

where user is the login name for the account with the password you want to change. In all cases, you will be required to enter the new password twice. If you happen to make a typing error, then the password will not be changed, and you will be warned that the two password strings entered did not match. Here's an example for the user www:

```
bash-2.03 # passwd www
New password:
Re-enter new password:
passwd(SYSTEM): They don't match; try again.
New password:
Re-enter new password:
passwd (SYSTEM): passwd successfully changed for www
```

After a passwd has been entered for a user, such as the www user, it should appear as an encrypted string in the shadow password database (/etc/shadow):

```
bash-2.03# grep www /etc/shadow
www:C4dMH8As4bGTM::::::
```

Once a user has been granted an initial password, he or she can then enter a new password by using the passwd command with no options.

Deleting Users

Now imagine that one of your prized employees has moved into greener pastures unexpectedly. Although you will eventually be able to change the ownership on all of her files, you cannot immediately restart some production applications. In this case, it is possible to temporarily disable logins to a specific account by using a command like the following:

```
bash-2.03# passwd -l natashia
```

This command would lock Natashia's account until the root user once again used the passwd command on this account to set a new password. A locked account can be identified in the password database by the characters LK:

```
bash-2.03# grep natashia /etc/shadow
natashia:*LK*::::::
```

Once all of the user's files have been backed up, and any active processes have been killed by the super-user, the user account may be permanently deleted by using the userdel command. For example, to delete the user account natashia, and remove that user's home directory, and all of the files underneath that directory, you would use the command

```
bash-2.03# userdel -r natashia
```

Alternatively, you could edit both the password and shadow password databases, and remove the appropriate lines containing the entries for the user natashia. You would also need to manually remove the user's home directory, and all of her files underneath that directory.

Also, several system accounts should remain locked at all times to prevent interactive logins, including adm, bin, listen, nobody, lp, sys, and uucp.

Although it is possible to re-use usernames and UIDs, this is unwise, given that other local systems may still trust relationships set up for a previous user.

Groups

Solaris provides a facility for identifying sets of related users into groups. Each user is associated with a primary group ID (GID), which is associated with a name. The group name and GID can be used interchangeably. In addition, users can also be associated with one or more secondary groups. This flexibility means that while users might have primary group memberships based on their employment or organizational status (such as staff or managers), they can actively share data and system privileges with other groups based on their workgroup needs (such as sales or engineer).

Group Characteristics

All information about groups in Solaris is stored in the groups database (/etc/group). Let's examine a typical set of groups:

```
bash-2.03 # cat /etc/group
root::0:root
other::1:
bin::2:root,bin,daemon
sys::3:root,bin,sys,adm
adm::4:root,adm,daemon
uucp::5:root,uucp
mail::6:root
tty::7:root,tty,adm
lp::8:root,lp,adm
nuucp::9:root,nuucp
staff::10:paul,maya,brad,natashia
```

```
postgres::a.mBzQnr1ei2D.:100:postgres, paul
daemon::12:root,daemon
sysadmin::14:
nobody::60001:
noaccess::60002:
nogroup::65534:
```

We can see that the lower group numbers are associated with all of the system functions and accounts, such as the bin group, which has the members root, bin, and daemon, and the sys group, which has the members root, bin, sys, and adm. Higher numbered groups, such as staff, contain several different users, such as paul, maya, brad, and natashia. Notice also that paul has a secondary group membership in the postgres group, giving him database access privileges. A group password can also be set for each group, although most groups don't use this facility. In this group database, we can see that the postgres group is the only group that has an encrypted password (a.mBzQnr1ei2D.).

You can obtain a list of all groups that a user belongs to by using the **groups** command. For example, to view all of the groups that the root users belong to, we use the command

```
bash-2.03# groups root
other root bin sys adm uucp mail tty lp nuucp daemon
```

Adding Groups

To add a new group to the system, you can either manually edit the /etc/group file or use the groupadd command, which has the following syntax:

```
/usr/sbin/groupadd -g gid  group_name
```

Thus, to add a group called managers to the system with a GID of 500, you would use the command

```
bash-2.03# groupadd -g 500 managers
```

You would then be able to verify the new group's existence by searching the groups database:

```
bash-2.03# grep management /etc/group
managers:500:
```

The **groupadd** command will fail if the GID that you specify has already been allocated to an existing group or if the group_name is greater than eight characters.

Managing Groups

If you want to change your group from the primary to secondary during an interactive session to ensure that all of the files that you create are associated with the correct GID, you need to use the newgrp command. For example, the root user has the following primary group membership:

```
bash-2.03# id
uid=0(root) gid=0(root)
```

However, if the root user wants to act as a member of another group, such as sys, the following command would have to be used:

```
bash-2.03# newgrp sys
```

The effective GID would then change to sys:

```
bash-2.03# id
uid=0(root) gid=3(sys)
```

Any operations that the root user performs after using newgrp, such as creating files, will be associated with the GID of 3 (sys), rather than 0 (root). For example, if we created a new file with the primary group, the group associated with the new file would be GID 0:

```
bash-2.03# touch root.txt
bash-2.03# ls -l root.txt
-rw-r--r--   1 root      root   0 Oct 12 11:17 root.txt
```

However, if the root user then changes groups to sys and creates a new file, then the group associated with the file will be sys, rather than root:

```
bash-2.03# newgrp sys
bash-2.03# touch sys.txt
bash-2.03# ls -l sys.txt
-rw-r--r--   1 root      sys    0 Oct 12 11:18 sys.txt
```

Passwords

All Solaris users have a username and password associated with their account, except when a user account has been explicitly locked (designated *LK*), or when a system account has been specified not to have a password at all (NP). Many early exploits of Solaris systems were associated with default passwords used on some system accounts, and the most common method of gaining unauthorized access to a Solaris system remains password cracking and/or guessing. In this section, we examine the password database (/etc/passwd), and its more secure counterpart, the shadow database (/etc/shadow). We also examine strategies for making passwords safer.

The standard password database is stored in the file /etc/passwd and looks like this:

```
bash-2.03 # cat /etc/passwd
root:x:0:1:Super-User:/:/sbin/sh
daemon:x:1:1:/:
bin:x:2:2:/usr/bin:
sys:x:3:3:/:
adm:x:4:4:Admin:/var/adm:
lp:x:71:8:Line Printer Admin:/usr/spool/lp:
uucp:x:5:5:uucp Admin:/usr/lib/uucp:
nuucp:x:9:9:uucp Admin:/var/spool/uucppublic:/usr/lib/uucp/uucico
listen:x:37:4:Network Admin:/usr/net/nls:
nobody:x:60001:60001:Nobody:/:
noaccess:x:60002:60002:No Access User:/:
nobody4:x:65534:65534:SunOS 4.x Nobody:/:
postgres:x:1001:100:Postgres User:/usr/local/postgres:/bin/sh
htdig:x:1002:10:htdig:/opt/www:/usr/local/bin/bash
apache:x:1003:10:apache user:/usr/local/apache:/bin/sh
```

We have already seen some of the fields shown here when adding users to the system:

- **Username field**   Has a maximum of eight characters

- **Encrypted password field**   In a system using shadow passwords is crossed with an x

- **User ID field**   Contains the numeric and unique UID

- **Primary group ID field**   Contains the numeric GID

- **User comment**   Contains a description of the user

- **Path to the user's home directory**

- **User's default shell**

In older versions of Solaris, the encrypted password field would have contained an encrypted password string like X14oLaiYg7bO2. However, this presented a security problem, as the login program required all users to have read access to the password file:

```
bash-2.03# ls -l /etc/passwd
-rw-r--r--   1 root     sys             605 Jul 24 11:04 /etc/passwd
```

Thus, any user with the lowest form privilege would be able to access the encrypted password field for the root user and attempt to gain root access by guessing the password. A number of programs were specifically developed for this purpose, such as "crack," which takes a standard Solaris password file and uses a dictionary and some clever lexical rules to guess passwords. Once a root password has been obtained, a rogue user may perform any operation on a Solaris system, including formatting hard disks, installing trojan horses, and launching attacks on other systems.

The cryptographic algorithm used by Solaris is not easy to crack. Indeed, a brute-force guess of a password composed of a completely random set of characters would take many central processing unit (CPU) years to compute. The task would be made even more difficult (if not impossible) if the root password was changed weekly, again with a random set of characters. However, the reality is that most users enter passwords that are easily guessed from a dictionary or from some knowledge about the user. Since we are constantly required to use PINs and passwords, people generally choose pass-words that are easy to remember. However, easily remembered passwords are also the easiest to crack.

Solaris has reduced the chances of a rogue user obtaining the password file in the first place by implementing a shadow password facility. This creates a file called /etc/shadow, which is similar to the password file (/etc/passwd), but is only readable by root and contains the encrypted password fields for each UID. Thus, if a rogue user can-not obtain the encrypted password entries, it is impossible to use them as the basis for a crack attack.

Managing Users and Groups with admintool

So far, we have only examined user and group administration by using command-line tools, such as useradd and groupadd. Fortunately, Solaris also provides an easy-to-use administrative interface for adding users and groups to the system called admintool. The admintool interface is shown in Figure 10-1. The interface shown is for user management, displaying the username, UID, and user comments. In addition to man-aging users and groups, admintool is also useful for managing hosts, printers, serial ports, and software. Each management option has its own interface, which is accessible from the Browse menu. When an interface is selected, such as the printer's interface, administrators can then add, modify, or delete the entries that exist in the current data-base (in this case, administrators can add, delete, or modify the entries for printers).

Let's examine how to modify existing user information using the admintool, as shown in Figure 10-1. Firstly, select the user whose data you want to modify (such as the adm user, one of the preconfigured system accounts, which is created during Solaris installation). Next, select the Modify . . . option from the admintool Edit menu. The

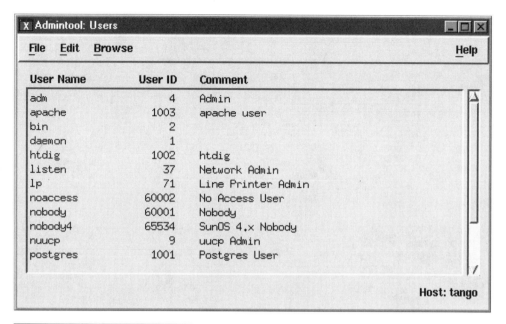

Figure 10-1   The Solaris admintool

user entry modification window is shown in Figure 10-2 for the adm user. Here it is possible to modify the following options:

- Username

- Primary group

- All secondary groups

- User comments

- Login shell, which is selected from a drop-down menu containing all the valid shells defined in the shells database (/etc/shells)

- Minimum and maximum days required before a password change

- Maximum number of inactive days for an account

- An expiration date for the user's account

- Number of days warning to give a user before his or her password must be changed

- Path to the user's home directory

Of course, all of this information can be set on the command line by using the **passwd** command. However, the admintool interface is easier to use and provides some

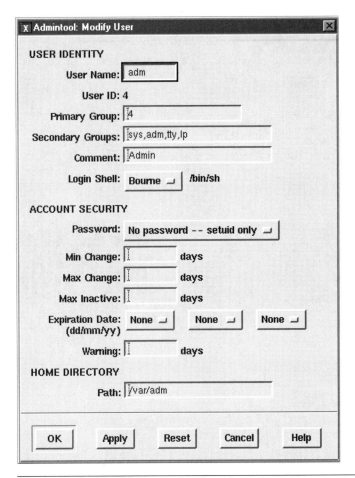

Figure 10-2 Modifying user details with admintool

additional functionality. For example, it is impossible to enter an invalid expiration date, because the day, month, and year are selected from drop-down boxes. In addition, if any problems are encountered during modification, no changes will be recorded.

Adding a user to the system involves entering data into the same interface used for modifying user details, as shown in Figure 10-3. The UID is sequentially generated, as it contains a default primary group, user shell, password option (not set until first login), and the option to create a new directory for the user as their home directory. Again, admintool has advanced error-checking facilities that make it difficult to damage or overwrite system files with invalid data.

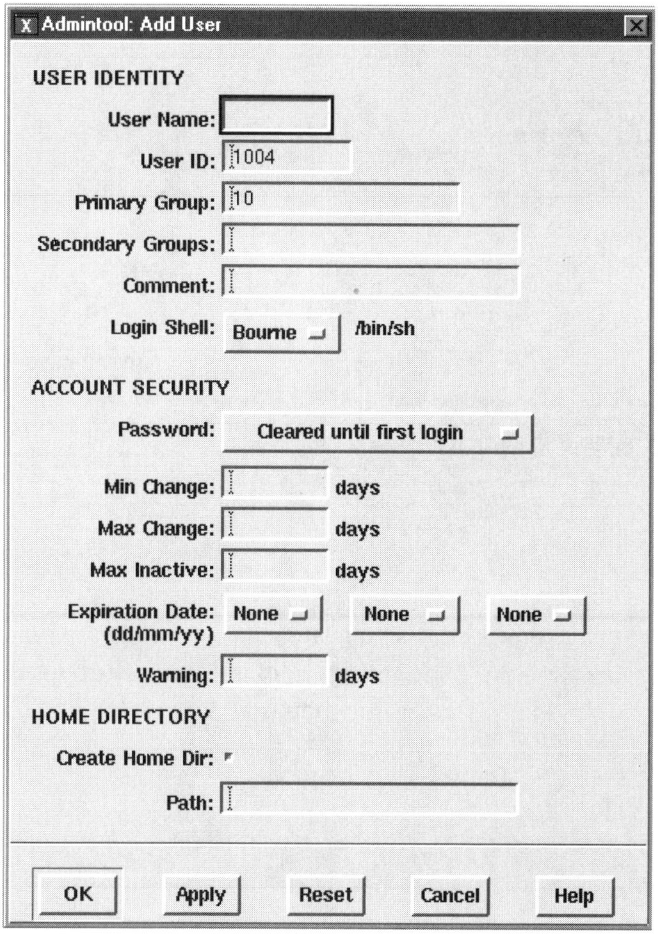

Figure 10-3   Adding user details with admintool

Admintool can also be used as a group administration tool. Groups can be created, and users can be added to specific groups or removed from groups. In addition, groups can also be deleted using admintool. The group administration interface is shown in Figure 10-4. Here five groups are shown. The adm group (GID 4) has three members: root, adm, and daemon. To add a user to the group, simply select the adm group and click on the Add . . . entry in the Edit menu. A comma-delimited list of users in the group would then be displayed. The bin user could be added to the adm group by inserting a comma after the last entry and adding the name "bin" to the list.

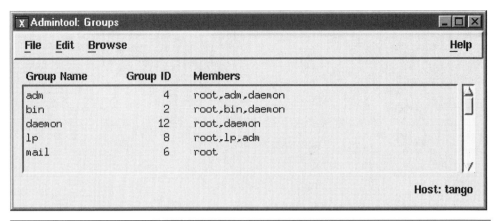

Figure 10-4 The group administration interface

Summary

In this chapter, we have examined a number of issues relating to user and group management under Solaris, including password management, adding users and groups on the command line, and managing groups using the graphical administration tool (admintool).

Questions

1. What are the typical uses for a Solaris user account? (Choose two.)
   A. Spawning a shell
   B. Connecting networks together
   C. Performing hardware maintenance
   D. Scheduling applications to run on specific times and dates

2. Which of the following groups contain only default system accounts?
   A. root, daemon, bin, sys, lp, adm, www
   B. root, samba, bin, sys, lp, adm, uucp
   C. root, daemon, bin, sys, lp, adm, uucp
   D. oracle, daemon, bin, sys, lp, adm, uucp

3. What are the names of the two password files used by Solaris?
   A. /etc/passwd, /etc/secure
   B. /etc/password, /etc/secure
   C. /bin/passwd, /etc/group
   D. /etc/passwd, /etc/shadow

4. Which of the following users has a default UID of 0?
   A. bin
   B. root
   C. sys
   D. adm

5. Which of the following useradd command is valid?
   A. useradd -u abc -g 10 -d /home/abc -s /bin/sh -c "ABC" abc
   B. useradd -u 1023 -g abc -d /home/abc -s /bin/sh -c "ABC" abc
   C. useradd -u 1023 -g 10 -d /home/abc -s /bin/sh -c "ABC" abc
   D. useradd -u abc -g abc -d /home/abc -s /bin/sh -c "ABC" abc

6. Which of the following usermod commands would change the UID of the www account from 1004 to 1005?
   A. usermod -u 1005 www
   B. usermod -u 1004 -n 1005 www
   C. usermod www -n 1005
   D. usermod www 1004 1004

7. A locked account can be identified in /etc/passwd by which entry?
   A. *LOCKED*
   B. LOCKED
   C. *LK*
   D. *

8. Which of the following userdel commands would delete account melissa (UID 1002)?
   A. userdel -r melissa
   B. userdel -u 1002
   C. userdel -uid melissa
   D. userdel -r 1002

9. Which of the following useradd command is valid?
   A. groupadd —g 100 staff
   B. groupadd —g 100 -s staff
   C. groupadd staff -gid 100
   D. groupadd —g staff 100

10. Which of the following characteristics cannot explicitly be set using admintool?
   A. The primary group
   B. The login shell
   C. An expiry date for the user's account
   D. File permissions for home directory

Answers

1. A, D

2. C

3. D

4. B

5. C

6. A

7. C

8. B

9. A

10. D

Administration of Initialization Files

The following objectives will be met upon completing this chapter's material:

- Understanding default shell variables set in .profile
- Modifying system-wide templates for .profile in /etc/skel/profile.local
- Reviewing commonly used commands for use in .profile
- Basic shell scripting

Using the command line (or shell) has the following advantages over Graphic User Interface (GUI) environments:

- The shell is essential for programming repetitive tasks, which can only be performed laboriously through a GUI. Such tasks would include searching a filesystem for all document files that have changed each day and making a copying of all these files (with the extension .doc) to a backup directory (with the extension .bak).

- The shell can be used to search for, modify, edit, and replace Solaris configuration files, which are typically storied in a text format. This is much like the approach taken with Windows .ini configuration files, which were text-based. However, versions of Windows after Windows 95 used the Registry to store configuration information in a binary format, making it impossible to manually edit. All Solaris configuration files are text-based.

- The shell has a number of built-in commands that typically mirror those provided in the C programming language. This means it is possible to write small programs as shell statements that are executed as sequential steps, without having to use a compiler (just like MS-DOS batch files are interpreted without requiring a compiler).

- The shell can be used to launch applications that use a CUI, which is especially useful for logging in to a remote system, and it can use all the commands that the administrator uses on the console. In the era of global information systems, this is very useful. Although Windows applications like Symantec's pcAnywhere can be used for remote access to the Windows desktop, they don't easily support multi-user access (or multiuser access where one user requires a Character User Interface [CUI] and another a GUI).

- The shell can be used to execute commands for which there is no equivalent GUI application. Although many operations could conceivably be performed using a GUI, it is usually easier to write a shell script than create a completely new GUI application.

Every time a user logs into a system, a shell is spawned. The type of shell spawned is determined by the default shell entry in /etc/passwd for the user concerned:

```
apache:x:1003:10:apache user:/usr/local/apache:/bin/sh
```

In this case, the apache user has the Bourne shell (/bin/sh) set as the default. To be a valid login shell, /bin/sh must also be included in the shells database (stored in the file /etc/shells). The default system shell is the Bourne shell (/bin/sh). When a login shell is spawned, an initialization script is executed by the shell, which contains a series of commands that are executed sequentially, in addition to a number of environment variables being set. Each shell has its own initialization script. In the case of Bourne shell, the initialization script is called .profile. The .profile is typically located in the user's home directory, although a system-wide /etc/profile script is also executed.

The .profile Script

The .profile file can contain any commands and environment settings that a normal shell script can. Environment variables are used to store information in a form that is accessible to commands within the shell, and other applications that are spawned from the shell. You can obtain a list of all the environment variables that have been set in a shell by using the following command:

```
$ set
COLUMNS=80
DIRSTACK=()
DISPLAY=cassowary:0.0
EDITOR=/usr/bin/vi
ENV=/.kshrc
EUID=0
GROUPS=()
HELPPATH=/usr/openwin/lib/locale:/usr/openwin/lib/help
HISTFILE=/.sh_history
HISTFILESIZE=500
HISTSIZE=500
HOME=/
HOSTNAME=cassowary
HOSTTYPE=i386
IFS=' '
LANG=en_AU
LC_COLLATE=en_AU
LC_CTYPE=en_AU
LC_MESSAGES=C
LC_MONETARY=en_AU
LC_NUMERIC=en_AU
LC_TIME=en_AU
LD_LIBRARY_PATH=/usr/local/lib:/usr/openwin/lib:/usr/dt/lib
LINES=24
LOGNAME=root
MACHTYPE=i386-pc-solaris2.8
MAIL=/var/mail/root
MAILCHECK=60
MANPATH=/usr/dt/man:/usr/man:/usr/openwin/share/man
OPENWINHOME=/usr/openwin
OPTERR=1
OPTIND=1
OSTYPE=solaris2.8
PATH=/usr/sbin:/usr/bin:/bin:/usr/ucb:/usr/local/bin:/usr/openwin/
bin:/usr/ccs/bin
PIPESTATUS=([0]="1")
PPID=1584
PS1='\s-\v\$ '
PS2='> '
PS4='+ '
PWD=/etc
SESSION_SVR=tango
SHELL=/bin/ksh
SHLVL=1
TERM=dtterm
TERMINAL_EMULATOR=dtterm
TZ=Australia/NSW
UID=0
USER=root
WINDOWID=58720265
```

Although this seems to be a lot of shell variables, the most significant ones include the following:

- **COLUMNS**   The columns' width for the terminal
- **DISPLAY**   The display variable that is used for X11 graphics
- **HOME**   The default home directory for the user
- **HOSTNAME**   The hostname of the current system
- **LD_LIBRARY_PATH**   The path to system and user libraries
- **LOGNAME**   The username of the shell owner
- **MANPATH**   The path to the system manuals
- **NNTPSERVER**   The hostname of the NNTP server
- **PATH**   The path that is searched to find applications where no absolute path is specified on the command line
- **PPID**   The parent process ID
- **TERM**   The terminal type (usually VT100)
- **UID**   The user ID
- **WINDOWMANAGER**   The name of the X11 window manager

The values of all shell variables can be set in .profile. For example, if we wanted to set the current terminal type to VT220, we would insert the following environment variable definition into the .profile file:

```
TERM=vt220; export TERM
```

In this example, the TERM variable is created and the value vt220 is assigned to it. At this point, the scope of the variable is just the .profile script itself. In order to ensure that the value is exported to shell proper, the export command should be used as shown.

Because many environment variables are set system-wide (such as the location of database files), each user will expect to have variables consistently set. One way to ensure that users are using the correct variables is to define the /etc/skel/profile.local file. This skeleton file contains variable definitions that will be copied to new user's accounts when they are created with admintool or useradd.

Common .profile Commands

If the default shell prompt is not to your liking, its format can easily be changed by setting two environment variables: PS1 and PS2. We will cover environment variables in more detail later, but the Solaris environment is equivalent to that found in Linux and Windows NT. For example, to set the prompt to display the username and host, we would use the following command:

```
PS1='\u@\H> ' export PS1
```

The prompt displayed by the shell would then look like this:

```
oracle@db>
```

Many users like to display their current username, hostname, and current working directory, which can be set using the following command:

```
PS1='\u@\H:\w> '; export PS1
```

When executed, this shell prompt is changed to the following:

```
oracle@db:/usr/local>
```

Here oracle is the current user, db is the hostname, and /usr/local is the current working directory. A list of different customization options for the shell prompts is given in Table 11-1.

We will now look at some common examples for executing commands within the .profile script.

Source (.)

The source command reads in and executes the lines of a shell script. The format of this command is

```
. file
```

file is a valid filename that contains a Bourne shell script. The first line should contain a directive that points to the absolute location of the shell:

```
#!/bin/sh
```

Alternatively, Bourne shell scripts can be executed by calling them with a new shell invocation, or by calling them directly if the executable bit is set for the executing user.

Table 11-1   Environment Variable Setting for Different Command Prompts under the Bourne Shell

Setting	Description	Output
\a	ASCII beep character	Beep
\d	Date string	Wed Sep 6
\h	Short hostname	www
\H	Full hostname	www.paulwatters.com
\s	Shell name	sh
\t	Current time (12-hour format)	10:53:44
\T	Current time (24-hour format)	10:53:55
\@	Current time (A.M./P.M. format)	10:54am
\u	Username	Root
\v	Shell version	2.03
\W	Shell version with revision	2.03.0
\!	Command history number	223
\$	Privilege indicator	#
\u\$	Username and privilege indicator	root#
\u:\!:\$	Username, command history number, and privilege indicator	root:173:#

However, only the source command (.) preserves any environment variable settings made in the script. If the .profile is large, it can be logically divided into a number of smaller scripts that can be more easily administered.

basename

The basename command strips a filename of its extension. The format of this command is

```
basename filename.ext
```

filename.ext is a valid filename like mydata.dat. The basename command parses mydata.dat and extracts mydata. Because file extensions are not mandatory in Solaris, this command is very useful for processing files copied from Windows or MS-DOS.

cat

The cat command prints out the contents of the file without any special screen control features like scrolling backwards or forwards in a file. The format of this command is

```
cat filename
```

To display the groups database, for example, we could insert the following command:

```
cat /etc/group
```

This would display the following result:

```
root::0:root
other::1:
bin:2::root,bin,daemon
sys::3:root,bin,sys,adm
adm::4:root,adm,daemon
uucp::5:root,uucp
mail::6:root
tty::7:root,tty,adm
lp::8:root,lp,adm
nuucp::9:root,nuucp
staff::10:
```

cd

The cd command changes the current working directory to a new directory location, which can be specified in both absolute or relative terms. The format of this command is

```
cd directory
```

For example, if the current working directory is /usr/local, and we insert the command

```
cd bin
```

then the new working directory would be /usr/local/bin. However, if we insert the command

```
cd /bin
```

then the new working directory would be /bin. For security reasons, scripts should always contain absolute directory references, making no assumptions about relative file locations.

chgrp

The chgrp command modifies the default group membership of a file. The format of this command is

```
chgrp group file
```

group is a valid group name, defined in the groups database (/etc/groups), and file is a valid filename. Because permissions can be assigned to individual users or groups of users, assigning a non-default group membership can be useful for users who need to exchange data with members of different organizational units (such as the Webmaster who swaps configuration files with the database administrator and also exchanges HTML files with Web developers). Only the file owner or the super-user can modify the group membership of a file.

chmod

This command modifies the file access permissions for users, groups, and the file owner, and it is similar to the ATTRIB command in Windows NT. File permissions enable users in different classes to have read, write, or execute access to a file. Only the file owner or the super-user can modify the permissions of a file. The format of this command is

```
chmod permission file
```

where permission is a permission code (symbolic or octal format) and filename is a valid filename.

date

This command prints the current system date and time. The format of this command is

```
date
```

The default output for the command output is of the following form:

```
Wednesday September  6 13:43:23 EST 2000
```

It is also possible to modify the output format by using a number of parameters corresponding to days, months, hours, minutes, and so on. For example, the command

```
date '+Current Date: %d/%m/%y%nCurrent Time:%H:%M:%S'
```

produces the following output:

```
Current Date: 06/09/00
Current Time:13:45:43
```

grep

The grep command searches a file for a string (specified by string) and prints the line wherever a match is found. The format of this command is

```
grep string file
```

The grep command is useful for interpreting log files, where you only want to display a line that contains a particular code (for example, a Web server logfile can be grepped for the string 404, which indicates a page not found).

head

The head command displays the first page of a file. The format of this command is

```
head filename
```

The head command is useful for examining the first few lines of a long file. For example, to display the first page of the name service switch configuration file (/etc/nsswitch.conf), we would use the command

```
head /etc/nsswitch.conf
```

The following output would be displayed:

```
# /etc/nsswitch.nisplus:
# An example file that could be copied over to /etc/nsswitch.conf; it
# uses NIS+ (NIS Version 3) in conjunction with files.
# "hosts:" and "services:" in this file are used only if the
# /etc/netconfig file has a "-" for nametoaddr_libs of "inet"
transports.
# the following two lines obviate the "+" entry in /etc/passwd and
/etc/group.
```

less

The less command prints a file on the screen and enables searching backwards and forwards through the file. The format of this command is

```
less filename
```

To scroll through the contents of the system log configuration file (/etc/syslog.conf), you would use the following command:

```
less /etc/syslog.conf
#ident  "@(#)syslog.conf    1.4    96/10/11 SMI"    /* SunOS 5.0 */
# Copyright (c) 1991-1993, by Sun Microsystems, Inc.
# syslog configuration file.
# This file is processed by m4 so be careful to quote (") names
# that match m4 reserved words.  Also, within ifdef's, arguments
# containing commas must be quoted.
*.notice                                        @loghost
*.err;kern.notice;auth.notice                   /dev/console
*.err;kern.debug;daemon.notice;mail.crit;daemon.info
/var/adm/messages
*.alert;kern.err;daemon.err                     operator
*.alert                                         root
```

The less command has a number of commands that can be issued interactively. For example, to move forward one window, just type **f**, or to move back one window, just type **b**. Less also supports searching with the /pattern command.

ls

The ls command prints the names of files contained in the directory dir (by default, the contents of the current working directory are displayed). The format of the command is

```
ls directory
```

directory is the name of the directory that contains the contents you want to list. For example, to list the contents of the /var/adm directory, which contains a number of system logs, you could insert the following command:

```
ls /var/adm
```

The following output would then be displayed:

```
aculog        log          messages.1   passwd      utmp       wtmp
ftpmessages   messages     messages.2   spellhist   utmpx      wtmpx
lastlog       messages.0   messages.3   sulog       vold.log
```

more

The more command prints the contents of a file, like the less command, but it only permits the scrolling forward through a file. The format of this command is

```
more filename
```

To scroll through the contents of the disk device configuration file (/etc/format.dat), you would use the command:

```
more /etc/format.dat
#pragma ident    "@(#)format.dat 1.21    98/01/24 SMI"
# Copyright (c) 1991,1998 by Sun Microsystems, Inc.
# All rights reserved.
# Data file for the 'format' program.  This file defines the known
# disks, disk types, and partition maps.
# This is the list of supported disks for the Emulex MD21 controller.
disk_type = "Micropolis 1355" \
        : ctlr = MD21 \
        : ncyl = 1018 : acyl = 2 : pcyl = 1024 : nhead = 8 : nsect = 34 \
        : rpm = 3600 : bpt = 20832
```

The more command has a number of commands that can be issued interactively. For example, to move forward one window, just hit the spacebar, or to move forward one line, just hit the Enter key. more also supports searching with the /pattern command.

pwd

The pwd command prints the current working directory in absolute terms. The format of the command is

```
pwd
```

For example, if we change directory to /etc and issue the pwd command, we would see the following result:

```
cd /etc; pwd
/etc
```

tail

The tail command displays the last page of a file. The format of this command is

```
tail filename
```

The tail command is useful for examining the last few lines of a long file. For example, to display the first page of a Web log file (/usr/local/apache/logs/access_log), we could use the following command:

```
tail /usr/local/apache/logs/access_log
192.168.205.238 - - [31/Aug/2000:09:35:59 +1000] "GET
/images/picture10.gif HTTP/1.1" 200 53
192.168.205.238 - - [31/Aug/2000:09:35:59 +1000] "GET /images/
picture1.gif HTTP/1.1" 200 712
```

```
192.168.205.238 - - [31/Aug/2000:09:35:59 +1000] "GET /images/
picture5.gif HTTP/1.1" 200 7090
192.168.205.238 - - [31/Aug/2000:09:35:59 +1000] "GET /images/
picture66.gif HTTP/1.1" 200 997
192.168.205.238 - - [31/Aug/2000:09:35:59 +1000] "GET /images/
picture49.gif HTTP/1.1" 200 2386
192.168.205.238 - - [31/Aug/2000:09:36:09 +1000] "GET
/servlet/SimpleServlet HTTP/1.1" 200 10497
```

Writing Shell Scripts

Shell scripts are combinations of shell and user commands that are executed in non-interactive mode for a wide variety of purposes. Whether you require a script that converts a set of filename extensions, or whether you need to alert the system administrator by e-mail that disk space is running low, shell scripts can be used. The commands that you place inside a shell script should normally execute in the interactive shell mode as well, making it easy to take apart large scripts and debug them line by line in your normal login shell. In this section, we will only examine shell scripts that run under the Bourne shell. Although many of the scripts will work without modification using other shells, it is always best to check the syntax chart of your own shell before attempting to run the scripts on another shell.

Processing Shell Arguments

A common goal of writing shell scripts is to make them as general as possible, so that they can be used with many different kinds of input. For example, in the cat examples presented previously, we wouldn't want to have to create an entirely new script for every file that we wanted to insert data into. Fortunately, shell scripts are able to make use of command-line parameters, which are numerically ordered arguments that are accessible from within a shell script. A shell script to move files from one computer to another, for instance, might require parameters for the source host, the destination host, and the name of the file to be moved. Obviously, we want to be able to pass these arguments to the script, rather than hard-wiring them into the code. This is one advantage of shell scripts (and Perl programs) over compiled languages like C. Scripts are easy to modify, and their operation is completely transparent to the user.

Arguments to shell scripts can be identified by a simple scheme. The command executed is referred to with the argument $0, with the first parameter identified as $1, the second parameter identified by $2, and so on, up to a maximum of nine parameters. Thus, a script executed with the parameters

```
display_hardware.sh cdrom scsi ide
```

would refer internally to cdrom as $1, scsi as $2, and ide as $3. This approach would be particularly useful when calling smaller scripts from the main .profile script.

Let's see how arguments can be used effectively within a script to process input parameters. The first script we will create simply counts the number of lines in a file (using the wc command), specified by a single command-line argument ($1). To begin with, we create an empty script file:

```
touch count_lines.sh
```

Next, we set the permissions on the file to be executable:

```
chmod +x count_lines.sh
```

Next, we edit the file

```
vi count_lines.sh
```

and add the appropriate code:

```
#!/bin/sh
echo "Number of lines in file " $1
wc -l $1
```

The script takes the first command-line argument, prints the number of lines, and then exits. We run the script with the command

```
./count_lines.sh /etc/group
```

which gives the output:

```
Number of lines in file /etc/group
43
```

Although the individual activity of scripts is quite variable, the procedure of creating the script file, setting its permissions, editing its contents, and executing it on the command line remains the same across scripts. Of course, you may want to make the script only available to certain users or groups for execution. This can be enabled by using the chmod command and explicitly adding or removing permissions when necessary.

Testing File Properties

One of the assumptions that we made in the previous script is that the file specified by $1 actually existed. If it didn't exist, then we obviously would not be able to count the number of lines it contained. If the script is running from the command line, we can safely debug it and interpret any error conditions that arise (such as a file not existing or having incorrect permissions). However, if a script is intended to run as a scheduled job (using the cron or at facility), then it is impossible to debug in real time. Thus, it is often useful to write scripts that can handle error conditions gracefully and intelligently, rather than leaving administrators wondering why a job didn't produce any output when it was scheduled to run.

The number one cause of run-time execution errors is the incorrect setting of file permissions. Although most users remember to set the executable bit on the script file itself, they often neglect to include error checking for the existence of data files that are used by the script. For example, if we wanted to write a script that checked the syntax of a configuration file (like the Apache configuration file, httpd.conf), then we need to check that the file actually exists before performing the check. Otherwise, the script may not return an error message, and we may erroneously assume that the script file is correctly configured.

Fortunately, Bourne shell makes it easy to test for the existence of files by using the (conveniently named) test facility. In addition to testing for file existence, files that exist can also be tested for read, write, and execute permissions prior to any read, write, or execute file access being attempted by the script. Let's revise our previous script that counted the number of lines in a file by first verifying that the target file (specified by $1) exists and printing the result. Otherwise, an error message will be displayed:

```
#!/bin/sh
if test -a $1 then
echo "Number of lines in file " $1
wc [nd]l $1
else
        echo "The file" $1 "does not exist"
fi
```

When we run this command, if a file exists, it should count the number of lines in the target file as before. Otherwise, an error message will be printed. If the /etc/group file did not exist, for example, we'd really want to know about it:

```
./count_lines.sh /etc/group
The file /etc/group does not exist
```

Situations may occur where we will want to test another file property. For example, the /etc/shadow password database must only be readable by the super-user. Thus, if we execute a script to check whether or not the /etc/shadow file is readable by a non-privileged user, it should not return a positive result. We can check file readability by using the -r option, rather than the -a option. Here's the revised script:

```
#!/bin/sh
if test [nd]r $1 then
echo "I can read the file " $1
else
        echo "I can't read the file" $1
fi
```

The following file permissions can also be tested using the test facility:

- **-b** The file is a special block file.
- **-c** The file is a special character file.
- **-d** The file is a directory.
- **-f** The file is a normal file.
- **-h** The file is a symbolic link.
- **-p** The file is a named piped.
- **-s** The file has non-zero size.
- **-w** The file is writable by the current user.
- **-x** The file is executable by the current user.

Looping

All programming languages have the capability to repeat blocks of code for a specified number of iterations. This makes performing repetitive actions very easy for a well-written program. The Bourne shell is no exception; it features a for loop, which repeats the actions of a code block for a specified number of iterations, as defined by a set of consecutive arguments to the for command. In addition, an iterator is available within the code block to indicate which sequence of iterations that will be performed is currently being performed. If that sounds a little complicated, let's have a look at a concrete example, which uses a for loop to generate a set of filenames. These filenames are then tested using the test facility to determine whether or not they exist:

```
#!/bin/sh
for i in apple orange lemon kiwi guava
do
        DATAFILE=$i".dat"
        echo "Checking" $DATAFILE
        if test -s $FILENAME
        then
                echo "$DATAFILE "has zero-length"
        else
                echo $FILENAME "is OK"
        fi
done
```

The for loop is repeated nine times with the variable $i taking on the values apple, orange, lemon, kiwi, and guava. Thus, on the first iteration when $i = apple, the shell interprets the for loop in the following way:

```
FILENAME="apple.dat"
echo "Checking apple.dat"
if test -s apple.dat
then
echo "apple.dat has zero-length"
else
echo "apple.dat is OK"
fi
```

If we run this script in a directory with files of zero-length, we would expect to see the following output:

```
./zero_length_check.sh
Checking apple.dat
apple.dat is zero-length
Checking orange.dat
orange.dat is zero-length
Checking lemon.dat
lemon.dat is zero-length
Checking kiwi.dat
kiwi.dat is zero-length
Checking guava.dat
guava.dat is zero-length
```

However, if we entered data into each of the files, we should see them receive the OK message:

```
./zero_length_check.sh
Checking apple.dat
apple.dat is OK
Checking orange.dat
orange.dat is OK
Checking lemon.dat
lemon.dat is OK
Checking kiwi.dat
kiwi.dat is OK
Checking guava.dat
guava.dat is OK
```

Using Shell Variables

In the previous example, we assigned different values to a shell variable, which was used to generate filenames for checking. It is common to modify variables within scripts by using export and to attach error codes to instances where variables are not defined within a script. This is particularly useful if a variable that is available within a user's interactive shell is not available in their non-interactive shell. For example, we can create a script called show_errors.sh that returns an error message if the PATH variable is not set:

```
#!/bin/sh
echo ${PATH:?PATH_NOT_SET}
```

Of course, because the PATH variable is usually set, we should see output similar to the following:

```
# ./path_set.sh
/sbin:/bin:/usr/games/bin:/usr/sbin:/root/bin:/usr/local/bin:/usr/
local/sbin/:/usr/bin:
/usr/X11R6/bin: /usr/games:/opt/gnome/bin:/opt/kde/bin
```

However, if the PATH is not set, we would see the following error message:

```
./show_errors.sh: PATH_NOT_SET
```

It is also possible to use system-supplied error messages as well by not specifying the optional error string:

```
#!/bin/sh
echo ${PATH:?}
```

Thus, if the PATH variable is not set, we would see the following error message:

```
# ./path_set.sh
./showargs: PATH: parameter null or not set
```

We can also use the numbered shell variables ($1, $2, $3, and so on) to capture the space-delimited output of certain commands and perform actions based on the value of these variables using the set command. For example, the command

```
# set 'ls'
```

will sequentially assign each of the fields within the returned directory listing to a numbered shell variable. For example, if our directory listing contained the entries

```
apple.dat   guava.dat   kiwi.dat   lemon.dat   orange.dat
```

we could retrieve the values of these filenames by using the echo command:

```
# echo $1
apple.dat
# echo $2
guava.dat
# echo $3
```

```
kiwi.dat
# echo $4
lemon.dat
# echo $5
orange.dat
```

This approach is useful if your script needs to perform some action based on only one component of the data. For example, if you wanted to create a unique filename to assign to a compressed file, then you could combine the values of each variable with a .Z extension to produce a set of strings like orange.dat.Z.

Summary

In this chapter, we examined how to create shell initialization scripts by examining how to set environment variables and execute commonly used script commands. In addition, we reviewed some basic shell script patterns that can be used within .profile (and other shell scripts) to perform a wide variety of repetitive actions.

Questions

1. What is the name of the Bourne shell initialization script?
   A. .cshrc
   B. .login
   C. .profile
   D. .init

2. What is the name of the site-wide skeleton file for the Bourne shell initialization file?
   A. /etc/skel/local.cshrc
   B. /etc/skel/local.login
   C. /etc/skel/local.profile
   D. /etc/skel/local.init

3. Which command would be used to set the value of the environment variable TERM to be vt220?
   A. TERM=vt220
   B. TERM='vt220'
   C. set TERM=vt200
   D. setenv TERM='vt220'

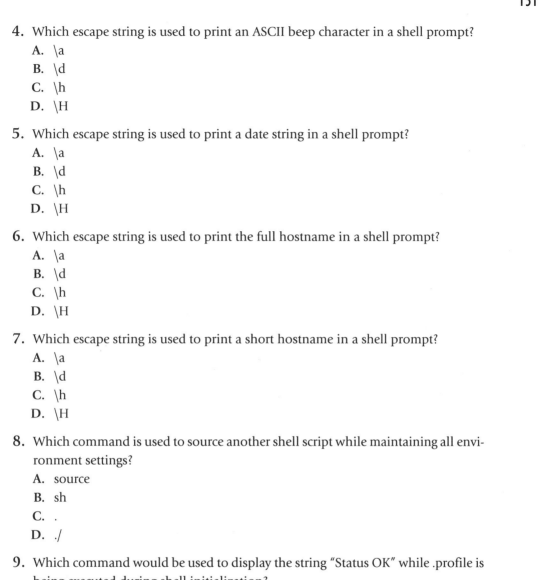

4. Which escape string is used to print an ASCII beep character in a shell prompt?
   A. \a
   B. \d
   C. \h
   D. \H

5. Which escape string is used to print a date string in a shell prompt?
   A. \a
   B. \d
   C. \h
   D. \H

6. Which escape string is used to print the full hostname in a shell prompt?
   A. \a
   B. \d
   C. \h
   D. \H

7. Which escape string is used to print a short hostname in a shell prompt?
   A. \a
   B. \d
   C. \h
   D. \H

8. Which command is used to source another shell script while maintaining all environment settings?
   A. source
   B. sh
   C. .
   D. ./

9. Which command would be used to display the string "Status OK" while .profile is being executed during shell initialization?
   A. println "Status OK"
   B. printf "Status OK"
   C. echo "Status OK"
   D. cat "Status OK" > /dev/null

10. Which parameter is used with the test command to determine whether a file is a special block file?
    A. -b
    B. -block
    C. -blockfile
    D. -bf

Answers

1. C

2. C

3. A

4. A

5. B

6. D

7. C

8. C

9. C

10. A

12

Advanced File Permissions

The following objectives will be met upon completing this chapter's material:

- Understanding file ownership
- Setting file access permissions
- Setting default file permissions (umask)
- Setuid and setgid permissions
- Setting the sticky bit

File Ownership

One of the most confusing issues for novice users of Solaris is understanding the Solaris file access permissions system. The basic approach to setting and interpreting relative file permissions is using a set of symbolic codes to represent users and permission types. However, even advanced users might find it difficult to understand the octal permissions codes that are used to set absolute permissions. When combined with a default permission mask set in the user's shell (the umask), octal permission codes are more powerful than symbolic permission codes.

The Solaris filesystem permits three basic kinds of file access: the ability to read (r), to write (w), and to execute (x) a file or directory. These permissions can be granted exclusively or nonexclusively, on individual files, or on a group of files specified by a wildcard (*). These permissions can be set by using the chmod command, in combination with a + operator. Permissions can be easily removed with the chmod command by using the − operator.

For example, to set read permissions (for the current user) on the file /usr/local/lib/libproxy.a, we would use the command

```
bash-2.03$ chmod +r /usr/local/lib/libproxy.a
```

Alternatively, to set read permissions for all users on the file /usr/local/lib/libproxy.a, we would use the command

```
bash-2.03$ chmod a+r /usr/local/lib/libproxy.a
```

To remove read permissions on the file /usr/local/lib/libproxy.a for all users who are not members of the current user's default group, we would use the command

```
bash-2.03$ chmod o-r /usr/local/lib/libproxy.a
```

This does not remove the group and user read permissions that were set previously. Similarly, execute and write permissions can be set. For example, to set execute permissions on the /usr/local/bin/gcc files for each class of user (current, group, and world), we would use the command

```
bash-2.03$ chmod u+x /usr/local/bin/gcc; chmod g+x
/usr/local/bin/gcc; chmod o+x /usr/local/bin/gcc
```

To explicitly remove write permissions on the /usr/local/bin/gcc files for each class of user (current, group, and world), we would use the command

```
bash-2.03$ chmod u-w /usr/local/bin/gcc; chmod g-w
/usr/local/bin/gcc; chmod o-w /usr/local/bin/gcc
```

The rationale behind using read and write permissions should be clear: Permitting read access on a file enables an identified user to access the text of a file by reading it byte by byte. Write access enables the user to modify or delete any file on which the write permission is granted, regardless of who originally created the file. Thus, individual users can create files with read and write access for any other user on the system.

The permission to execute a file must be granted on scripts (such as shell scripts or Perl scripts), while compiled and linked applications must also have the execute bit set on a specific application. The executable permission must also be granted on the special files that represent directories on the filesystem, if the directory's contents are to be accessed by a specific class of user.

The different options available for granting file access permissions can sometimes lead to interesting, but confusing scenarios: For example, permissions can be set to allow a group to delete a file, but not to execute it. More usefully, a group might be given execute permission on an application, but be unable to write over it. In addition, setting file permissions using relative permission strings (rather than absolute octal permission codes) means that permissions set by a previous change of permission command (chmod) are not revoked by any subsequent chmod commands.

However, the permissions themselves are only half the story: Unlike single-user filesystems, permissions on Solaris are associated with different file owners. (All files and processes on a Solaris system are owned by a specific user.) In addition, groups of users can be granted read, write, and execute permissions on a file or a set of files stored in a directory. Alternatively, file permissions can be granted on a systemwide basis, effectively granting file access without respect to file ownership. Because filesystems can be exported using Network File System (NFS) and/or Samba, it's bad practice to grant systemwide read, write, and execute permissions on any file—unless every user needs access to that file. For example, all users need to read the password database (/etc/passwd), but only the root user should have read access to the shadow password database (/etc/shadow). Blindly exporting all files with world-read, -write, or -execute permissions on an NFS-shared volume is inviting trouble!

The three filesystem categories of ownership are defined by three permission-setting categories: the user (u), who owns the file, group members (g), who have access to the file, and all other users (o) on the system. The group specified by g can be the user's primary group (as defined in /etc/passwd) or a secondary group to which the file has been assigned (defined in /etc/group). It is important to remember that a Solaris filesystem ultimately has few secrets. The root user has full access at all times (read, write, and execute) on all files on the filesystem—even if a user removes all permissions on a file. (The rule of root is absolute.) If the contents of a file really need to be hidden, it is best to encrypt a file's contents using Pretty Good Privacy (PGP), crypt or similar. A root user can also change the ownership of a file. Thus, a user's files do not absolutely belong to a specific user. The chown command can only be used by the super-user for this purpose.

Policies regarding default file permissions need to be set selectively in different environments. For example, in a production Web server system that processes credit card data, access should be denied by default to all users except those who are required to conduct online transactions (for example, the apache user for the Apache Web server). On a system that supports team-based development, obviously permissions need to be set that enable the exchange of data between team partners, but that prevent the access to development files by others. Few Solaris systems would allow a default world writable policy on any filesystem, except for the temporary swap (/tmp) filesystem.

It is possible to enforce systemwide permissions by using a default umask, which sets the read, write, and execute permissions on all new files created by a specific user. If a user wants to use a umask other than the default systemwide setting, this can be achieved by setting it on the command line when required or in the user's shell startup file (for example, .kshrc for Korn shell).

We start our examination of Solaris file permissions by examining how to create files, set permissions, change ownerships, group memberships, and use the ls command to examine existing file permissions. All these commands can be used by nonprivileged users, except the chown command.

The ls command is the main directory and file permission-listing program used in Solaris. When displaying a long listing, it prints file access permissions, user and group ownerships, file size and creation date, and the filename. For example, the output from ls for the password file /etc/passwd looks like this:

```
bash-2.03# ls -l /etc/passwd
-r--r--r--   1 root     other         256 Sep  18 00:40 passwd
```

This directory entry can be read from left to right in the following ways:

- The password file is not a directory, indicated by the first -.
- The password file has read-only permissions for the owner (r--), but not execute or write permissions.
- The password file has read-only permissions for group members (r--).
- The password file has read-only permissions for other staff (r--).
- The password file is owned by the root user.
- The password file has other group permissions.
- The password file size is 256K.
- The password file was created on September 18 at 12:40 A.M.
- The name of the password file is passwd.

The permissions string shows changes depending on the permissions that have been set by the owner. For example, if the password file had execute and write permissions for the root user, the permissions string would read -rwxr--r--, rather than just -r--r--r--. Each of the permissions can be set using symbolic or octal permissions code, with the chmod command.

We've seen how a normal file looks under ls, but let's compare this with a directory entry, which is a special kind of file, that is usually created by the mkdir command:

```
bash-2.03# mkdir samples
```

We can check the permissions of the directory entry by using the ls command:

```
bash-2.03# ls -l
total 8
drwxrwxr-x   2 root      other        512 Sep  5 13:41 samples
```

The directory entry for the directory samples can be read from left to right in the following way:

- The directory entry is a special file denoted by a leading d.
- The directory entry has read, write, and execute permissions for the owner (rwx).
- The directory entry has read, write, and execute permissions for group members (rwx).
- The directory entry has read and execute permissions for other staff (r-x).
- The directory entry is owned by the root user.
- The directory entry has other group permissions.
- The directory entry size is 512K.
- The directory entry was created on September 5 at 1:41 P.M.
- The name of the directory is samples.

For a directory to be accessible to a particular class of user, the executable bit must be set using the chmod command.

Some expert users prefer not to separate user and permission information with the user symbols (u, g, o) and the permission symbols (r, w, x). Instead, a numeric code can be used to combine both user and permission information. If you use lots of common permissions settings, it might be easier for you to remember a single octal code than to work out the permissions string symbolically. The octal code consists of three numbers, which represent owner permissions, group permissions, and other user permissions respectively (from left to right). The higher the number, the greater the permissions for each user. For example, to give a file read, write, and execute permissions for the file owner, the octal code 700 can be used with the chmod command:

```
bash-2.03$ chmod 700 *
```

We can now check to see if the correct permissions have been granted:

```
bash-2.03$ ls -l
total 4
drwx------   2 root      users       4096 Jun  8 20:10 test
-rwx------   1 root      users          0 Jun  8 20:10 test.txt
```

We can also grant read, write, and execute permissions to members of the group by changing the middle number from 0 to 7:

```
bash-2.03$ chmod 770 *
```

Again, the changes are reflected in the symbolic permissions string displayed by ls:

```
bash-2.03$ ls -l
total 4
drwxrwx---   2 root      users         4096 Jun  8 20:10 test
-rwxrwx---   1 root      users            0 Jun  8 20:10 test.txt
```

If you want to grant read, write, and execute permissions to all users, simply change the third permissions number from 0 to 7:

```
bash-2.03$ chmod 777 *
```

Now, all users on the system have read, write, and execute permissions on all files in the directory:

```
bash-2.03$ ls -l
total 4
drwxrwxrwx   2 root      users         4096 Jun  8 20:10 test
-rwxrwxrwx   1 root      users            0 Jun  8 20:10 test.txt
```

Of course, the codes that can be used to specify permissions are usually not just 0 or 7. For example, the code 5 gives read and execute access, but not write access. So, if we wanted to grant read and execute access to members of the group, but deny write access, we could use the code 750:

```
bash-2.03$ chmod 750 *
```

This produces the following result:

```
bash-2.03$ ls -l
total 4
drwxr-x---   2 root      users         4096 Jun  8 20:10 test
-rwxr-x---   1 root      users            0 Jun  8 20:10 test.txt
```

If we wanted to remove all access permissions from the files in the current directory, we could use the code 000: (You should not normally need to do this.)

```
bash-2.03$ chmod 000 *
```

Let's examine the result of that command:

```
bash-2.03$ ls -l
total 4
```

```
d---------    2 root      users        4096 Jun  8 20:10 test
----------    1 root      users           0 Jun  8 20:10 test.txt
```

All access permissions have been removed, except the directory indicator on the special file test. It's important to note the main difference between setting files using symbolic codes rather than octal codes: Symbolic codes are relative, but numeric codes are absolute. This means that unless you explicitly revoke a file permission when setting another using symbolic codes, it will persist. Thus, if a file already has group-write access, and we grant group-execute access (or remove group-execute access), the write-access permission is not removed. However, if we specify only group-execute access using an octal code, the group-write access is automatically removed (if it has been previously set). You may well find in startup scripts and in situations where the permissions are not known in advance, that it is wiser to use octal codes.

Display and Change the Default Permissions (umask)

It is possible to enforce systemwide permissions by using a default user mask (umask), which sets the read, write, and execute permissions on all new files created by a specific user. If a user wishes to use a umask other than the default systemwide setting, this can be achieved by setting it on the command line when required, or in the user's shell startup file (for example, .kshrc for Korn shell). In addition, the mask that is set for the current user can be displayed by using the umask command by itself.

Like file permissions, the umask is set using octal codes. (Symbolic codes cannot be used.) Two different strategies exist for computing umasks: For directories, the octal value of the default permission that you want to set must be subtracted from octal 777. For files, the octal value of the default permission that you want to set must be subtracted from octal 666. For example, to set the default permission to 444 (all read-only), we would subtract 444 from 666 for files, deriving the umask of 222. Alternatively, for the default permission 600 (user read/write, no other access), we would subtract 600 from 666, leaving a umask of 066 (which will often be displayed as 66).

If you want all users to have full access permissions on all files that you create, you would set the umask to 000 (666−000=666):

```
bash-2.03$ umask 000
```

Let's examine the results, after creating a file called data.txt, and setting the umask to 000:

```
bash-2.03$ touch data.txt
bash-2.03$ ls -l
total 4
-rwxrwxrwx   1 root      users               0 Jun  8 20:20 data.txt
```

Everyone now has full access permissions. However, you are more likely to set a umask like 022, which would give new files the permissions 755 (777−022=755). This would give the file owner read, write, and execute access, but give only read permissions to group members and other users:

```
bash-2.03$ umask 022
```

If we now create a new file called newdata.txt with the new umask, we should see that the default permissions have changed:

```
bash-2.03$ touch newtest.txt
bash-2.03$ ls -l
total 4
-rw-r--r--   1 root      root                0 Jun  8 20:21 newdata.txt
-rwxrwxrwx   1 root      users               0 Jun  8 20:20 data.txt
```

If you're more conservative, and you don't want to grant any access permissions to other users (including group members), you can set the umask to 077, which still gives the file owner full access permissions:

```
bash-2.03$ umask 077
```

Let's see what happens when we create a new file called lastminute.txt:

```
bash-2.03$ touch lastminute.txt
bash-2.03$ ls -l
total 4
-rw-r--r--   1 root      root            0 Jun  8 20:21 newdata.txt
-rw-------   1 root      root            0 Jun  8 20:22 lastminute.txt
-rwxrwxrwx   1 root      users           0 Jun  8 20:20 data.txt
```

The new file has full access permissions for the owner, but no access permissions for other users. Resetting the umask does not affect the permissions of other files that have already been created.

Setuid and Setgid Permissions

The file permissions we've covered so far are employed by users in their day-to-day file management strategies. However, administrators can make use of a different set of file permissions that enable files to be executed as a particular user (setuid), and/or as a member of a particular group (setgid). These facilities are very powerful because they enable unprivileged users to gain access to limited super-user privileges in many cases (without requiring super-user authentication). For example, the volume daemon (vold) enables unprivileged users who are logged into the console to mount and unmount CD-ROMs and floppy disks, an operation that required super-user privileges in previous Solaris releases. Here, the effective user ID is set to 0, meaning that unprivileged users can effectively run processes as root. The downside to this is obvious. Setgid and setuid permissions open a Pandora's box in terms of security because normal authentication procedures are bypassed. For example, imagine a device management tool that needed to run as setuid 0 to read and write device files. If the tool had a standard feature of many UNIX programs (the capability to spawn a shell), the shell spawned would have full root privileges, rather than the privileges of the original user. For this reason, some administrators refuse to allow setgid and setuid permissions to be set. The find command, for example, can be used to scan all filesystems and remove any files with setuid or setgid privileges automatically.

You can determine whether a file is setuid by root in two ways:

- Checking for files that are owned by root

- Checking whether these files have the s flag assigned to the user's permissions

For example, if a file management tool called filetool is setuid by root, the following directory listing would clearly indicate this property:

```
-r-sr-sr-x 3 root sys 1220334 Jul 18 11:01 /usr/local/bin/filetool
```

The first s in the permissions table refers to setuid root. In addition, this file is setgid for the sys group, which is indicated by the second s in the permissions table.

The setuid bit can be set using a command like

```
bash-2.03# chmod u+s file.txt
```

where file.txt is the file that requires setuid to be set. The setgid bit can be set by using a command like

```
bash-2.03# chmod g+s file.txt
```

where file.txt is the file that requires setgid to be set.

Sticky Bit Permissions

A network administrator once explained to me that sticky bits were those bits that slowed network transmission rates because they were highly attracted to the magnetic qualities of the Ethernet. This is not true! A sticky bit is a special permission that prevents files in common file areas from being deleted by other users. For example, a download area consisting of a large 10G partition can be set aside for user downloads, which are not counted against individual user quotas. This means that users could download up to 10G of data without infringing on their allocated directory space. Although a shared public file area sounds like a great idea, it would be unwise to allow users to overwrite one another's files. In this case, the sticky bit can be set on the top-level directory of the public file area, allowing only users who created individual files to delete them.

The sticky bit can be set using a command like

```
bash-2.03# chmod +t somedir
```

where somedir is the directory that requires the sticky bit to be set.

Summary

In this chapter, we have examined how to list and modify access permissions for files and directories. In addition, we reviewed methods that enable files to be executed with the permissions of privileged users and groups. Finally, we examined how to set the sticky bit to protect user files in common file areas.

Questions

1. What command would be used to set read permissions (for the current user) on the file /usr/local/lib/libproxy.a?
   A. chmod +r /usr/local/lib/libproxy.a
   B. chmod a+r /usr/local/lib/libproxy.a
   C. chmod g+r /usr/local/lib/libproxy.a
   D. chmod u+r /usr/local/lib/libproxy.a

2. What command would be used to set read permissions for all users on the file /usr/local/lib/libproxy.a?
   A. chmod +r /usr/local/lib/libproxy.a
   B. chmod a+r /usr/local/lib/libproxy.a
   C. chmod g+r /usr/local/lib/libproxy.a
   D. chmod u+r /usr/local/lib/libproxy.a

3. What command would be used to set write permissions for the current user's group on the file /usr/local/lib/libproxy.a?
   A. chgrp +w /usr/local/lib/libproxy.a
   B. chmod a+w /usr/local/lib/libproxy.a
   C. chmod g+w /usr/local/lib/libproxy.a
   D. chmod u+w /usr/local/lib/libproxy.a

4. What command would be used to remove write permissions for the current user's group on the file /usr/local/lib/libproxy.a?
   A. chgrp -w /usr/local/lib/libproxy.a
   B. chmod a-w /usr/local/lib/libproxy.a
   C. chmod g-w /usr/local/lib/libproxy.a
   D. chmod u-w /usr/local/lib/libproxy.a

5. What command would be used to set the sticky bit on /public?
   A. chmod +t /public
   B. chmod +s /public
   C. chmod +S /public
   D. chmod t+s /public

6. What command would be used to remove the sticky bit on /public?
   A. chmod -t /public
   B. chmod -s /public
   C. chmod -S /public
   D. chmod t-s /public

7. What command would be used to set the permission setuid on /public/shell?
   A. chmod +t /public/shell
   B. chmod +s /public/shell
   C. chmod +S /public/shell
   D. chmod t+s /public/shell

Answers

1. A
2. B
3. C
4. C
5. A
6. A
7. B

Process Control

The following objectives will be met upon completing this chapter's material:

- Understanding how the **ps** command can be used to monitor system processes
- Sending signals to processes to modify their behavior using the **kill** command
- Configure the at daemon to schedule the execution of a job
- Configure the cron daemon to regularly schedule the execution of a job

Processes lie at the heart of modern multi-user operating systems and provide the capability to run applications and services on top of the kernel. In user terms, job management is a central feature of using a single login shell to start and stop multiple jobs running concurrently, often suspending their execution while waiting for input. Solaris 8 provides many tools for process management. In this chapter, we will highlight the process management tools and command formats found in Solaris 8 as well as task automation using the cron and at daemons.

Processes

One of the appealing characteristics of Solaris and other UNIX-like systems is that applications can execute (or "spawn") other applications. After all, user shells are nothing more than applications themselves. A shell can spawn another shell or application, which can spawn another shell or application, and so on. Instances of applications, such as the sendmail mail transport agent or the telnet remote access application, can be uniquely identified as individual processes and are associated with a unique process identifier (pid), which is an integer.

You may be wondering why process identifiers are not content-addressable, that is, why the sendmail process cannot be just identified as "sendmail." Such a scheme would be quite sensible if it was impossible to execute multiple, independent instances of the same application (like MacOS). However, Solaris allows the same user or different users to concurrently execute the same application independently, meaning that an independent identifier is required for each process. This means that each pid is related to a user's identifier (UID) and to that user's group identifier (GID). The UID in this case can either be the real UID of the user who executed the process or the effective UID if the file executed is setuid. Similarly, the GID in this case can either be the real GID, which the user who executed the process belongs to, or the effective GID if the file executed is setgid. When an application can be executed as setuid and setgid, other users can execute such a program as the user who owns the file. This means that setting a file as setgid for root can be dangerous in some situations, although necessary in others.

An application, such as a shell, can spawn another application by using the system call system() in a C program. (For more details on system(), see the system man page.) This is expensive performance-wise, because a new shell process is spawned in addition to the target application. However, an alternative is to use the fork() system call, which spawns child processes directly, with an application executed using exec(). Each child process is linked back to its parent process. If the parent process exits, then the parent process automatically reverts to pid 1, which exits when the system is shutdown or rebooted.

In the following sections, we look at ways to determine which processes are currently running on your system and how to examine process lists and tables to determine which system resources are being used by specific processes.

The main command used to list commands is **ps**, which is highly configurable and has many command-line options. **ps** takes a snapshot of the current process list; many administrators find that they need to interactively monitor processes on systems that have a high load, so that they kill processes that are consuming too much memory, or at least assign them a lower execution priority. One popular process-monitoring tool is the CDE graphical process finder, which also lists currently active processes, shown in Figure 13-1. It is possible to list processes here by pid, name, owner, percentage of central processing unit (CPU) time consumed, physical memory used, virtual memory used, date started, parent pid, and the actual command executed.

```
                          Process Manager:root@austin
 Process  Edit  View  Sample                                                        Help

 Filter:                        Sample Every 30      Secs    Find: |

 ID | Name   | Owner  |CPU% | RAM | Swap | Started | Parent |        Command
1095 ux_passw    root   88.3   1816    2208 16:18:41       1 /opt/local/bin/ux_password_svr
1169 Xsun        root    3.1  72288   30600 16:25:29     395 /usr/openwin/bin/Xsun :0 -nobanner -auth /var/dt/A:0-DiayXa
1304 dtwm        root    1.8   7112    9168 20:11:59    1298 dtwm
1334 sdtimage    root    1.5  10368   15392 20:12:24    1333 /usr/dt/bin/sdtimage -snapshot
1331 dtfile      root    0.7   6648    8680 20:12:16    1330 dtfile -noview
1319 sdtproce    root    0.5   6544    9040 20:12:10    1318 sdtprocess
1336 ps          root    0.4   1160    1952 20:12:41    1335 /usr/bin/ps -A -o pid=ID -o fname=Name -o user=Owner -o pcpu,rss
1335 sort        root    0.2    872   17544 20:12:41    1319 sort -bf -rn +3
1333 dtexec      root    0.2   2344    3120 20:12:24    1304 /usr/dt/bin/dtexec -open 0 -ttprocid 2.wqjnj 01 1297 1289637086
1305 sdtperfm    root    0.2   4784    7224 20:12:02    1298 /usr/dt/bin/sdtperfmeter -f -H -t cpu -t disk -s 1 -name fpperfr
1298 dtsessio    root    0.2   4800    8088 20:11:58    1284 /usr/dt/bin/dtsession
1297 ttsessio    root    0.2   3696    4976 20:11:57       1 /usr/dt/bin/ttsession
1330 sh          root    0.1    792    1072 20:12:16    1297 /bin/sh -c dtfile -noview
1318 dtexec      root    0.1   2328    3120 20:12:10    1304 /usr/dt/bin/dtexec -open 0 -ttprocid 2.wqjnj 01 1297 1289637086
1307 sdtvolch    root    0.1   1280    1864 20:12:02       1 /bin/ksh /usr/dt/bin/sdtvolcheck -d -z 5 cdrom,zip,jaz,dvdrom,r
1282 sdt_shel    root    0.1   2008    3888 20:11:55    1236 /usr/dt/bin/sdt_shell -c           unset DT;        DISPLAY=:0;
1236 Xsession    root    0.1   1280    1880 20:11:54    1170 /bin/ksh /usr/dt/bin/Xsession
 497 rpc.ttdb    root    0.1   2416    3440 14:24:27     213 rpc.ttdbserverd
   3 fsflush     root    0.1      0       0 14:04:56       0 fsflush
1337 tail        root    0.0    680    1024 20:12:41    1335 tail +2
1329 cat         root    0.0    704     952 20:12:13    1307 /bin/cat /tmp/.removable/notify1307
1312 rpc.rsta    root    0.0   1256    1800 20:12:03     213 rpc.rstatd
1286 dsdm        root    0.0    768    2328 20:11:55       1 /usr/dt/bin/dsdm
1284 sh          root    0.0    304     304 20:11:55    1282 -sh -c           unset DT;        DISPLAY=:0;        /usr/dt
1250 speckeys    root    0.0    984    5080 20:11:54       1 /usr/openwin/bin/speckeysd
1246 fbconsol    root    0.0   1288    2304 20:11:54    1236 /usr/openwin/bin/fbconsole
1232 smbd        root    0.0   2224    4144 20:10:56    1217 ./smbd
1219 nmbd        root    0.0   1576    2192 19:18:56       1 ./nmbd
1217 smbd        root    0.0   2464    3752 19:18:55       1 ./smbd
1172 fbconsol    root    0.0   1288    2304 16:25:30       1 /usr/openwin/bin/fbconsole -d :0
1170 dtlogin     root    0.0   2688    5272 16:25:29     395 /usr/dt/bin/dtlogin -daemon
1080 ux_passw    root    0.0   1480    2144 16:18:10       1 /bin/cat /tmp/.removable/notify1307
 415 mibiisa     root    0.0   1760    2440 14:24:07     393 mibiisa -r -p 328/6
 413 ttymon      root    0.0   1072    1752 14:24:04     410 /usr/lib/saf/ttymon
 411 ttymon      root    0.0    944    1752 14:24:03       1 /usr/lib/saf/ttymon -g -h -p austin console login:   -T sun -d /
 410 sac         root    0.0   1008    1752 14:24:03       1 /usr/lib/saf/sac -t 300
 404 snmpXdmi    root    0.0   1824    3768 14:24:03       1 /usr/lib/dmi/snmpXdmid -s austin
 403 dmispd      root    0.0   1720    3176 14:24:03       1 /usr/lib/dmi/dmispd
 395 dtlogin     root    0.0   2192    4976 14:24:02       1 /usr/dt/bin/dtlogin -daemon
 393 snmpdx      root    0.0   1264    2160 14:24:02       1 /usr/lib/snmp/snmpdx -y -c /etc/snmp/conf
 375 atokmngd    root    0.0    608     976 14:24:00       1 /usr/lib/locale/ja/atokserver/atokmngdaemon
 349 dwhttpd   daemon    0.0   3208   10432 14:23:58     348 /usr/lib/ab2/dweb/sunos5/bin/dwhttpd /usr/lib/ab2/dweb/data
 348 dwhttpd   daemon    0.0   1624    9720 14:23:58       1 /usr/lib/ab2/dweb/sunos5/bin/dwhttpd /usr/lib/ab2/dweb/data
 330 htt_serv    root    0.0   1472    3048 14:23:49     329 htt_server -port 9010 -syslog -message_locale C
 329 htt         root    0.0    616     944 14:23:49       1 /usr/lib/im/htt -port 9010 -syslog -message_locale C
 326 jserver_    root    0.0   1384    2576 14:23:49     325 /usr/lib/locale/ja/wnn/jserver_m
 325 jserver     root    0.0    456    1592 14:23:49       1 /usr/lib/locale/ja/wnn/jserver
```

Figure 13-1   CDE's graphical process finder

The ps Command

ps lists all currently active processes on the local system. By default, **ps** just prints the
processes belonging to the user who issues the **ps** command:

```
bash-2.03$ ps
PID TTY        TIME CMD
 29081 pts/8    0:00 bash
```

The columns in the default ps list are the process identifier (PID), the terminal
from which the command was executed (TTY), the CPU time consumed by the
process (TIME), and the actual command that was executed (CMD), including any

command-line options passed to the program. Alternatively, if you would like more information about the current user's processes, you can add the -f parameter:

```
bash-2.03$ ps -f
     UID     PID   PPID  C STIME     TTY      TIME CMD
   pwatters 29081 29079  0 10:40:30 pts/8    0:00 /bin/ksh
```

Again, the pid, tty, CPU time, and command are displayed. However, the uid is also displayed (UID), as is the pid of the parent process (PPID), along with the starting time of the process (STIME). In addition, a deprecated column (C) is used to display processor utilization. To obtain the maximum detail possible, you can also use the -l option, which means long, and long it certainly is, as shown in this example:

```
bash-2.03$ ps -l
 F S   UID    PID  PPID  C PRI NI    ADDR      SZ    WCHAN TTY
 TIME CMD
 8 S  6049  29081 29079  0  51 20 e11b4830    372 e11b489c pts/8
 0:00 ksh
 8 R  6049  29085 29081  0  51 20 e101b0d0    512          pts/8
 0:00 bash
```

Here we can see the

- Flags (F) associated with the processes

- State (S) of the processes (29081 is sleeping "S," 29085 is running "R")

- Process identifier (29081 and 29085)

- Parent process identifier (29079 and 29081)

- Processor utilization (deprecated)

- Process priority (PRI), which is 51

- Nice value (NI), which is 20

- Memory address (ADDR), which is expressed in hex (e11b4830 and e101b0d0)

- Size (SZ) in kilobytes, which is 372K and 512K

- Memory address for sleeping process events (WCHAN), which is e11b489c for pid 29081

- CPU time used (TIME)

- Command executed (CMD)

If you're a system administrator, you're probably not interested in the status of just your own processes, but all or some of the processes actively running on the system. You can determine these statuses in many different ways. One is to generate a process list using the -A or the -e option. Either one of these lists information for all processes currently running on the machine:

```
bash-2.03$ ps -A
   PID TTY        TIME CMD
     0 ?          0:00 sched
     1 ?          0:01 init
     2 ?          0:01 pageout
     3 ?          9:49 fsflush
   258 ?          0:00 ttymon
   108 ?          0:00 rpcbind
   255 ?          0:00 sac
    60 ?          0:00 devfseve
    62 ?          0:00 devfsadm
   157 ?          0:03 automount
   110 ?          0:01 keyserv
   112 ?          0:04 nis_cache
   165 ?          0:00 syslogd
```

Again, the default display of pid, tty, CPU time, and the command executed is generated. The processes listed relate to the scheduler, init, the system logging facility, the NIS cache, and several other standard applications and services. Alternatively, the **time** command can be used to measure how long individual processes take to execute.

It is good practice to become familiar with the main processes on your system and the relative CPU times they usually consume. This can be very useful when troubleshooting or when evaluating security. One of the nice features of **ps** is the capability to combine multiple flags to print out a more elaborate process list. For example, we can combine the -A option (all processes) with the -f option (full details) to produce a process list with full details. Here are the full details for the same process list:

```
bash-2.03$ ps -Af
     UID    PID   PPID   C    STIME TTY    TIME CMD
    root      0      0   0   Mar 20 ?      0:00 sched
    root      1      0   0   Mar 20 ?      0:01 /etc/init -
    root      2      0   0   Mar 20 ?      0:01 pageout
    root      3      0   0   Mar 20 ?      9:51 fsflush
    root    258    255   0   Mar 20 ?      0:00 /usr/lib/saf/ttymon
    root    108      1   0   Mar 20 ?      0:00 /usr/sbin/rpcbind
    root    255      1   0   Mar 20 ?      0:00 /usr/lib/saf/sac -t 300
    root     60      1   0   Mar 20 ?      0:00 /usr/lib/devfsadm/
                                                devfseventd
    root     62      1   0   Mar 20 ?      0:00 /usr/lib/devfsadm/
                                                devfsadmd
    root    157      1   0   Mar 20 ?      0:03 /usr/lib/autofs/
                                                automountd
    root    110      1   0   Mar 20 ?      0:01 /usr/sbin/keyserv
    root    112      1   0   Mar 20 ?      0:05 /usr/sbin/nis_cachemgr
    root    165      1   0   Mar 20 ?      0:00 /usr/sbin/syslogd
```

Another common use for **ps** is to print process information in a format that is suitable for the scheduler:

```
bash-2.03$ ps -c
   PID  CLS PRI TTY       TIME CMD
 29081   TS  48 pts/8     0:00 ksh
 29085   TS  48 pts/8     0:00 bash
```

This can be useful when used in conjunction with the **priocntl** command, which displays the parameters used for process scheduling. This allows administrators in particular to determine the process classes currently available on the system, or to set the class of a specific process to interactive or time-sharing. You can obtain a list of all supported classes by passing the -l parameter to priocntl:

```
bash-2.03$ priocntl -l
CONFIGURED CLASSES
==================
SYS (System Class)
TS (Time Sharing)
        Configured TS User Priority Range: -60 through 60
IA (Interactive)
        Configured IA User Priority Range: -60 through 60
```

You can combine this with a -f full display flag to create ps -c in order to obtain more information:

```
bash-2.03$ ps -cf
    UID    PID  PPID CLS PRI     STIME TTY       TIME CMD
   paul 29081 29079  TS  48 10:40:30 pts/8     0:00 /bin/ksh
   paul 29085 29081  TS  48 10:40:51 pts/8     0:00
   /usr/local/bin/bash
```

If you want to obtain information about processes being executed by a particular group of users, this can be specified on the command line by using the -g option, followed by the gid of the target group. In this example, we print out all processes from users in group zero:

```
bash-2.03$ ps -g 0
   PID TTY       TIME CMD
     0 ?         0:00 sched
     1 ?         0:01 init
     2 ?         0:01 pageout
     3 ?         9:51 fsflush
```

Another common configuration option used with **ps** is -j, which displays the session identifier (SID) and the process group identifier (PGID), as shown here:

```
bash-2.03$ ps -j
   PID  PGID   SID TTY        TIME CMD
 29081 29081 29081 pts/8      0:00 ksh
 29085 29085 29081 pts/8      0:00 bash
```

Finally, you can print out the status of lightweight processes (LWP) in your system. These are virtual CPU or execution resources, which are designed to make the best use of available CPU resources based on their priority and scheduling class. Here is an example:

```
bash-2.03$ ps -L
   PID  LWP TTY        LTIME CMD
 29081    1 pts/8      0:00 ksh
 29085    1 pts/8      0:00 bash
```

Table 13-1 summarizes the main options for **ps**.

Table 13-1 Main Options for Listing Processes with **ps**

Option	Description
-a	Lists the most frequently requested processes.
-A, -e	Lists all processes.
-c	Lists processes in scheduler format.
-d	Lists all processes.
-f	Prints comprehensive process information.
-g	Prints process information on a group basis for a single group.
-G	Prints process information on a group basis for a list of groups.
-j	Includes SID and PGID in printout.
-l	Prints complete process information.
-L	Displays LWP details.
-p	Lists process details for a list of specified process.
-P	Lists the CPU ID to which a process is bound.
-s	Lists session leaders.
-t	Lists all processes associated with a specific terminal.
-u	Lists all processes for a specific user.

Signals

Since all processes are identifiable by a single PID, it can be used to manage that process by means of a signal. Signals can be sent to other processes in C programs using the signal() function or they can be sent directly from the shell. Solaris supports a number of standard signal types, which can be used as a means of interprocess communication.

A common use for signals is to manage user applications that are launched from a shell. A suspend signal can be sent to an application running in the foreground by pressing CTRL+Z at any time. To actually run this application in the background in C-shell, for example, you need to type **bg**. A unique background job number is then assigned to the job, and typing **fg n**, where n is that number, brings the process back to the foreground. You can run as many applications as you like in the background.

In this example, we run httpd in the foreground, which is process number 123. When we press CTRL+Z, the process is suspended, and when we type **bg**, it is assigned the background process number one. We can then execute other commands, like ls, while httpd runs in the background. When we then type **fg**, the process is bought once again into the foreground:

```
bash-2.03$ httpd
^z

Suspended
bash-2.03$ bg
[1] httpd&
bash-2.03$ ls
httpd.conf  access.conf   srm.conf
bash-2.03$ fg
```

The kill Command

A useful process management tool is the **kill** command. **kill** is used to send signals directly to any process on the system. It is usually called with two parameters: the signal type and the pid. For example, if you have made changes to the configuration file for the Internet super daemon, you must send a signal to the daemon to tell it to re-read its configuration file. Note that you don't need to restart the daemon itself. This is one of the advantages of a process-based operating system that facilitates interprocess communication. If inetd had the pid 167, then typing

```
bash-2.03$ kill -1 167
```

would force inetd to re-read its configuration file and update its internal settings. The -1 parameter stands for the SIGHUP signal, which means hangup. However, imagine a situation in which we would want to switch off inetd temporarily to perform a security check. We can send a kill signal to the process by using the -9 parameter (the SIGKILL signal):

```
bash-2.03$ kill -1 167
```

Although SIGHUP and SIGKILL are the most commonly used signals in the shell, several others are used by programmers and are defined in the signal.h header file. Also, another potential consequence of sending a signal to a process exists. Instead of "hanging up" or "being killed," it could exit and dump a core file, which is a memory image of the process to which the message was sent. This is very useful for debugging, although too many core files will quickly fill up your filesystem. Table 13-2 shows the most commonly used signals, as originally defined in UNIX version 7. Alternatively, for

Table 13-2   Commonly Used Signals

Signal	Code	Action	Description
SIGHUP	1	Exit	Hangup
SIGINT	2	Exit	Interrupt
SIGQUIT	3	Core	Quit
SIGILL	4	Core	Illegal instruction
SIGTRAP	5	Core	Trace
SIGABRT	6	Core	Abort
SIGEMT	7	Core	Emulation trap
SIGFPE	8	Core	Arithmetic exception
SIGKILL	9	Exit	Killed
SIGBUS	10	Core	Bus error
SIGSEGV	11	Core	Segmentation fault
SIGSYS	12	Core	Bad system call
SIGPIPE	13	Exit	Broken pipe
SIGALRM	14	Exit	Alarm clock
SIGTERM	15	Exit	Terminate

the Solaris version you are using (including Solaris 8), you can obtain a list of available signals to the **kill** command, by passing the -l option:

```
bash-2.03$ kill -l
HUP INT QUIT ILL TRAP ABRT EMT FPE KILL BUS SEGV SYS PIPE ALRM
TERM USR1 USR2
CLD PWR WINCH URG POLL STOP TSTP CONT TTIN TTOU VTALRM PROF XCPU
XFSZ WAITING
LWP FREEZE THAW RTMIN RTMIN+1 RTMIN+2 RTMIN+3 RTMAX-3 RTMAX-2
RTMAX-1 RTMAX
```

Scheduling Jobs

Many system administration tasks need to be performed on a regular basis. For example, log files for various applications need to be archived nightly, and a new log file created. Often a short script is created to perform this by following these steps:

1. Kill the daemon affected using the **kill** command.

2. Compress the logfile using the **gzip** or **compress** command.

3. Change the log filename to include a timestamp, so that it can be distinguished from other logfiles by using the **time** command.

4. Move it to an archive directory using the **mv** command.

5. Create a new logfile by using the **touch** command.

6. Restart the daemon by calling the appropriate /etc/init.d script.

Instead of the administrator having to execute these commands interactively at midnight, they can be scheduled to run daily using the **cron** scheduling command. Alternatively, if a job needs to be run only once at a particular time, like bringing a new Web site online at 7 A.M. one particular morning, then the **at scheduler** can be used. In this section, we look at the advantages and disadvantages of each scheduling method.

The at Command

You can schedule a single system event for execution at a specified time by using the **at** command. The jobs are specified by files in the /var/spool/cron/atjobs, while configuration is managed by the file /etc/cron.d/at.deny. The job can be a single command or can refer to a script that contains a set of commands.

Let's imagine that we wanted to start up sendmail at a particular time. The reason for this could be because some scheduled maintenance of the network infrastructure is scheduled to occur until 8:30 A.M. tomorrow morning. However, you really don't feel like logging in early and starting up sendmail (you've switched it off completely during the outage to prevent users from filling the queue). Let's add a job to the queue, which is scheduled to run at 8:40 A.M., giving the network guys a ten-minute window:

```
bash-2.03$ at 0840
at> /usr/lib/sendmail -bd
at> <EOT>
commands will be executed using /bin/ksh
job 954715200.a at Mon Apr  3 08:40:00 2000
```

After submitting a job using **at**, we can check that the job is properly scheduled by checking to see whether an atjob has been created:

```
bash-2.03$ cd /var/spool/cron/atjobs
bash-2.03$ ls -l
total 8
-r-Sr--r--   1 paul     other        3701 Apr  3 08:35 954715200.a
```

The file exists, which is a good start. Let's check that it contains the appropriate commands to run the job:

```
bash-2.03$ cat 954715200.a
 :at job
 :jobname: stdin
 :notify by mail: no
export PWD; PWD='/home/paul'
export _; _='/usr/bin/at'
cd /home/paul
umask 22
ulimit unlimited
/usr/lib/sendmail -bd
```

This looks good. After 8:40 A.M. the next morning, the command should have executed at the appropriate time, and some output should have been generated and sent to you as a mail message. Let's see what the message contains:

```
From paul Sat Apr  1 08:40:00 2000
Date: Sat Apr  1 2000 08:40:00 +1000 (EST)
From: paul <paul>
To: paul
Subject: Output from "at" job
Your "at" job on tango
"/var/spool/cron/atjobs/954715200.a"
produced the following output:
/bin/ksh[5]: sendmail: 501 Permission denied
```

Oops! We forgot to submit the job as root. Normal users don't have permission to start sendmail in the background daemon mode. We would need to submit this job as root to be successful.

The cron Command

An **at** job executes only once at a particular time. However, **cron** is much more flexible, because you can schedule system events to execute repetitively at regular intervals by using the **crontab** command. Each user on the system can have a crontab, which allows him or her to schedule multiple events to occur at multiple times on multiple dates. The jobs are specified by files in the /var/spool/cron/cronjobs, while configuration is managed by the files /etc/cron.d/cron.allow and /etc/cron.d/cron.deny.

To check your own crontab, you can use the **crontab -l** command:

```
bash-2.03$ crontab -l root
10 3 * * 0,4 /etc/cron.d/logchecker
10 3 * * 0   /usr/lib/newsyslog
15 3 * * 0 /usr/lib/fs/nfs/nfsfind
1 2 * * * [ -x /usr/sbin/rtc ] && /usr/sbin/rtc -c > /dev/null
2>&1
30 3 * * * [ -x /usr/lib/gss/gsscred_clean ] && /usr/lib/gss/gss-
cred_clean
```

This is the standard crontab generated by Solaris for root. It performs tasks like checking if the cron logfile is approaching the system ulimit at 3:10 A.M. on Sundays and Thursdays, creating a new system log at 3:10 A.M. only on Sundays, and reconciling time differences at 2:01 A.M. every day of the year.

The six fields in the crontab stand for

- **Minutes**   In the range 0 to 59
- **Hours**   In the range 0 to 23
- **Days of the month**   In the range 1 to 31
- **Months of the year**   In the range 1 to 12
- **Days of the week**   In the range 0 to 6, starting with Sundays
- **The command to execute**

If you want to add or delete an entry from your crontab, you can use the **crontab -e** command. This will start up your default editor (vi on the command line, textedit in CDE), and you can make changes interactively. After saving your job, you then need to run **crontab** by itself to make the changes.

Summary

In this chapter, we have examined the most commonly used process and scheduling management tools under Solaris. Processes are at the very core of multi-user systems. For users to make the best of the Solaris environment by managing jobs with **kill** and the proc tools, and scheduling their own regular jobs with **cron**, they need to understand how processes are represented and executed.

Questions

1. Which of the following statements is true?
   A. A shell can spawn another shell or application.
   B. A shell can spawn another shell, not an application.
   C. A shell cannot spawn another shell but can spawn an application.
   D. A shell can never spawn another shell or application.

2. What is a process ID?
   A. A string corresponding to the name of the application executed
   B. A randomly generated string that distinguishes one process from another
   C. A class associated with a process's allocated priority
   D. A sequentially allocated integer that distinguishes one process from another

3. A process that can have its effective ownership changed is known as what?
   A. A setgid process
   B. A magic number process
   C. A setuid process
   D. A process that has a magic cookie

4. What is the ultimate parent PID for all processes on a system?
   A. a
   B. 1
   C. 0
   D. init

5. What does the acronym PPID stand for?
   A. Processor PID
   B. Priority PID
   C. Personal PID
   D. Parent PID

6. What does the acronym STIME stand for
   A. Process starting time
   B. Standard process execution time
   C. Single process execution time
   D. Timezone environment variable

7. What is the acronym for the memory address of sleeping processes?
   A. SLPADDR
   B. ADDR
   C. WCHAN
   D. CHANADDR

8. Which command sequence is used to suspend a process?
   A. CTRL+C
   B. ESC+C
   C. CTRL+Z
   D. ESC+Z

9. How can the kill command be used to send a SIGHUP to pid 2192?
   A. kill -1 2192
   B. kill -2 2192
   C. kill -3 2192
   D. kill -9 2192

10. How can the kill command be used to send a SIGKILL to pid 2192?
    A. kill -1 2192
    B. kill -2 2192
    C. kill -3 2192
    D. kill -9 2192

Answers

1. A

2. D

3. C

4. B

PART I

 5. D

 6. A

 7. C

 8. C

 9. A

10. D

## CHAPTER 14

Disk Configuration and Naming

The following objectives will be met upon completing this chapter's material:

- Understanding Solaris physical device names
- Understanding Solaris logical device names
- Learning how to use the format and dmesg commands to review system hardware
- Displaying the system configuration with the prtconf command

Physical and Logical Device Names

One of the most challenging aspects of understanding Solaris hardware is the device names and references used by Solaris to manage devices. Solaris uses a very specific set of naming conventions to associate physical devices with instance names on the operating system. For administrators new to Solaris, this can be incredibly confusing. In addition, devices can also be referred to by their device name, which is associated with a device file created in the /dev directory after configuration. For example, a hard disk may have the physical device name/pci@1f,0/pci@1,1/ide@3/dad@0,0, which is associated with the device file /dev/dsk/c0t0d0. In most versions of Microsoft Windows, disks are simply labeled by their drive letter (C:, D:, E:, and so on), although in Linux, device files are much simplified (for example, /dev/hda for an IDE hard disk, or /dev/sda for a SCSI hard disk). The benefit of the more complex Solaris logical device names and physical device references is that it is easy to interpret the characteristics of each device by simply looking at its name. For the disk example given above, we can see that the IDE hard drive is located on a PCI bus at target 0. When we view the amount of free disk space on the system, for example, it is easy to identify slices on the same disk by looking at the device name:

```
bash-2.03# df -k
Filesystem          kbytes    used    avail   capacity  Mounted on
/proc                    0       0        0        0%   /proc
/dev/dsk/c0t0d0s0  1982988  615991  1307508       33%   /
fd                       0       0        0        0%   /dev/fd
/dev/dsk/c0t0d0s3  1487119  357511  1070124       26%   /usr
swap                182040     416   181624        1%   /tmp
```

Here, we can see that /dev/dsk/c0t0d0s0 and /dev/dsk/c0t0d0s3 are slice 0 and slice 3 of the disk /dev/dsk/c0t0d0.

The Format Command

If you're ever unsure of which physical disk is associated with a specific disk device name, then the format command will tell you:

```
bash-2.03# format
Searching for disks...done
AVAILABLE DISK SELECTIONS:
0. c1t3d0 <SUN2.1G cyl 2733 alt 2 hd 19 sec 80>
/pci@1f,0/pci@1/scsi@1/sd@3,0
```

Here, we can see that physical device /pci@1f,0/pci@1/scsi@1/sd@3,0 is matched with the disk device /dev/dsk/c1t3d0 from the df output shown above.

The /etc/path_to_inst File

A list of mappings between physical devices to instance names is always kept in the /etc/path_to_inst file. In the following example, we review the device to instance name mapping for a SBUS-based SPARC system:

```
"/sbus@1f,0" 0 "sbus"
"/sbus@1f,0/sbusmem@2,0" 2 "sbusmem"
"/sbus@1f,0/sbusmem@3,0" 3 "sbusmem"
"/sbus@1f,0/sbusmem@0,0" 0 "sbusmem"
"/sbus@1f,0/sbusmem@1,0" 1 "sbusmem"
"/sbus@1f,0/SUNW,fas@2,8800000" 1 "fas"
"/sbus@1f,0/SUNW,fas@2,8800000/ses@f,0" 1 "ses"
"/sbus@1f,0/SUNW,fas@2,8800000/sd@1,0" 16 "sd"
```

```
"/sbus@1f,0/SUNW,fas@2,8800000/sd@0,0" 15 "sd"
"/sbus@1f,0/SUNW,fas@2,8800000/sd@3,0" 18 "sd"
"/sbus@1f,0/SUNW,fas@2,8800000/sd@2,0" 17 "sd"
"/sbus@1f,0/SUNW,fas@2,8800000/sd@5,0" 20 "sd"
"/sbus@1f,0/SUNW,fas@2,8800000/sd@4,0" 19 "sd"
"/sbus@1f,0/SUNW,fas@2,8800000/sd@6,0" 21 "sd"
"/sbus@1f,0/SUNW,fas@2,8800000/sd@9,0" 23 "sd"
"/sbus@1f,0/SUNW,fas@2,8800000/sd@8,0" 22 "sd"
"/sbus@1f,0/SUNW,fas@2,8800000/sd@a,0" 24 "sd"
"/sbus@1f,0/SUNW,fas@2,8800000/st@1,0" 8 "st"
"/sbus@1f,0/SUNW,fas@2,8800000/st@0,0" 7 "st"
"/sbus@1f,0/SUNW,fas@2,8800000/sd@c,0" 26 "sd"
"/sbus@1f,0/SUNW,fas@2,8800000/st@3,0" 10 "st"
"/sbus@1f,0/SUNW,fas@2,8800000/sd@b,0" 25 "sd"
"/sbus@1f,0/SUNW,fas@2,8800000/st@2,0" 9 "st"
"/sbus@1f,0/SUNW,fas@2,8800000/sd@e,0" 28 "sd"
"/sbus@1f,0/SUNW,fas@2,8800000/st@5,0" 12 "st"
"/sbus@1f,0/SUNW,fas@2,8800000/sd@d,0" 27 "sd"
"/sbus@1f,0/SUNW,fas@2,8800000/st@4,0" 11 "st"
"/sbus@1f,0/SUNW,fas@2,8800000/sd@f,0" 29 "sd"
"/sbus@1f,0/SUNW,fas@2,8800000/st@6,0" 13 "st"
"/sbus@1f,0/SUNW,CS4231@d,c000000" 0 "audiocs"
"/sbus@1f,0/dma@0,81000" 0 "dma"
"/sbus@1f,0/dma@0,81000/esp@0,80000" 0 "esp"
"/sbus@1f,0/dma@0,81000/esp@0,80000/sd@0,0" 30 "sd"
"/sbus@1f,0/dma@0,81000/esp@0,80000/sd@1,0" 31 "sd"
"/sbus@1f,0/dma@0,81000/esp@0,80000/sd@2,0" 32 "sd"
"/sbus@1f,0/dma@0,81000/esp@0,80000/sd@3,0" 33 "sd"
"/sbus@1f,0/dma@0,81000/esp@0,80000/sd@4,0" 34 "sd"
"/sbus@1f,0/dma@0,81000/esp@0,80000/sd@5,0" 35 "sd"
"/sbus@1f,0/dma@0,81000/esp@0,80000/sd@6,0" 36 "sd"
"/sbus@1f,0/dma@0,81000/esp@0,80000/st@0,0" 14 "st"
"/sbus@1f,0/dma@0,81000/esp@0,80000/st@1,0" 15 "st"
"/sbus@1f,0/dma@0,81000/esp@0,80000/st@2,0" 16 "st"
"/sbus@1f,0/dma@0,81000/esp@0,80000/st@3,0" 17 "st"
"/sbus@1f,0/dma@0,81000/esp@0,80000/st@4,0" 18 "st"
"/sbus@1f,0/dma@0,81000/esp@0,80000/st@5,0" 19 "st"
"/sbus@1f,0/dma@0,81000/esp@0,80000/st@6,0" 20 "st"
"/sbus@1f,0/sbusmem@f,0" 15 "sbusmem"
"/sbus@1f,0/sbusmem@d,0" 13 "sbusmem"
"/sbus@1f,0/sbusmem@e,0" 14 "sbusmem"
"/sbus@1f,0/cgthree@1,0" 0 "cgthree"
"/sbus@1f,0/SUNW,hme@e,8c00000" 0 "hme"
"/sbus@1f,0/zs@f,1000000" 1 "zs"
"/sbus@1f,0/zs@f,1100000" 0 "zs"
"/sbus@1f,0/SUNW,bpp@e,c800000" 0 "bpp"
"/sbus@1f,0/lebuffer@0,40000" 0 "lebuffer"
"/sbus@1f,0/lebuffer@0,40000/le@0,60000" 0 "le"
"/sbus@1f,0/SUNW,hme@2,8c00000" 1 "hme"
"/sbus@1f,0/SUNW,fdtwo@f,1400000" 0 "fd"
"/options" 0 "options"
"/pseudo" 0 "pseudo"
```

Here, we can see entries for the network interface /sbus@1f,0/SUNW,hme@2, 8c00000, as well as the floppy disk /sbus@1f,0/SUNW,fdtwo@f,1400000 and the SBUS sbus@1f,0. For a PCI-based system, like a Sun Blade 100, the output would look like this:

```
"/pci@1f,0" 0 "pcipsy"
"/pci@1f,0/isa@7" 0 "ebus"
"/pci@1f,0/isa@7/power@0,800" 0 "power"
"/pci@1f,0/isa@7/dma@0,0" 0 "isadma"
"/pci@1f,0/isa@7/dma@0,0/parallel@0,378" 0 "ecpp"
"/pci@1f,0/isa@7/dma@0,0/floppy@0,3f0" 0 "fd"
"/pci@1f,0/isa@7/serial@0,2e8" 1 "su"
"/pci@1f,0/isa@7/serial@0,3f8" 0 "su"
"/pci@1f,0/pmu@3" 0 "pmubus"
"/pci@1f,0/pmu@3/i2c@0" 0 "smbus"
"/pci@1f,0/pmu@3/i2c@0/temperature@30" 0 "max1617"
"/pci@1f,0/pmu@3/i2c@0/card-reader@40" 0 "scmi2c"
"/pci@1f,0/pmu@3/i2c@0/dimm@a0" 0 "seeprom"
"/pci@1f,0/pmu@3/fan-control@0" 0 "grfans"
"/pci@1f,0/pmu@3/ppm@0" 0 "grppm"
"/pci@1f,0/pmu@3/beep@0" 0 "grbeep"
"/pci@1f,0/ebus@c" 1 "ebus"
"/pci@1f,0/usb@c,3" 0 "ohci"
"/pci@1f,0/usb@c,3/mouse@2" 0 "hid"
"/pci@1f,0/usb@c,3/keyboard@4" 1 "hid"
"/pci@1f,0/firewire@c,2" 0 "hci1394"
"/pci@1f,0/ide@d" 0 "uata"
"/pci@1f,0/ide@d/dad@0,0" 0 "dad"
"/pci@1f,0/ide@d/sd@1,0" 0 "sd"
"/pci@1f,0/sound@8" 0 "audiots"
"/pci@1f,0/SUNW,m64B@13" 0 "m64"
"/pci@1f,0/network@c,1" 0 "eri"
"/pci@1f,0/pci@5" 0 "pci_pci"
"/options" 0 "options"
"/SUNW,UltraSPARC-IIe@0,0" 0 "us"
"/pseudo" 0 "pseudo"
```

Here, we can see that all of the sbus entries have been replaced by the pci entries, and that the network interface is no longer a hme, but an eri ("/pci@1f,0/ network@c,1" 0 "eri"). In addition, some completely new types of hardware, such as a smart card reader ("/pci@1f,0/pmu@3/i2c@0/card-reader@40" 0 "scmi2c"), are also available.

The dmesg Command

The dmesg command is often used to determine whether specific device drivers, for network interfaces and mass storage devices, have been correctly loaded at boot time.

While its functions have largely been taken over by the syslog daemon (syslogd), dmesg provides a useful record of error and status messages printed by the kernel.

When the system boots, several status messages of log level kern.notice will be recorded, and can be subsequently retrieved by using dmesg:

```
May 15 14:23:16 austin genunix: [ID 540533 kern.notice] SunOS
Release 5.8 Version Generic_108528-06 64-bit
May 15 14:23:16 austin genunix: [ID 784649 kern.notice] Copyright
1983-2000 Sun Microsystems, Inc.  All rights reserved.
May 15 14:23:16 austin genunix: [ID 678236 kern.info] Ethernet
address = 0:3:ba:4:a4:e8
May 15 14:23:16 austin unix: [ID 389951 kern.info]
mem = 131072K (0x8000000)
May 15 14:23:16 austin unix: [ID 930857 kern.info]
avail mem = 121085952
```

Here, we can see that a 64-bit kernel has been loaded successfully, for SunOS 5.8 (Solaris 8). Sun's copyright banner is also recorded, along with the ethernet address of the primary network interface card (0:3:ba:4:a4:e8), the amount of installed RAM, and the amount of currently available RAM after the kernel has been loaded.

Before the kernel begins loading device drivers, it performs an integrity check to determine if any naming conflicts exist. If a conflict is found, it is logged for future reference and action:

```
May 15 14:23:16 austin genunix: [ID 723599 kern.warning] WARNING:
Driver alias "cal" conflicts with an existing driver name
or alias.
```

Here, we can see that the device driver alias "cal" has been used more than once, giving rise to a naming conflict. Next, details about the system architecture and its main bus type are displayed:

```
May 15 14:23:16 austin rootnex: [ID 466748 kern.info] root nexus =
Sun Blade 100 (UltraSPARC-IIe)
May 15 14:23:16 austin rootnex: [ID 349649 kern.info] pcipsy0 at
root: UPA 0x1f 0x0
May 15 14:23:16 austin genunix: [ID 936769 kern.info] pcipsy0 is
/pci@1f,0
May 15 14:23:16 austin pcipsy: [ID 370704 kern.info] PCI-device:
pmu@3, pmubus0
May 15 14:23:16 austin pcipsy: [ID 370704 kern.info] PCI-device:
ppm@0, grppm0
May 15 14:23:16 austin genunix: [ID 936769 kern.info] grppm0 is
/pci@1f,0/pmu@3/ppm@0
```

Here, we can see that the system is a Sun Blade 100, and that its PCI bus architecture has been correctly identified. The next stage involves identifying the hard drives attached to the system, as follows:

```
May 15 14:23:27 austin pcipsy: [ID 370704 kern.info] PCI-device:
ide@d, uata0
May 15 14:23:27 austin genunix: [ID 936769 kern.info] uata0 is
/pci@1f,0/ide@d
May 15 14:23:28 austin uata: [ID 114370 kern.info] dad0 at
pci10b9,52290
May 15 14:23:28 austin uata: [ID 347839 kern.info]  target 0 lun 0
May 15 14:23:28 austin genunix: [ID 936769 kern.info] dad0 is
/pci@1f,0/ide@d/dad@0,0
May 15 14:23:28 austin dada: [ID 365881 kern.info] <ST315320A cyl
29649 alt 2 hd 16 sec 63>
May 15 14:23:29 austin swapgeneric: [ID 308332 kern.info] root on
/pci@1f,0/ide@d/disk@0,0:a fstype ufs
```

The IDE hard drive installed on the system has been correctly detected (/pci@1f,0/ ide@d/dad@0,0), and has the label "ST315320A cyl 29649 alt 2 hd 16 sec 63." In addition, the filesystem type has been identified as native UFS.

The status of every device on the system is logged during device driver loading, so it's possible to use the dmesg command to determine whether drivers have been correctly loaded. In the following entry, the FDDI interface cannot be activated since it is not correctly installed:

```
May 15 14:26:38 austin smt: [ID 272566 kern.notice] smt0: nf FDDI
driver is not active. Initialization of this driver cannot be com-
pleted.                                                          .
```

The prtconf Command

If you're ever confused about the devices which have been detected on a system, and are currently active, you can use the prtconf command to display their configuration details:

```
bash-2.03# prtconf
System Configuration: Sun Microsystems   sun4u
Memory size: 128 Megabytes
```

Initially, the system architecture is displayed (sun4u in the case of an Ultra 5 workstation), along with the amount of physical RAM. What follows is a hierarchical list of all system peripherals and attached drivers (where appropriate), arranged in logical order. For example, all PCI devices listed under the pci node, being associated with either pci instance #0 or pci instance #1:

```
System Peripherals (Software Nodes):
SUNW,Ultra-5_10
    packages (driver not attached)
        terminal-emulator (driver not attached)
        deblocker (driver not attached)
        obp-tftp (driver not attached)
        disk-label (driver not attached)
        SUNW,builtin-drivers (driver not attached)
        sun-keyboard (driver not attached)
        ufs-file-system (driver not attached)
    chosen (driver not attached)
    openprom (driver not attached)
        client-services (driver not attached)
    options, instance #0
    aliases (driver not attached)
    memory (driver not attached)
    virtual-memory (driver not attached)
    pci, instance #0
        pci, instance #0
            ebus, instance #0
                auxio (driver not attached)
                power, instance #0
                SUNW,pll (driver not attached)
                se, instance #0
                su, instance #0
                su, instance #1
                ecpp (driver not attached)
                fdthree, instance #0
                eeprom (driver not attached)
                flashprom (driver not attached)
                SUNW,CS4231 (driver not attached)
            network, instance #0
            SUNW,m64B (driver not attached)
            ide, instance #0
                disk (driver not attached)
                cdrom (driver not attached)
                dad, instance #0
                sd, instance #30
        pci, instance #1
            scsi, instance #0
                disk (driver not attached)
                tape (driver not attached)
                sd, instance #0 (driver not attached)
                sd, instance #1 (driver not attached)
                sd, instance #2 (driver not attached)
                sd, instance #3
                sd, instance #4 (driver not attached)
                sd, instance #5 (driver not attached)
                sd, instance #6 (driver not attached)
                sd, instance #7 (driver not attached)
                sd, instance #8 (driver not attached)
                sd, instance #9 (driver not attached)
                sd, instance #10 (driver not attached)
```

```
              sd, instance #11 (driver not attached)
              sd, instance #12 (driver not attached)
              sd, instance #13 (driver not attached)
              sd, instance #14 (driver not attached)
          scsi, instance #1
              disk (driver not attached)
              tape (driver not attached)
              sd, instance #15 (driver not attached)
              sd, instance #16 (driver not attached)
              sd, instance #17 (driver not attached)
              sd, instance #18 (driver not attached)
              sd, instance #19 (driver not attached)
              sd, instance #20 (driver not attached)
              sd, instance #21 (driver not attached)
              sd, instance #22 (driver not attached)
              sd, instance #23 (driver not attached)
              sd, instance #24 (driver not attached)
              sd, instance #25 (driver not attached)
              sd, instance #26 (driver not attached)
              sd, instance #27 (driver not attached)
              sd, instance #28 (driver not attached)
              sd, instance #29 (driver not attached)
      SUNW,UltraSPARC-IIi (driver not attached)
      SUNW,ffb, instance #0
      pseudo, instance #0
```

Summary

In this chapter, we've examined how to use various commands to determine the status of devices (particularly disk devices) which are attached to the system. In addition, we looked at how to match up Solaris logical device names to physical device references, which can be difficult for newcomers.

Questions

1. Which of the following is a valid device name for an IDE hard drive?
    A. /pci@1f,0/pci@1,1/ide@3/dad@0,0
    B. /sbus@1f,0/SUNW,fas@2,8800000/sd@c,0
    C. /sbus@1f,0/SUNW,fas@2,8800000/ide@c,0
    D. /pci@1f,0/pci@1,1/ide@3/dad@x,x

2. Which of the following is a valid "available device" selection for the format command?

    A. c1t3d0 <SUN2.1G cyl 2733 alt 2 hd 19 sec 80>

    B. /pci@1f,0/pci@1/scsi@1/sd@3,0

    C. /pci@1f,0/pci@1/scsi@1/sd@3,0 <SUN2.1G cyl 2733 alt 2 hd 19 sec 80>

    D. c1t3d0 </pci@1f,0/pci@1/scsi@1/sd@3,0>

3. The /etc/path_to_inst file contains what?

    A. A list of all physical device names.

    B. A list of all installed device drivers.

    C. A list of mappings between device drivers and their filenames.

    D. A list of mappings between physical devices to instance names.

4. What error message might be displayed if a hardware device was not installed, but the kernel loaded its device driver?

    A. May 15 14:23:16 hostname genunix: [ID 723599 kern.warning] WARNING: Driver alias "name" conflicts with an existing driver name or alias.

    B. May 15 14:26:38 hostname smt: [ID 272566 kern.notice] device is not active (conflicts with an existing driver name or alias). Initialization of this driver cannot be completed.

    C. May 15 14:26:38 hostname smt: [ID 272566 kern.notice] device is not active. Initialization of this driver cannot be completed.

    D. May 15 14:26:38 hostname smt: [ID 272566 kern.info] device is not active. Initialization of this driver cannot be completed.

5. What does prtconf not display?

    A. System peripherals (Software Nodes).

    B. System architecture type.

    C. Physical memory installed.

    D. Virtual memory installed.

Answers

1. A

2. A

3. D

4. C

5. D

## CHAPTER 15

Disk Partitions and Format

The following objectives will be met upon completing this chapter's material:

- Understanding hard disk layouts
- Formatting disks
- Creating new filesystems

Hard Disk Layout

When formatted for operation with the Solaris 8 operating system, hard disks are logically divided into one or more *slices* (or partitions), on which a single filesystem resides. Filesystems contain sets of files, which are hierarchically organized around a number of directories. The Solaris 8 system contains a number of predefined directories that often form the top level of a filesystem hierarchy. Many of these directories lie one level below the root directory, often denoted by /, which exists on the primary system disk of any Solaris 8 system. In addition to a primary disk, many Solaris 8 systems will have additional disks that provide storage space for user and daemon files. Each filesystem has a mount point that is usually created in the top level of the root filesystem. For example, the /export filesystem is obviously mounted in the top level of /. The mount point is created by using the mkdir command:

```
server# mkdir /export
```

In contrast, the /export/home filesystem, which usually holds the home directories of users and user files, is mounted in the top level of the /export filesystem. Thus, the mount point is created by using the command

```
server# mkdir /export/home
```

A single, logical filesystem can be created on a single slice, but cannot exist on more than one slice, unless there is an extra level of abstraction between the logical and physical filesystems (for example, a metadevice can be created using DiskSuite, providing striping across many physical disks). A physical disk can also contain more than one slice. Sparc architecture systems have eight slices which can be used, numbered zero through seven. Intel architecture systems, however, have ten available slices, numbered zero through nine.

The actual assignment of logical filesystems to physical slices is a matter of discretion for the individual administrator, and although customary assignments are recommended by Sun and other hardware vendors, it is possible that a specific site policy, or an application's requirements, necessitate the development of a local policy. For example, database servers often make quite specific requirements about the allocation of disk slices to improve performance. However, with modern high-performance RAID systems, these recommendations are often redundant. Because many organizations will have many different kinds of systems deployed, it is useful to maintain compatibility between systems as much as possible.

Figure 15-1 shows the typical filesystem layout for a Sparc architecture system following customary disk slice allocations. Slice 0 holds the root partition, while Slice 1 is allocated to swap space. For systems with changing virtual memory requirements, it might be better to use a swap file on the filesystem, rather than allocating an entire slice for swap. Slice 2 often refers to the entire disk, while /export on Slice 3 traditionally holds older versions of the operating system, which are used by client systems with

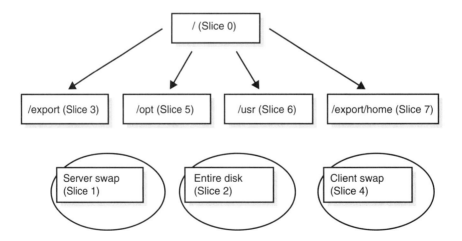

Figure 15-1 Typical filesystem layout for a Sparc architecture system

lower performance (for example, Classic or LX systems that use the trivial FTP daemon, tftpd, to download their operating system upon boot). These systems may also use Slice 4 as exported swap space. Export may also be used for file sharing using the networked file system, NFS. Slice 5 holds the /opt filesystem, which is the default location under Solaris 8 for local packages installed using the pkgadd command. Under earlier versions of Solaris, the /usr/local filesystem held local packages, and this convention is still used by many sites. The system package filesystem /usr is usually located on Slice 6, while /export/home usually contains user home directories on Slice 7. Again, earlier systems located user home directories under /home, but because this is used by the automounter program in Solaris 8, some contention can be expected.

Figure 15-2 shows the typical filesystem layout for an Intel architecture system following customary disk slice allocations. Slice 0 again holds the root partition, while Slice 1 is also allocated to swap space. Slice 2 continues to refer to the entire disk, while /export on Slice 3 again holds older versions of the operating system, which are used by client systems, and Slice 4 contains exported swap space for these clients. The local package filesystem, /opt, is still located on Slice 5, and the system package filesystem

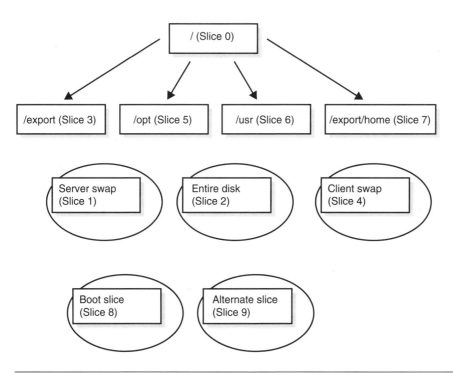

Figure 15-2 Typical filesystem layout for an Intel architecture system

/usr is again located on Slice 6. Slice 7 contains the user home directories on /export/ home. However, the two extra slices serve very different purposes: Boot information for Solaris is located on Slice 8, and is known as the boot slice; Slice 9 provides space for alternative disk blocks and is known as the alternative slice.

Formatting

Hard disk installation and configuration on Solaris is often more complicated than on other UNIX systems. However, this complexity is required to support the sophisticated hardware operations typically undertaken by Solaris systems. For example, Linux refers to hard disks using a simple BSD-style scheme: /dev/hd*n* are the IDE hard disks on a system, and /dev/sd*n* are the SCSI hard disks on a system, where *n* refers to the hard disk number. A system with two IDE hard disks and two SCSI hard disks will therefore have the following device files configured:

```
/dev/hda
/dev/hdb
/dev/sda
/dev/sdb
```

Partitions created on each drive are also sequentially numbered: If /dev/hda is the boot disk, it may contain several partitions on the disk, reflecting the basic UNIX system directories:

```
/dev/hda1 (/ partition)
/dev/hda2 (/usr)
/dev/hda3 (/var)
/dev/hda4 (swap)
```

Instead of simply referring to the disk type, disk number, and partition number, the device filename for each partition (slice) on a Solaris disk contains four identifiers: controller (c), target (t), disk (d), and slice (s). Thus, the device file

```
/dev/dsk/c0t3d0s0
```

identifies Slice 0 (s0) of Disk 0 (d0), Controller 0 (c0) at SCSI Target ID 3 (t3). To complicate matters further, disk device files exist in both the /dev/dsk and /dev/rdsk directories, which correspond to block device and raw device entries respectively. Raw and block devices refer to the same physical partition, but are used in different contexts: Using raw devices only allows operations of small amounts of data, which is very useful for RDBMS systems, whereas a buffer can be used with a block device to increase the data read size. It is not always clear whether to use a block or raw device interface, however, low-level system commands (the fsck command, which performs disk maintenance) typically use raw device interfaces, whereas commands that operate on the entire disk (such as df, which reports disk usage), will most likely use block devices.

To install a new hard drive on a Solaris system, just follow these steps:

1. Prepare the system for a reconfiguration boot, by issuing the command:

```
server# touch /reconfigure
```

2. Synchronize disk data, and power-down the system using the commands:

```
server# sync; init 0
```

3. Switch off power to the system, and attach the new hard disk to the external SCSI chain, or install it internally into an appropriate disk bay

4. Check that the SCSI device ID does not conflict with any existing SCSI devices. If a conflict exists, simply change the ID using the switch

5. Power-on the system, and use the boot command to load the kernel if the Open-Boot monitor appears:

```
ok boot
```

The next step, assuming that you have decided which partitions you wish to create on your drive using the information supplied above, is to run the format program. In addition to creating slices, format also displays information about existing disks and slices, and can be used to repair a faulty disk. When format is invoked without a command-line argument

```
server# format
```

it displays the current disks, and asks the administrator to enter the number of the disk to format. Selecting a disk for formatting at this point is nondestructive, so even if you make a mistake, you can always exit the format program without damaging data. For example, on a Sparc-20 system with three 1.05G SCSI disks, format opens with the screen

```
Searching for disks...done
AVAILABLE DISK SELECTIONS:
0. c0t1d0 <SUN1.05 cyl 2036 alt 2 hd 14 sec 72>
/iommu@f,e0000000/sbus@f,e0001000/espdma@f,400000/esp@f,800000/
sd@1,0
1. c0t2d0 <SUN1.05 cyl 2036 alt 2 hd 14 sec 72>
/iommu@f,e0000000/sbus@f,e0001000/espdma@f,400000/esp@f,800000/
sd@2,0
2. c0t3d0 <SUN1.05 cyl 2036 alt 2 hd 14 sec 72>
/iommu@f,e0000000/sbus@f,e0001000/espdma@f,400000/esp@f,800000/
sd@3,0
Specify disk (enter its number):
```

It is also possible to pass a command-line option to format, comprising the disk (or disks) to be formatted, such as

```
# format /dev/rdsk/c0t2d0
```

After selecting the appropriate disk, the message

```
[disk formatted]
```

will appear if the disk has previously been formatted. This is an important message, as it is a common mistake to misidentify a target disk from the available selection of both formatted and unformatted disks. The menu looks like this:

```
FORMAT MENU:
        disk       - select a disk
        type       - select (define) a disk type
        partition  - select (define) a partition table
        current    - describe the current disk
        format     - format and analyze the disk
        fdisk      - run the fdisk program
        repair     - repair a defective sector
        show       - translate a disk address
        label      - write label to the disk
        analyze    - surface analysis
        defect     - defect list management
        backup     - search for backup labels
        verify     - read and display labels
        save       - save new disk/partition definitions
        volname    - set 8-character volume name
        !<cmd>     - execute <cmd>, then return
        quit
format>
```

If the disk has not been formatted, the first step is to prepare the disk to contain slices and filesystems by formatting the disk. This is done by issuing the command format:

```
format> format
Ready to format. Formatting cannot be interrupted
and takes 15 minutes (estimated). Continue? yes
```

The purpose of formatting is to identify defective blocks, mark them as bad, and generally to verify that the disk is operational from a hardware perspective. After this has been completed, new slices can be created and sized by using the partition option at the main menu:

```
format> partition
```

In this case, we want to create a new Slice 5 on Disk 0 at Target 3, which will be used to store user files when mounted as /export/home, and corresponding to block device

/dev/dsk/c0t3d0s5. After determining the maximum amount of space available, enter that size in gigabytes (in this case, 1.05G) when requested to do so by the format program for Slice 5. (Enter 0 for the other slices.) If the disk is not labeled, you will also be prompted to enter a label, which contains details of the disk's current slices, which is useful for recovering data. This is an important step, as the operating system will not be able to find any newly created slices unless the volume is labeled. To view the disk label, use the prtvtoc command. Here's the output from the primary drive in an x86 system:

```
# prtvtoc /dev/dsk/c0d0s2
* /dev/dsk/c0d0s2 partition map
*
* Dimensions:
*     512 bytes/sector
*      63 sectors/track
*     255 tracks/cylinder
*   16065 sectors/cylinder
*    1020 cylinders
*    1018 accessible cylinders
*
* Flags:
*    1: unmountable
*   10: read-only
*
*                         First     Sector    Last
* Partition  Tag  Flags   Sector    Count     Sector    Mount
                                                         Directory
            0     2    00      48195    160650    208844    /
            1     7    00     208845     64260    273104    /var
            2     5    00          0  16354170  16354169
            3     3    01     273105    321300    594404
            6     4    00     594405   1317330   1911734    /usr
            7     8    00    1911735  14442435  16354169
                                                         /export/home
            8     1    01          0     16065     16064
            9     9    01      16065     32130     48194
```

The disk label contains a full partition table, which can be printed for each disk using the print command:

```
format> print
```

For our 1.05G disk, the partition table will look like this:

```
Part Tag Flag Cylinders Size Blocks
0 root wm 0 0 (0/0/0) 0
1 swap wu 0 0 (0/0/0) 0
2 backup wm 0 - 3732 (3732/0/0) 2089920
3 unassigned wm 0 0 (0/0/0) 0
4 unassigned wm 0 0 (0/0/0) 0
```

```
5 home wm 0 - 3732 1075MB (3732/0/0) 2089920
6 usr wm 0 0 (0/0/0) 0
7 unassigned wm 0 0 (0/0/0) 0
```

After saving the changes to the disk's partition table, exit the format program, and create a new UFS filesystem on the target slice using the newfs command:

```
server# newfs /dev/rdsk/c0t3d0s5
```

After a new filesystem is constructed, it is ready to be mounted. First, a mount point is created:

```
server# mkdir /export/home
```

followed by the appropriate mount command:

```
server# mount /dev/dsk/c0t3d0s5 /export/home
```

At this point, the disk is available to the system for the current session. However, if you want the disk to be available after reboot, it is necessary to create an entry in the virtual filesystems table, which is created from /etc/vfstab file. An entry like

```
/dev/dsk/c0t3d0s5 /dev/rdsk/c0t3d0s5 /export/home ufs 2 yes -
```

contains details of the slice's block and raw devices, the mount point, the filesystem type, instructions for fsck, and most importantly, a flag to force mount at boot.

For an x86 system, the output of format looks slightly different, given the differences in the way that devices are denoted:

```
AVAILABLE DISK SELECTIONS:
       0. c0d0 <DEFAULT cyl 1018 alt 2 hd 255 sec 63>
          /pci@0,0/pci-ide@7,1/ata@0/cmdk@0,0
Specify disk (enter its number):
```

The partition table is similar to that for the Sparc architecture systems:

```
partition> print
Current partition table (original):
Total disk cylinders available: 1018 + 2 (reserved cylinders)

Part      Tag    Flag  Cylinders      Size            Blocks
  0      root    wm     3 -   12    78.44MB   (10/0/0)      160650
  1       var    wm    13 -   16    31.38MB   (4/0/0)        64260
  2    backup    wm     0 - 1017     7.80GB   (1018/0/0)  16354170
  3      swap    wu    17 -   36   156.88MB   (20/0/0)      321300
  4 unassigned   wm     0             0        (0/0/0          0
  5 unassigned   wm     0             0        (0/0/0)         0
```

```
6          usr    wm     37 -  118     643.23MB  (82/0/0)     1317330
7          home   wm    119 - 1017      6.89GB  (899/0/0)    14442435
8          boot   wu      0 -    0       7.84MB   (1/0/0)       16065
9 alternates      wu      1 -    2      15.69MB   (2/0/0)       32130
```

Summary

In this chapter, we've examined the physical and logical layout of Solaris filesystems, and how filesystems can be created and configured. We also reviewed the differences between Solaris Sparc and Solaris Intel filesystems, and examined how to mount filesystems after they've been formatted.

Questions

1. What command would be used to create the mount point /work?
   A. mkpoint /work
   B. mkmountpoint /work
   C. touch /work
   D. mkdir /work

2. On a Sparcsystem, which partition is traditionally located on Slice 0?
   A. /
   B. swap
   C. /export
   D. /opt

3. On a Sparc system, which partition is traditionally located on Slice 1?
   A. /
   B. swap
   C. /export
   D. /opt

4. On a Sparc system, which partition is traditionally located on Slice 3?
   A. /
   B. swap
   C. /export
   D. /opt

5. On a Sparc system, which partition is traditionally located on Slice 5?
   A. /
   B. swap
   C. /export
   D. /opt

6. What device file identifies Slice 0 of Disk 0, Controller 0 at SCSI Target ID 3? (Choose one only.)
   A. /dev/dsk/c0t3d0s0
   B. /dev/dsk/c3t0d0s0
   C. /dev/dsk/c0t0d0s3
   D. /dev/dsk/c0t3d0s3

7. Which of the following is NOT a valid option under the format menu?
   A. disk
   B. slice
   C. partition
   D. format

Answers

1. D
2. A
3. B
4. C
5. D
6. A
7. B

Introduction to File Systems

The following objectives will be met upon completing this chapter's material:

- The structure of Solaris filesystems
- Creating new filesystems
- Monitoring disk space usage
- Repairing filesystems using fsck

Filesystem Structure

Solaris filesystems are generally of the type UFS (UNIX File System), although other filesystem types can be defined in /etc/default/fs. UFS filesystems are found on hard disks which have both a raw and block device interface on Solaris, as found in the /dev/dsk and /dev/rdsk directories respectively. Every partition created on a Solaris filesystem will have its own entry in /dev/dsk and /dev/rdsk. A UFS filesystem contains the following elements:

- **A boot block**   Contains booting data if the filesystem is bootable
- **A super block**   Contains the location of inodes, filesystem size, number of blocks, and status
- **Inodes**   Store the details of files on the filesystem
- **Data blocks**   Store the files

To create a new UFS filesystem, a disk needs to be partitioned into different slices. These slices can then be used for creating new filesystems by using the mkfs or newfs command. For example, the following two commands are equivalent for the purposes of creating a new filesystem on the partition c0t0d0s1:

```
bash-2.03# newfs /dev/rdsk/c0t0d0s1
bash-2.03# mkfs -F ufs /dev/rdsk/c0t0d0s1
```

Monitoring Disk Usage

The most commonly used command for monitoring disk space usage is /usr/bin/df, which by default displays the number of free blocks and files on all currently mounted volumes. Alternatively, many Administrators create an alias for df in their shell initialization script (for example, ~/.cshrc for C-shell) like df -k, which displays the amount of free disk space in kilobytes. The basic output for df for a Sparc system looks like

```
server# df
Filesystem              kbytes      used      avail capacity  Mounted on
/dev/dsk/c0t0d0s0       245911     30754     190566    14%    /
/dev/dsk/c0t0d0s4      1015679    430787     523952    46%    /usr
/proc                        0         0          0     0%    /proc
fd                           0         0          0     0%    /dev/fd
/dev/dsk/c0t0d0s3       492871    226184     217400    51%    /var
/dev/md/dsk/d1         4119256   3599121     478943    89%    /opt
swap                    256000     43480     212520    17%    /tmp
/dev/dsk/c0t2d0s3      4119256   3684920     393144    91%    /disks/vol1
/dev/md/dsk/d0        17398449  12889927    4334538    75%
/disks/vol2
/dev/md/dsk/d3         6162349   5990984     109742    99%    /disks/vol3
/dev/dsk/c1t1d0s0      8574909   5868862    1848557    77%    /disks/vol4
/dev/dsk/c2t3d0s2      1820189   1551628     177552    90%    /disks/vol5
/dev/dsk/c1t2d0s0      4124422   3548988     575434    87%    /disks/vol6
/dev/dsk/c2t2d0s3      8737664   8281113     456551    95%    /disks/vol7
/dev/md/dsk/d2         8181953   6803556    1296578    84%    /disks/vol8
client:/disks/junior_developers
                      4124560   3469376     613944    85%
                                                      /disks/junior_developers
```

For an Intel system, the output is similar, although disk slices have a different naming convention:

```
server# df
Filesystem              kbytes      used      avail capacity  Mounted on
/proc                        0         0          0     0%    /proc
/dev/dsk/c0d0s0          73684     22104      44212    34%    /
/dev/dsk/c0d0s6         618904    401877     161326    72%    /usr
fd                           0         0          0     0%    /dev/fd
/dev/dsk/c0d0s1          29905      4388      22527    17%    /var
/dev/dsk/c0d0s7        7111598         9    7040474     1%    /export/home
```

```
swap                     222516    272  222244    1%   /tmp
/vol/dev/diskette0/unnamed_floppy
                           1423    131    1292   10%
/floppy/unnamed_floppy
```

df has a number of command line options which can be used to customize the collection and display the information. For example,

```
server# df -a
Filesystem            kbytes       used      avail  capacity  Mounted on
/dev/dsk/c0t0d0s0     245911      30754     190566     14%    /
/dev/dsk/c0t0d0s4    1015679     430787     523952     46%    /usr
/proc                      0          0          0      0%    /proc
fd                         0          0          0      0%    /dev/fd
/dev/dsk/c0t0d0s3     492871     226185     217399     51%    /var
/dev/md/dsk/d1       4119256    3599121     478943     89%    /opt
swap                  256000      43480     212520     17%    /tmp
/dev/dsk/c0t2d0s3    4119256    3684920     393144     91%    /disks/vol1
/dev/md/dsk/d0      17398449   12889927    4334538     75%    /disks/vol2
/dev/md/dsk/d3       6162349    5990984     109742     99%    /disks/vol3
/dev/dsk/c1t1d0s0    8574909    5868862    1848557     77%    /disks/vol4
/dev/dsk/c2t3d0s2    1820189    1551628     177552     90%    /disks/vol5
/dev/dsk/c1t2d0s0    4124422    3548988     575434     87%    /disks/vol6
auto_direct          4124560    3469376     613944     85%    /disks/www
auto_direct                0          0          0      0%    /disks/ftp
server:vold(pid329)
                           0          0          0      0%    /vol
/dev/dsk/c2t2d0s3    8737664    8281113     456551     95%    /disks/vol7
/dev/md/dsk/d2       8181953    6803556    1296578     84%    /disks/vol8
client:/disks/junior_developers
                     4124560    3469376     613944     85%
                                                             /junior_developers
```

prints usage data for all filesystems, even those which have the "ignore" option set in their entries in /etc/mnttab:

```
server# cat /etc/mnttab
/dev/dsk/c0t0d0s0       /       ufs      rw,suid,dev=800000,largefiles
944543087
/dev/dsk/c0t0d0s4       /usr    ufs      rw,suid,dev=800004,largefiles
944543087
/proc   /proc   proc    rw,suid,dev=29c0000     944543087
fd      /dev/fd fd      rw,suid,dev=2a80000     944543087
/dev/dsk/c0t0d0s3       /var    ufs      rw,suid,dev=800003,largefiles
944543087
/dev/md/dsk/d1  /opt    ufs     suid,rw,largefiles,dev=1540001
944543105
swap    /tmp    tmpfs    ,dev=1 944543105
/dev/dsk/c0t2d0s3       /disks/vol1     ufs
suid,rw,largefiles,dev=800013   944543105
/dev/md/dsk/d0  /disks/vol2     ufs
```

```
nosuid,rw,largefiles,quota,dev=1540000  944543105
/dev/md/dsk/d3  /disks/vol3     ufs
nosuid,rw,largefiles,dev=1540003        944543106
/dev/dsk/c1t1d0s0        /disks/vol4 ufs
nosuid,rw,largefiles,dev=800080 944543105
/dev/dsk/c2t3d0s2        /disks/vol5     ufs
nosuid,rw,largefiles,dev=80010a 944543106
/dev/dsk/c1t2d0s0        /disks/vol6 ufs
suid,rw,largefiles,dev=800088   944543106
auto_direct     /disks/www      autofs
ignore,direct,nosuid,dev=2c00001        944543181
auto_direct     /disks/ftp autofs  ignore,direct,nosuid,dev=2c00002
944543181
server:vold(pid329)  /vol    nfs     ignore,noquota,dev=2bc0002
944543192
/dev/dsk/c2t2d0s3       /disks/vol7 ufs
nosuid,rw,largefiles,dev=800103 944548661
/dev/md/dsk/d2  /disks/vol8 ufs
nosuid,rw,largefiles,quota,dev=1540002  944553321
client:/disks/junior_developers   /disks/junior_developers
nfs     nosuid,dev=2bc0040      944604066
```

To avoid delays in printing resource information on NFS-mounted volumes, it is also possible to just check local filesystems with the command:

```
server# df -l
Filesystem              kbytes      used     avail capacity    Mounted on
/dev/dsk/c0t0d0s0       245911     30754    190566    14%      /
/dev/dsk/c0t0d0s4      1015679    430787    523952    46%      /usr
/proc                        0         0         0     0%      /proc
fd                           0         0         0     0%      /dev/fd
/dev/dsk/c0t0d0s3       492871    226184    217400    51%      /var
/dev/md/dsk/d1         4119256   3599121    478943    89%      /opt
swap                    256000     43488    212512    17%      /tmp
/dev/dsk/c0t2d0s3      4119256   3684920    393144    91%      /disks/vol1
/dev/md/dsk/d0        17398449  12889901   4334564    75%      /disks/vol2
/dev/md/dsk/d3         6162349   5990984    109742    99%      /disks/vol3
/dev/dsk/c1t1d0s0      8574909   5868862   1848557    77%      /disks/vol4
/dev/dsk/c2t3d0s2      1820189   1551628    177552    90%      /disks/vol5
/dev/dsk/c1t2d0s0      4124422   3548988    575434    87%      /disks/vol6
/dev/dsk/c2t2d0s3      8737664   8281113    456551    95%      /disks/vol7
/dev/md/dsk/d2         8181953   6803556   1296578    84%      /disks/vol8
```

A block device can be specified on the command line, and its individual usage measured, for example, a slice on controller 1:

```
server# df /dev/dsk/c1d0d2
Filesystem              kbytes      used     avail capacity   Mounted on
/dev/dsk/c1t1d0s0      8574909   5868862   1848557    77%     /disks/vol4
```

Users can also check the status of the disks holding their individual user directories and files by using df. For example,

```
server# df /staff/pwatters
Filesystem          kbytes     used     avail   capacity  Mounted on
/dev/md/dsk/d0     17398449 12889146  4335319     75%     /disks/vol2
```

will display the disk space usage for the disk on which the home directory exists for user pwatters, whereas:

```
server# df /tmp/mbox.pwatters
Filesystem          kbytes     used    avail  capacity  Mounted on
swap                256000    45392   210608    18%     /tmp
```

checks the size of the partition on which the temporary mailbox for the user pwatters was created by the elm mail-reading program. This is a good thing to check if you intend sending a lot of mail messages!

Another way of obtaining disk space usage information with more directory-by-directory detail is by using the /usr/bin/du command. This command prints the sum of the sizes of every file in the current directory, and performs the same task recursively for any subdirectories. The size is calculated by adding together all of the file sizes in the directory, where the size for each file is rounded up to the nearest 512-byte block. For example, taking a du of the /etc directory looks like:

```
server# cd /etc
server# du
14        ./default
7         ./cron.d
6         ./dfs
8         ./dhcp
201       ./fs/hsfs
681       ./fs/nfs
1         ./fs/proc
209       ./fs/ufs
1093      ./fs
26        ./inet
127       ./init.d
339       ./lib
37        ./mail
4         ./net/ticlts
4         ./net/ticots
4         ./net/ticotsord
13        ./net
3         ./opt/SUNWleo/bin
4         ./opt/SUNWleo
92        ./opt/licenses/from-zoul
118       ./opt/licenses
13        ./opt/SUNWmd
```

```
1          ./opt/SUNWimap/license_dir
2          ./opt/SUNWimap
1          ./opt/SUNWicg
32         ./opt/totalnet/httpd/conf
33         ./opt/totalnet/httpd
37         ./opt/totalnet
7          ./opt/ssh
2          ./opt/SUNWneo
13         ./opt/SUNWsymon
198        ./opt
3          ./rc0.d
2          ./rc1.d
13         ./rc2.d
14         ./rc3.d
5          ./rcS.d
3          ./saf/zsmon
6          ./saf
2          ./security/audit/localhost
3          ./security/audit
1          ./security/dev
18         ./security/lib
1          ./security/spool
53         ./security
5          ./skel
1          ./tm
2          ./acct
32         ./uucp
2          ./fn
1          ./openwin/devdata/profiles
2          ./openwin/devdata
3          ./openwin
9          ./lp/alerts
1          ./lp/classes
15         ./lp/fd
1          ./lp/forms
1          ./lp/interfaces
1          ./lp/printers
1          ./lp/pwheels
36         ./lp
2          ./dmi/ciagent
3          ./dmi/conf
6          ./dmi
42         ./snmp/conf
43         ./snmp
7          ./http
2          ./ski
2          ./totalnet
2429       .
```

Thus, /etc and all its subdirectories contain a total of 2,429 kilobytes of data. Of course, this kind of output is fairly verbose, and probably not much use in its current form.

Fixing Problems with fsck

/usr/sbin/fsck is a filesystem checking and repair program commonly found on Solaris and other UNIX platforms. It is usually executed by the superuser when the system is in a single-user mode state (for example, after entering run level S), but can also be performed on individual volumes during multiuser run levels. However, there is one golden rule for using fsck: never, ever apply fsck to a mounted filesystem. To do so could leave the filesystem in an inconsistent state and cause a kernel panic, at which point, its best to head for the backup tape locker! Any fixes to potential problems on a mounted filesystem could end up creating more damage than the original problem. In this section, we will examine the output of fsck, as well as look at some examples of common problems, and investigate how fsck repairs corrupt and inconsistent disk data.

Although Solaris 7 and 8 still retain fsck, it is really only necessary for Solaris 2.6 and prior releases. This is because logging is now provided for UNIX filesystems. Thus, before any changes are made to a filesystem, details of the change are recorded in a log prior to their physical application. Although this consumes some extra CPU and disk overhead (approximately 1% of disk space on each volume with logging enabled is required), it does ensure that the filesystem is never left in an inconsistent state. In addition, boot time is reduced, because fsck does not need to be executed.

Why do inconsistencies occur in the first place? In theory, they shouldn't, but there are three common reasons:

- Switching off a Solaris server like an old MS-DOS machine, without powering down first

- Halting a system without synchronizing disk data (it is advisable to explicitly use sync before shutting down using halt)

- Defective hardware, including damage to disk blocks and heads, which can be caused by moving the system and/or power surges

These problems realize themselves in corruption to the internal set of tables which every UNIX filesystem keeps to manage free disk blocks and inodes, leading to blocks that are actually free being reported as already allocated, and conversely, some blocks occupied by a program, but which might be recorded as being free. This is obviously problematic for mission-critical data, which is a good advertisement for RAID storage (or at least, reliable backups).

The Phases of fsck

The first step to running fsck is to enable filesystem checking to occur during boot. To do this, it is necessary to specify an integer value in the 'fsck' field in the virtual filesystem configuration file/etc/vfstab. Entering a '1' in this field ensures sequential fsck checking, although entering '2' does not ensure sequential checking, as in the following example:

```
#device device mount FS fsck mount mount
#to mount to fsck point type pass at boot options
#
/dev/dsk/c1t2d1s3 /dev/rdsk/c1t2d1s3 /usr ufs 2 yes -/
-
```

After being enabled for a particular filesystem, fsck can be executed. fsck checks the integrity of several different features of the filesystem. Most significant is the superblock, which stores summary information for the volume. Since the superblock is the most modified item on the filesystem being written and rewritten when data is changed on a disk, it is the most commonly corrupted feature. Checks on the superblock include

- A check of the filesystem size, which obviously must be greater than the size computed from the number of blocks identified in the superblock

- The total number of inodes, which must be less than the maximum number of inodes

- A tally of reported free blocks and inodes

If any of these values are identified as corrupt by fsck, the superuser can select one of the many superblock backups which were created during initial filesystem creation as a replacement for the current superblock. We will examine superblock corruption and how to fix it in the next section. In addition to superblock, the number and status of cylinder group blocks, inodes, indirect blocks, and data blocks are also checked. Since free blocks are located by maps stored in the cylinder group, fsck verifiers that all the blocks marked as free are not actually being used by any files—if they are, files could be corrupted. If all blocks are correctly accounted for, fsck determines whether the number of free blocks plus the number of used blocks equals the total number of blocks in the file system. If fsck detects any incongruity, the maps of unallocated blocks are rebuilt, although there is obviously a risk of data loss whenever there is a disagreement over the actual state of the filesystem. fsck always uses the actual count of inodes and/or blocks if the superblock information is wrong, and replaces the incorrect value if this is verified by the superuser. We will revisit this issue in the next section.

When inodes are examined by fsck the process is sequential in nature, and aims to identify inconsistencies in format and type, link count, duplicate blocks, bad block numbers, and inode size. Inodes should always be in one of three states: allocated (being used by a file), unallocated (not being used by a file), and partially allocated, meaning that during an allocation or unallocation procedure, data has been left behind which should have been deleted, or completed. Alternatively, partial allocation could result from a physical hardware failure. In both of these cases, fsck will attempt to clear the inode.

The link count is the number of directory entries which are linked to a particular inode. fsck always checks that the number of directory entries listed is correct, by examining the entire directory structure, beginning with the root directory, and tallying the number of links for every inode. Clearly, the stored link count and the actual link count should agree, however, the stored link count can occasionally be different to the actual link count. This could result from a disk not being synchronized before a shutdown, for example, and although changes to the filesystem have been saved, the link count has not been correctly updated. If the stored count is not zero, but the actual count is zero, then disconnected files are placed in the lost+found directory found in the top level of the filesystem concerned. In other cases, the actual count replaces the stored count.

An indirect block is a pointer to a list of every block claimed by an inode. fsck checks every block number against a list of allocated blocks: if two inodes claim the same block number, that block number is added to a list of duplicate block numbers. The administrator may be asked to choose which inode is correct—obviously a difficult decision, and usually time to verify files against backups. fsck also checks the integrity of the actual block numbers which can also become corrupt—it should always lie in the interval between the first data block and the last data block. If a bad block number is detected, the inode is cleared.

Directories are also checked for integrity by fsck. Directory entries are equivalent to other files on the filesystem, except they have a different mode entry in the inode. fsck checks the validity of directory data blocks, checking for the following problems: unallocated nodes associated with inode numbers; inode numbers exceeding the maximum number of inodes for a particular filesystem; incorrect inode numbers for the standard directory entries "." and ".."; and directories actually being accidentally disconnected from the file system. We will examine some of these errors and how they are rectified in the next section.

fsck examines each disk volume in five distinct stages, performing all of the checks discussed above: phase 1, in which blocks and sizes are checked; phase 2, where pathnames are verified; phase 3, where connectivity is examined; phase 4, where an investigation of reference counts is undertaken; and phase 5, where the actual cylinder groups are checked.

fsck Examples

In this section, we will examine a full run of fsck, outlining the most common problems, and how they are rectified, as well as presenting some examples of less-commonly encountered problems. On a Sparc 20 system, fsck for the / filesystem looks like

```
** /dev/rdsk/c0d0s0
** Currently Mounted on /
** Phase 1 - Check Blocks and Sizes
** Phase 2 - Check Pathnames
** Phase 3 - Check Connectivity
** Phase 4 - Check Reference Counts
** Phase 5 - Check Cyl groups
FREE BLK COUNT(S) WRONG IN SUPERBLK
SALVAGE?
```

Clearly, the actual block count and the block count recorded in the superblock are at odds with each other. At this point, fsck requires superuser permission to install the actual block count in the superblock, which the Administrator indicates by pressing Y. The scan continues with the /usr partition:

```
1731 files, 22100 used, 51584 free (24 frags, 6445 blocks,  0.0%
fragmentation)
** /dev/rdsk/c0d0s6
** Currently Mounted on /usr
** Phase 1 - Check Blocks and Sizes
** Phase 2 - Check Pathnames
** Phase 3 - Check Connectivity
** Phase 4 - Check Reference Counts
** Phase 5 - Check Cyl groups

FILE SYSTEM STATE IN SUPERBLOCK IS WRONG; FIX?
```

In this case, the filesystem state in the superblock records is incorrect, and again, the Administrator is required to give consent for it to be repaired. The scan then continues with the /var and /export/home partitions:

```
26266 files, 401877 used, 217027 free (283 frags, 27093 blocks,
0.0% fragmentation)
** /dev/rdsk/c0d0s1
** Currently Mounted on /var
** Phase 1 - Check Blocks and Sizes
** Phase 2 - Check Pathnames
** Phase 3 - Check Connectivity
** Phase 4 - Check Reference Counts
** Phase 5 - Check Cyl groups
1581 files, 4360 used, 25545 free (41 frags, 3188 blocks,  0.1%
fragmentation)
```

```
** /dev/rdsk/c0d0s7
** Currently Mounted on /export/home
** Phase 1 - Check Blocks and Sizes
** Phase 2 - Check Pathnames
** Phase 3 - Check Connectivity
** Phase 4 - Check Reference Counts
** Phase 5 - Check Cyl groups
2 files, 9 used, 7111589 free (13 frags, 888947 blocks,  0.0%
fragmentation)
```

Obviously, the /var partition and /export/home have passed examination by fsck, and are intact. However, the fact that the / and /usr filesystems were in an inconsistent state suggests that the filesystems were not cleanly unmounted, perhaps during the last reboot. Fortunately, the superblock itself was intact. However, this is not always the case. In this example, the superblock of /dev/dsk/c0t0d0s2 has a bad magic number, indicating that it is damaged beyond repair:

```
server# fsck /dev/dsk/c0t0d0s2
 BAD SUPER BLOCK: MAGIC NUMBER WRONG
 USE ALTERNATE SUPER-BLOCK TO SUPPLY NEEDED INFORMATION
eg. fsck [-F ufs] -o b=# [special ...]

where # is the alternate super block. SEE fsck_ufs(1M).
```

In this case, you need to specify one of the alternative superblocks which were created by the newfs command. When a filesystem is created, there is a message printed about the creation of superblock backups:

```
super-block backups (for fsck -b #) at:
32, 5264, 10496, 15728, 20960, 26192, 31424, 36656, 41888,
47120, 52352, 57584, 62816, 68048, 73280, 78512, 82976, 88208,
93440, 98672, 103904, 109136, 114368, 119600, 124832, 130064,
135296, 140528, 145760, 150992, 156224, 161456.
```

In the example above, you may need to specify one of these alternative superblocks, so that the disk contents are once again readable. If you didn't record the superblock backups during the creation of the filesystem, you can easily retrieve them by using newfs (and using -N to prevent the creation of a new filesystem):

```
server# newfs -Nv /dev/dsk/c0t0d0s2
```

Once you have determined an appropriate superblock replacement number (for example, 32), use fsck again to replace the older superblock with the new one:

```
server# fsck -o b=32 /dev/dsk/c0t0d0s2
```

Disks which have physical hardware errors often report being unable to read inodes beyond a particular point. For example, the error message

```
Error reading block 31821 (Attempt to read from filesystem
resulted in short read) while doing inode scan. Ignore error
<y> ?
```

stops the user from continuing with the fsck scan, and correcting the problem. This is probably a good time to replace a disk, rather than attempting any corrective action. Never be tempted to ignore these errors, and hope for the best—especially in commercial organizations, you will ultimately have to take responsibility for lost and damaged data. Users will be particularly unforgiving if you had advance warning of a problem.

Here is an example of what can happen there is a link count problem:

```
server # fsck /
** /dev/rdsk/c0t1d0s0
** Currently Mounted on /
** Phase 1 - Check Blocks and Sizes
** Phase 2 - Check Pathnames
** Phase 3 - Check Connectivity
** Phase 4 - Check Reference Counts
LINK COUNT DIR I=4  OWNER=root MODE=40700
SIZE=4096 MTIME=Nov  1 11:56 1999  COUNT 2 SHOULD BE 4
ADJUST? y
```

If the adjustment does not fix the error, use find to track down the problem file and delete it:

```
server# find / -mount -inum 4 -ls
```

It should be in the lost+found directory for the partition in question (in this case, /lost+found).

As outlined above, duplicate inodes can also be a problem:

```
** Phase 1 - Check Blocks and Sizes
 314415 DUP I=5009
 345504 DUP I=12011
 345505 DUP I=12011
 854711 DUP I=91040
 856134 DUP I=93474
 856135 DUP I=93474
```

This problem is often found in Solaris 2.5 and 2.6, although not usually seen in Solaris 7 or 8, and so an upgrade may correct the problem.

Summary

In this chapter, we examined methods for filesystem management and usage monitoring In addition, we examined how to setup and configure UFS filesystems which are standard for all Solaris releases.

Questions

1. Which file specifies the default filesystem type?
   A. /etc/defaultfs
   B. /etc/defaultfstype
   C. /etc/default/fs
   D. /etc/default/fstype

2. What does a super block contain?
   A. The location of inodes, filesystem size, number of blocks, and status
   B. The location of files in a map
   C. A list of supported filesystem types
   D. The location of backup blocks, filesystem size, number of blocks, and status

3. What is the df command used for?
   A. Monitoring disk space usage
   B. Adding a disk to the system
   C. Creating default filesystems (dfs)
   D. Recovering deleted files (dfs)

4. What does the du command do?
   A. Checks for duplicate inodes
   B. Checks for duplicate files in the same directory
   C. Prints number of blocks used in each directory
   D. Script for retrieving DNS data using dig (that is, "dig up" DNS data)

5. What operation should never be performed using fsck?
   A. Attempting to work on an unmounted filesystem
   B. Attempting to work on a mounted filesystem
   C. Checking UFS filesystems
   D. Running fsck as root

6. Which of the following does not cause filesystem inconsistencies?
   A. Switching off a Solaris server without powering down first
   B. Halting a system without synchronizing disk data
   C. Defective hardware, including damage to disk blocks and heads
   D. Copying files between filesystems

7. What does phase 1 of fsck involve?
   A. Checking blocks and sizes
   B. Pathname verification
   C. Connectivity check
   D. Reference count check

8. What does phase 2 of fsck involve?
   A. Checking blocks and sizes
   B. Pathname verification
   C. Connectivity check
   D. Reference count check

9. What does phase 3 of fsck involve?
   A. Checking blocks and sizes
   B. Pathname verification
   C. Connectivity check
   D. Reference count check

10. What does phase 4 of fsck involve?
    A. Checking blocks and sizes
    B. Pathname verification
    C. Checking cylinder groups
    D. Reference count check

11. What does phase 5 of fsck involve?
    A. Checking blocks and sizes
    B. Pathname verification
    C. Checking cylinder groups
    D. Reference count check

Answers

1. C

2. A

3. A

4. C

5. B

6. D

7. A

8. B

9. C

10. D

11. C

## CHAPTER 17

Mounting File Systems

The following objectives will be met upon completing this chapter's material:

- Mounting local filesystems
- Unmounting local filesystems
- Understanding mounting options
- Configuring /etc/vfstab

Mounting Local Filesystems

Solaris (UFS) filesystems are mapped in a one-to-one relationship with physical slices. This makes it easy to associate filesystems with partitions, even if the physical and logical device references are complex. For example, the slice /dev/dsk/c0t3d0s5 may be mounted on the mount point /export/home. Mount points are simply empty directories that have been created using the mkdir command.

One of the nice features of the UFS filesystem is that it has a one-to-many mapping to potential mount points. This means that a filesystem can be mounted, and its files and directories manipulated, unmounted, and then remounted on a different mount point. All of the data that were modified when the filesystem was mounted using a different mount point are retained. For example, if we mount /dev/dsk/c0t3d0s5 on /export/home, creating a directory called pwatters (that is, /export/home/pwatters), unmount the filesystem, and then remount it on /usr/local, the directory pwatters will still be available, albeit with a different absolute path (/usr/local/pwatters). Let's review the steps involved:

```
# mkdir /export/home
# mount  /dev/dsk/c0t3d0s5 /export/home
# cd /export/home
```

```
# mkdir pwatters
# ls
pwatters
# umount /export/home
# mkdir /usr/local
# mount /dev/dsk/c0t3d0s5 /usr/local
# cd /usr/local
# ls
pwatters
```

The mkdir command is used to create mount points, which are equivalent to directories. If you want to make a mount point one level below an existing directory, you can simply use the mkdir command with no options. However, if you want to make a mount point several directory levels below an existing directory, you will need to pass the option -p to the mkdir command. For example, the following command will create the mount point /staff, because the parent directory already exists:

```
# mkdir /staff
```

However, to create the mount point /staff/nfs/pwatters, you would have to use the -p option if the directory /staff/nfs did not already exist:

```
# mkdir -p /staff/nfs/pwatters
```

Once a mount point has been created, the mount command is used to attach the filesystem to the mount point. For example, to mount the filesystem /dev/dsk/c0t3d0s5 on the mount point /export/home, you would use the following command:

```
# mount /dev/dsk/c0t3d0s5 /export/home
```

The mount command assumes a UFS filesystem will be mounted. If the target filesystem is non-UFS, then an option specifying the filesystem type will need to be passed on the command line using the -F options. Supported filesystem types include the following:

- **nfs** Network File System (NFS) filesystem
- **pcfs** MS-DOS-formatted filesystem
- **s5fs** System V-compliant filesystem

The details of all the currently mounted files are kept in the /etc/mnttab file. This file should never be directly edited by the super-user. The /etc/mnttab will contain entries similar to the following:

```
# cat /etc/mnttab
/dev/dsk/c0t0d0s0 / ufs rw,intr,largefiles,suid,dev=1100000
921334412
```

```
/proc /proc proc dev=2280000 922234443
fd /dev/fd fd rw,suid,dev=2240000 922234448
mnttab /etc/mnttab mntfs dev=2340000 922234442
swap /tmp tmpfs dev=1 922234451
/dev/dsk/c0t0d0s5 /usr ufs rw,intr,onerror=panic,suid,dev=1100005
922234441
```

The mount command, executed without any options, provides a list of all the
mounted filesystems:

```
# mount
/ on /dev/dsk/c0t0d0s0 read/write/setuid/intr/largefiles/
onerror=panic on Tue Jul 10 09:10:01 2001
/usr on /dev/dsk/c0t0d0s6
read/write/setuid/intr/largefiles/onerror=panic on Tue Jul 10
09:10:02 2001
/proc on /proc read/write/setuid on Tue Jul 10 09:10:03 2001
/etc/mnttab on mnttab read/write/setuid on Tue Jul 10 09:10:04
2001
/tmp on swap read/write/setuid on Tue Jul 10 09:10:05 2001
/export/home on /dev/dsk/c0t0d0s7
read/write/setuid/intr/largefiles/onerror=panic on Tue Jul 10
09:10:06 2001
```

Unmounting Local Filesystems

In normal operations, a filesystem is mounted at boot time if its mount point and
options are specified in the virtual filesystems table (/etc/vfstab), and it is unmounted
before the system is shut down. However, times may occur when it is necessary to manually unmount a filesystem. For example, if the filesystem's integrity needs to be
checked using the fsck command, then the target filesystem must be unmounted. Alternatively, if the mount point of a filesystem is going to be modified, then the filesystem
needs to be unmounted from its current mount point and remounted on the new
mount point. You cannot mount a filesystem on two different mount points.

Unmounting local filesystems is easy using the umount command. The filesystem to
be unmounted is specified on the command line. For example, to unmount the filesystem mounted on /export/home, the following command would be used:

```
# umount /export/home
```

However, if open files are on the filesystem or users are logging into their home
directories on the target filesystem, it's obviously a bad idea to unmount the filesystem
without giving some kind of notice. In fact, umount requires that no processes have
files opened on the target filesystem. In order to check which users are accessing a

particular filesystem, the fuser command can be used. For example, to check whether any processes have open files on the /export/home partition, the following command could be used:

```
# fuser -c /export/home
```

To give a listing of the User IDs (UIDs) associated with each process, the following command could be used:

```
# fuser -c -u /export/home
```

In order to warn users about the impending unmounting of the filesystem, the wall command can be used to send a message to all logged-in users. For example, the following message could be sent:

```
# wall
Attention all users
/export/home is going down for maintenance at 6:00 p.m.
Please kill all processes accessing this filesystem (or I will)
```

At 6:00 p.m., a fuser check should show that no processes are accessing the filesystem. However, if some users did not heed the warning, the fuser command can be used to kill all processes that are still active:

```
# fuser -c -k /export/home
```

This is obviously a drastic step, but may be necessary in emergency or urgent repair situations.

To save time, if you want to unmount all user filesystems (excluding /, /proc, /usr, and /var), you could use the umountall command:

```
# umountall
```

This only unmounts filesystems that are listed in the virtual filesystem table, subject to the previous exclusions.

Understanding Mounting Options

The mount command has several options, which are described here:

- *largefiles* enables support for large filesystems (those greater than 2G in size). To remove support for large filesystems, the *nolargefiles* option is used.

- *logging* enables a log of all UFS transactions to be maintained. In the event of a system crash, the log can be consulted, and all transactions verified. This virtually eliminates the need to run lengthy fsck passes on filesystems at boot. The default option is *nologging* because logs occupy around 1 percent of filesystem space.

- *noatime* prevents access timestamps from being touched on files. This significantly speeds up access times on large filesystems with many small files.

- *remount* permits a filesystem's properties to be modified while it is still mounted, reducing downtime.

- *rw* specifies that the filesystem is to be mounted read-write. Some filesystems, however, are read-only (such as CD-ROM). In this case, the *ro* option should be specified. Note that it is not physically possible to write to a read-only filesystem.

- *suid* permits set UID applications to be executed from the filesystem, while *nosuid* prevents set UID applications from executing.

Configuring /etc/vfstab

If you want a disk to be available after reboot, it is necessary to create an entry in the virtual filesystems table (/etc/vfstab). An entry such as

```
/dev/dsk/c0t3d0s5 /dev/rdsk/c0t3d0s5 /export/home ufs 2 yes -
```

contains details of the slice's block and raw devices, the mount point, the filesystem type, instructions for fsck, and, most importantly, a flag to force mount at boot. These options are largely equivalent to those used with the mount command.

All filesystems, including floppy disks, can be listed in the virtual filesystems table. The mount point configuration for the floppy drive is typically similar to the following:

```
fd          -          /dev/fd    fd     -       no      -
```

Instead of mounting filesystems individually using the mount command, all filesystems defined in /etc/vfstab can be mounted by using the mountall command:

```
# mountall
mount: /tmp already mounted
mount: /dev/dsk/c0t0d0s5 is already mounted
```

This attempts to mount all listed filesystems and reports filesystems that have previously been mounted. Obviously, filesystems that are currently mounted cannot be mounted twice.

Summary

In this chapter, we've examined how to mount and unmount local filesystems. In addition to exploring the various mounting options available for different filesystem types, we examined how to identify filesystems that are ready to be unmounted and how to unmount them gracefully or otherwise.

Questions

1. Can a filesystem be concurrently mounted on more than one mount point?
   A. Yes
   B. No
   C. Only filesystems of type s5fs
   D. Only filesystems of type pcfs

2. Can a filesystem initially mounted on one mount point be mounted later on a different mount point?
   A. Yes
   B. No
   C. Only filesystems of type s5fs
   D. Only filesystems of type pcfs

3. Can a filesystem be mounted on a mount point that has not been previously created?
   A. Yes
   B. No
   C. Only filesystems of type s5fs
   D. Only filesystems of type pcfs

4. Which command is used to create a mount point?
   A. mkpoint
   B. createpoint
   C. mkdir
   D. mkmountpoint

5. Which command is used to mount a filesystem?
   A. mount
   B. share

   C. attach

   D. join

6. Which command is used to unmount a filesystem?

   A. unmount

   B. umount

   C. unattach

   D. disjoin

7. Which of the following filesystem types cannot be mounted under Solaris?

   A. s5fs

   B. ntfs

   C. pcfs

   D. ufs

8. Which command would be used to check whether any processes have open files on the /export/home partition?

   A. checkusr /export/home

   B. chkusr /export/home

   C. ps -eaf | grep /export/home

   D. fuser -c /export/home

Answers

1. A

2. A

3. B

4. C

5. A

6. B

7. B

8. D

## CHAPTER 18

Backups

The following objectives will be met upon completing this chapter's material:

- Understanding backups
- Determiuning appropriate backup strategies
- Selecting a suitable backup medium
- Using ufsdump and ufsrestore
- Using tar, dd, and cpio

Software and hardware failures are an unfortunate fact of life in the Information Technology industry. These incidents often cause a sense of panic in organizations when missing or corrupt data is revealed during a peak service period. However, a system crash or a disk failure should not be a cause for alarm. It should be the signal to a well-armed and well-prepared Administrator to determine the cause of the problem, rectify any hardware faults, and restore any lost data by using a recovery procedure. This general procedure can be followed, regardless of whether user files or database tables have been lost or corrupted. Fortunately, Solaris provides a wide variety of backup and restore software that can be used in conjunction with any number of media, for example, magnetic and digital audio tapes, writeable CD-ROM's, Zip drives, and redundant hard drives. In this chapter, we will examine the development and implementation of backup and recovery procedures with Solaris.

Understanding Backups

In many companies, valuable data is stored on Solaris server systems, in user files, and in database tables. The variety of information stored is endless: personnel files, supplier invoices, receipts, and all kinds of intellectual property. In addition, many organizations provide some kind of service which relies on server uptime and information availability to generate income, or maintain prestige. For example, if a major Business-2-Consumer Web site or Business-2-Business hub experiences any downtime, every minute that the system is unavailable costs money in lost sales, frustrated consumers, and reduced customer confidence. Alternatively, a government site like the Government Accounting Office (**http://www.gao.gov/**) provides valuable advice to government, business, and consumers which is expected to be available continuously. The reputation of online service providers suffers greatly if servers go down.

On a smaller scale, but just as significant, is the departmental server, which might provide file serving, authentication services, and print access for several hundred PC systems or Sun Rays. If the server hard disk crashes, the affected users who can't read their mail or retrieve their files are going to be very angry at 9 A.M., if system data cannot be restored in a timely fashion. In this section, we will examine the background and rationale for providing a reliable backup and restore service which will in turn ensure a high level of service provision, even in the event of hardware failure. Backups should always form one component of a disaster recovery plan.

Why Do You Need Backups?

The first requirement of a backup service is the ability to rapidly restore a dysfunctional system to a functional state. The relationship between time of restoration and user satisfaction is inverse, as shown in Figure 18-1. The longer a restore takes, the faster users will become angry, whereas the rapid restoration of service will give users confidence in the service they are using. For this reason, many sites will take incremental backups of their complete filesystems each night, but may take a weekly "full dump" snapshot which can be used to rapidly rebuild an entire system from a single tape or disk.

The second requirement for a backup service is data integrity: It is not sufficient just to restore some data, and hope that it's close enough to the original. It is essential that all restored data can actually be used by applications, as if no break in service had occurred. This is particularly important for database applications, which may have several different kinds of files associated with them. Table indices, data files, and rollback segments must all be synchronized if the database is to operate correctly, and user data must be consistent with the internal structure and table ownership rights. If files are

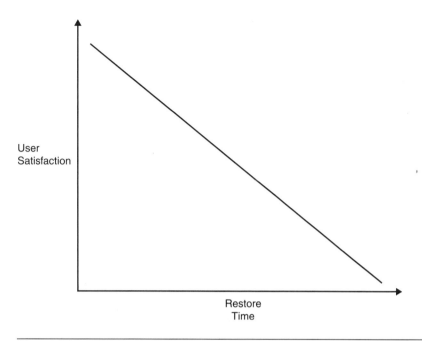

User
Satisfaction

Restore
Time

Figure 18-1 The relationship between time to restore and user satisfaction is inverse.

simply backed up onto disk when the database is open, these files can be restored, but the database system may not be able to use the files. It is essential to understand the restoration and data integrity requirements for all key applications on your system, and identify any risks to service provisions associated with data corruption. Thus, a comprehensive backup and restore plan should include provision for regular cold and warm dumps of databases to a filesystem which is regularly backed up.

A third requirement for a backup and restore service is flexibility: Data should be recorded and compressed on media which can potentially be read on a different machine, using a different operating system. In addition, using alternative media concurrently for concurrent backups is also useful for ensuring availability in case of hardware failure of a backup device. For example, you may use a DDS-3 DAT tape drive as your main backup device for nightly incremental backups, but you may also decide to burn a weekly CD-R containing a full dump of the database. If your server was affected by a power surge, and the DAT drive was damaged, and a replacement would take one week to arrive, then the CD-R dump can be used as a fallback, even though it may not be completely up-to-date.

Determining a Backup Strategy

Typical backup and restore strategies employ two related methods for recording data to any medium: incremental and full dumps. A full dump involves taking a copy of an entire filesystem or set of filesystems, and copying it to a backup medium. Historically, large filesystems have taken a long time to backup because of slow tape speeds and poor I/O performance, leading to the development of the incremental method. An incremental dump is an iterative method which involves taking a baseline dump on a regular basis (usually once every week), and then taking a further dump of files which have changed since the previous full dump. Although this approach can require the maintenance of complex lists of files and file sizes, it reduces the overall time to backup a filesystem because, on most filesystems, only a small proportion of the total number of files changes from week to week. This reduces the overall load on the backup server, and improves tape performance by minimizing friction on drive heads. However, using incremental backups can increase the time to restore a system, as there can be up to seven backup tapes which must be processed in order to restore data files fully. Therefore, a balance must be struck between convenience and the requirement for a speedy restore in the event of an emergency. Many sites use a combination of incremental and full daily dumps on multiple media to ensure that full restores can be performed rapidly, and to ensure redundant recording of key data.

After deciding on an incremental or full dump backup strategy, it is important to then plan how backups can be integrated into an existing network. There are four possible configurations which can be considered. The simplest approach is to attach a single backup device to each server, so that it acts as its own backup host. A possible configuration is shown in Figure 18-2.

This approach is appealing because it allows data to be backed up and restored using the same device, without any requirement for network connectivity. However, it does not provide for redundancy through the use of multiple backup devices. This can be rectified by including multiple backup devices for a single host. This configuration is shown in Figure 18-3.

The cost of maintaining single or multiple backup devices for each server in an organization can be very expensive. In order to reduce cost, many organizations have moved

Figure 18-2   Single server and single backup device configuration

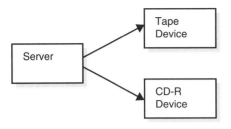

Figure 18-3   Single server and multiple backup device configuration

to centralize the management and storage of data for entire departments or sites, on a single server. This approach is detailed in Figure 18-4. Multiple client machines can have their local hard drives backed up to a central Solaris server, whether or not those clients are PC's running windows, or other Solaris servers. The central backup server can also be attached to multiple backup devices, providing different levels of redundancy for more or less significant data. For example, data from user PC's may not require double or triple redundancy, which financial records might well deserve.

There is also an increasing trend towards developing storage area networks (SANs), where backup management and data storage is distributed across multiple backup hosts, and multiple devices. Thus, a client's data could be potentially stored on many different backup servers, and management of that data could be performed from a remote manager running on the client. This configuration is shown in Figure 18-5. For example, there is a Veritas client for Windows called Backup Exec, which can connect to many different Solaris servers through an Server Message Block (SMB) service, backing up data to

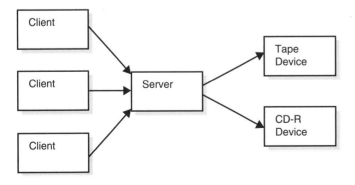

Figure 18-4   Centralized backup server with multiple storage devices

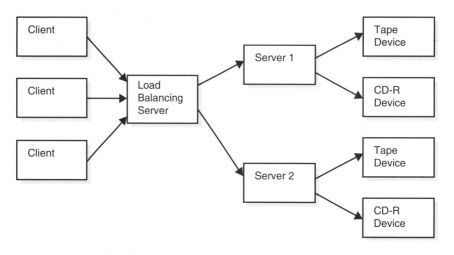

Figure 18-5 Distributed storage and management of backup services

multiple mediums. Other server-side packages, such as Legato Networker, offer distributed management of all backup services. New to the game is Sun's own Java-based Jiro
technology, which implements the proposed Federated Management Architecture
(FMA) standard. FMA is one proposal for implementing distributed storage across networks in a standard way, and is receiving support from major hardware manufacturers
like Hitachi, Quantum, Veritas and Fujitsu for future integration with their products.
More information on Jiro and FMA can be found at **http://www.jiro.com/**.

Selecting a Backup Media

Selecting a backup medium should always attempt to best meet the requirements of
rapid restoration, data integrity, and flexibility. The four main media currently in use
include tapes, disk drives, Zip and Jaz drives, and CD writing and CD rewriting technologies. Capacity and reliability criteria must also be considered: For example,
whereas tapes are generally considered very reliable for bulk storage, tape drives are
much slower than a hard drive. However, a 20G tape is much cheaper than an equivalent capacity hard drive, so the cost of any backup solutions must be weighed against
the value of the data being stored. For more information on choosing a bulk storage
device, see the FAQ for the USENET forum comp.arch.storage at **http://alumni.
caltech.edu/~rdv/comp-arch-storage/FAQ-1.html.**

Tape

Solaris supports tape drives from the old Archive Quarter-Inch Cartridge (QIC 150) tape drives (with a maximum 250M capacity), up to modern digital audio tape (DAT) and DLT systems. The QIC is a low-end drive which takes a two-reel cassette, which was widely used in many early Sun workstations. DAT tapes for DDS-2 drives have a capacity of 4 to 8G, whereas tapes for the newer DDS-3 standard have 12 to 24G capacity, depending on compression ratios. DDS-2 drives can typically record between 400K and 800K per second, again depending on compression ratios. The transition from analogue-to-digital encoding methods has increased the performance and reliability of tape-based backup methods, and they are still the most commonly used methods today. On the other hand, Digital Linear Tape (DLT) drives are becoming more popular in the enterprise because of their very large storage capacities: for example, a Compaq 1624 DLT drive can store between 35 to 70G, depending on compression, which is much more than the DAT drives. They also feature much higher transfer rates of between 1.25 to 2.5 Mbps. Of course, DLT drives are more expensive than DAT drives, and DAT drives have always been more costly than a QIC, although a QIC is generally much too small to be useful for most systems today.

Hard Drives

Since hard drives have the fastest seek times of all backup media, they are often used to store archives of user files, copied from client drives using an SMB service. In addition, hard drives form the basis of so-called RAID systems, or Redundant Array of Inexpensive Disks. Thus, an array of RAID drives can work together as a single, logical storage device, or collectively act as a single storage system, which can withstand the loss of one or more of its constituent devices. For example, if a single drive is damaged by a power surge, then depending on the "level" of RAID protection, your system may be able to continue its functions with a minimum of Administrator interference, with no impact on functionality, until the drive is replaced. Many systems now support hot-swapping of drives, so that the faulty drive could be removed and replaced, with the new drive coming seamlessly on-line. You may be wondering why, in the days of RAID, would anybody consider still using backups: the answer is that entire RAID arrays are just as vulnerable to power surges as a single drive, and so in the event of a full hardware failure, all your data could still be lost unless it is stored safely offsite, in a tape or CD-ROM. To circumvent concurrent drive corruption at the end of a disk's life, many Administrators use drives of equivalent capacities from different manufacturers, some new and some used, in a RAID array. This ensures that drives are least likely to fail concurrently.

RAID has six levels which are numbered zero through five, although RAID Levels 0 and 1 are most commonly used. RAID Level 0 involves parallelizing data transfer between disks, spreading data across multiple drives thereby improving overall data transmission rates. This technique is known as "striping." However, while RAID Level 0 has the ability to write multiple disks concurrently, it does not support redundancy, which is provided with RAID Level 1. This Level makes an identical copy of a primary disk onto a secondary disk. This kind of "mirroring" provides complete redundancy: if the primary disk fails, the secondary disk is then able to provide all data contained on the primary disk, until the primary disk is replaced. Because striping and mirroring consume large amounts of disk space, they are costly to maintain per megabyte of actual data. Thus, higher RAID Levels attempt to use heuristic techniques to provide similar functionality to the lower RAID Levels, whereas reducing the overall cost. For example, RAID Level 4 stores parity information on only a single drive, which reduces the overall amount of disk space required, but is more risky than RAID Level 1.

Software RAID solutions typically support both striping and mirroring. This speeds up data writing, and makes provision for automating the transfer of control from the primary disk to the secondary disk in the event of a primary disk failure. In addition, many software solutions support different RAID Levels on different partitions on a disk, which may also be useful in reducing the overall amount of disk space required to safely store data. For example, whereas users might require access to a fast partition using RAID Level 0, there may be another partition which is dedicated to a financial database, which requires mirroring (thus RAID Level 1). Sun's DiskSuite product is currently one of the most popular software RAID solutions.

Alternatively, custom hardware RAID solutions are also proving popular, because of the minimal administrative overhead involved with installing and configuring such systems. Although not exactly "plug and play," external RAID arrays such as the StorEdge A1000 have many individual disks that can be used to support both mirroring and striping, with data transfer rates of up to 40 Mbps. In addition, banks of fast caching memory (up to 80M) speed up disk writes by temporarily storing them in RAM before writing them to one or more disks in the array. This makes the RAID solution not only safe but significantly faster than a normal disk drive.

Zip/Jaz Disks

Zip and Jaz drives are portable, magnetic storage media which are ideal as a backup medium. Only SCSI interfaces are fully supported under Solaris, although it may be possible to use ATAPI interfaces on Solaris x86. USB and Parallel port interfaces are presently unsupported under Solaris. Zip drives come in two storage capacities: the standard 100M drive, and the expanded 250M drive, which is backwards compatible with the 100M drive. 100M and 250M drives are not going to get you very far with backups, even though Zip drives have relatively fast write speeds compared to tape drives. Zip drives are most useful for dumps of database tables, and/or user files that need to be interchanged with PCs and other client systems.

Jaz drives offer several improvements over Zip technology, the most distinguishing characteristic being increased storage capacity. Jaz drives also come in two flavors: the standard 1G drive, and a newer 2G version, which is backwards compatible with the standard drive. The Jaz drive is also much faster than the Zip drive, with reported average seek times of around 10 ms. This makes Jaz drives comparable in speed terms to many IDE hard drives, and provides the flexibility of easily sharing data between server and client systems.

Zip drive technology has improved in recent years. However, early versions of the 100M suffered from a problem known as the "click of death," where a drive would fail to read or write, and a number of repetitive clicks were heard from inside the drive. This problem has now completely disappeared with new models, and users should feel confident in using Zip as a storage medium. For historical information on the "click of death" problem, see Steve Gibson's page: **http://grc.com/clickdeath.htm**.

Further discussion of Zip and Jaz drives can be found on the **alt.iomega.zip.jazz** USENET forum.

CD-Rs and CD-RWs

CD writing and CD rewriting devices are rapidly gaining momentum as desktop backup systems, which are cheap, fast and, in the case of CD-RW, reusable. CD-R and CD-RW devices serve two distinct purposes in backup systems: whereas CD-RW disks are very useful for day-to-day backup operations, because they can be reused, CD-R technology is more useful for archiving and auditing purposes. For example, many organizations outsource their development projects to third-party contractors: In this case, it is useful for both the contractor and the client to have an archival copy of what has been developed, in case there is some later disagreement concerning developmental goals and milestones. Alternatively, contracts involved with government organizations may require regular snapshots to satisfy auditing requirements. Because CD-R is a write-once, read-only technology it is best suited to this purpose. CD-R is wasteful as a normal backup medium, because writeable CD's can only be used once. CD-RWs can be rewritten hundreds of times, and with over 600M of storage, they are competitive with Zip drives for storage, and much cheaper per unit than Jaz drives.

Backup and Restore

Backup and restore software falls into three different categories:

- Standard Solaris tools like tar, dd, cpio, ufsdump, and ufsrestore. These tools are quite adequate for backing up single machines, with multiple backup devices

- Centralized backup tools like AMANDA and Legato Networker, which are useful for backing up multiple machines through a single backup server

- Distributed backup tools like Veritas NetBackup, which are capable of remotely managing storage for multiple machines

In this section, we will examine the standard Solaris backup and restore tools, which are generally used for single machines with one or two backup devices. In addition, these tools are often useful for normal users to manage their own accounts on the server. For example, users can create "tape archives" using the tar command, whose output can be written to a single disk file. This is a standard way of distributing source trees in the Solaris and broader UNIX community. Users can also make copies of disks and tapes using the dd command. It is also possible to backup database files in combination with standard Solaris tools. For example, Oracle server is supplied with an exp utility, which can be used to take a dump of the database while it is still running

```
exp system/manager FULL=Y
```

where system is the username for an Administrator with DBA privileges, and manager is the password. This will create a file called expat.dmp which can then be scheduled to be backed up every night using a cron job such as

```
0 3 * * * exp system/manager FULL=Y
```

Some sites prefer to take full dumps every night. This involves transferring an entire file to a backup medium, which is a small system overhead if the file is only a few megabytes, but for a database with a tablespace of 50G, this would place a great strain on a backup server, especially if it was used for other purposes. Thus, it might be more appropriate to take an incremental dump, which only records data that has changed. Incremental dumps will be discussed in the section on ufsdump.

Using tar

The tar command is used to create a "tape archive," or to extract the files contained in a tape archive. Although tar was originally conceived with a tape device in mind, in fact, any device can hold a tar file, including a normal disk filesystem. For this reason users have adopted tar as their standard archiving utility, even though it does not perform compression like the Zip tools for PCs. Tape archives are easy to transport between systems using FTP or secure-copy in binary transfer mode, and are the standard means of exchanging data between Solaris systems.

As an example, let's create a tar file of the /opt/totalnet package. First, check the potential size of the tape archive by using the du command:

```
server% cd /opt/totalnet
server% du
4395    ./bin
367     ./lib/charset
744     ./lib/drv
434     ./lib/pcbin
777     ./lib/tds
5731    ./lib
5373    ./sbin
145     ./man/man1
135     ./man/man1m
281     ./man
53      ./docs/images
56      ./docs
15837   .
```

The estimated size of the archive is therefore 15,387 blocks. To create a tape archive in the /tmp directory for the whole package, including subdirectories, execute the following command:

```
server# tar cvf /tmp/totalnet.tar *
a bin/ 0K
a bin/atattr 54K
a bin/atconvert 58K
a bin/atkprobe 27K
a bin/csr.tn 6K
a bin/ddpinfo 10K
a bin/desk 17K
a bin/ipxprobe 35K
a bin/m2u 4K
a bin/maccp 3K
a bin/macfsck 3K
a bin/macmd 3K
a bin/macmv 3K
a bin/macrd 3K
a bin/macrm 3K
a bin/nbmessage 141K
a bin/nbq 33K
a bin/nbucheck 8K
a bin/ncget 65K
a bin/ncprint 66K
a bin/ncput 65K
a bin/nctime 32K
```

```
a bin/nwmessage 239K
a bin/nwq 2`6K
a bin/pfinfo 70K
a bin/ruattr 122K
a bin/rucopy 129K
a bin/rudel 121K
a bin/rudir 121K
a bin/ruhelp 9K
a bin/u2m 4K
a bin/rumd 120K
a bin/rumessage 192K
a bin/ruprint 124K
a bin/rurd 120K
a bin/ruren 121K
```

To extract the tar file's contents to disks, execute the following command:

```
server# cd /tmp
server# tar xvf totalnet.tar
x bin, 0 bytes, 0 tape blocks
x bin/atattr, 54676 bytes, 107 tape blocks
x bin/atconvert, 58972 bytes, 116 tape blocks
x bin/atkprobe, 27524 bytes, 54 tape blocks
x bin/csr.tn, 5422 bytes, 11 tape blocks
x bin/ddpinfo, 9800 bytes, 20 tape blocks
x bin/desk, 16456 bytes, 33 tape blocks
x bin/ipxprobe, 35284 bytes, 69 tape blocks
x bin/m2u, 3125 bytes, 7 tape blocks
x bin/maccp, 2882 bytes, 6 tape blocks
x bin/macfsck, 2592 bytes, 6 tape blocks
x bin/macmd, 2255 bytes, 5 tape blocks
x bin/macmv, 2866 bytes, 6 tape blocks
x bin/macrd, 2633 bytes, 6 tape blocks
x bin/macrm, 2509 bytes, 5 tape blocks
x bin/nbmessage, 143796 bytes, 281 tape blocks
x bin/nbq, 33068 bytes, 65 tape blocks
x bin/nbucheck, 7572 bytes, 15 tape blocks
x bin/ncget, 66532 bytes, 130 tape blocks
x bin/ncprint, 67204 bytes, 132 tape blocks
x bin/ncput, 65868 bytes, 129 tape blocks
x bin/nctime, 32596 bytes, 64 tape blocks
x bin/nwmessage, 244076 bytes, 477 tape blocks
x bin/nwq, 26076 bytes, 51 tape blocks
x bin/pfinfo, 71192 bytes, 140 tape blocks
x bin/ruattr, 123988 bytes, 243 tape blocks
x bin/rucopy, 131636 bytes, 258 tape blocks
x bin/rudel, 122940 bytes, 241 tape blocks
x bin/rudir, 123220 bytes, 241 tape blocks
x bin/ruhelp, 8356 bytes, 17 tape blocks
x bin/u2m, 3140 bytes, 7 tape blocks
x bin/rumd, 122572 bytes, 240 tape blocks
```

```
x bin/rumessage, 195772 bytes, 383 tape blocks
x bin/ruprint, 126532 bytes, 248 tape blocks
x bin/rurd, 122572 bytes, 240 tape blocks
x bin/ruren, 123484 bytes, 242 tape blocks
```

Tape archives are not compressed by default in Solaris. This means that they should be compressed with normal Solaris compress:

```
server% compress file.tar
```

This will create a compressed file called file.tar.Z. Alternatively, the GNU gzip utility often achieves better compression ratios than standard compress, so it should be downloaded and installed. When executed, it creates a file call file.tar.gz:

```
server% gzip file.tar
```

Although Solaris does come with tar installed, it is advisable to download, compile, and install GNU tar, because of the increased functionality that it includes with respect to compression. For example, to create a compressed tape archive file.tar.gz, use the z flag in addition to the normal cvf flags:

```
server% tar zcvf file.tar *
```

Using cpio

cpio is used for copying file archives, and is much more flexible than tar, because a cpio archive can span multiple volumes. cpio can be used in three different modes:

- Copy in mode, executed with cpio -i, extracts files from standard input, from a stream created by cat or similar

- Copy out mode, denoted by cpio -o, obtains a list of files from standard input, and creates an archive from these files, including their path name

- Copy pass mode, performed by cpio -p, is equivalent to copy out mode, except that no archive is actually created

The basic idea behind cpio for archiving is to generate a list of files to be archived, print it to standard output, and then pipe it through cpio in copy out mode. For example, to archive all of the text files in one's home directory, and store them in an archive called myarchive in the /staff/pwatters directory, use the command

```
server% find . -name '*.txt' -print | cpio -oc >
/staff/pwatters/myarchive
```

When the command completes, the number of blocks required to store the files is reported:

```
8048 blocks
```

The files themselves are stored in text format, with an identifying header, which we can examine with cat or head:

```
server% head myarchive
0707010009298a00008180000011fc0000005400000001380bb9b600001e9b0000
005500000000000000000000000000000001f00000003Directory/file.txtThe
quick brown fox jumps over the lazy dog.
```

Recording headers in ASCII is portable, and is achieved by using the -c option. This means that files can be extracted from the archive by using the cat command:

```
server% cat myarchive | cpio -icd "*"
```

This extracts all files and directories as required (specified by using the -d option). It is just as easy to extract a single file: to extract Directory/file.txt, we use the command:

```
server% cat myarchive | cpio -ic "Directory/file.txt"
```

If you are copying files directly to tape, it is important to use the same blocking factor when you retrieve or copy files from the tape to the hard disk as you did when you copied files from the hard disk to the tape. If you use the defaults, there should be no problems, although you can specify a particular blocking factor by using the -B directive.

Using dd

dd is a program which copies raw disk or tape slices block-by-block to other disk or tape slices: it is like cp for slices. It is often used for backing up disk slices to other disk slices and/or to a tape drive, and for copying tapes. To use dd, it is necessary to specify an input file if and an output file "of," and a block size. For example, to copy the root partition "/" on /dev/rdsk/c1t0d0s0 to /dev/rdsk/c1t4d0s0, you can use the command

```
server# dd if=/dev/rdsk/c1t0d0s0 of=/dev/rdsk/c1t4d0s0 bs=128k
```

To actually make the new partition bootable, you will also need to use the install-boot command after dd. Another use for dd is backing up tape data from one tape to another tape. This is particularly useful for re-creating archival backup tapes which may be aging. For example, to copy from tape drive 0 (/devrmt/0) to tape drive 2 (/dev/rmt/2), use the command

```
server# dd if=/dev/rmt/0h  of=/dev/rmt/1h
```

It is also possible to copy the contents of a floppy drive, by redirecting the contents of the floppy disk and piping it through dd:

```
server# dd < /floppy/floppy0 > /tmp/floppy.disk
```

Using ufsdump and ufsrestore

ufsdump and ufsrestore are standard backup and restore applications for UNIX filesystems. ufsdump is often set to run from cron jobs late at night to minimize load on server systems. ufsrestore is normally run in single-user mode after a system crash. ufsdump can be run on a mounted filesystem, however, it may be wise to unmount it first, perform a filesystem check (using fsck), remount it, and then perform the backup.

The key concept in planning ufsdump's is the "dump level" of any particular backup. The dump level determines whether or not ufsdump performs a full or incremental dump. A full dump is represented by a dump level of zero, while the numbers one through nine can be arbitrarily assigned to incremental dump levels. The only restriction on the assignment of dump level numbers for incremental backups is their numerical relationship to each other: A high number should be used for normal daily incremental dumps, followed once a week by a lower number which specifies that the process should be restarted. This approach uses the same set of tapes for all files, regardless of on which day they were recorded. For example, Monday through Saturday would have a dump level of 9, whereas Sunday would have a dump level of 1. After cycling through incremental backups during the weekdays and Saturday, the process starts again on Sunday.

Some organizations like to keep a day's work separate from other days in a single tape. Keeping work separate in this manner makes it easier to recover work from an incremental dump in which speed is important, and/or whether or not backups from a particular day wish to be retrieved. For example, someone may want to retrieve a version of a file that was edited on a Wednesday and the following Thursday, but they want the version just prior to the latest (for example, Wednesday). The Wednesday tape can then be used in conjunction with ufsdump to retrieve the file. A weekly full dump is scheduled to occur on Sunday, when there are few people using the system. Thus, Sunday would have a dump level of 0, followed by Monday, Tuesday, Wednesday, Thursday, and Friday with dump levels of 5, 6, 7, 8, and 9, respectively. To signal the end of a backup cycle, Saturday then has a lower dump level than Monday, which could be one of 1, 2, 3, or 4.

Prior to beginning a ufsdump, it is often useful to estimate the size of a dump, to determine how many tapes will be required. This estimate can be obtained by dividing the size of the partition by the capacity of the tape. For example, to determine how many tapes would be required to backup the /dev/rdsk/c0t0d0s4 filesystem:

```
server# ufsdump S /dev/rdsk/c0t0d0s4
50765536
```

The approximately 49M on the drive will therefore easily fit onto a QIC, DAT, or DLT tape. To perform a full dump of a x86 partition (/dev/rdsk/c0d0s0) at Level 0, we can use the following approach:

```
# ufsdump 0cu /dev/rmt/0 /dev/rdsk/c0d0s0
  DUMP: Writing 63 Kilobyte records
  DUMP: Date of this level 0 dump: Mon Feb 03 13:26:33 1997
  DUMP: Date of last level 0 dump: the epoch
  DUMP: Dumping /dev/rdsk/c0d0s0 (solaris:/) to /dev/rmt/0.
  DUMP: Mapping (Pass I) [regular files]
  DUMP: Mapping (Pass II) [directories]
  DUMP: Estimated 46998 blocks (22.95MB).
  DUMP: Dumping (Pass III) [directories]
  DUMP: Dumping (Pass IV) [regular files]
  DUMP: 46996 blocks (22.95MB) on 1 volume at 1167 KB/sec
  DUMP: DUMP IS DONE
  DUMP: Level 0 dump on Mon Feb 03 13:26:33 1997
```

The parameters passed to ufsdump include 0 (dump level), c (cartridge: blocking factor 126), and u (updates the dump record /etc/dumpdates). The dump record is used by ufsdump and ufsrestore to track the last dump of each individual filesystem:

```
server# cat /etc/dumpdates
/dev/rdsk/c0t0d0s0            0 Wed Feb  2 20:23:31 2000
/dev/md/rdsk/d0              0 Tue Feb  1 20:23:31 2000
/dev/md/rdsk/d2              0 Tue Feb  1 22:19:19 2000
/dev/md/rdsk/d3              0 Wed Feb  2 22:55:16 2000
/dev/rdsk/c0t0d0s3           0 Wed Feb  2 20:29:21 2000
/dev/md/rdsk/d1              0 Wed Feb  2 21:20:04 2000
/dev/rdsk/c0t0d0s4           0 Wed Feb  2 20:24:56 2000
/dev/rdsk/c2t3d0s2           0 Wed Feb  2 20:57:34 2000
/dev/rdsk/c0t2d0s3           0 Wed Feb  2 20:32:00 2000
/dev/rdsk/c1t1d0s0           0 Wed Feb  2 21:46:23 2000
/dev/rdsk/c0t0d0s0           3 Fri Feb  4 01:10:03 2000
/dev/rdsk/c0t0d0s3           3 Fri Feb  4 01:10:12 2000
```

ufsdump is very flexible, because it can be used in conjunction with rsh (remote shell) and remote access authorization files (.rhosts and /etc/hosts.equiv) to remotely login to another server and dump the files to one of the remote server's backup devices. However, the problem with this approach is that using .rhosts leaves the host system vulnerable to attack: If an intruder gains access to the client, he can then remotely login to a remote backup server without a username and password. The severity of the issue is compounded by the fact that a backup server which serves many clients has access to most of that client's information in the form of tape archives. Thus, a concerted attack on a single client, leading to an unchallenged remote login to a backup server, can greatly expose an organization's data.

A handy trick often used by Administrators is to use ufsdump to move directories across filesystems. A ufsdump is taken of a particular filesystem, which is then piped through ufsrestore to a different destination directory. For example, to move existing staff files to a larger filesystem, use the commands

```
server# mkdir /newstaff
server# cd /staff
server# ufsdump 0f - /dev/rdsk/c0t0d0s2 | (cd /newstaff;
ufsrestore xf -)
```

After backing up data using ufsdump, it is easy to restore the same data using the ufsrestore program. To extract data from a tape volume on /dev/rmt/0, use the command

```
# ufsrestore xf /dev/rmt/0
You have not read any volumes yet.
Unless you know which volume your file(s) are on you should start
with the last volume and work towards the first.
Specify next volume #: 1
set owner/mode for '.'? [yn] y
```

ufsrestore then extracts all of the files on that volume. However, you can also list the table of contents of the volume to standard output, if you are not sure of the contents of a particular tape:

```
# ufsrestore tf /dev/rmt/0
1          ./openwin/devdata/profiles
2          ./openwin/devdata
3          ./openwin
9          ./lp/alerts
1          ./lp/classes
15         ./lp/fd
1          ./lp/forms
1          ./lp/interfaces
1          ./lp/printers
1          ./lp/pwheels
36         ./lp
2          ./dmi/ciagent
3          ./dmi/conf
6          ./dmi
42         ./snmp/conf
```

ufsrestore also supports an interactive mode, which has on-line help to assist you in finding the correct volume to restore from

```
# ufsrestore i
ufsrestore > help
Available commands are:
        ls [arg] - list directory
        cd arg - change directory
        pwd - print current directory
        add [arg] - add 'arg' to list of files to be extracted
        delete [arg] - delete 'arg' from list of files to be
        extracted
        extract - extract requested files
        setmodes - set modes of requested directories
        quit - immediately exit program
        what - list dump header information
        verbose - toggle verbose flag (useful with "ls")
        help or '?' - print this list
If no 'arg' is supplied, the current directory is used
ufsrestore >
```

Summary

In this chapter, we have examined basic approaches to backup and restore which are suitable for most systems which act as their own backup server. In addition, we have reviewed more sophisticated centralized and distributed commercial and freeware software solutions for reducing the overall cost of backups, making better use of existing hardware, even if devices are attached to remote systems. Many sites will combine RAID technologies with backups to ensure data integrity.

Questions

1. What is a full dump?
    A. A filesystem or set of filesystems which is copied to a backup medium
    B. An uncompressed tape archive
    C. A compressed tape archive
    D. A selective backup strategy based on only recently modified files being backed up

2. What is an incremental dump?
   A. A filesystem or set of filesystems which is copied to a backup medium
   B. An uncompressed tape archive
   C. A compressed tape archive
   D. A selective backup strategy based on only recently modified files being backed up

3. What media can be used for a backup?
   A. Hard disk, zip drive, DAT tape, or CD-RW
   B. Zip drive, DAT tape, CD-RW only
   C. DAT tape or QIC tape only
   D. Hard disk, zip drive, DAT tape, or EPROM

4. What is a RAID Level 0?
   A. Mirroring
   B. Striping
   C. Mirroring 1 Striping
   D. Blocking

5. What is a RAID Level 1?
   A. Mirroring
   B. Striping
   C. Mirroring 1 Striping
   D. Blocking

6. What command would be used to extract a tar file called backup.tar using verbose output?
   A. tar zvf backup.tar
   B. tar xvf backup.tar
   C. tar evf backup.tar
   D. tar zevf backup.tar

7. What does cpio "copy in" mode do?
   A. Inserts files into an archive, with data sourced from a stream created by cat or similar
   B. Inserts files into an archive by extracting them directly from the filesystem (using the -f option)
   C. Acts like cp for slices
   D. Extracts files from standard input, from a stream created by cat or similar

8. What does dd do?
   A. Inserts files into an archive, with data sourced from a stream created by cat or similar
   B. Inserts files into an archive by extracting them directly from the filesystem (using the -f option)
   C. Acts like cp for slices
   D. Extracts files from standard input, from a stream created by cat or similar

Answers

1. A

2. D

3. A

4. B

5. A

6. B

7. D

8. C

The lp Print Service

The following objectives will be met upon completing this chapter's material:

- Exploring supported Solaris printers and the terminfo database
- Configuring name services for printing
- Setting printer environment variables
- Using admintool to add and configure printers

Managing print services is an important function of Solaris services. In addition to supporting both BSD and System V style print services, Solaris also provides a wide variety of text processing tools that can be used to render material suitable for printing. In Chapter 20, readers will learn to install and configure printing services.

Supported Printers

Solaris supports a wide variety of printers, whose details are stored in the terminfo database (/usr/share/lib/terminfo). Most plaintext and PostScript printers are supported. However, some older, SPARC-specific printing hardware, which relied on the proprietary NeWSPrint software, is no longer supported in Solaris 8. To correctly install a printer for Solaris, it is necessary to verify that a driver exists in the terminfo database, as this defines printer interface data.

The terminfo database is just a set of hierarchical directories which contain files that define communication settings for each printer type. Printers from different vendors are defined in files that sit in a subdirectory whose name is defined by the first letter of the vendor's name. Thus, the directory /usr/share/lib/terminfo contains the following entries:

```
bash-2.03# ls /usr/share/lib/terminfo
1  3  5  7  9  a  b  d  f  g  h  j  l  m  o  p  r  s  u  w  y
2  4  6  8  A  B  c  e  G  H  i  k  M  n  P  q  S  t  v  x  z
```

For example, if we wanted to see which Epson printers are supported under Solaris 8, we would change to the root directory of the terminfo database, and then to the subdirectory in which Epson drivers are found (/usr/share/lib/terminfo/e). This directory contains drivers for the following printers:

```
bash-2.03# ls -l
total 80
-rw-r--r--   2 bin      bin       1424 Sep  1  1998 emots
-rw-r--r--   2 bin      bin       1505 Sep  1  1998 env230
-rw-r--r--   2 bin      bin       1505 Sep  1  1998 envision230
-rw-r--r--   1 bin      bin       1717 Sep  1  1998 ep2500+basic
-rw-r--r--   1 bin      bin       1221 Sep  1  1998 ep2500+color
-rw-r--r--   1 bin      bin       1093 Sep  1  1998 ep2500+high
-rw-r--r--   1 bin      bin       1040 Sep  1  1998 ep2500+low
-rw-r--r--   2 bin      bin        971 Sep  1  1998 ep40
-rw-r--r--   2 bin      bin        971 Sep  1  1998 ep4000
-rw-r--r--   2 bin      bin        971 Sep  1  1998 ep4080
-rw-r--r--   2 bin      bin        971 Sep  1  1998 ep48
-rw-r--r--   1 bin      bin       2179 Sep  1  1998 epson2500
-rw-r--r--   1 bin      bin       2200 Sep  1  1998 epson2500-80
-rw-r--r--   1 bin      bin       2237 Sep  1  1998 epson2500-hi
-rw-r--r--   1 bin      bin       2257 Sep  1  1998 epson2500-hi80
-rw-r--r--   2 bin      bin       1209 Sep  1  1998 ergo4000
-rw-r--r--   1 bin      bin       1095 Sep  1  1998 esprit
-rw-r--r--   1 bin      bin        929 Sep  1  1998 ethernet
-rw-r--r--   1 bin      bin        927 Sep  1  1998 ex3000
-rw-r--r--   2 bin      bin       1053 Sep  1  1998 exidy
-rw-r--r--   2 bin      bin       1053 Sep  1  1998 exidy2500
```

Here, we can see that the Epson 2500, for example, has its settings contained within the file ep2500+basic. However, several other versions of the printer driver are available, including ep2500+color, ep2500+high, and ep2500+low.

There are several important system configuration issues to keep in mind when planning to set up printing services on a Solaris system. First, you must ensure that there is plenty of disk space in the /var partition, so that print jobs may be spooled in /var/spool. This is particularly important when spooling PostScript print jobs, which may be several megabytes in size. When several PostScript jobs are submitted concurrently, the system will require 10-20M of disk space. In addition, you need to ensure that sufficient physical RAM is available: Otherwise, spooling will be slowed down by the use of virtual RAM. If you must use virtual RAM for spooling, ensure that enough virtual RAM is available (more can be added by using the swap command). In addition, when spooling print jobs, it pays to invest in fast SCSI disks for the /var partition:

10,000 RPM disks are now available as standard in all new UltraSPARC systems, and these give excellent print spooling performance.

Configuring Print Services

The first place to start is the configuration of the printers entry in the /etc/nsswitch.conf file, where your local naming service is used to resolve printer names. For example, if you only use file-based naming resolution, then the printers entry in /etc/nsswitch.conf would look like this:

```
printers: files
```

Alternatively, if you use NIS, then the entry would look like this:

```
printers: files nis
```

Finally, if you use NIS+, then the entry would contain the following:

```
printers: nisplus files xfn
```

It is also possible that individual users will define printers in the file ~/.printers, in which case the entry user can also be added to the /etc/nsswitch.conf printer configuration entry in the order in which the ~/.printers file should be consulted. In addition, the environment variables LPDEST and PRINTER can be set to indicate which printer should be used as the default. For example, the following command will set the default printer for the current user to be the local hp1 printer:

```
bash-2.03$ PRINTER=hp1; export PRINTER
```

The LPDEST environment variable can be set in the same manner:

```
bash-2.03$ LPDEST=hp1; export LPDEST
```

Next, we need to examine entries within the /etc/printers.conf file, which determines, for file-based name resolution, which printers are available for use by users of the local system. The printers concerned may be connected locally, through the parallel port, or could be mounted remotely by using NFS or Samba. A typical /etc/printers.conf file looks like this:

```
bash-2.03$ cat /etc/printers.conf
hp1:\
        :bsdaddr=pserver,hp1,Solaris:\
        :description=HP Primary:
```

```
hp2:\
        :bsdaddr=pserver,hp2,Solaris:\
        :description=HP Secondary:
_default:\
        :use=hp1:
```

Admintool

The easiest way to add printers to a Solaris system is by using the admintool, as shown in Figure 19-1. There are several fields which can be used to define a printer entry:

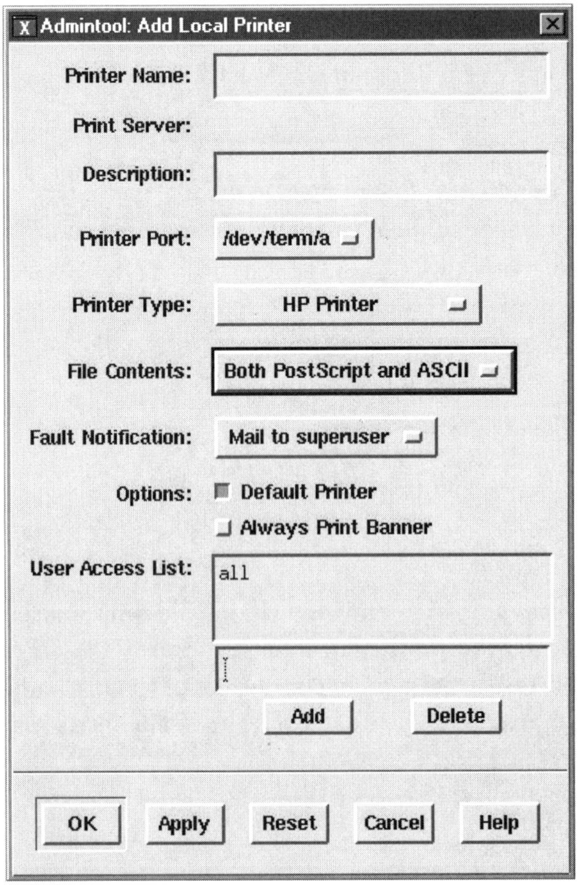

Figure 19-1 Using admintool to add a printer

- A printer name, such as hp1, must be set. This should uniquely identify a printer with respect to the local host, so that there is no confusion about which printer a job should be sent to.

- The name of the server on which the printer is attached, such as admin or finance.

- A description of the printer, which could refer to its physical location, such as Building C Level 2 Room 143.

- A printer port, such as /dev/term/a, which identifies the parallel port.

- The printer type, such as a Hewlett Packard (HP) Printer.

- The file types that will be accepted for printing, usually both PostScript and ASCII for supported printers.

- Who should be notified in case of faults, such as sending an email message to the superuser.

- Several optional settings, such as whether the current printer is the default printer, and whether or not to always print a banner.

- A list of users who can submit jobs to the printer queue. Many printers have no user restrictions on printing, so all can be entered into the user list.

The admintool can also be used to modify all current settings for installed printers when necessary.

Solaris Print Manager

The Solaris Print Manager provides a more sophisticated view of current printer settings, by displaying a list of all printers that are known to the local system, as well as their configuration settings. In addition, it is possible to set display options for the Print Manager that make it easy to customize views based on local site preferences. In Figure 19-2, for example, we show the default view on a network that has three printers available: yasimov, henryov, and prova. The entry [Empty] appears next to the icon for each printer because no jobs are currently being processed by any of the printers. The details of print jobs can be minimized for each printer by clicking the - symbol next to the appropriate icon.

The printer properties window can be raised for each printer defined on the system. For the printer yasimov, the current properties are shown in Figure 19-3. There are several key characteristics noted:

- The icon label, which is usually the name of the printer (yasimov).

- The icon set to be used for the printer.

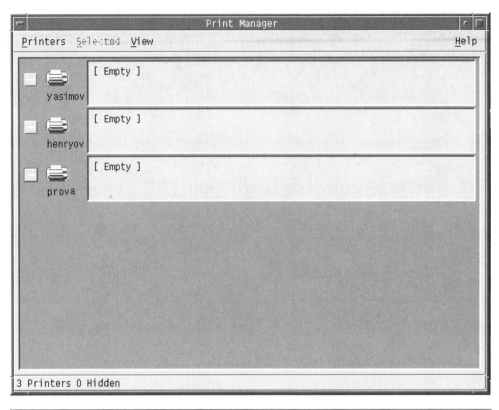

Figure 19-2 Viewing configured printers

- A description of the printer.
- The name of the printer queue.
- The status of the printer queue.
- The name of the printer device.
- The status of the printer device.

It is possible to further modify the display of printer sets by selecting the Set Options item from the View menu, as shown in Figure 19-4:

- Representation of printers by using large or small icons, names only, or full details.
- Whether or not to show all jobs on the printer, or only the jobs of the current user.

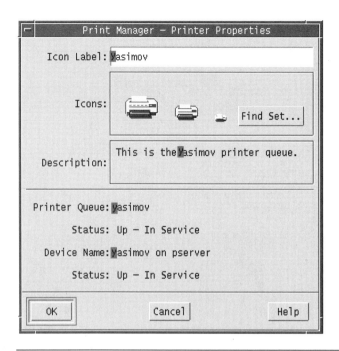

Figure 19-3   Viewing printer properties for individual printers

Figure 19-4   Setting Print Manager options

- Whether to display various flags when errors are encountered.
- How often to update the display of printers on the system.

Summary

In this chapter, we have examined how to install and configure printers with Solaris, and explored supported Solaris printers. In addition to reviewing the contents of the terminfo database, we examined how to configure name services for printing, and to use admintool to add and configure printers.

Questions

1. Where is the terminfo database stored?
   A. /usr/lib/terminfo
   B. /share/lib/terminfo
   C. /lib/terminfo
   D. /usr/share/lib/terminfo

2. What is the role of the LPDEST environment variables?
   A. Sets the default printer name
   B. Sets the default local printer name only
   C. Sets the default remote printer name only
   D. Specifies a list of printers used for printer spooling

3. What is the role of the PRINTER environment variables?
   A. Sets the default printer name
   B. Sets the default local printer name only
   C. Sets the default remote printer name only
   D. Specifies a list of printers used for printer spooling

4. Which file specifies the default printer name on a per-user basis?
   A. ~/.printcap
   B. ~/.printers
   C. ~/.defaultprinter
   D. None—it must be specified per user by using an environment variable

Answers

1. D

2. A

3. A

4. B

## CHAPTER 20

Print Commands

The following objectives will be met upon completing this chapter's material:

- Printing using the lp command
- Checking printer status with lpstat
- Setting up printer classes
- Using lpadmin to manage a printer

Printing Using lp

The lp (line printer) commands predate the admintool and Solaris Print Manager interfaces, and are most likely to be used by experienced Solaris administrators. They are typically used to add and delete local and remote printer entries, and a number of other administrative tasks.

After a printer is configured, it's then very easy to submit jobs. Let's look at some examples. To submit a PostScript job to the printer hp1 on the local server, we would use the command:

```
bash-2.03$ lp -d hp1 file.ps
```

Once the job has been spooled, the printer will interpret the PostScript commands embedded in the file correctly. If your printer does not support PostScript, then you will be printing the embedded PostScript codes, and not the rendered document. The -d flag is used to specify the name of the printer (hp1). If a printer is not specified, the job will be sent to the default printer. (In this case, hp1 is the default printer, so it's not necessary to use the -d option.) A similar command can be used to spool a text file to the same printer:

```
bash-2.03$ lp file.txt
```

Alternatively, the POSIX-style of printing can be used to submit jobs. This involves specifying both the print server and printer name, rather than just the printer name. This ensures that there is no conflict between printers with the same names that are attached to different hosts. For example, the server admin could have a printer called hp1 as could the server finance: If we just pass -d hp1 on the command line with lp, which printer would be selected for our job? The answer is to specify both the server and printer on the command line. Let's revisit our PostScript example, using a POSIX-compliant format:

```
bash-2.03$ lpr -P admin:hp1 file.ps
```

If you wanted to print to the hp1 server attached to the server finance, you could use the following command instead:

```
bash-2.03$ lpr -P finance:hp1 file.ps
```

A print job can be easily cancelled by using the cancel command, and passing the job's ID to the command. For example, to cancel the job hp1-212, we would use the following command:

```
bash-2.03# cancel hp1-212
```

Monitoring Print Jobs

You can check the status of a particular printer by using the lpstat command. To check the status of the printer hp1, you could use the following command:

```
bash-2.03$ lpstat -D -p hp1
printer hp1 is idle. enabled since Nov 06 16:13 2000. available.
```

Here, we can see that hp1 is idle, and has been up since November 6th, 2000.

Managing a Printer Using lpadmin

lpadmin is a printing administration utility that is used to add and configure printers. Adding a printer, or modifying its operating characteristics is usually performed with a number of lpadmin commands.

To set a printer name and port, we would use the following command:

```
bash-2.03# lpadmin -p hp2 -v /dev/null
```

This command sets the port to /dev/null for the printer hp2. To specify the printer software type to be used, we would use the following command:

```
bash-2.03# lpadmin -p hp2 -m netstandard
```

This command would force the hp2 printer to use the netstandard printing software. To set the protocol and timeout parameters, we would use the following command:

```
bash-2.03#  lpadmin -p hp2 -o dest=lithgow:hp2 -o protocol=tcp
-o timeout=5
```

This command specifies that hp2 (being mounted from the server lithgow) would use the TCP protocol, and have a timeout of five seconds. If the hp2 printer was no longer attached to the system, its data could be removed by using the following command:

```
bash-2.03# lpadmin -x hp2
```

If a printer is temporarily unavailable due to maintenance, the reject command can be used to prevent new jobs from being sent to a local printer. In the following example, the hp2 printer is temporarily removed from access:

```
bash-2.03# reject hp2
```

To actually stop all print jobs from proceeding, the disable command is typically used. Thus, to disable all print jobs on the printer hp2, the following command would be used:

```
bash-2.03# disable hp2
```

To add a more meaningful description to a printer entry, an optional description string can be used. For example, to add the description "HP printer on lithgow" to the hp2 printer, we would use the following command:

```
bash-2.03# lpadmin -p hp2 -D "HP printer on lithgow"
```

By default, a banner page is printed when using the lp print commands. However, to disable the banner page from printing, to conserve paper, the nobanner option can be set. For example, to set the nobanner option on hp2, we would use the command:

```
bash-2.03# lpadmin -p hp2 -o nobanner=never
```

Alternatively, to make banner printing optional on hp2, the following command would be used:

```
bash-2.03# lpadmin -p hp2 -o nobanner=optional
```

Setting Printer Classes

A set of printers can be grouped together to form a class. These class definitions are stored in the directory /etc/lp/classes. A file is created for each printer class, with the filename set to the name of the class. The file contains a list of all printers belonging to the class. To add a printer to the class, we can either manually edit the appropriate class file, or use the lpadmin command. For example, either of the following commands would add the printer hp2 to the class bubblejets:

```
bash-2.03# cat "hp2" >> /etc/lp/classes/bubblejets
bash-2.03# lpadmin -p hp2 -c bubblejets
```

Adding Remote Access Using lpadmin

If you want to refer to a remote printer as if it were a locally attached printer, you can do so by using lpadmin. In the following example, the server lithgow has the printer katoomba attached, so we can add it using this command:

```
bash-2.03# lpadmin -p katoomba -s lithgow
```

To verify that the printer is available for remote printing, simply use the lpstat command:

```
bash-2.03$ lpstat -p katoomba
printer katoomba is idle. enabled since Dec 07 17:23 2000.
available.
```

Summary

In this chapter, we examined how to use the lp commands and related tools to enable remote printing access, print jobs, create printer classes, and check printer status. In addition, we examined how lpadmin can be used to manage individual printer configurations.

Questions

1. How could a PostScript job (file1.ps) be submitted to the printer hp1 on the remote server admin?
   A. lp -d admin:hp1 -f file.ps
   B. lp -d admin:hp1 file.ps

C. lp -d hp1 file.ps

D. lp -p admin:hp1 file.ps

2. How could a print job with the ID hp1-212 (filename: file1.ps) be cancelled on the default printer hp1?

A. cancel hp1-212

B. cancel -p hp1

C. cancel file1.ps

D. cancel hp1 -f file1.ps

3. What command is used to monitor printer status?

A. lpmonitor

B. lpview

C. openview

D. lpstat

4. What command is used to prevent new jobs from being spooled to a printer?

A. remove

B. cancel

C. disable

D. reject

5. What command is used to stop all jobs from being spooled to a printer?

A. remove

B. cancel

C. disable

D. reject

Answers

1. B

2. A

3. D

4. D

5. C

PART II

Sun Certified System Administrator for Solaris 8

The Solaris 8 Network Environment

The following objectives will be met upon completing this chapter's material:

- Understanding Solaris networking functions
- Reviewing networking capabilities
- Investigating routing

In this chapter, we will examine how to connect multiple machines in subnets and how to connect subnets to form local area networks (LANs) through routers. Inter-router connections enable the formation of wide area networks (WANs) and ultimately the Internet. Communication between different machines, through the transmission of data packets, can only take place through the process of routing. Routing involves finding a route between two hosts, whether they exist on the same network or are separated by thousands of miles and hundreds of intermediate hosts. Fortunately, the basic principles are the same in both cases. In this chapter, we will examine static and dynamic methods for configuring routes between hosts.

Network Configuration

Solaris supports many different kinds of network interfaces for local area and wide area transmissions. Ethernet and the Fiber Distributed Data Interface (FDDI) are commonly used for creating networks of two or more systems at a single site through a LAN while supporting high-speed, wide area connections through T1 and X.25 lines and, most recently, Asynchronous Transfer Mode (ATM) networks.

In its simplest form, a Solaris local area Class C network for a fictitious organization called cassowary.net could consist of two servers with a single Ethernet interface, each connected to a hub, which could then be connected to a router. A hub is a device that can interconnect many devices so that they can be channeled directly to a router for wide area connections. For example, each physical floor of a building may have a hub, and each of these hubs then connects to a single hub for the whole building. This hub is connected to an Internet Service Provider (ISP) through a router (router.cassowary. net) and a dedicated Integrated Services Digital Network (ISDN) service.

A general rule of thumb for connecting routable networks is not to have more than three levels of connection between a server and a router. Otherwise, the number of errors increases dramatically. Figure 21-1 shows a possible Class C network configuration for this building.

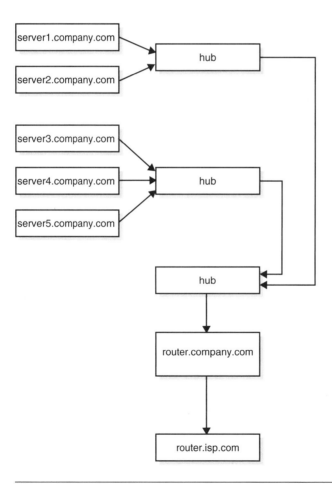

Figure 21-1 Class C network configuration (203.17.64.0)

This configuration is fine if a single company (cassowary.net) owns and occupies this building. However, let's imagine that cassowary.net downsizes and leases the second floor to a government department paulwatters.com. The government department wants to make use of the existing ISP arrangements and is happy to share the cost of the ISDN connection. Yet they want to logically isolate their network from that of cassowary.net for security purposes. They intend to install a packet filter on their own router, which explicitly denies or enables packets to cross into the government department's network.

This logical separation can be easily achieved by separating the existing network into two subnets, allowing the government department to install their own router, and by connecting the two networks through that router. Traffic to the ISP can still flow through the existing connection, although there are now two internal connections to the router. The way that the department's traffic can "find" the ISP is the kind of problem that routing can solve. More generally, routing enables one host to find a path to any other host on the Internet. Figure 21-2 shows the revised configuration for this building, incorporating the

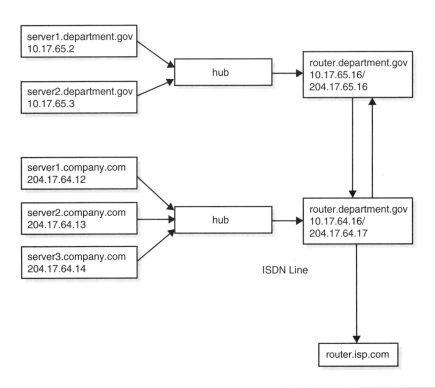

Figure 21-2 Connecting two Class C networks (203.17.64.0 and 203.17.65.0)

changes required by the government department, forming two Class C networks whose routers are connected to each other.

It should be clear from these examples that from a network perspective, a host must either be a router or a host. A router can be a Solaris server, which performs other functions (as a Domain Name System [DNS] server or a Network Information Service [NIS] server); however, it can also be a dedicated, hardware-based system supplied by another manufacturer (such as Cisco or Ascend). In this chapter, we will examine ways of setting up and configuring a host to be a router, although it may be that your organization prefers to use a dedicated system for routing.

The basic function of a router, as displayed in Figures 21-1 and 21-2, is to pass information from one network to another. In the examples, information is passed from one Class C network to another, but also to the router of an ISP. The ISP's router then connects with many other ISP's routers, eventually giving global coverage. The information passed between networks is contained in discrete packets, and because the router passes this information along, it follows that the router can potentially make a copy of the data and save it to a local disk. This is the basis of many security-related problems on the Internet, because usernames and passwords are also transmitted as packets and can be intercepted by any intermediate router between the client and server.

To be a router, a system must have multiple network interfaces. Thus, the router for cassowary.net has the interfaces 204.17.64.16 and 204.17.64.17. The first interface accepts traffic from the internal network and passes it to the second interface, while the second interface accepts traffic from the other routers and passes it to the internal network or to other routers as appropriate. Having two network interfaces enables data to be passed through the machine and exchanged across different networks. In the previous example, the cassowary.net router is able to exchange information between the paulwatters.com router and the ISP's router. Thus, many routers can be interconnected to form networks, in which packets can be passed from a source to a destination host transparently.

Since the paulwatters.com router serves as a packet-filtering firewall, it is likely that the network has a non-routable, internal structure, which is not directly accessible to the external network, but is visible from the router (the 10.17.65.0 network). Thus, a rogue user from cassowary.net will be able to "see" the external interface for the paulwatters.com router, but will not be able to see the internal interface, or any of the hosts beyond, unless he or she manages to break into the router through the external interface. This adds a second layer of protection against intrusion. A packet filter can then be used to explicitly deny connections to machines in the internal network, except for very specific ports.

For example, a departmental mail server may reside on server1.paulwatters.com, and external machines will ultimately need access to the sendmail ports on this server. This can be achieved by port forwarding, or the capability of the router to map a port on its external interface to a port on a machine on the internal network. For example, a Web server on server1.paulwatters.com:80 could be accessed from the external network by connecting to router.paulwatters.com:8080 if the mapping was enabled. These techniques can achieve the necessary logical isolation between external users and an actual network configuration, which can be useful for security planning.

A machine with more than one network interface may not be configured to act as a router, in which case it is referred to a multihomed host. Multihoming can be useful for performing such functions as load balancing and directly serving different Class C networks without passing information between them.

In order to configure routing, it is necessary to enable the appropriate network interfaces. In this chapter, we will assume that an Ethernet network is being used; thus, each system that acts as a router must have at least one Ethernet interface installed. In addition, Solaris also supports multiple Ethernet interfaces to be installed on a single machine. These are usually designated by files like

```
/etc/hostname.hmen
```

or for older machines

```
/etc/hostname.len
```

where *n* is the interface number. Interface files contain a single IP address, with the primary network interface being designated with an interface number of zero. Thus, the primary interface of a machine called server would be defined by the file /etc/server.hme0, which might contain the IP address 203.17.64.28. A secondary network interface connected to a different subnet might be defined in the file /etc/server.hme1.

In this case, the file might contain the IP address 10.17.65.28. This setup is commonly used in organizations that have a provision for a failure of the primary network interface or to enable the load balancing of server requests across multiple subnets (such as for an intranet Web server processing HTTP requests). A system with a second network interface can either act as a router or as a multihomed host. Hostnames and IP addresses are locally administered through a naming service, which is usually the Domain Name Service (DNS) for companies connected to the Internet, and the Network Information Service (NIS/NIS+) for companies with large internal networks that require administrative functions beyond what DNS provides, including centralized authentication.

It is also worth mentioning at this point that it is quite possible to assign different IP addresses to the same network interface, which can be useful for hosting "virtual" domains that require their own IP addresses, rather than relying on application-level support for multihoming (such as when using the Apache Web server). Simply create a new /etc/hostname.hmeX:Y file for each IP address required, where X represents the physical device interface, and Y represents the virtual interface number.

In the examples presented, each of the routers has two interfaces, one for the internal network, and one for the external Internet. The subnet mask used by each of these interfaces must also be defined in /etc/netmasks. This is particularly important if the interfaces lie on different subnets or if they serve different network classes. In addition, it might also be appropriate to assign a fully qualified domain name to each of the interfaces, although this will depend on the purpose to which each interface is assigned. For the system router.paulwatters.com, two hostname files will be created in the /etc directory. The /etc/hostname.hme0 file will contain the entry 10.17.65.16, while the /etc/hostname.hme0 file will contain the entry 204.17.65.16.

When installing a system as a router, it is necessary to determine which network interface to use as the external interface for passing information between networks. This interface must be defined in the file /etc/defaultrouter by including that interface's IP address. These addresses can be matched to hostnames if appropriate. For example, the interfaces for router.paulwatters.com will be defined in /etc/hosts as

```
127.0.0.1      localhost       loghost
10.17.65.16    internal
               204.17.65.16    router        router.paulwatters.com
```

If the server is to be multihomed instead of being a router, ensure that /etc/defaultrouter does not exist, and create an /etc/notrouter file:

```
server# rm /etc/defaultrouter
server# touch /etc/notrouter
```

For both routing and multihomed hosts, the status of all network interfaces can be checked by using the netstat -i command:

```
router# netstat -i
Name  Mtu  Net/Dest   Address        Ipkts    Ierrs Opkts    Oerrs Collis Queue
lo0   8232 loopback   localhost      199875   0     199875   0            0
hme0  1500 203.17.65.0 paulwatters.com 16970779 623190 19543549 0    0    0
hme1  1500 10.17.65.0 internal.gov    68674644 54543 65673376 0    0      0
```

In this example, Mtu is the maximum transfer rate, which is much higher for the loopback address than the network interface (as would be expected), and the number of Ipkts (inbound packets) and Opkts (outbound packets) is equivalent for lo0 (as one would hope). The loopback interface significantly increases the efficiency of a host that transmits packets to itself.

Here an almost six-fold increase takes place in the Mtu for the lo0 interface over either of the standard network interfaces. The primary network interface hme0 is connected to the 203.17.65.0 network and has transmitted a large number of packets in and out since booting (16,970,779 and 19,543,549 respectively). A number of inbound errors (623,190) have taken place, but no outbound errors or collisions have occurred. Examining how these figures change over time can indicate potential problems in network topology, which may need to be addressed.

For example, if you are testing a Web server, and it doesn't appear to be working, the Ipkts count can reveal whether or not the connections are actually being made. If the counter does not increase as expected, it may indicate an intermediate hardware failure (a dead hub). Another example of identifying intermittent hardware failure might be revealed by a large number of inbound packets, representing requests, but only a small number of outbound packets.

The following example consists of 1,000,847 inbound packets, but of only 30,159 outbound packets since boot. Because it is unlikely in most situations that a 33:1 imbalance exists in the ratio of inbound to outbound packets, the hme0 network interface should be checked. Also, many collisions are being experienced by the hme0 interface. Collisions between packets render them useless, and the figure reported here indicates a significant loss of bandwidth. If the interface is working as expected, it can also be worthwhile to investigate other causes arising from software (such as the incorrect configuration of a packet filter):

```
server# netstat -i
Name  Mtu  Net/Dest      Address     Ipkts   Ierrs Opkts  Oerrs Collis Queue
lo0   8232 loopback      localhost   7513    0     7513   0     0      0
hme0  1500 204.17.64.0   1000847 5   30159   0     3979   0
```

netstat -s also enables these per-interface statistics to be viewed on a per-protocol basis, which can be very useful in determining potential problems with routing, especially if the router is packet filtering. The following example shows output from the netstat -s command, which displays the per-protocol statistics for the User Datagram Protocol (UDP), the Transmission Control Protocol (TCP), and the Internet Control Message Protocol (ICMP):

```
router# netstat -s
UDP
        udpInDatagrams      =502856     udpInErrors        =        0
        udpOutDatagrams     =459357
TCP     tcpRtoAlgorithm     =      4    tcpRtoMin          =      200
        tcpRtoMax           =240000     tcpMaxConn         =       -1
        tcpActiveOpens      =  33786    tcpPassiveOpens    =    12296
        tcpAttemptFails     =    324    tcpEstabResets     =      909
```

```
              tcpCurrEstab          =    384     tcpOutSegs            =19158723
              tcpOutDataSegs        =13666668    tcpOutDataBytes       =981537148
              tcpRetransSegs        = 33038      tcpRetransBytes       =41629885
              tcpOutAck             =5490764     tcpOutAckDelayed      =462511
              tcpOutUrg             =     51     tcpOutWinUpdate       =    456
              tcpOutWinProbe        =    290     tcpOutControl         = 92218
              tcpOutRsts            =   1455     tcpOutFastRetrans     = 18954
              tcpInSegs             =15617893
              tcpInAckSegs          =9161810     tcpInAckBytes         =981315052
              tcpInDupAck           =4559921     tcpInAckUnsent        =      0
              tcpInInorderSegs      =5741788     tcpInInorderBytes
      =1120389303
              tcpInUnorderSegs      = 25045      tcpInUnorderBytes     =16972517
              tcpInDupSegs          =4390218     tcpInDupBytes         =4889714
              tcpInPartDupSegs      =    375     tcpInPartDupBytes     =130424
              tcpInPastWinSegs      =     17     tcpInPastWinBytes     =1808990872
              tcpInWinProbe         =    162     tcpInWinUpdate        =    270
              tcpInClosed           =    313     tcpRttNoUpdate        = 28077
              tcpRttUpdate          =9096791     tcpTimRetrans         = 18098
              tcpTimRetransDrop     =     26     tcpTimKeepalive       =    509
              tcpTimKeepaliveProbe=       76     tcpTimKeepaliveDrop   =      1
              tcpListenDrop         =      0     tcpListenDropQ0       =      0
              tcpHalfOpenDrop       =      0
      IP      ipForwarding          =      2     ipDefaultTTL          =    255
              ipInReceives          =16081438    ipInHdrErrors         =      8
              ipInAddrErrors        =      0     ipInCksumErrs         =      1
              ipForwDatagrams       =      0     ipForwProhibits       =      2
              ipInUnknownProtos     =    274     ipInDiscards          =      0
              ipInDelivers          =16146712    ipOutRequests         =19560145
              ipOutDiscards         =      0     ipOutNoRoutes         =      0
              ipReasmTimeout        =     60     ipReasmReqds          =      0
              ipReasmOKs            =      0     ipReasmFails          =      0
              ipReasmDuplicates     =      0     ipReasmPartDups       =      0
              ipFragOKs             =   7780     ipFragFails           =      0
              ipFragCreates         = 40837      ipRoutingDiscards     =      0
              tcpInErrs             =    291     udpNoPorts            =144065
              udpInCksumErrs        =      2     udpInOverflows        =      0
              rawipInOverflows      =      0
      ICMP    icmpInMsgs            = 17469      icmpInErrors          =      0
              icmpInCksumErrs       =      0     icmpInUnknowns        =      0
              icmpInDestUnreachs    =   2343     icmpInTimeExcds       =     26
              icmpInParmProbs       =      0     icmpInSrcQuenchs      =      0
              icmpInRedirects       =     19     icmpInBadRedirects    =     19
              icmpInEchos           =   9580     icmpInEchoReps        =   5226
              icmpInTimestamps      =      0     icmpInTimestampReps   =      0
              icmpInAddrMasks       =      0     icmpInAddrMaskReps    =      0
              icmpInFragNeeded      =      0     icmpOutMsgs           = 11693
              icmpOutDrops          =140883      icmpOutErrors         =      0
              icmpOutDestUnreachs   =   2113     icmpOutTimeExcds      =      0
              icmpOutParmProbs      =      0     icmpOutSrcQuenchs     =      0
              icmpOutRedirects      =      0     icmpOutEchos          =      0
              icmpOutEchoReps       =   9580     icmpOutTimestamps     =      0
              icmpOutTimestampReps=        0     icmpOutAddrMasks      =      0
```

```
icmpOutAddrMaskReps =      0    icmpOutFragNeeded   =      0
icmpInOverflows     =      0
```

This system appears to be working well. No UDP problems exist (udpInErrors=0), and on the ICMP front, icmpOutErrors and icmpInErrors are both zero. However, some IP errors have occurred (ipInHdrErrors=8). It is often useful to run a cron job to extract these figures from a file and then to write a Perl script to compare the values of concern. It is also possible that errors could be masked by integers being "wrapped around" and starting at zero after they reach values that are greater than the maximum available for a machine's architecture. This should not be a problem for 64-bit kernels.

Viewing Network Interfaces

The ifconfig command is responsible for configuring each network interface at boot time. ifconfig can also be used to check the status of active network interfaces by passing the -a parameter:

```
router# ifconfig -a
lo0: flags=849<UP,LOOPBACK,RUNNING,MULTICAST> mtu 8232
        inet 127.0.0.1 netmask ff000000
hme0: flags=863<UP,BROADCAST,NOTRAILERS,RUNNING,MULTICAST> mtu 1500
        inet 10.17.65.16 netmask ffffff00 broadcast 10.17.65.255
hme1: flags=863<UP,BROADCAST,NOTRAILERS,RUNNING,MULTICAST> mtu 1500
        inet 204.17.65.16 netmask ffffff00 broadcast 204.17.65.255
```

In this case, the primary interface hme0 is running on the internal network, while the secondary interface hme1 is visible to the external network. The netmask for a Class C network is used on both interfaces, while both have a distinct broadcast address. This ensures that information broadcast on the internal network is not visible to the external network. Several parameters are shown with ifconfig -a, including whether or not the interface is up or down (active or inactive). In the following example, the interface has not been enabled at boot time:

```
server# ifconfig hme1
hme1: flags=863<DOWN,BROADCAST,NOTRAILERS,RUNNING,MULTICAST> mtu 1500
        inet 204.17.64.16 netmask ffffff00 broadcast 204.17.64.255
```

If the /etc/ethers database has been updated by the administrator to include details of the Ethernet addresses of hosts on the local network, then an entry is also displayed about the corresponding interface when using ifconfig:

```
server# cat /etc/ethers
8:0:19:7:f2:a1 server
server# ifconfig hme1
```

```
hme1: flags=863<UP,BROADCAST,NOTRAILERS,RUNNING,MULTICAST> mtu 1500
        inet 204.17.128.16 netmask ffffff00 broadcast 204.17.128.255
ether 8:0:19:7:f2:a1
```

It can also be useful when detecting problems with a routing network interface to examine the address resolution protocol results for the LAN. This will determine whether or not the interface is visible to its clients:

```
server# arp -a
Net to Media Table
Device   IP Address                        Mask         Flags   Phys Addr
------   -------------------  ---------------  -----   ---------------
hme0    server1.cassowary.net 255.255.255.255          00:c0:ff:19:48:d8
hme0    server2.cassowary.net 255.255.255.255          c2:d4:78:00:15:56
hme0    server3.cassowary.net 255.255.255.255          87:b3:9a:c2:e9:ea
```

Modifying Interface Parameters

Two methods are available for modifying network interface parameters. Firstly, the ifconfig command can be used to modify operational parameters and to bring an interface online (up), or shut it down (down). Secondly, one can use ndd to set parameters for a TCP/IP transmission, which will affect all network interfaces. In this section, we will examine both of these methods, and how they can be used to manage interfaces and improve performance.

It is sometimes necessary to shut down and start up a network interface in order to upgrade drivers or install patches affecting network service. To shut down a network interface, for example, one can use the command

```
server# ifconfig hme1 down
server# ifconfig hme1
hme1: flags=863<DOWN,BROADCAST,NOTRAILERS,RUNNING,MULTICAST> mtu 1500
        inet 204.17.64.16 netmask ffffff00 broadcast 204.17.64.255
```

It is also possible to bring this interface back up by using ifconfig:

```
server# ifconfig hme1 up
server# ifconfig hme1
hme1: flags=863<UP,BROADCAST,NOTRAILERS,RUNNING,MULTICAST> mtu 1500
        inet 204.17.64.16 netmask ffffff00 broadcast 204.17.64.255
```

ndd is used to set parameters for network protocols, including TCP, IP, UDP, and the Address Resolution Protocol (ARP). It can be used to modify the parameters associated with IP forwarding and routing. For example, let's look at the set of configurable parameters for TCP transmission:

```
server# ndd /dev/tcp \?
?                              (read only)
tcp_close_wait_interval        (read and write)
tcp_conn_req_max_q             (read and write)
tcp_conn_req_max_q0            (read and write)
tcp_conn_req_min               (read and write)
tcp_conn_grace_period          (read and write)
tcp_cwnd_max                   (read and write)
tcp_debug                      (read and write)
tcp_smallest_nonpriv_port      (read and write)
tcp_ip_abort_cinterval         (read and write)
tcp_ip_abort_linterval         (read and write)
tcp_ip_abort_interval          (read and write)
tcp_ip_notify_cinterval        (read and write)
tcp_ip_notify_interval         (read and write)
tcp_ip_ttl                     (read and write)
tcp_keepalive_interval         (read and write)
tcp_maxpsz_multiplier          (read and write)
tcp_mss_def                    (read and write)
tcp_mss_max                    (read and write)
tcp_mss_min                    (read and write)
tcp_naglim_def                 (read and write)
tcp_rexmit_interval_initial    (read and write)
tcp_rexmit_interval_max        (read and write)
tcp_rexmit_interval_min        (read and write)
tcp_wroff_xtra                 (read and write)
tcp_deferred_ack_interval      (read and write)
tcp_snd_lowat_fraction         (read and write)
tcp_sth_rcv_hiwat              (read and write)
tcp_sth_rcv_lowat              (read and write)
tcp_dupack_fast_retransmit     (read and write)
tcp_ignore_path_mtu            (read and write)
tcp_rcv_push_wait              (read and write)
tcp_smallest_anon_port         (read and write)
tcp_largest_anon_port          (read and write)
tcp_xmit_hiwat                 (read and write)
tcp_xmit_lowat                 (read and write)
tcp_recv_hiwat                 (read and write)
tcp_recv_hiwat_minmss          (read and write)
tcp_fin_wait_2_flush_interval  (read and write)
tcp_co_min                     (read and write)
tcp_max_buf                    (read and write)
tcp_zero_win_probesize         (read and write)
tcp_strong_iss                 (read and write)
tcp_rtt_updates                (read and write)
tcp_wscale_always              (read and write)
tcp_tstamp_always              (read and write)
tcp_tstamp_if_wscale           (read and write)
tcp_rexmit_interval_extra      (read and write)
tcp_deferred_acks_max          (read and write)
tcp_slow_start_after_idle      (read and write)
tcp_slow_start_initial         (read and write)
tcp_co_timer_interval          (read and write)
```

```
tcp_extra_priv_ports          (read only)
tcp_extra_priv_ports_add      (write only)
tcp_extra_priv_ports_del      (write only)
tcp_status                    (read only)
tcp_bind_hash                 (read only)
tcp_listen_hash               (read only)
tcp_conn_hash                 (read only)
tcp_queue_hash                (read only)
tcp_host_param                (read and write)
tcp_1948_phrase               (write only)
```

Parameters can also be set for IP as well as TCP. For example, if the parameter ip_forwarding has a value of two (the default), it will only perform routing when two or more interfaces are active. However, if this parameter is set to zero, then ip_forwarding will never be performed (that is, to ensure that multihoming is enabled rather than routing). This can be set by using the command:

```
server# ndd -set /dev/ip ip_forwarding 0
```

To ensure that this configuration is preserved from boot to boot, it is possible to edit the networking startup file /etc/rc2.d/S69inet and add this line to any others that configure the network interfaces.

It may be necessary to set several of these parameters in a production environment to ensure optimal performance, especially when application servers and Web servers are in use. For example, when a Web server makes a request to port 80 using TCP, a connection is opened and closed. However, the connection is kept open for a default time of two minutes to ensure that all packets are correctly received. For a system with a large number of clients, this can lead to a bottleneck of stale TCP connections, which can significantly impact the performance of the Web server. Fortunately, the parameter that controls this behavior (tcp_close_wait_interval) can be set using ndd to something more sensible (like 30 seconds):

```
server# ndd -set /dev/tcp tcp_close_wait_interval 30000
```

However, administrators should be aware that altering this parameter will affect all TCP services, so although a Web server might perform optimally with tcp_close_wait_interval equal to 30 seconds, a database listener that handles large datasets may require a much wider time window. The best way to determine optimal values is to perform experiments with low, moderate, and peak levels of traffic for both the Web server and the database listener to determine a value that will provide reasonable performance for both applications. It is also important to check SunSolve for the latest patches and updates for recently discovered kernel bugs.

IP Routing

Now that we have discussed how to install, configure, and tune network interfaces, we shall turn our attention to setting up routing by explaining how packets are transferred by hosts to routers and are exchanged between routers. We will also examine how to troubleshoot routing problems with traceroute and introduce the different routing protocols that are currently being used on the Internet.

Two kinds of routing exist: static and dynamic. Static routing is common in simple networks with only a few hosts and networks interconnected. Static routing is much simpler to implement than dynamic routing, which is suitable for large networks, where the routes between networks cannot be readily specified. For example, if your organizational network has only two routers connecting three networks, then the number of routes that need to be installed statically is four (the square of the number of routers). In contrast, for a building with five routers, the number of routes that needs to specified statically is 25. If a router configuration changes, then all of the static configuration files on all of the routers need to be changed (no mechanism exists for the "discovery" of routes). Alternatively, if a router fails because of a hardware fault, then packets may not be able to be correctly routed. Dynamic routing solves all of these problems, but requires more processing overhead on each router. Two related dynamic routing daemons are available: in.rdisc, the router discovery daemon, and in.routed, the route daemon; the latter's configuration will be discussed at length in this section.

Overview of Packet Delivery

Before we examine the differences between static and dynamic routing in detail, let's take a step back and consider how information is passed between two systems, whether the exchange is host-host, host-router, or router-router. All information is exchanged in the form of discrete packets, which is the smallest unit of information that is transmitted between hosts using TCP/IP. A packet contains both a header, and a message component, as shown in Figure 21-3.

In order to deliver packets from one host to another host successfully, each packet contains information in the header that is similar to an envelope; it contains the address of the destination machine and the address of the source machine. The message section of the packet contains the actual data to be transferred. Packets are often transferred on the transport layer using the Transmission Control Protocol (TCP), which guarantees the delivery of packets, while some applications use UDP, where the continuity of a connection cannot be guaranteed. In normal TCP transmission mode, only 64K of data can be transferred in a single session, unless large window support is enabled, in which case, up to 1G of data can be transmitted. The header can also have

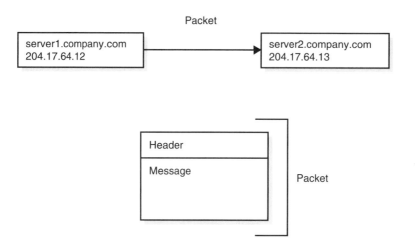

Packet

server1.company.com
204.17.64.12

server2.company.com
204.17.64.13

Header

Message

Packet

Figure 21-3 A packet has both a message and a header.

information inserted by the source machine, which is referred to as data encapsulation. The action of passing a packet is referred to as a hop, so routing involves enabling packets to hop from a source host to any arbitrary host on the Internet.

In order for packets to be delivered correctly between two hosts, all intermediate routers must be able to determine where the packets have come from and where they must be delivered to. This can be achieved by referring to a host by using its IP address (such as 203.16.42.58) or its fully qualified domain name (server.cassowary.net). Although it is also possible to refer to a machine by its Ethernet (hardware) address, it is often preferred in TCP/IP to use a logical rather than a physical representation of a machine's network interface card (NIC).

Sending a packet across a network makes full use of all network layers. For example, if a telnet session is to be established between two machines, the application protocol specifies how the message and header are to be constructed, which is information that is then passed to the Transport Layer protocol. For a telnet session, the Transport Layer protocol is TCP, which proceeds with encapsulation of the packet's data, that is split into segments. The data is divided depending on the size of the TCP window enabled by the system. Each segment has a header and a checksum, which is used by the destination host to determine whether a received packet is likely to be free of corruption.

When a segment is due to be transmitted from the source host, a three-way handshake occurs between the source and the destination. A synchronization (SYN) segment is sent to the destination host requesting a connection, and an acknowledgement (ACK) is returned to the source when the destination host is ready to receive.

When the ACK is received by the source host, its receipt is acknowledged back to the destination, and transmission proceeds with data being passed to the IP layer, where segments are realized as IP datagrams. IP also adds a header to the segment and passes it to the physical networking layer for transport.

A common method of enacting a "denial of service" attack on a remote host involves sending many SYN requests to a remote host, without completing the three-way handshake. Solaris now limits the maximum number of connections with "handshake incomplete," in order to solve the problem. When a packet finally arrives at the destination host, it travels through the TCP/IP protocol stack in the reverse order from that which it took on the sender, just like a deck of cards that has been dealt onto a playing table and retrieved from the top of the pack.

The story becomes more complicated when packets need to be passed through several hosts to reach their ultimate destination. Although the method of passing data from source to destination is the same, the next hop along the route needs to be determined somehow. The path that a packet takes across the network depends on the IP address of the destination host, as specified in the packet header. If the destination host is on the local network, it can be delivered immediately without the intervention of a separate router.

For example, a source host 204.12.60.24 on the Class C network 204.12.60.0 can directly pass a packet to a destination 204.12.60.32. However, once a packet needs to be delivered beyond the local network, the process becomes more complicated. The packet is passed to the router on the local network (which may be defined in /etc/defaultrouter), and a router table is consulted. The router table contains a list of the hosts on the local network and other routers to which the router has a connection.

The router for the 204.12.60.0 network might be 204.12.60.64. Thus, a packet from 204.12.60.24 would be passed to 204.12.60.64 if the destination host is not on the 204.12.60.0 network. The router 204.12.60.64 may have a second interface 204.12.61.64 that connects the 204.12.60.0 and 204.12.59.0 networks. If the destination host is 204.12.59.28, the packet could now be delivered directly to the host because the router bridges the two networks. However, if the packet is not deliverable to a host on the 204.12.59.0 network, then it must be passed to another router defined in the current router's tables.

traceroute

If the process of finding a route is difficult to conceptualize, Solaris provides the traceroute tool to literally display the route taken by a packet between two hosts. The traceroute utility measures the time taken to reach each intermediate host from source to destination. If an intermediate host cannot be reached in a specified time period (usually the time to live [TTL] field), an error message is reported. A maximum number of hops (usually 30) is specified to prevent traceroute from looping infinitely if an operational route cannot be found. traceroute is also very useful for determining network points of failure due to misconfiguration and hardware problems.

Here is an example of a traceroute between a host on the AT&T network and a host on the Sun network:

```
client% traceroute www.sun.com
Tracing route to wwwwseast.usec.sun.com [192.9.49.30]
over a maximum of 30 hops:
  1   184 ms   142 ms   138 ms   202.10.4.131
  2   147 ms   144 ms   138 ms   202.10.4.129
  3   150 ms   142 ms   144 ms   202.10.1.73
  4   150 ms   144 ms   141 ms   atm11-0-0-11.ia4.optus.net.au [202.139.32.17]
  5   148 ms   143 ms   139 ms   202.139.1.197
  6   490 ms   489 ms   474 ms   hssi9-0-0.sf1.optus.net.au [192.65.89.246]
  7   526 ms   480 ms   485 ms   g-sfd-br-02-f12-0.gn.cwix.net [207.124.109.57]
  8   494 ms   482 ms   485 ms   core7-hssi6-0-0.SanFrancisco.cw.net
[204.70.10.9]
  9   483 ms   489 ms   484 ms   corerouter2.SanFrancisco.cw.net [204.70.9.132]
 10   557 ms   552 ms   561 ms   xcore3.Boston.cw.net [204.70.150.81]
 11   566 ms   572 ms   554 ms   sun-micro-system.Boston.cw.net
[204.70.179.102]
 12   577 ms   574 ms   558 ms   wwwwseast.usec.sun.com [192.9.49.30]
Trace complete.
```

Static Routes

On hosts, routing information can be extracted in two ways: by building a full routing table, exactly as it does on a router, or by creating a minimal kernel table, containing a single default route for each available router (static routing). The most common static route is from a host to a local router, as specified in the /etc/defaultrouter file. For example, for the host 204.12.60.24, the entry in /etc/defaultrouter might be

```
204.12.60.64
```

This places a single route in the local routing table. The responsibility for determining the next hop for the message is then passed to the router. Static routes can also be added for servers using in.routed by defining them in the /etc/gateways file. When using static routing, routing tables in the kernel are defined when the system boots and do not normally change, unless modified by using the route or ifconfig command. When a local network has a single gateway to the rest of the Internet, static routing is the most appropriate choice.

Routing Protocols

The Routing Information Protocol (RIP) and the Router Discovery Protocol (RDISC) are the two standard routing protocols for TCP/IP networks, and Solaris supports both. RIP is implemented by in.routed, the routing daemon, and is usually configured to start during multi-user mode startup. The route daemon always populates the routing table with a route to every reachable network, but whether or not it advertises its routing availability to other systems is optional.

Hosts use the RDISC daemon (in.rdisc) to collect information about routing availability from routers. RDISC is implemented by in.rdisc, which should run on both routers and hosts. in.rdisc typically creates a default route for each router that responds to requests. This route discovery is central to the capability of RDISC-enabled hosts to dynamically adjust to network changes. Routers that only run in.routed cannot be discovered by RDISC-enabled hosts. For hosts running both in.rdisc and in.routed, the latter will operate until an RDISC-enabled router is discovered on the network, in which case, RDISC will take over routing.

The Kernel Routing Table

The routing table maintains an index of routes to networks and routers that are available to the local host. Routes can be determined dynamically, by using RDISC for example, or can be added manually by using route or ifconfig. These commands are normally used at boot time to initialize network services.

Three kinds of routes exist: host routes, which map a path from the local host to another host on the local network; network routes, which enable packets to be transferred from the local hosts to other hosts on the local network; and default routes, which pass the task of finding a route to a router. Both RIP and RDISC daemons can use default routes. Dynamic routing often causes changes in the routing table after booting, when a minimal routing table is configured by ifconfig when initializing each network interface, as the daemons manage changes in the network configuration and router availability.

Viewing the Routing Table (netstat -r)

The command netstat -r shows the current routing table. Routes are always specified as a connection between the local server and a remote machine, via some kind of gateway. The output from the netstat -r command contains several different flags. Flag U indicates that the route between the destination and gateway is up, while flag G shows that the route passes through a gateway. Flag H indicates that the route connects to a host, while the D flag signifies that the route was dynamically created using a redirect.

Three other columns are shown in the routing table. Ref indicates the number of concurrent routes occupying the same link layer, while Use indicates the number of packets transmitted along the route (on a specific Interface).

The following example shows an example server (server.cassowary.net) that has four routes. The first is for the loopback address (lo0), which is up and is connected through a host, and the second route is for the local Class C network (204.16.64.0) through the gateway gateway.cassowary.net., which is also up. The third route is the special multicast route, which is up, while the fourth route is the default route, pointing to the local network router, which is also up.

```
bash-2.03$ netstat -r

Routing Table:
   Destination              Gateway                  Flags  Ref   Use   Interface
-------------------- ------------------------ ----- ----- ----- ---------
127.0.0.1                localhost                UH     0     877   lo0
204.17.64.0              gateway.cassowary.net    U      3      85   hme0
BASE-ADDRESS.MCAST.NET   host.cassowary.net       U      3       0   hme0
default                  router.cassowary.net     UG     0     303
```

Manipulating the Routing Table (route)

The route command is used to manually manipulate the routing tables. If dynamic routing is working correctly, it should not normally be necessary to do this. However, if static is being used, or the RDISC daemon does not discover any routes, it may be necessary to add routes manually. In addition, it may also be necessary to delete routes explicitly for security purposes. You should be aware, though, that except for interface changes, the routing daemon may not respond to any modifications to the routing table that may have been enacted manually. It is best to shutdown the routing daemon first before making changes and then restart it after all changes have been initiated.

Adding Host Routes

To add a direct route to another host, the route command is used with the syntax:

```
route add -host destination_ip local_ip -interface
```

Thus, if we wanted to add a route between the local host (204.12.17.1) and a host on a neighboring Class C network (204.12.16.100) for the primary interface hme0, we would use the command:

```
add -host 204.12.16.100 204.12.17.1 -interface hme0
```

Adding Network Routes

To add a direct route to another network, the route command is used with the syntax:

```
route add -net destination_network_ip local_ip" -netmask
```

If we wanted to add a route between the local host (204.12.17.1) and the same network as the host we specified previously (the 204.12.16.0 network) for the Class C netmask (255.255.255.0), we would use the command:

```
route add -net 204.12.16.0 204.12.17.1 -netmask 255.255.255.0
```

Adding a Default Route

To add a default route, the route command can be used with the syntax

```
route add default hostname -interface
```

For example, to add a default route to a local router (204.54.56.1) for a secondary interface hme1, you can use the command:

```
route add default 204.54.56.1 -interface hme1
```

Dynamic Routing

In this section, we will look more closely at the RIP and RDISC dynamic routing protocols. A prerequisite for dynamic routing to operate is that the /etc/defaultrouter file should be empty.

routed

in.routed is the network routing daemon and is responsible for dynamically managing entries in the kernel routing tables, as described previously. It usually starts from a line during multi-user boot (/etc/rc2.d/S69inet) using the command

```
/usr/sbin/in.routed -q
```

The routing daemon uses port 520 to route packets and to establish which interfaces are currently up and which are down. in.routed listens for requests for packets and for known routes from remote hosts. This supplies hosts on a network with the information they need to determine how many hops it is to a host. When it is initialized, the routing daemon checks both the passive and active gateways specified in /etc/gateways.

It is also possible to run the routing daemon in a special space-saving mode that retains only the default routes in the routing table. Although this may leave a system at the mercy of a faulty router, it does save space and reduces the resources that in.routed requires to maintain lists of active routes that are periodically updated. This can be enabled by initializing in.routed with the -S parameter.

rdisc

The rdisc daemon uses the ICMP router discovery protocol and is usually executed on both hosts and routers at boot time, when routers broadcast their availability and hosts start listening for available routers. Routers broadcast their availability using the 224.0.0.1 multicast address. Routers that share a network with a host are selected first as the default route, if one is found. Another approach is for the host to send out a broadcast on the 224.0.0.2 multicast address to solicit any available routers. In either case, if a router is available, it will accept packet-forwarding requests from the host concerned.

Summary

In this chapter, we've examined how Solaris networks can be built around subnets connected by routers. These routers can be dedicated hardware devices or Solaris servers. In addition, we looked at the different daemons that have the responsibility of routing.

Questions

1. Name the three major types of subnets supported by Solaris.
    A. Class 1, Class 2, Class 3
    B. Class A, Class B, Class C
    C. T1, broadband, cable
    D. None of the above

2. What is the purpose of a router?
    A. To pass information from one network to another
    B. To pass information between two hosts only
    C. To provide two independent network interfaces on a single host
    D. None of the above

3. What is the main requirement of a router?
    A. To be connected to the Internet
    B. To run Solaris 8

   C. To have multiple network interfaces

   D. None of the above

4. What would be contained in the file /etc/hostname.hme0?

   A. A hostname

   B. A fully qualified domain name

   C. An IP address

   D. The default router's hostname

5. What is contained in the file /etc/defaultrouter?

   A. The local router's hostname

   B. The local router's IP address

   C. The local router's hostname or IP address

   D. The local router's netmask

6. Which file should be created for a non-routing, multihomed host?

   A. /etc/noroute

   B. /etc/notrouter

   C. /etc/notroute

   D. /etc/!route

7. Which command is used to set parameters for network protocols?

   A. tcp

   B. ip

   C. tip

   D. ndd

Answers

1. B

2. A

3. C

4. C

5. C

6. B

7. D

Installing a Server

The following objectives will be met upon completing this chapter's material:

- Understanding the differences between a client and server system.
- Reviewing the new features of Solaris 8 servers.
- Reviewing which software packages and CD-ROMs make up the Solaris 8 server distribution.
- Understanding hardware configurations that are supported by Solaris 8 servers.
- Learning about server pre-installation tasks.
- Installing Solaris 8 servers using the Web Start wizard.

Clients and Servers

In Chapter 4, we examined the procedures behind the installation of a single host. In Solaris networks, hosts are either clients or servers (or in some cases, both). A client is simply a host that uses another host (the server) to perform some operation that is greater than its own capacity to carry out the task. For example, an E10000 system with 64 central processing units (CPUs) can obviously compute more floating-point operations per second than a Sparc 10. If a Mathematica user on the Sparc 10 uses a graphic user interface (GUI) to display graphics but uses MathLink to connect through to the E10000 to perform the majority of computations, then the Sparc 10 is said to be a client of the E10000 server.

Why are client-server relationships so critical to Solaris networks, when the average desktop PC is now hundreds of times faster than its predecessors? A client-server arrangement can be preferred to a peer-to-peer arrangement for several good reasons:

- The management of mission-critical services can be centrally administered on a single host, rather than having to administer multiple systems. This saves time and protects data.

- Fast CPUs and memory can be centralized to provide a large pool of processing capacity for all users of the server, rather than enabling each user to have a single, fast CPU on their desktop. Most PCs spend their days displaying screensavers, while centralized server systems operate at peak loads constantly. The client-server approach is cost-effective.

- The administration of software can be centralized, while software installation and updates on client systems can be minimized. This reduces the number of administrators required to manage entire networks.

Notice in each of these points that we've used the term "centralize" quite often. Centralization is the key characteristic of client-server networks that promotes the cost- and time-effective utilization of host resources in the long term. Take the suggested client-server scenario suggested by Sun, which is based around departments and organizational units putting so-called "thin clients" in the form of Sun Ray systems on desktops that connect to E450 servers over high-speed Ethernet switches. This removes bulky PCs from desktops, replacing them with a small footprint client that's about the size of this book. In addition, no local software installation is required, apart from firmware updates. The systems boot across the network using the Reverse Address Resolution Protocol (RARP) daemon and the Network File System (NFS). Sun Rays provide a full Common Desktop Environment (CDE) interface, and all clients share the CPU capacity of their centralized servers.

Client-server architectures do have their drawbacks. If a centralized system fails, all of the clients will be unable to work. However, with appropriate high-availability strategies in place, this issue should not affect most systems.

Solaris 8 Server Innovations

Sun has released a new batch of server-side products to improve upon the existing functionality of SunOS with Solaris 8. Of interest to those in the data center will be the new 2.2 release of Sun's Cluster product, which offers high system availability through management of hardware redundancy. This offering caters largely to the corporate world, but developers who are more interested in championing open-source technologies will also be pleased with the inclusion of lxrun, a platform for binary compatibility between Linux applications and the Solaris operating environment. Originally developed for

UNIX systems distributed by the Santa Cruz Operation (SCO), lxrun enables applications developed for Linux and released with a binary-only codebase to be executed natively on the Solaris x86 platform without recompilation or modification. This will ultimately lead to a greater exchange of technology and ideas between Solaris and Linux users.

Clustering Technology

Confidence in server reliability is often gained by the use of hardware redundancy, which can be achieved on a filesystem-by-filesystem basis, by using a software solution like DiskSuite, or a hardware-based solution like an A1000 RAID drive. This enables partitions to be actively mirrored, so that in the event of a hardware failure, service can be rapidly resumed, and missing data can be rapidly restored.

This approach is fine for single-server systems that do not require close to 100 percent uptime. However, for mission-critical applications, where the integrity of the whole server is at stake, it makes sense to invest in clustering technology. Quite simply, clusters are what the name suggests: groups of similar servers (or nodes) that have similar functions and that share responsibility for providing system and application services. Clustering is commonly found in the financial world, where downtime is measured in hundreds of thousands of dollars, and not in minutes. Large organizations need to undertake a cost-benefit analysis to determine whether clustering is an effective technology for their needs. However, Sun has made the transition to clustering easier by integrating the Cluster product with Solaris 8.

Although Solaris 8 currently ships with Cluster 2.2, Cluster 3.0 will ship with a later Solaris 8 release. It offers even more functionality, with a clustered virtual file system, and cluster-wide load balancing. For more information on introducing clustering technology using Sun Cluster, see Paul Korzeniowski's technical article at **www.sun.com/ clusters/article.**

lxrun

One of the advantages of Solaris 8 for Intel x86 over its Sparc companion is the greater interoperability between computers based on Intel architectures. This means that a greater potential exists for cooperation between Linux and Solaris, which both operate on Intel. This potential has been realized recently with the efforts of Steve Ginzburg and Solaris engineers, who developed lxrun, which remaps system calls embedded in Linux software binaries to those appropriate for the Solaris environment. This means that Linux binaries can run without recompilation or modification on Solaris. In some ways, lxrun is like the Java virtual machine in that Linux applications execute through a layer that separates the application from the operating system. This means that your favorite Linux applications are now directly available through Solaris, including the following:

- KDE
- Gnome
- WordPerfect 7 and 8
- Applix
- Quake 2
- GIMP

For more information on lxrun, see its home page at **www.ugcs.caltech.edu/ ~steven/lxrun**.

Solaris 8 Security Innovations

Security is a major concern for Solaris administrators. The Internet is rapidly expanding with the new IPv6 protocol set to completely supercede IPv4 sometime in the next few years. This will enable many more addresses to be available for Internet hosts than are currently available. It also means that the number of crackers, thieves, and rogue users will also increase exponentially. Solaris 8 prepares your network for this "virtual onslaught" by embracing IPv6, not only for its autoconfiguration and network numbering features, but because of the built-in security measures that form part of the protocol. In particular, authentication is a key issue, after many highly publicized IP-spoofing breaches reported in the popular press over the past few years.

A second layer of authentication for internal networks and intranets is provided in Solaris 8 by the provision of Kerberos version 5 clients and daemons. Previous releases, such as Solaris 7, only included support for Kerberos version 4.

Kerberos Version 5

Kerberos is the primary means of network authentication employed by many organizations to centralize authentication services. As a protocol, it is designed to provide strong authentication for client/server applications by using secret-key cryptography. Recall that Kerberos is designed to provide authentication to hosts inside and outside a firewall, as long as the appropriate realms have been created. The protocol requires a certificate granting and validation system based around "tickets," which are distributed between clients and the server. A connection request from a client to a server takes a convoluted but secure route from a centralized authentication server before being forwarded to the target server. This ticket authorizes the client to request a specific service from a specific host, generally for a specific time period. A common analogy is a parking ticket machine that grants the drivers of motor vehicles permission to park in a specific street for one or two hours only.

Kerberos version 5 contains many enhancements over Kerberos version 4, including ticket renewal, which removes some of the overhead involved in repetitive network requests. In addition, a pluggable authentication module features support for RPC. The new version of Kerberos also provides both server- and user-level authentication, featuring a role-based access control feature that assigns access rights and permissions more stringently, ensuring system integrity. In addition to advances on the software front, Solaris 8 also provides integrated support for Kerberos and Smart card technology using the Open Card Framework (OCF) 1.1. More information concerning Kerberos is available from MIT at **http://web.mit.edu/network/kerberos-form.html**.

IPv6

IPv6, described in RFC 2471, is the replacement IP protocol for IPv4, which is currently deployed worldwide. The Internet relies on IP for negotiating many transport-related transactions on the Internet, including routing and the domain name service (DNS). This means that host information is often stored locally (and inefficiently) at each network node. It is clearly important to establish a protocol that is more general in function, but more centralized for administration, and that can deal with the expanding requirements of the Internet.

One of the growing areas of the Internet is obviously the number of hosts that need to be addressed. Many subnets are already exhausted, and the situation is likely to get worse. In addition, every IP address needs to be manually allocated to each individual machine on the Internet, which makes the usage of addresses within a subnet sparse and less than optimal. Clearly, a need exists for a degree of centralization when organizing IP addresses that can be handled through local administration, and through protocols like the Dynamic Host Configuration Protocol (DHCP). However, one of the key improvements of IPv6 over IPv4 is its auto-configuration capabilities, which make it easier to configure entire subnets and to renumber existing hosts.

In addition, security is now included at the IP level, making host-to-host authentication more efficient and reliable, even enabling data encryption. One way that this is achieved is by authentication header extensions. This enables a target host to determine whether or not a packet actually originates from a source host. This prevents common attacks, like IP spoofing and denial of service, and reduces reliance on a third-party firewall by locking in security at the packet level. Although IPv6 is included with the Solaris 8 distribution, it is also now available separately for Solaris at **http://playground. sun.com/pub/solaris2-ipv6/html/solaris2-ipv6.html**. Tools are also included with Solaris 8 to assist with IPv4-to-IPv6 migration.

IP Security (IPSec)

Virtual Private Network (VPN) technology is also provided with Solaris 8, using IP Security (IPSec). IPSec is compatible with both IPv4 and IPv6, making it easier to connect hosts using both new and existing networking protocols. IPSec consists of a combination of IP tunneling and encryption technologies in order to create sessions across the Internet that are as secure as possible. IP tunneling makes it difficult for unauthorized users (such as intruders) to access data that is being transmitted between two hosts on different sites. This is supported by encryption technologies and an improved method for exchanging keys using the Internet key exchange (IKE) method. IKE facilitates interprotocol negotiation and selection during host-to-host transactions, ensuring data integrity. By implementing encryption at the IP layer, it will be even more difficult for rogue users to "pretend" to be a target host, intercepting data with authorization.

Solaris 8 Distribution

The Solaris server operating environment is typically not available in your local computer store. It must be obtained directly from Sun or through an authorized reseller. The good news is that if your Sparc system has eight CPUs or less, you may now obtain a Solaris license free of charge by applying directly to Sun. The catch is that you must pay for postage and handling, which Sun calculates to be $75 per package. This is an increase of the previous shipping and handling charges associated with previous editions of the "free" Solaris program. However, the new package has a number of value-added extras, including the Oracle database server. It is also possible to obtain the source code to Solaris at **www.sun.com/software/solaris/source**.

The free Solaris license program is targeted at both home users who want to take advantage of the Solaris platform's stability for using Star Office and other productivity applications as well as Solaris developers who want to deploy on the Solaris platform. More information is available from **www.sun.com/software/solaris/binaries**.

The Solaris 8 media pack comes with several CDs, including the following:

- A Web Start Installation CD, which is used to install the Solaris operating environment

- Two Solaris software CDs, which contain all of the standard Solaris packages

- Solaris documentation CDs, which contain all of the Solaris documentation in Answer Book format

- A languages CD, which contains local customizations for nine different languages

- The Star Office 5.2 productivity suite

- Forte for Java-integrated development environments

- A GNU software CD

- The iPlanet software suite, which provides a Web server, a directory server, a certificate manager, a Sun screen firewall, and an application server

- An Oracle database server

- A supplemental software CD, including support for OpenGL, Java 3D, and advanced networking support, including SunATM, SunFDDI, and Sun Gigabit-Ethernet

The server configuration for Solaris Scalable Processor Architecture (SPARC) is approximately 2.4 G in size (the entire distribution plus Original Equipment Manufacturer [OEM] support).

Supported Hardware

Sun has developed a wide range of hardware systems over the past few years, much of which are still supported by Solaris 8. These systems are based on the SPARC, which is managed by a SPARC member organization (**www.sparc.org**). In addition to Sun Microsystems, Fujitsu (**www.fujitsu.com**) and T.Sqware (**www.tsqware.com**) also build SPARC-compliant CPU systems. System vendors who sell systems based on SPARC CPUs include Amdahl Corporation (**www.amdahl.com**), Tatung (**www.tatung.com**), Tadpole (**www.tadpole.com**), and Toshiba (**www.toshiba.com**). Vendors of system boards and peripherals for SPARC CPU-based systems include Hitachi (**www. hitachi.com**), Seagate (**www.seagate.com**), and Kingston Technology (**www.kingston. com**). Although media critics and competitors often paint SPARC systems from Sun as standalone, vendor-specific traps for the unwary, the reality is that a large number of hardware vendors also support the SPARC platform. It should also be noted that software vendors, such as Red Hat, also support SPARC versions of Linux, meaning that Solaris is not the only operating system that powers the SPARC platform. The SPARC standards can be downloaded free of charge from **www.sparc.org/standards.html**.

Often, administrators of Linux and Microsoft Windows systems, who are used to PC hardware, are incredulous to discover that some supported systems (such as the

SPARCclassic) have CPUs that run at sub-100 MHz. This must seem a slow CPU speed in the age of Intel CPUs and their clones reaching the 1-GHz mark. However, CPU speed is only one component that contributes to the overall performance of a system. SPARC systems are renowned for their high-speed buses and very fast I/O performance. In addition, many SPARC systems were designed for continuous operation. It is not unheard of for systems to have several years of uptime, compared to several days for other operating systems. The many impressive features of the Solaris operating systems were developed with the SPARC hardware platform as a target, and these systems naturally have the best performance.

However, Sun has not ignored hardware developments and emerging standards. In recent years, they have created the Ultra series of workstations and servers, which feature a PCI bus and compatibility with Super VGA (SVGA) multi-sync monitors commonly sold with PC systems. Of course, SPARC systems have always supported the Small Computer Systems Interface (SCSI) standard, and all SCSI devices will work with Solaris. At the same time, Sun has proceeded with innovations, such as the 64-CPU Enterprise 10000 system, which can operate as a single system with massively parallel computational capabilities, or it can be logically partitioned to act as up to 64 different systems. Imagine being able to control an entire Application Service Provider (ASP), with no apparent "shared hosting" to the client, which is actually being serviced by a single physical system. Although the upfront cost of an E10000 far exceeds that required for 64 systems running Linux or Microsoft Windows, only one administrator is required to manage an E10000, while 64 different systems might require more than one administrator.

Supported SPARC Platforms

The following SPARC systems are supported under Solaris 8:

- SPARCclassic
- SPARCstation LX
- SPARCstation 4
- SPARCstation 5
- SPARCstation 10
- SPARCstation 20
- Ultra 1 (including Creator and Creator 3D models)
- Enterprise 1
- Ultra 2 (including Creator and Creator 3D models)

- Ultra 5
- Ultra 10
- Ultra 30
- Ultra 60
- Ultra 450
- Blade 100
- Blade 1000
- Enterprise 2
- Enterprise 150
- Enterprise 250
- Enterprise 450
- Enterprise 3000
- Enterprise 3500
- Enterprise 4000
- Enterprise 4500
- Enterprise 5000
- Enterprise 5500
- Enterprise 6000
- Enterprise 10000
- SPARCserver 1000
- SPARCcenter 2000

Some popular systems are no longer supported, such as the SPARCstation 1 and SPARCstation 2. Often, these can be upgraded with a firmware or CPU change to be compatible with Solaris 8. In addition, a minimum of 64MB of RAM is required to install Solaris 8. The installer will not let you proceed unless it can detect this amount of physical RAM, so be sure to check that your system meets the basic requirements before attempting to install Solaris 8.

Device Nomenclature

One of the most challenging aspects of understanding Solaris hardware is the device names and references used by Solaris to manage devices. Solaris uses a specific set of naming conventions to associate physical devices with instance names on the operating system. In addition, devices can also be referred to by their device name, which is associated with a device file created in the /dev directory after configuration.

For example, a hard disk may have the physical device name /pci@1f,0/pci@1,1/ ide@3/dad@0,0, which is associated with the device file /dev/dsk/c0t0d0. The benefit of the more complex Solaris device names and physical device references is that it is easy to interpret the characteristics of each device by looking at its name. For the disk example given previously, we can see that the IDE hard drive is located on a PCI bus at target 0. When we view the amount of free disk space on the system, for example, it is easy to identify slices on the same disk by looking at the device name:

```
bash-2.03# df -k
Filesystem           kbytes     used    avail capacity  Mounted on
/proc                     0        0        0     0%     /proc
/dev/dsk/c0t0d0s0   1982988   615991  1307508    33%     /
fd                        0        0        0     0%     /dev/fd
/dev/dsk/c0t0d0s3   1487119   357511  1070124    26%     /usr
swap                 182040      416   181624     1%     /tmp
```

Here we can see that /dev/dsk/c0t0d0s0 and /dev/dsk/c0t0d0s3 are slice 0 and slice 3 of the disk /dev/dsk/c0t0d0. If you're ever unsure of which physical disk is associated with a specific disk device name, then the format command will tell you:

```
bash-2.03# format
Searching for disks...done
AVAILABLE DISK SELECTIONS:
0. c1t3d0 <SUN2.1G cyl 2733 alt 2 hd 19 sec 80>
        /pci@1f,0/pci@1/scsi@1/sd@3,0
```

Here we can see that physical device /pci@1f,0/pci@1/scsi@1/sd@3,0 is matched with the disk device /dev/dsk/c1t3d0. In addition, a list of mappings between physical devices to instance names is always kept in the /etc/path_to_inst file:

```
"/sbus@1f,0" 0 "sbus"
"/sbus@1f,0/sbusmem@2,0" 2 "sbusmem"
"/sbus@1f,0/sbusmem@3,0" 3 "sbusmem"
"/sbus@1f,0/sbusmem@0,0" 0 "sbusmem"
"/sbus@1f,0/sbusmem@1,0" 1 "sbusmem"
"/sbus@1f,0/SUNW,fas@2,8800000" 1 "fas"
"/sbus@1f,0/SUNW,fas@2,8800000/ses@f,0" 1 "ses"
"/sbus@1f,0/SUNW,fas@2,8800000/sd@1,0" 16 "sd"
"/sbus@1f,0/SUNW,fas@2,8800000/sd@0,0" 15 "sd"
"/sbus@1f,0/SUNW,fas@2,8800000/sd@3,0" 18 "sd"
"/sbus@1f,0/SUNW,fas@2,8800000/sd@2,0" 17 "sd"
"/sbus@1f,0/SUNW,fas@2,8800000/sd@5,0" 20 "sd"
"/sbus@1f,0/SUNW,fas@2,8800000/sd@4,0" 19 "sd"
"/sbus@1f,0/SUNW,fas@2,8800000/sd@6,0" 21 "sd"
"/sbus@1f,0/SUNW,fas@2,8800000/sd@9,0" 23 "sd"
```

```
"/sbus@1f,0/SUNW,fas@2,8800000/sd@8,0" 22 "sd"
"/sbus@1f,0/SUNW,fas@2,8800000/sd@a,0" 24 "sd"
"/sbus@1f,0/SUNW,fas@2,8800000/st@1,0" 8 "st"
"/sbus@1f,0/SUNW,fas@2,8800000/st@0,0" 7 "st"
"/sbus@1f,0/SUNW,fas@2,8800000/sd@c,0" 26 "sd"
"/sbus@1f,0/SUNW,fas@2,8800000/st@3,0" 10 "st"
"/sbus@1f,0/SUNW,fas@2,8800000/sd@b,0" 25 "sd"
"/sbus@1f,0/SUNW,fas@2,8800000/st@2,0" 9 "st"
"/sbus@1f,0/SUNW,fas@2,8800000/sd@e,0" 28 "sd"
"/sbus@1f,0/SUNW,fas@2,8800000/st@5,0" 12 "st"
"/sbus@1f,0/SUNW,fas@2,8800000/sd@d,0" 27 "sd"
"/sbus@1f,0/SUNW,fas@2,8800000/st@4,0" 11 "st"
"/sbus@1f,0/SUNW,fas@2,8800000/sd@f,0" 29 "sd"
"/sbus@1f,0/SUNW,fas@2,8800000/st@6,0" 13 "st"
"/sbus@1f,0/SUNW,CS4231@d,c000000" 0 "audiocs"
"/sbus@1f,0/dma@0,81000" 0 "dma"
"/sbus@1f,0/dma@0,81000/esp@0,80000" 0 "esp"
"/sbus@1f,0/dma@0,81000/esp@0,80000/sd@0,0" 30 "sd"
"/sbus@1f,0/dma@0,81000/esp@0,80000/sd@1,0" 31 "sd"
"/sbus@1f,0/dma@0,81000/esp@0,80000/sd@2,0" 32 "sd"
"/sbus@1f,0/dma@0,81000/esp@0,80000/sd@3,0" 33 "sd"
"/sbus@1f,0/dma@0,81000/esp@0,80000/sd@4,0" 34 "sd"
"/sbus@1f,0/dma@0,81000/esp@0,80000/sd@5,0" 35 "sd"
"/sbus@1f,0/dma@0,81000/esp@0,80000/sd@6,0" 36 "sd"
"/sbus@1f,0/dma@0,81000/esp@0,80000/st@0,0" 14 "st"
"/sbus@1f,0/dma@0,81000/esp@0,80000/st@1,0" 15 "st"
"/sbus@1f,0/dma@0,81000/esp@0,80000/st@2,0" 16 "st"
"/sbus@1f,0/dma@0,81000/esp@0,80000/st@3,0" 17 "st"
"/sbus@1f,0/dma@0,81000/esp@0,80000/st@4,0" 18 "st"
"/sbus@1f,0/dma@0,81000/esp@0,80000/st@5,0" 19 "st"
"/sbus@1f,0/dma@0,81000/esp@0,80000/st@6,0" 20 "st"
"/sbus@1f,0/sbusmem@f,0" 15 "sbusmem"
"/sbus@1f,0/sbusmem@d,0" 13 "sbusmem"
"/sbus@1f,0/sbusmem@e,0" 14 "sbusmem"
"/sbus@1f,0/cgthree@1,0" 0 "cgthree"
"/sbus@1f,0/SUNW,hme@e,8c00000" 0 "hme"
"/sbus@1f,0/zs@f,1000000" 1 "zs"
"/sbus@1f,0/zs@f,1100000" 0 "zs"
"/sbus@1f,0/SUNW,bpp@e,c800000" 0 "bpp"
"/sbus@1f,0/lebuffer@0,40000" 0 "lebuffer"
"/sbus@1f,0/lebuffer@0,40000/le@0,60000" 0 "le"
"/sbus@1f,0/SUNW,hme@2,8c00000" 1 "hme"
"/sbus@1f,0/SUNW,fdtwo@f,1400000" 0 "fd"
"/options" 0 "options"
"/pseudo" 0 "pseudo"
```

Here we can see entries for the network interface /sbus@1f,0/
SUNW,hme@2,8c00000 as well as the floppy disk /sbus@1f,0/SUNW,fdtwo@
f,1400000 and the SBUS sbus@1f,0.

Pre-Installation Tasks

Before installing your system, you will require the following information from your network administrator:

- **Hostname (www)**   This is the name that you want to give your host to identify it uniquely on the local area network (LAN).

- **IP address (such as 204.58.32.46)**   The IP address is used by the transport layer to locate a specific host on the Internet.

- **Domain name (such as paulwatters.com)**   The domain name is the organizational to which your host belongs. All hosts on the Internet must belong to a domain.

- **DNS server (such as ns)**   The DNS server maps IP addresses to domain names, and domain names to IP addresses.

- **Subnet mask (e.g., 255.255.255.0)**   The mask that is used to locate hosts that form part of the same subnet on the LAN.

You will also need to decide which language you want to use when installing Solaris. The following languages are supported for performing the installation process:

- English
- French
- German
- Italian
- Japanese
- Korean
- Simplified Chinese
- Spanish
- Swedish
- Traditional Chinese

If the system has never had Solaris installed, you can simply insert the CD-ROM into its caddy and/or CD-ROM drive, and the Web Start installer will start. Alternatively, once the system has started booting, you can press the Stop+a keys, and when you get the OK prompt, you can simply type the following:

```
ok boot cdrom
```

You will then see output similar to the following:

```
Boot device: /sbus/espdma@e,8400000/esp@e,8800000/sd@6,0:f File and args:
SunOS Release 5.8 Version Generic 32-bit
Copyright 1983-2000 Sun Microsystems, Inc. All rights reserved.
Configuring /dev and /devices
Using RPC Bootparams for network configuration information.
Solaris Web Start 3.0 installer
English has been selected as the language in which to perform the install.
Starting the Web Start 3.0 Solaris installer
Solaris installer is searching the system's hard disks for a
location to place the Solaris installer software.
Your system appears to be upgradeable.
Do you want to do a Initial Install or Upgrade?
1) Initial Install
2) Upgrade
Please Enter 1 or 2 >
```

If the following message appears in the boot messages, then you can elect to perform an upgrade of the existing Solaris installation. However, most administrators backup their existing software, perform a fresh install, and then restore their data and applications once their system is operational. In this case, we will choose to perform an initial install, which will overwrite the existing operating system.

After you enter 1 and hit Enter, you will see a message like this:

```
The default root disk is /dev/dsk/c0t0d0.
The Solaris installer needs to format
/dev/dsk/c0t0d0 to install Solaris.
WARNING: ALL INFORMATION ON THE DISK WILL BE ERASED!
Do you want to format /dev/dsk/c0t0d0? [y,n,?,q]
```

Formatting the hard drive will overwrite all existing data on the drive. You must ensure that, if you have previously installed an operating system on the target drive (c0t0d0), you have backed up all the data that you will need in the future. This includes both user directories and application installations.

After answering "y", the following screen will appear:

```
NOTE: The swap size cannot be changed during filesystem layout.
Enter a swap slice size between 384MB and 2027MB, default = 512MB [?]
```

Just hit the Enter key to accept the default on 512MB if your system has 256MB of physical RAM, as the sample system has. However, as a general rule, you should only allocate twice the amount of physical RAM as swap space; otherwise, system performance will be impaired. The swap partition should be placed at the beginning of the drive, as the following message indicates, so that other slices are not dependent on its physical location:

```
The Installer prefers that the swap slice is at the beginning of the
disk. This will allow the most flexible filesystem partitioning later
in the installation.
Can the swap slice start at the beginning of the disk [y,n,?,q]
```

After answering "y" to this question, you will see be asked to confirm the formatting settings:

```
You have selected the following to be used by the Solaris installer:
Disk Slice : /dev/dsk/c0t0d0
Size : 1024 MB
Start Cyl. : 0
WARNING: ALL INFORMATION ON THE DISK WILL BE ERASED!
Is this OK [y,n,?,q]
```

If you answer "y," then the disk will be formatted, and a mini-root filesystem will be copied to the disk, after which the system will be rebooted, and the Web Start wizard installation process can begin:

```
The Solaris installer will use disk slice, /dev/dsk/c0t0d0s1.
After files are copied, the system will automatically reboot, and
installation will continue.
Please Wait...
Copying mini-root to local disk....done.
Copying platform specific files....done.
Preparing to reboot and continue installation.
Rebooting to continue the installation.
Syncing file systems... 41 done
rebooting...
Resetting ...
SPARCstation 20 (1 X 390Z50), Keyboard Present
ROM Rev. 2.4, 256 MB memory installed, Serial #456543
Ethernet address 5:2:12:c:ee:5a HostID 456543
Rebooting with command:
boot /sbus@1f,0/espdma@e,8400000/esp@e,8800000/sd@0,0:b
Boot device: /sbus@1f,0/espdma@e,8400000/esp@e,8800000/sd@0,0:b
File and args:
SunOS Release 5.8 Version Generic 32-bit
Copyright 1983-2000 Sun Microsystems, Inc. All rights reserved.
Configuring /dev and /devices
Using RPC Bootparams for network configuration information.
```

Web Start Installation

Using the Web Start wizard is the easiest way to install and configure Solaris. Although it is possible to use the Solaris Interactive Installer supplied with previous Solaris versions, the Web Start wizard enables users to install entire distributions or groups of packages and automatically size, layout, and create slices on the filesystem. It also configures the boot disk and other disks that are installed locally. However, if you want to install individual packages or change the size of the swap file, then you will not be able to use the Web Start wizard.

Network

The first section of the wizard involves setting up the network. The Network Connectivity screen gives users the option to select a networked or non-networked system. If you don't need to install network support, you will still need a unique hostname, and this must then be entered. Network users will have to enter a hostname, but must first identify how their system obtains IP support. One possibility is that the system will use DHCP, which is useful when IP addresses are becoming scarce on a Class C network. DHCP enables individual systems to be allocated only for the period during which they are up. Thus, if a client machine is only operated between 9 a.m. and 5 p.m. every day, it is only "leased" an IP address for that period of time. When an IP address is not leased to a specific host, it can be reused by another host. Solaris DHCP servers can service Solaris clients as well as Microsoft Windows and Linux clients. Chapter 17 provides more information about DHCP services under Solaris.

Next, you need to indicate whether IPv6 needs to be supported by this system. The decision to use DHCP will depend on whether your network is part of the Multicast Backbone (Mbone), the IPv6-enabled version of the Internet. As proposed in RFC 2471, IPv6 will replace IPv4 in the years to come, as it provides for many more IP addresses than IPv4. Once IPv6 is adopted worldwide, there will be less reliance on stop-gap measures like DHCP. However, IPv6 also incorporates a number of innovations above and beyond the addition of more IP addresses for the Internet. Enhanced security provided by authenticating header information, for example, will reduce the risk of IP spoofing and denial of service attacks succeeding. Since IPv6 support does not interfere with existing IPv4 support, most administrators will want to support it.

Finally, you need to enter the IP address assigned to this system by the network administrator. It is important not to use an IP address that is currently being used by another host, since packets may be misrouted. You will also need to enter the netmask for the system, which will be 255.0.0.0 (Class A), 255.255.0.0 (Class B), or 255.255.255.0 (Class C). If you're not sure, ask your network administrator.

Name Service

A name service enables your system to find other hosts on the Internet or on the LAN. Solaris supports several different naming servers, including the Network Information

Service (NIS/NIS+), the DNS, or file-based name resolution. NIS/NIS+ is used to manage large domains by creating maps of hosts, services, and resources that are shared between hosts and can be centrally managed. The DNS, on the other hand, only stores maps of IP addresses and hostnames. Solaris supports the concurrent operation of different naming services, so it's possible to select NIS/NIS+ at this point and set up DNS manually later. However, because most hosts are now connected to the Internet, it may be more appropriate to install DNS first and install NIS/NIS+ after.

If you select DNS or NIS/NIS+, you will be asked to enter a domain name for the local system. This should be the fully qualified domain name (paulwatters.com). If you selected DNS, you will either need to search the local subnet for a DNS server or enter the IP address of the primary DNS server that is authoritative for your domain. You may also enter up to two secondary DNS servers that have records of your domain. This can be a useful backup if your primary DNS server goes down. It is also possible that, when searching for hosts with a hostname rather than a fully qualified domain name, you would want to search multiple local domains. For example, the host www.finance.paulwatters.com belongs to the finance.paulwatters.com domain. However, your users may want to locate other hosts within the broader paulwatters.com domain by using the simple hostname, in which case, you can add the paulwatters.com domain to a list of domains to be searched for hosts.

Date and Time

The next section requires that you enter your timezone, as specified by geographic region, and the number of hours beyond or before Greenwich Mean Time (GMT) or by timezone file. Using the geographic region is the easiest method, although if you already know the GMT offset and/or the name of the timezone file, you may enter that instead. Next, you are required to enter the current time and date, with a four-digit year, a month, day, hour, and minute.

Root Password

The most important stage of the installation procedure occurs next, the selection of the root password. The root user has the same powers as the root user on Linux, or the Administrator account on Windows NT. If an intruder gains root access, he/she is free to roam the system, deleting or stealing data, removing or adding user accounts, or installing Trojan horses that transparently modify the way that your system operates.

One way to protect against an authorized user gaining root access is to use a difficult-to-guess root password. This makes it difficult for a cracker to use a password-cracking program to guess your password to be successful. The optimal password is a completely random string of alphanumeric and punctuation characters. Some applications, discussed in Chapter 15, can be used to generate passwords that are easy to remember, but which contain almost random combinations of characters.

In addition, the root password should never be written down, unless it is locked in the company safe or told to anyone who doesn't need to know it. If users require levels of access that are typically privileged (such as mounting CD-ROMs), it is better to use the sudo utility to limit the access of each user to specific applications for execution as the super-user, rather than giving out the root password to everyone who asks for it.

The root password must be entered twice just in case you should happen to make a typographical error, as the characters that you type are masked on the screen.

Power Management

Do you want your system to switch off automatically after 30 minutes of inactivity? If you can honestly answer yes to this question (because you have a workstation that does not run services), then you should enable power management, as it can save costly power bills. However, if you're administering a server, then you'll definitely want to turn power management off.

Proxy Server

A proxy server acts as a buffer between hosts on a local network and the rest of the Internet. A proxy server passes connections back and forth between local hosts and any other host on the Internet. It usually acts in conjunction with a firewall to block access to internal systems, thereby protecting sensitive data. One of the most popular firewalls is squid, which also acts as a caching server.

To enable access to the Internet through a proxy server, you need to enter the hostname of the proxy server, and the port on which the proxy operates.

Kiosk

After all of the configuration settings have been entered, the following message will be seen on the screen:

```
Please wait while the system is configured with your settings...
```

The installation kiosk will then appear on the screen. The kiosk is primarily used to select the type of installation that you want to perform. To begin the software selection process, you need to eject the Web Start CD-ROM and insert the software (1) CD-ROM. Next, you have the option of installing all Solaris software using the default options or customizing your selection before copying the files from the CD-ROM. Obviously, if you have a lot of disk space and a fast system, you may prefer to install the entire distribution and delete packages after installation that you no longer require. This is definitely the fastest method. Alternatively, you can elect to perform a customized installation.

You are then presented with a screen of all the available software groups. Here you can select or deselect individual package groups or package clusters, depending on your requirements. For example, you may decide to install the Netscape Navigator software, but not install the NIS/NIS+ server for Solaris. After choosing the packages that you want to install, you are then required to enter your locale based on geographic region (the U.S. entry is selected by default). You may also elect to install third-party software during the Solaris installation process. This is particularly useful if you have a standard operating environment that consists of using the Oracle database server in conjunction with the Solaris operating environment, for example. You would need to insert the product CD-ROM at this point so that it could be identified.

After selecting your software, you will need to layout the disks. This involves defining disk slices that will store the different kinds of data on your system. The fastest configuration option involves selecting the boot disk and allowing the installer to automatically layout the partitions according to the software selection that you have chosen. For example, you may want to expand the size of the /var partition to enable large print jobs to be spooled or Web servers logs to be recorded.

Finally, you will be asked to confirm your software selections and proceed with installation. All of the packages will then be installed to your system. A progress bar displayed on the screen indicates which packages have been installed at any particular point and how many remain to be installed. After you have installed all of the software, you will have to reboot the system. After restarting, your system should boot directly into Solaris unless you have a dual-booting system, in which case you will need to select the Solaris boot partition from the Solaris boot manager.

After installation, the system will reboot and display a status message when starting up, which is printed on the console. A sample console display during booting will look something like the following:

```
ok boot
Resetting ...
SPARCstation 20 (1 X 390Z50), Keyboard Present
ROM Rev. 2.4, 256 MB memory installed, Serial #456543
Ethernet address 5:2:12:c:ee:5a HostID 456543
Boot device: /iommu/sbus/espdma@f,400000/esp@f,800000/sd@1,0
File and args:
SunOS Release 5.8 Version generic [UNIX(R) System V Release 4.0]
Copyright (c) 1983-2000, Sun Microsystems, Inc.
configuring network interfaces: le0.
Hostname: server
```

```
The system is coming up. Please wait.
add net default: gateway 204.58.62.33
NIS domainname is paulwatters.net
starting rpc services: rpcbind keyserv ypbind done.
Setting netmask of le0 to 255.255.255.0
Setting default interface for multicast: add net 224.0.0.0: gateway emu
syslog service starting.
Print services started.
volume management starting.
The system is ready.
emu console login:
```

By default, the CDE login screen is then displayed.

Summary

In this chapter, we've examined what makes a Solaris server different from a standard Solaris host and reviewed some of the new features of Solaris 8 that servers typically make use of. In addition, we reviewed the key pre-installation tasks that must be undertaken prior to beginning a Web Start installation, which is also covered in detail.

Practice Questions

1. Which one of the following Solaris 8 installation types is required for servers?
   A. Entire distribution without OEM support
   B. Entire distribution plus OEM support
   C. Developer system
   D. End user system

2. What is a key benefit of client-server architectures?
   A. Clients rely less on centralized servers
   B. Clients have faster CPUs on the desktop
   C. Centralization of system administration
   D. None of the above

3. What is the main advantage of clustering?
   A. Load balancing
   B. Cheaper servers
   C. Slower input/output (I/O) performance
   D. Compatibility with Intel CPUs

4. Which of the following SPARC systems are supported under Solaris 8? (Choose two only.)
   A. SPARCclassic
   B. SPARCstation LX
   C. SPARCstation 1
   D. SPARCstation 2

5. What is the minimum amount of RAM required to run Solaris 8?
   A. 16MB
   B. 32MB
   C. 64MB
   D. 128MB

6. Which is a valid physical device for /pci@1f,0/pci@1,1/ide@3/dad@0,0?
   A. /dev/dsk/c0t0d0
   B. /dev/dsk/c0t0d1
   C. /dev/dsk/c1t0d0
   D. /dev/dsk/c0t1d0

7. What is a hostname?
   A. A network name that identifies a group of hosts
   B. A special username that has super-user privileges
   C. A unique name that is associated with a system
   D. A network name that identifies an entire network

8. What is an IP address?
   A. A network address that identifies a group of hosts
   B. A number that is used to locate hosts on the same local subnet
   C. A unique name that is associated with a system
   D. A network number that identifies a single host

9. What is a domain name?
   A. An IP address that identifies a group of hosts
   B. A number that is used to locate hosts on the same local subnet
   C. A unique name that is associated with a system
   D. A network name that identifies a group of hosts

10. What is a subnet mask?
    A. An IP address that identifies a group of hosts
    B. A number that is used to locate hosts on the same local subnet

    C. A unique name that is associated with a system

    D. A network name that identifies a group of hosts

11. What is a root password?

    A. An authentication token for the super-user

    B. A hacking tool used to crack low-level accounts

    C. A password that cannot be used to gain indirect access to the nobody account

    D. A network name that identifies a group of hosts

12. What is DHCP?

    A. A protocol for permanently assigning IP addresses to hosts

    B. A protocol for leasing IP addresses to hosts

    C. A method for invoking super-user privileges

    D. A protocol for identifying a group of hosts

Answers

1. A

2. C

3. A

4. A, B

5. C

6. A

7. C

8. D

9. D

10. B

11. A

12. B

Solaris Syslog and Auditing Utilities

The following objectives will be met upon completing this chapter's material:

- Understanding the syslog facility
- Using TCP wrappers
- Exploring how to monitor system processes using the ps command

Syslog

The Solaris system log daemon (syslogd) is optimized to provide this logging on a per-machine or per-site basis, the latter requiring a dedicated loghost declared in /etc/hosts. In this section, we'll examine the role of syslogd in recording remote access requests.

What Is Syslog?

Syslog is a centralized logging facility that provides different classes of events that are logged to a logfile and also provides an alerting service for certain events. Because syslogd is configurable by root, it is very flexible in its operations. Multiple log files can exist for each daemon whose activity is being logged, or a single logfile can be created. The syslog service is controlled by the configuration file /etc/syslog.conf, which is read at boot time, or whenever the syslog daemon receives a HUP signal. This file defines the facility levels or system source of logged messages and conditions. Priority levels are also assigned to system events recorded in the system log, while an action field defines which action is taken when a particular class of event is encountered. These events can range from normal system usage, such as File Transport Protocol (FTP) connections and remote shells, to system crashes.

The source facilities defined by Solaris are for the kernel (kern), authentication (auth), daemon (daemon), mail system (mail), print spooling (lp), and user processes (user). Priority levels are classified as system emergencies (emerg), errors requiring immediate attention (attn), critical errors (crit), messages (info), debugging output (debug), and other errors (err). These priority levels are defined for individual systems and architectures in <sys/syslog.h>. It is easy to see how logging applications, such as TCP wrappers, can take advantage of the different error levels and source facilities provided by syslogd.

On the Solaris platform, the syslog daemon depends on the m4 macro processor being present. m4 is typically installed with the software developer packages and is usually located in /usr/ccs/bin/m4. This version has been installed by default since Solaris 2.4. Users should note that the syslogd supplied by Sun has been error-prone in previous releases. With early Solaris 2.x versions, the syslog daemon left behind zombie processes when alerting logged-in users (such as notifying root of an emerg). In addition, the syslogd supplied in Solaris 2.6 appears to be unstable, and patch 106439 should be installed. If syslogd does not work, check that m4 exists and is in the path for root and/or run the syslogd program interactively by invoking it with a -d parameter.

Examining Log Files

Log files are fairly straightforward in their contents, and what events are recorded can be stipulated by instructions in the syslog.conf file. Records of mail messages can be useful for billing purposes and for detecting the bulk sending of unsolicited commercial e-mail (spam). The system log will record the details supplied by sendmail: a message ID, when a message is sent or received, a destination, and a delivery result, which is typically delivered or deferred. Connections are usually deferred when a connection to a site is down. Sendmail usually tries to redeliver failed deliveries in four-hour intervals.

When using TCP wrappers, connections to supported Internet daemons are also logged. For example, an FTP connection to a server will result in the connection time and date being recorded, along with the hostname of the client. A similar result is achieved for Telnet connections.

A delivered mail message is recorded as

```
Feb 20 14:07:05 server sendmail[238]: AA00238: message-
id=<bulk.11403.19990219175554@sun.com>
Feb 20 14:07:05 server sendmail[238]: AA00238:
from=<sun-developers-l@sun.com>, size=1551, class=0, received from
gateway.site.com (172.16.1.1)
Feb 20 14:07:06 server sendmail[243]: AA00238:
to=<pwatters@mail.site.com>, delay=00:00:01, stat=Sent,
mailer=local
```

while a deferred mail message is recorded differently:

```
Feb 21 07:11:10 server sendmail[855]: AA00855:
message-id=<Pine.SOL.3.96.990220200723.5291A-100000@oracle.com>
Feb 21 07:11:10 server sendmail[855]: AA00855:
from=<support@oracle.com>, size=1290, class=0, received
from gateway.site.com (172.16.1.1)
Feb 21 07:12:25 server sendmail[857]: AA00855:
to=pwatters@mail.site.com, delay=00:01:16, stat=Deferred:
Connection timed out during user open with mail.site.com,
mailer=TCP
```

An FTP connection is recorded in a single line:

```
Feb 20 14:35:00 server in.ftpd[277]: connect from
workstation.site.com
```

in the same way that a telnet connection is recorded:

```
Feb 20 14:35:31 server in.telnetd[279]: connect from
workstation.site.com
```

The syslog.conf File

The file /etc/syslog.conf contains information used by the system log daemon, syslogd, to forward a system message to appropriate log files and/or users. syslogd preprocesses this file through m4 to obtain the correct information for certain log files, defining LOGHOST if the address of loghost is the same as one of the addresses of the host that is running syslogd.

The default syslogd configuration is not optimal for all installations. Many configuration decisions depend on the degree to which the system administrator wants to be alerted immediately, should an alert or emergency occur, or whether it is sufficient for all auth notices to be logged, and a cron job run every night to filter the results for a review in the morning. For non-commercial installations, the latter is probably a reasonable approach. A crontab entry such as the following

```
0 1 * * * cat /var/adm/messages | grep auth | mail root
```

will send the root user a mail message at 1 A.M. every morning with all authentication messages.

A basic syslog.conf should contain a provision for sending emergency notices to all users as well as alters to the root user and other non-privileged administrator accounts. Errors, kernel notices, and authentication notices probably need to be displayed on the system console (in OpenWindows, a console can be created by cmdtool+C). It is generally sufficient to log daemon notices, alerts, and all other authentication information to the system log file, unless the administrator is watching for cracking attempts, as shown here:

```
*.alert                                          root,pwatters
*.emerg                                          *
*.err;kern.notice;auth.notice                    /dev/console
daemon.notice                         /var/adm/messages
auth.none;kern.err;daemon.err;mail.crit;*.alert  /var/adm/messages
auth.info                                        /var/adm/authlog
```

Monitoring System Access

System access can be monitored interactively using a number of measures. For example, syslog entries can be automatically viewed in real time by using the command

```
client% tail -f /var/adm/messages
```

However, most administrators want to interactively view what remote users are doing on a system at any one time. Process-viewing commands are covered in the following section, but we will examine two methods here for viewing remote user activity. The who command displays who is currently logged into the system. The output of who displays the username, the connecting line, the date of login, the idle time, the process ID, and a comment. An example output is

```
client% who | more
root         console     Nov 22 12:39
pwatters     pts/0       Nov 19 21:05     (client.site.com)
```

This command can be automated to update the list of active users. An alternative to who is the w command, which displays a more detailed summary of the current activity on the system, including the current process name for each user. The header output from w shows the current time, the uptime of the current system, and the number of users actively logged into the system. The average system load is also displayed as a series of three numbers at the end of the w header, indicating the average number of jobs in the run queue for the previous one, five, and 15 minutes. In addition to the output generated by who, the w command displays the current foreground process for each user, which is usually a shell. For example, the output

```
root     console     Thu12pm 3days    6     6  /usr/openwin/bin/shelltool
pwatters  pts/12      Thu11am 8:45     9        /usr/local/bin/tcsh
```

shows that the root user has an active shelltool running under OpenWindows, while the user pwatters is running the Cornell shell. The w and who commands are useful tools for getting an overview of current and historical usage patterns on any Solaris system.

TCP Wrappers

Although the security measures we have examined so far have been concerned with directly modifying the identification and authentication sequences used by clients to access server resources, we have neglected an important aspect of evaluating security: access logging. As the first step in developing a secure access policy, logging access information can reveal whether an organization's networks have an authentication problem. In addition, specific instances of unauthorized access to various resources can be collated, and using statistical methods, they can be assessed for regular patterns of abuse. The monitoring of log files can also be used by applications to accept or reject connections, based on historical data contained in centralized logging mechanisms provided under Solaris, such as the syslogd system logging daemon.

One reason access monitoring is not often discussed is that implementations of the standard Unix network daemons that are spawned by the Internet super server, inetd (discussed previously), do not have a provision to write directly to a syslog file. Later Internet service daemons, such as the Apache Web server, run as standalone services not requiring inetd, but have enhanced logging facilities that are used to track Web site usage.

Wietse Venema's TCP wrappers are a popular method of enabling daemons launched from inetd to log their accepted and rejected connections. This is because the wrapper programs that are installed for each service do not require alterations to existing binary software distributions or to existing configuration files.

In their simplest form, TCP wrappers are used for monitoring only, but they could be used to build better applications that can reject connections on the basis of failed connections. For example, a flood of requests to login using rsh from an untrusted host could be terminated after three failed attempts from a single host. TCP wrappers work by compiling a replacement daemon that points to the real daemon file, often located in a subdirectory below the daemon wrappers. The wrappers log the date and time of a service request with a client hostname and whether the request was rejected or accepted.

The current version of TCP wrappers (Release 7.6) supports the System V Release 4 (SVR4) TLI network-programming interface under Solaris, which has equivalent functionality to the Berkeley socket-programming interface. In addition, the latest release supports access control and detection of host address or hostname spoofing. The latter is particularly important in the context of authentication services that provide access to services based on IP subnet ranges or specific hostnames in a local area network (LAN). If these are spoofed and access is granted to a rogue client, then the entire security infrastructure has failed. It is critical to detect and reject any unauthorized connections at an early stage, and TCP wrappers are an integral part of this mechanism. The sequence of events involved in logging TCP connections is shown in Figure 23-1.

When writing access information to syslog, the output looks like the following:

```
Nov 18 11:00:52 server in.telnetd[1493]: connect from client.site.com
Nov 18 11:25:03 server in.telnetd[1510]: connect from workstation.site.com
Nov 18 11:25:22 server in.telnetd[1511]: connect from client.site.com
Nov 18 12:16:30 server in.ftpd[1556]: connect from workstation.site.com
```

These entries indicate that between 11:00 A.M. and 1:00 P.M. on November 18, some clients connected using telnet from client.site.com and workstation. site.com. In addition, an FTP connection was made from workstation.site.com. Although we've only examined wrappers for in.ftpd and in.telnetd, wrappers can be compiled for most services launched from inetd, including finger, talk, tftp (trivial ftp), and rsh (remote shell).

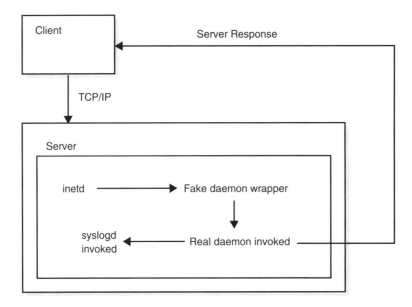

Figure 23-1   Logging TCP requests using TCP wrappers

Process Monitoring

So far, we've examined how to monitor logs and logged-in user details to examine what's happening on a system. Because Solaris is designed to handle many different concurrent users who all own their applications, which can be executed in the foreground or in the background, the operating system needs an intelligent method to keep track of these applications.

Each program that runs on a Solaris system is associated with a unique process ID (PID), which distinguishes that program from all others. A PID is necessary because the same application can be started multiple times and thus cannot be referred to by a name alone. In addition, two different applications could be executed concurrently with the same name, or different users could both be executing the same application. Both Linux and Windows NT have a similar system for managing process IDs, but some important differences exist.

Identifying Processes

Although Windows NT only has the concept of a single PID for each process, the Solaris process model is more sophisticated because each PID is associated with a parent process ID (PPID). This is useful for grouping processes together that were spawned by the same parent process. For example, the Samba daemon spawns several child processes to serve individual clients making requests for file access. The PID of each spawned process is different, but the PPID of each child process is the same:

```
watashi:/usr/local/abw > ps -eaf | grep smbd
    root    238      1  0   Aug 31 ?         0:00
/usr/local/samba/bin/smbd -D -l /var/adm/smblogs/log -s
/usr/local/samba/lib/sm
    root    172    238  0 08:09:54 ?         0:05
/usr/local/samba/bin/smbd -D -l /var/adm/smblogs/log -s
/usr/local/samba/lib/sm
root    272    238  0 08:20:02 ?           0:07
/usr/local/samba/bin/smbd -D -l /var/adm/smblogs/log -s
/usr/local/samba/lib/sm
```

In this example, the original Samba PID is 238, which has the PPID of 1 (it was started at system boot time). However, the Samba application spawned two child processes (172 and 272), which both have the PPID of 238. As we have already seen, the shell is the main entry point for applications on a Solaris system, so any applications started from a shell will have the PPID equivalent to the PID of that shell.

In the Samba example, the root user owns all the Samba processes. However, any user on the system can potentially own the processes. Owning a process confers some privileges to the owner; the process can be killed or restarted only by that user or the super-user. Other users cannot interfere with your work. The user is identified by a user ID known as the UID, and that user's default group is associated with a group ID (GID).

The situation is also more complicated for some Solaris applications that can set the owner of a process to be a different user. These setuid programs are powerful because they enable unprivileged users to access some facilities that are normally reserved for the root user (such as mounting a CD-ROM). However, they are also potentially dangerous if their capabilities are not closely audited. For example, a dangerous setuid application would enable unprivileged users to spawn an external shell and execute commands as root. Also, some situations will occur where applications can be executed setgid, where the group ID of the application can be set to a privileged group.

Parent and Child Processes

Technically speaking, when Solaris boots, the process that is responsible for spawning all child processes on the system is PID 1. However, when PID 1 spawns a shell, it takes on its own PID. Although the shell's PPID is 1, all of its child processes will have the PPID of the shell's PID. However, if the shell is killed while an application is running in the background, the PPID of the shell's child processes reverts to PID 1. All processes that have the PPID 1 are shutdown only when the system is shutdown by sending a kill command to PID 1.

As we saw previously, the ps command reveals some useful information about the characteristics of processes on the system. In fact, ps has a large number of options that can be used to monitor all aspects of application performance on Solaris. Process lists can be obtained for the processes owned by the current user or for all processes currently running on the system. Linux users will have encountered the ps command before, yet they will be more used to the Berkeley style distribution (BSD) of ps options, which were found in early versions of Solaris, rather than the more modern System V commands.

The ps Command

The ps command, by default, only displays the process spawned by the current user from the current shell:

```
bash-2.03# ps
   PID TTY      TIME CMD
  1653 pts/4    0:00 bash
  1584 pts/4    0:00 ksh
  1654 pts/4    0:00 ps
```

Four columns are displayed: the PID, the teletype terminal (TTY) on which the commands were executed, the CPU time used by the process, and the command name as executed on the command line. If this doesn't seem like a whole lot of information, the trick is to determine which combinations of options to ps will give you the information that you're looking for. For example, if you pass the option -l to ps, you will receive the long style of output from the command:

```
bash-2.03# ps -l
  F S   UID   PID  PPID  C PRI NI     ADDR   SZ      WCHAN TTY      TIME CMD
  8 R     0  1653  1584  0  51 20 e0b0a030  504            pts/4   0:00 bash
  8 S     0  1584  1582  0  51 20 e0f42058  375 e0f420c4 pts/4   0:00 ksh
  8 R     0  1656  1653  0  41 20 e1286768  196            pts/4   0:00 ps
```

In addition to the PID, the TTY on which the commands were executed, the CPU time used by the process, and the command name as executed on the command line, several other parameters are displayed:

- Any flags (F) set by the process
- The memory address (ADDR) used by the process
- The memory address for processes that are sleeping (WCHAN)
- The memory consumption (SZ)
- The name of the command (CMD)
- The nice value (NI), which indicates the priority of the process
- The parent process ID (PPID)
- The process priority (PRI)
- The run state (S) of the process, where S indicates a sleeping process, and R indicates an active process

Any user can obtain information about all the other processes currently running on the system. This can be very useful if you suspect that another user is hogging all of the CPU time with his or her processes (the nice value, reported earlier, can be set to a lower value by the root user on these kinds of processes). A typical ps option combination is -Af, which prints a full list of all the processes on the system, including the following:

- The name of the user who started the process
- The PID of the process
- The PPID of the process
- The scheduling class (C) of the process

- The date/time when the process was started (STIME)

- The terminal (TTY) on which the process was started

- The CPU time consumed by the process since it was started

- The name of the command

A sample output from the ps -Af command is as follows:

```
bash-2.03# ps -Af
     UID   PID  PPID  C   STIME TTY        TIME CMD
    root     0     0  0   Apr 11 ?         0:00 sched
    root     1     0  0   Apr 11 ?         0:00 /etc/init -
    root     2     0  0   Apr 11 ?         0:03 pageout
    root     3     0  0   Apr 11 ?       119:21 fsflush
    root   190     1  0   Apr 11 ?         1:03 /usr/sbin/nscd -S passwd,yes
-S
group,yes
    root   111     1  0   Apr 11 ?         0:01 /usr/sbin/rpcbind
    root   265     1  0   Apr 11 ?         0:00 /usr/lib/saf/sac -t 300
    root    63     1  0   Apr 11 ?         0:00
/usr/lib/devfsadm/devfseventd
    root    65     1  0   Apr 11 ?         0:00 /usr/lib/devfsadm/devfsadmd
    root   160     1  0   Apr 11 ?         0:23 /usr/lib/autofs/automountd
    root   115     1  0   Apr 11 ?         1:14 /usr/sbin/nis_cachemgr
    root 10994   256  0   Jul 13 vt01      1:33 /usr/openwin/bin/Xsun :0 -
nobanner -auth /var/dt/A:0-XiaaGa
    root   177     1  0   Apr 11 ?         0:01 /usr/sbin/cron
    root   155     1  0   Apr 11 ?         0:00 /usr/lib/nfs/lockd
    root   249     1  0   Apr 11 ?         0:00 /usr/lib/snmp/snmpdx -y -c
/etc/snmp/conf
    root   202     1  0   Apr 11 ?         0:00 /usr/lib/lpsched
  daemon   156     1  0   Apr 11 ?         0:00 /usr/lib/nfs/statd
    root   157     1  0   Apr 11 ?         0:00 /usr/sbin/inetd -s
    root   223     1  0   Apr 11 ?         0:00 /usr/sbin/vold
    root   214     1  0   Apr 11 ?         0:00 /usr/lib/power/powerd
    root  1653  1584  0 13:22:55 pts/4     0:00 bash
    root   225     1  0   Apr 11 ?         0:00 /usr/lib/utmpd
    root   257     1  0   Apr 11 ?         0:00 /usr/lib/dmi/dmispd
    root   266     1  0   Apr 11 console   0:00 /usr/lib/saf/ttymon -g -h -p
tango console login:   -T AT386 -d /dev/console -l
    root   247     1  0   Apr 11 ?         0:04 /usr/lib/sendmail -bd -q15m
    root 11091     1  0   Jul 13 ?         0:00 /bin/ksh
/usr/dt/bin/sdtvolcheck -d -z 5 cdrom
    root 21276 11079  0   Jul 18 pts/2     0:00 /bin/sh -c dtpad -server
    root   256     1  0   Apr 11 ?         0:00 /usr/dt/bin/dtlogin -daemon
    root   272   249  0   Apr 11 ?         0:00 mibiisa -r -p 12416
```

The applications running on the system include the login daemon for the Common Desktop Environment (CDE) (PID 256), the sendmail mail transport agent (PID 247), the Internet super daemon (PID 157), and the Remote Procedure Call (RPC) server (PID 111). Table 23-1 summarizes the most commonly used options for ps.

Table 23-1 Main Options for Listing Processes with ps

Option	Description
-a	Lists the most frequently requested processes
-A, -e	Lists all processes
-c	Lists processes in scheduler format
-d	Lists all processes
-f	Prints comprehensive process information
-g	Prints process information on a group basis for a single group
-G	Prints process information on a group basis for a list of groups
-j	Includes SID and PGID in printout
-l	Prints complete process information
-L	Displays LWP details
-p	Lists process details for the list of specified processes
-P	Lists the CPU ID to which a process is bound
-s	Lists session leaders
-t	Lists all processes associated with a specific terminal
-u	Lists all processes for a specific user

Summary

In this chapter, we examined how to use system-, user-, and process-monitoring tools to accurately determine the types of activity being undertaken on a Solaris system. These tools are typically used to keep tabs on user and system activity to ensure high performance as well as the enforcement of security and usage policies.

Questions

1. Which file contains loghost definitions?
   A. /etc/loghost
   B. /etc/syslog.conf
   C. /etc/hosts
   D. /etc/system

2. What is the name of the syslog configuration file?
   A. /etc/loghost
   B. /etc/syslog.conf
   C. /etc/hosts
   D. /etc/system

3. Which of the following is *not* a source facility defined in the syslog configuration file?
   A. kern
   B. auth
   C. default
   D. mail

4. What is the name of the macro processor used to process syslog data?
   A. perl
   B. sed
   C. awk
   D. m4

5. Name the default syslog file.
   A. /var/log/syslog
   B. /var/adm/messages
   C. /etc/syslog
   D. /var/adm/messages/syslog

6. The w command displays the system load for which time intervals?
   A. One, two, and three minutes
   B. One, five, and 10 minutes
   C. One, 10, and 15 minutes
   D. One, five, and 15 minutes

Answers

1. C
2. B
3. C
4. D
5. B
6. A

Managing Devices

The following objectives will be met upon completing this chapter's material:

- Understanding device files
- Exploring the /dev and /devices directories
- Reviewing available storage devices
- Configuring serial devices
- Displaying device configuration data

One of the most important but most challenging roles of a system administrator is device management. Devices in this context can be defined as both physical and logical entities that together constitute a hardware system. Although some operating systems hide device configuration details from all users in proprietary, binary formats, a Solaris device configuration is easy to use, with configuration information stored in special files, known as device files. In addition to providing the technical background on how device files operate, and how device drivers can be installed, this chapter examines how to install standard devices, such as new hard drives, and more modern media, like CD-ROMs and zip disks.

Solaris 8 now supports the dynamic reconfiguration of many systems' devices on some SPARC platforms, particularly in the medium-level server range (E450) and above. This enables administrators to remove faulty hardware components, replace them without having to power-down a system, and perform a reconfiguration boot, which is necessary for older systems. This is particularly significant for systems that have a high redundancy of system components to guarantee uptime under all but the most critical of circumstances.

Device Files

Device files are special files that represent devices in the Solaris operating system and are located in the /dev directory as well as in the subdirectories (such as /dev/dsk). The /devices directory is a tree that completely characterizes the hardware layout of the system in the filesystem namespace. Although it may seem initially confusing that separate directories are used for devices and system hardware, the difference between the two systems will become apparent in the following discussion.

Solaris refers to both physical and logical devices in three separate ways, with physical device names, physical device files, and logical device names. Physical device names are easily identified as they are long strings that provide all the details relevant to the physical installation of the device. Every physical device has a physical name. For example, an SBUS could have the name /sbus@1f,0, while a disk device might have the name /sbus@1f,0/SUNW,fas@2,8800000/sd@1,0. Physical device names are usually displayed at boot time and when selected applications are used that access hardware directly, such as format.

On the other hand, physical device files that are located in the /devices directory comprise an instance name that is an abbreviation of a physical device name, which can be interpreted by the kernel. For example, the SBUS /sbus@1f,0 might be referred to as sbus, and a device disk, /sbus@1f,0/SUNW,fas@2,8800000/sd@1,0, might be referred to as sd1. The mapping of instance names to physical devices is not hard-wired. The /etc/path_to_inst file always contains these details, keeping them consistent between boots. For an Ultra 2, this file looks like the following:

```
"/sbus@1f,0" 0 "sbus"
"/sbus@1f,0/sbusmem@2,0" 2 "sbusmem"
"/sbus@1f,0/sbusmem@3,0" 3 "sbusmem"
"/sbus@1f,0/SUNW,fas@2,8800000" 1 "fas"
"/sbus@1f,0/SUNW,fas@2,8800000/ses@f,0" 1 "ses"
"/sbus@1f,0/SUNW,fas@2,8800000/sd@1,0" 16 "sd"
"/sbus@1f,0/SUNW,fas@2,8800000/sd@0,0" 15 "sd"
"/sbus@1f,0/SUNW,fas@2,8800000/sd@3,0" 18 "sd"
"/sbus@1f,0/SUNW,fas@2,8800000/sd@2,0" 17 "sd"
"/sbus@1f,0/SUNW,fas@2,8800000/sd@5,0" 20 "sd"
"/sbus@1f,0/SUNW,fas@2,8800000/sd@4,0" 19 "sd"
"/sbus@1f,0/SUNW,CS4231@d,c000000" 0 "audiocs"
"/sbus@1f,0/dma@0,81000" 0 "dma"
"/sbus@1f,0/dma@0,81000/esp@0,80000" 0 "esp"
"/sbus@1f,0/dma@0,81000/esp@0,80000/sd@0,0" 30 "sd"
"/sbus@1f,0/dma@0,81000/esp@0,80000/ses@1,0" 3 "ses"
"/sbus@1f,0/dma@0,81000/esp@0,80000/ses@2,0" 4 "ses"
"/sbus@1f,0/dma@0,81000/esp@0,80000/ses@3,0" 5 "ses"
"/sbus@1f,0/dma@0,81000/esp@0,80000/ses@4,0" 6 "ses"
"/sbus@1f,0/dma@0,81000/esp@0,80000/ses@5,0" 7 "ses"
```

```
"/sbus@1f,0/dma@0,81000/esp@0,80000/ses@6,0" 8 "ses"
"/sbus@1f,0/cgthree@1,0" 0 "cgthree"
"/sbus@1f,0/SUNW,hme@e,8c00000" 0 "hme"
"/sbus@1f,0/zs@f,1000000" 1 "zs"
"/sbus@1f,0/zs@f,1100000" 0 "zs"
"/sbus@1f,0/SUNW,bpp@e,c800000" 0 "bpp"
"/sbus@1f,0/lebuffer@0,40000" 0 "lebuffer"
"/sbus@1f,0/lebuffer@0,40000/le@0,60000" 0 "le"
"/sbus@1f,0/SUNW,hme@2,8c00000" 1 "hme"
"/sbus@1f,0/SUNW,fdtwo@f,1400000" 0 "fd"
"/options" 0 "options"
"/pseudo" 0 "pseudo"
```

In addition to physical devices, Solaris also needs to refer to logical devices. For example, physical disks may be divided into many different slices, so the physical disk device will need to be referred to using a logical name. Logical device files in the /dev directory are symbolically linked to physical device names in the /devices directory. Most user applications will refer to logical device names.

dev and /devices

A typical listing of /dev directory has numerous entries that look like the following:

arp	ptys0	ptyyb	rsd3a	sd3e	ttyu2
audio	ptys1	ptyyc	rsd3b	sd3f	ttyu3
audioctl	ptys2	ptyyd	rsd3c	sd3g	ttyu4
bd.off	ptys3	ptyye	rsd3d	sd3h	ttyu5
be	ptys4	ptyyf	rsd3e	skip_key	ttyu6
bpp0	ptys5	ptyz0	rsd3f	sound/	ttyu7
cgthree0	ptys6	ptyz1	rsd3g	sp	ttyu8
conslog	ptys7	ptyz2	rsd3h	sr0	ttyu9
console	ptys8	ptyz3	rsr0	stderr	ttyua
cua/	ptys9	ptyz4	rst11	stdin	ttyub
dsk/	ptysa	ptyz5	rst12	stdout	ttyuc
dtremote	ptysb	ptyz6	rst13	swap/	ttyud
dump	ptysc	ptyz7	rst19	syscon	ttyue
ptyqe	ptyx9	rsd31g	sd32c	ttyt0	ttyzb
ptyqf	ptyxa	rsd31h	sd32d	ttyt1	ttyzc
ptyr0	ptyxb	rsd32a	sd32e	ttyt2	ttyzd
ptyr1	ptyxc	rsd32b	sd32f	ttyt3	ttyze
ptyr2	ptyxd	rsd32c	sd32g	ttyt4	ttyzf
ptyr3	ptyxe	rsd32d	sd32h	ttyt5	udp
ptyr4	ptyxf	rsd32e	sd33a	ttyt6	volctl
ptyr5	ptyy0	rsd32f	sd33b	ttyt7	vvod
ptyr6	ptyy1	rsd32g	sd33c	ttyt8	winlock
ptyr7	ptyy2	rsd32h	sd33d	ttyt9	wscons
ptyr8	ptyy3	rsd33a	sd33e	ttyta	zero
ptyr9	ptyy4	rsd33b	sd33f	ttytb	zsh
ptyra	ptyy5	rsd33c	sd33g	ttytc	zsh0

ptyrb	ptyy6	rsd33d	sd33h	ttytd	zsh1
ptyrc	ptyy7	rsd33e	sd3a	ttyte	
ptyrd	ptyy8	rsd33f	sd3b	ttytf	
ptyre	ptyy9	rsd33g	sd3c	ttyu0	
ptyrf	ptyya	rsd33h	sd3d	ttyu1	

Many of these device filenames are self-explanatory:

- /dev/console represents the console device. Error and status messages are usually written to the console by daemons and applications using the syslog service. /dev/console typically corresponds to the monitor in text mode, but the console is also represented logically in windowing systems, such as OpenWindows, where the command server% cmdtool -C brings up a console window.

- /dev/hme is the network interface device file.

- /dev/dsk contains device files for disk slices.

- /dev/tty*n* and /dev/pty*n* are the *n* terminal and *n* pseudo-terminal devices attached to the system.

- /dev/null is the end point of discarded output. Many applications pipe their output.

The drvconfig command creates the /devices directory tree, which is a logical representation of the physical layout of devices attached to the system, and the pseudo-drivers. drvconfig is executed automatically after a reconfiguration boot. It reads file permission information for new nodes in the tree from /etc/minor_perm, which contains entries like

```
sd:* 0666 httpd staff
```

where sd is the node name for a disk device, 0666 is the default file permission, httpd is the owner, and staff is the group.

Storage Devices

Solaris supports many different kinds of mass-storage devices, including Small Computer Systems Interface (SCSI) hard drives (and Integrated Development Environment [IDE] drives on the x86 platform), reading and writing standard and rewriteable CD-ROMs, Iomega Zip and Jaz drives, tape drives, and floppy disks. Hard drives are the most common kind of storage device found on a Solaris system, ranging from individual drives used to create system and user filesystems to highly redundant, server-based Redundant Array of Inexpensive Disks (RAID) systems. These RAID configurations can comprise a set of internal disks, managed through software (such as DiskSuite), or high-speed, external arrays, like the A1000, which include dedicated RAM for write-caching. Because disk writing is one of the slowest operations in any modern server system, this greatly increases overall operational speed.

Hard drives have faced stiff competition in recent years, with new media such as Iomega's Zip and Jaz drives providing removeable media for both random and sequential file access. This makes them ideal media for archival backups, competing with the traditional magnetic tape drives. The latter have largely been replaced in modern systems by the digital audio tape (DAT) tape system, which has high reliability and data throughput rates (especially the DDS-3 standard).

In this section, we will look at the issues surrounding the installation and configuration of storage devices for Solaris, with a focus on CD-ROM and related technologies.

CD-ROMs

A popular format of read-only mass storage on many servers is the compact disc read-only memory (CD-ROM). Although earlier releases of Solaris worked best with Sun-branded CD-ROM drives, as of Solaris 2.6, the operating system fully supports all SCSI-2 CD-ROMs. For systems running older versions of Solaris, it may still be possible to use a third-party drive, but the drive must support 512-byte sectors (the Sun standard). A second Sun default to be aware of is that CD-ROMs must usually have the SCSI target ID of 6, although this limitation has again been overcome in later releases of the kernel. However, a number of third-party applications with auto-detect functions may still expect to see the CD-ROM drive at SCSI ID 6.

A number of different CD formats are also supported with the mount command, which is used to attach CDs to the filesystem. It is common to use the mount point /cdrom for the primary CD-ROM device in Solaris systems, although it is possible to use a different mount point for mounting the device by using a command-line argument to mount.

Zip and Jaz Drives

Zip and Jaz drives can be installed in two ways: by treating the drive as a SCSI disk, in which case format data needs to be added to the system to recognize it, or to use Andy Polyakov's ziptool, which will format and manage protection modes supported by Zip 100 and Jaz 1GB/2GB drives. Both of these techniques will only support SCSI and not parallel port drives.

Treating the Zip 100 SCSI drive or the Jaz 1G drive as a normal SCSI device is the easiest approach, as built-in Solaris support exists for these SCSI devices. However, only standard, non-write protected disks can be used. The steps for installation are similar for both the Zip and Jaz drives:

1. Set the SCSI ID switch to any ID that is not reserved.

2. Attach the Zip or Jaz drive to your SCSI adapter or chain, and ensure that it has power.

3. Create a device entry in /etc/format.dat by editing the file and inserting the following for a Zip drive:

```
disk_type="Zip 100"\
                        :ctlr=SCSI\
                        :ncyl=2406:acyl=2:pcyl=2408:nhead=2\
                        :nsect=40:rpm=3600:bpt=20480
        partition="Zip 100"\
                        :disk="Zip 100":ctlr=SCSI\
                        :2=0,192480
                        :2=0,1159168
```

4. For a Jaz drive, enter the following information in /etc/format.dat:

```
disk_type="Jaz 1GB"\
                        :ctlr=SCSI\
                        :ncyl=1018:acyl=2:pcyl=1020:nhead=64\
                        :nsect=32:rpm=3600:bpt=16384
        partition="Jaz 1GB"\
                        :disk="Jaz 1GB":ctlr=SCSI\
                        :2=0,2084864
```

5. Perform a reconfiguration boot by typing

```
ok boot -r
```

at the OpenBoot prompt or by using these commands from a super-user shell:

```
server# touch /reconfigure
server# sync; sync; init 6
```

The drive should now be visible to the system. To actually use the drive to mount a volume, insert a Zip or Jaz disk into the drive prior to booting the system. After booting, run the format program:

```
server# format
```

Assuming that the sd number for your drive is 3, select this sd as the disk to be formatted. Create the appropriate partition using the partition option, and follow the instructions for creating disk slices. First, create an appropriate label for the volume and quit the format program. Next, create a new filesystem on the drive by using the newfs command, such as the following:

```
server# newfs -v /dev/sd3c
```

After creating the filesystem, you can mount it by typing

```
server# mount /dev/sd3c /mount_point
```

where /mount_point is something self-documenting (such as /zip or /jaz). This needs to be created before mounting by typing

```
server# mkdir /zip
```

or

```
server# mkdir /jaz
```

Tape Drives

Solaris supports a wide variety of magnetic tapes using the Remote Magtape (RMT) protocol. Tapes are generally used as backup devices, rather than as interactive storage devices. What they lack in availability, they definitely make up for in storage capacity. Many DAT drives have capacities of 24GB, making it easy to perform a complete backup of many server systems on a single tape. This removes the need for late-night monitoring by operations staff to insert new tapes when full, as many administrators will have experienced in the past.

Device files for tape drives are found in the /dev/rmt directory. They are numbered sequentially from 0, so default drives will generally be available as /dev/rmt/0.

To backup to a remote drive, use the command ufsdump, which is an incremental file-system-dumping program. For example, to create a full backup of the /dev/rdsk/c0t1d0s1 filesystem to the tape system /dev/rmt/0, simply use the command:

```
example# ufsdump 0 /dev/rmt/0 /dev/rdsk/c0t1d0s1
```

This command specifies a level zero (complete) dump of the filesystem, specifying the target drive and data source as /dev/rmt/0 and /dev/rdsk/c0t1d0s1 respectively.

Floppy Disks

Floppy disk drives are usually standard on both SPARC and Intel architecture systems. In addition, detecting and mounting floppy disks is straightforward when using volume management. Insert the target disk into the drive and use the command

```
server# volcheck
```

This checks all volumes that are managed by volume management and will mount any valid filesystem that is found. The mount point for the floppy drive is determined by the settings in /etc/vfstab:

```
fd            -           /dev/fd        fd      -      no      -
```

Refer to the section on entering disk information into the virtual filesystem database for more details on configuring the /etc/vfstab file. A very useful feature of volcheck is to automatically check for new volumes, such as the following:

```
server# volcheck -i 60 -t 3600 /dev/diskette0 &
```

This works in the background to check every minute if a floppy is in the drive. However, this polling only takes place for one hour unless renewed.

Serial Devices

Like any modern server system, Solaris supports the connection of simple external devices through both a serial (RS-232-C or RS-423) and a parallel port. The two most common uses for serial devices on a SPARC system are connecting a VT-100 terminal or the equivalent, operating as the system console if no graphics device is installed, and as a modem, enabling dial-up Internet access using the Point-to-Point Protocol (PPP). The former is a common practice in many server rooms, where using a VT-100 terminal as the console can eliminate the expense of a monitor and video card, as many SPARC machines require a display device to boot at all.

On x86 systems, many more devices are available that often only have drivers available for other operating systems. Sun and other third-party hardware vendors are slowly making releases available for these devices through the Solaris Developer Connection. If you need to obtain an updated copy of the Solaris Device Configuration Assistant, and any updated device drivers for supported external devices, these are currently available for download at **http://soldc.sun.com/support/drivers/boot.html**.

Central to the idea of providing services through serial ports is the port monitor, which continuously monitors the serial ports for requests to login. The port monitor doesn't process the communication parameters directly, but accepts requests and passes them to the operating system. Newer releases of Solaris use the ttymon port monitor, which enables multiple concurrent getty requests from serial devices.

To configure the port for a terminal, start up admintool and enter the user mode, which can be either Basic, More, and Expert. In most cases, the Basic setup will be useful for most circumstances. admintool enables the configuration of most parameters for the port, including the baud rate for communications, the default terminal type, flow control, and carrier detection. The values entered here should match those on the matching VT-100 terminal. Once the settings have been saved, it is possible to check the validity of the settings by using the pmadm command:

```
server# pmadm -l -s ttyb
```

Modem access can be configured to be inbound-only, outbound-only, or bidirectional, which enables traffic in both directions using a similar scheme. To test the modem, use the tip command:

```
server# tip hardwire
```

Hardwire should be defined as /etc/remote. If the message

```
connected
```

appears on your terminal, then you've passed the first test. For Hayes-compatible modems, try and issue a command string like

```
ATE1V1
```

If you see OK, then the modem is communicating as expected and can now be configured to run PPP. More information about PPP and Solaris can be found at **ftp://cs.anu.edu.au/pub/software/ppp**.

Checking for Devices

Obtaining a listing of devices attached to a Solaris system is the best way to begin examining this import issue. In Solaris 8, obtaining system configuration information, including device information, can be done easily by using the print configuration command on any SPARC or Intel architecture system:

```
server% prtconf
```

On an Ultra 5 workstation, the system configuration looks like the following:

```
SUNW,Ultra-5_10
    packages (driver not attached)
        terminal-emulator (driver not attached)
        deblocker (driver not attached)
        obp-tftp (driver not attached)
        disk-label (driver not attached)
        SUNW,builtin-drivers (driver not attached)
```

```
        sun-keyboard (driver not attached)
        ufs-file-system (driver not attached)
chosen (driver not attached)
openprom (driver not attached)
        client-services (driver not attached)
options, instance #0
aliases (driver not attached)
memory (driver not attached)
virtual-memory (driver not attached)
pci, instance #0
    pci, instance #0
        ebus, instance #0
            auxio (driver not attached)
            power (driver not attached)
            SUNW,pll (driver not attached)
            se, instance #0
            su, instance #0
            su, instance #1
            ecpp (driver not attached)
            fdthree (driver not attached)
            eeprom (driver not attached)
            flashprom (driver not attached)
            SUNW,CS4231, instance #0
        network, instance #0
        SUNW,m64B, instance #0
        ide, instance #0
            disk (driver not attached)
            cdrom (driver not attached)
            dad, instance #0
            atapicd, instance #2
    pci, instance #1
        pci, instance #0
            pci108e,1000 (driver not attached)
            SUNW,hme, instance #1
            SUNW,isptwo, instance #0
                sd (driver not attached)
                st (driver not attached)
SUNW,UltraSPARC-IIi (driver not attached)
pseudo, instance #0
```

Never panic about the message that a driver is "not attached" to a particular device. Because device drivers are only loaded on demand in Solaris, only those devices that are actively being used will have their drivers loaded. When a device is no longer being used, the device driver is unloaded from memory. This is an efficient memory management strategy that optimizes the use of physical RAM by deallocating memory for devices when they are no longer required. In the case of the Ultra 5, we can see that devices like the PCI bus and the IDE disk drives have attached device drivers and were being used while prtconf was running.

For an x86 system, the devices found are quite different:

```
System Configuration:  Sun Microsystems   i86pc
Memory size: 128 Megabytes
System Peripherals (Software Nodes):
i86pc
    +boot (driver not attached)
        memory (driver not attached)
    aliases (driver not attached)
    chosen (driver not attached)
    i86pc-memory (driver not attached)
    i86pc-mmu (driver not attached)
    openprom (driver not attached)
    options, instance #0
    packages (driver not attached)
    delayed-writes (driver not attached)
    itu-props (driver not attached)
    isa, instance #0
        motherboard (driver not attached)
        asy, instance #0
        lp (driver not attached)
        asy, instance #1
        fdc, instance #0
            fd, instance #0
            fd, instance #1 (driver not attached)
        kd (driver not attached)
        bios (driver not attached)
        bios (driver not attached)
        pnpCTL,0041 (driver not attached)
        pnpCTL,7002 (driver not attached)
        kd, instance #0
        chanmux, instance #0
    pci, instance #0
        pci8086,1237 (driver not attached)
        pci8086,7000 (driver not attached)
        pci-ide, instance #0
            ata, instance #0
                cmdk, instance #0
                sd, instance #1
        pci10ec,8029 (driver not attached)
        pci5333,8901 (driver not attached)
    used-resources (driver not attached)
    objmgr, instance #0
    pseudo, instance #0
```

At Boot Time

The OpenBoot monitor has the capability to diagnose hardware errors on system devices before booting the kernel. This can be particularly useful for identifying bus connectivity issues, such as unterminated SCSI chains, but also some basic functional issues, such as whether or not devices are responding. Issuing the command

```
ok reset
```

will also force a self-test of the system.

Just after booting, it is also useful to review the system boot messages, which can be retrieved by using the dmesg command. This displays a list of all the devices that were successfully attached at boot time. It also displays any error messages that were detected. Let's look at the dmesg output for a SPARC Ultra architecture system:

```
server# dmesg
Jan 17 13:06
cpu0: SUNW,UltraSPARC-IIi (upaid 0 impl 0x12 ver 0x12 clock 270 MHz)
SunOS Release 5.5.1 Version Generic_103640-19 [UNIX(R) System V Release
4.0]
Copyright (c) 1983-1996, Sun Microsystems, Inc.
mem = 131072K (0x8000000)
avail mem = 127852544
Ethernet address = 8:0:20:90:b3:23
root nexus = Sun Ultra 5/10 UPA/PCI (UltraSPARC-IIi 270MHz)
pci0 at root: UPA 0x1f 0x0
PCI-device: pci@1,1, simba #0
PCI-device: pci@1, simba #1
dad0 at pci1095,6460 target 0 lun 0
dad0 is /pci@1f,0/pci@1,1/ide@3/dad@0,0
        <Seagate Medalist 34342A cyl 8892 alt 2 hd 15 sec 63>
root on /pci@1f,0/pci@1,1/ide@3/disk@0,0:a fstype ufs
su0 at ebus0: offset 14,3083f8
su0 is /pci@1f,0/pci@1,1/ebus@1/su@14,3083f8
su1 at ebus0: offset 14,3062f8
su1 is /pci@1f,0/pci@1,1/ebus@1/su@14,3062f8
keyboard is </pci@1f,0/pci@1,1/ebus@1/su@14,3083f8> major <37> minor <0>
mouse is </pci@1f,0/pci@1,1/ebus@1/su@14,3062f8> major <37> minor <1>
stdin is </pci@1f,0/pci@1,1/ebus@1/su@14,3083f8> major <37> minor <0>
SUNW,m64B0 is /pci@1f,0/pci@1,1/SUNW,m64B@2
m64#0: 1280x1024, 2M mappable, rev 4754.9a
stdout is </pci@1f,0/pci@1,1/SUNW,m64B@2> major <8> minor <0>
boot cpu (0) initialization complete - online
se0 at ebus0: offset 14,400000
se0 is /pci@1f,0/pci@1,1/ebus@1/se@14,400000
SUNW,hme0: CheerIO 2.0 (Rev Id = c1) Found
SUNW,hme0 is /pci@1f,0/pci@1,1/network@1,1
SUNW,hme1: Local Ethernet address = 8:0:20:93:b0:65
pci1011,240: SUNW,hme1
SUNW,hme1 is /pci@1f,0/pci@1/pci@1/SUNW,hme@0,1
dump on /dev/dsk/c0t0d0s1 size 131328K
SUNW,hme0: Using Internal Transceiver
SUNW,hme0: 10 Mbps half-duplex Link Up
pcmcia: no PCMCIA adapters found
```

PART II

dmesg first performs a memory test, sets the Ethernet address for the network inter-face, and then initializes the PCI bus. An IDE disk is then recognized and mapped into a physical device, and the appropriate partitions are activated. The standard input devices (keyboard and mouse) are then activated, and the boot sequence is largely complete. However, the output is slightly different for the x86 system:

```
Jan 17 08:32
SunOS Release 5.7 Version Generic [UNIX(R) System V Release 4.0]
Copyright (c) 1983-1998, Sun Microsystems, Inc.
mem = 130688K (0x7fa0000)
avail mem = 114434048
root nexus = i86pc
isa0 at root
pci0 at root: space 0 offset 0
        IDE device at targ 0, lun 0 lastlun 0x0
        model ST310230A, stat 50, err 0
                cfg 0xc5a, cyl 16383, hd 16, sec/trk 63
                mult1 0x8010, mult2 0x110, dwcap 0x0, cap 0x2f00
                piomode 0x200, dmamode 0x200, advpiomode 0x3
                minpio 240, minpioflow 120
                valid 0x7, dwdma 0x407, majver 0x1e
ata_set_feature: (0x66,0x0) failed
        ATAPI device at targ 1, lun 0 lastlun 0x0
        model CD-912E/ATK, stat 50, err 0
                cfg 0x85a0, cyl 0, hd 0, sec/trk 0
                mult1 0x0, mult2 0x0, dwcap 0x0, cap 0xb00
                piomode 0x200, dmamode 0x200, advpiomode 0x1
                minpio 209, minpioflow 180
                valid 0x2, dwdma 0x203, majver 0x0
PCI-device: ata@0, ata0
ata0 is /pci@0,0/pci-ide@7,1/ata@0
Disk0:  <Vendor 'Gen-ATA ' Product 'ST310230A          '>
cmdk0 at ata0 target 0 lun 0
cmdk0 is /pci@0,0/pci-ide@7,1/ata@0/cmdk@0,0
root on /pci@0,0/pci-ide@7,1/ide@0/cmdk@0,0:a fstype ufs
ISA-device: asy0
asy0 is /isa/asy@1,3f8
ISA-device: asy1
asy1 is /isa/asy@1,2f8
Number of console virtual screens = 13
cpu 0 initialization complete - online
dump on /dev/dsk/c0d0s3 size 156 MB
```

While the System Is up

If you are working remotely on a server system, and you are unsure of the system archi-tecture, the command

```
server# arch -k
```

returns sun4u on the Ultra 5 system, but sun4m on a Sparc 10 system.

For a complete view of a system's device configuration, you may also try the sysdef command, which displays more detailed information concerning pseudo-devices, kernel-loadable modules, and parameters. Here's the sysdef output for an x86 server:

```
server# sysdef
# sysdef
*
* Hostid
*
   0ae61183
*
* i86pc Configuration
*
*
* Devices
*
+boot (driver not attached)
        memory (driver not attached)
aliases (driver not attached)
chosen (driver not attached)
i86pc-memory (driver not attached)
i86pc-mmu (driver not attached)
openprom (driver not attached)
options, instance #0
packages (driver not attached)
delayed-writes (driver not attached)
itu-props (driver not attached)
isa, instance #0
        motherboard (driver not attached)
        asy, instance #0
        lp (driver not attached)
        asy, instance #1
        fdc, instance #0
                fd, instance #0
                fd, instance #1 (driver not attached)
        kd (driver not attached)
        bios (driver not attached)
        bios (driver not attached)
        pnpCTL,0041 (driver not attached)
        pnpCTL,7002 (driver not attached)
        kd, instance #0
        chanmux, instance #0
pci, instance #0
        pci8086,1237 (driver not attached)
        pci8086,7000 (driver not attached)
        pci-ide, instance #0
                ata, instance #0
                        cmdk, instance #0
                        sd, instance #1
        pci10ec,8029 (driver not attached)
        pci5333,8901 (driver not attached)
used-resources (driver not attached)
```

```
objmgr, instance #0
pseudo, instance #0
        clone, instance #0
        ip, instance #0
        tcp, instance #0
        udp, instance #0
        log, instance #0
        sad, instance #0
        iwscn, instance #0
        mm, instance #0
        tl, instance #0
        cn, instance #0
        openeepr, instance #0
        kstat, instance #0
        pm, instance #0
        sy, instance #0
        vol, instance #0
        xsvc, instance #0
        ptm, instance #0
        pts, instance #0
        devinfo, instance #0
        ksyms, instance #0
*
* Loadable Objects
*
* Loadable Object Path = /platform/i86pc/kernel
*
drv/eisa
drv/isa
drv/mc
drv/openeepr
drv/pci
drv/rootnex
mach/uppc
misc/bootdev
misc/emul_80387
misc/pci_autoconfig
mmu/mmu32
unix
drv/aha
drv/asy
drv/chanmux
drv/cnft
drv/elx
drv/fd
drv/fdc
drv/kd
drv/kdmouse
drv/logi
drv/lp
drv/mlx
drv/msm
drv/smartii
```

```
drv/smc
drv/tr
misc/mse
drv/eha
drv/ata
drv/dpt
drv/mscsi
drv/pci-ide
drv/sbpro
drv/mcis
strmod/ansi
strmod/char
strmod/emap
strmod/vuid2ps2
strmod/vuid3ps2
strmod/vuidkd
strmod/vuidm3p
strmod/vuidm4p
strmod/vuidm5p
*
* Loadable Object Path = /kernel
*
strmod/hwc
exec/coffexec
misc/kgssapi
misc/cis
misc/cs
misc/pcalloc
misc/pcmcia
misc/dadk
misc/gda
misc/sccd_audio
misc/scdk
misc/snlb
misc/strategy
misc/sysinit
misc/rpcsec_gss
drv/arp
        hard link:   strmod/arp
drv/clone
drv/cn
drv/devinfo
drv/i2o_bs
drv/i2o_scsi
drv/icmp
drv/ip
drv/iwscn
drv/llc1
drv/log
drv/mm
drv/options
drv/pci_to_i2o
drv/profile
```

```
drv/pseudo
drv/ptc
cdrv/ptsl
drv/rts
drv/sad
drv/st
drv/sy
drv/tcp
drv/tl
drv/udp
drv/wc
fs/cachefs
fs/fifofs
fs/hsfs
fs/lofs
fs/nfs
        hard link:   sys/nfs
fs/procfs
fs/sockfs
fs/specfs
fs/tmpfs
fs/ufs
sched/TS
sched/TS_DPTBL
sys/c2audit
sys/doorfs
sys/inst_sync
sys/kaio
sys/msgsys
sys/pipe
sys/pset
sys/semsys
sys/shmsys
drv/pci_pci
drv/adp
drv/aic
drv/blogic
drv/chs
drv/corvette
drv/cpqncr
drv/csa
drv/dnet
drv/eepro
drv/elxl
drv/esa
drv/flashpt
drv/iee
drv/ieef
drv/iprb
drv/mega
drv/mtok
drv/ncrs
drv/nee
```

PART II

```
        drv/nei
        drv/nfe
        drv/p9000
        drv/p9100
        drv/pcn
        drv/pcscsi
        drv/pe
        drv/sd
        drv/smce
        drv/smceu
        drv/smcf
        drv/spwr
        drv/trantor
        drv/xsvc
        mach/ast
        mach/compaq
        mach/corollary
        mach/pcplusmp
        mach/syspro
        mach/tpf
        mach/wysemp
        fs/autofs
        drv/pcic
        drv/pcs
        drv/pem
        drv/ra
        drv/pcelx
        drv/pcmem
        drv/pcram
        drv/pcser
        drv/cmdk
        drv/objmgr
        drv/pcata
        exec/elfexec
        exec/intpexec
        genunix
    misc/consconfig
      misc/des
      misc/gld
      misc/i2o_msg
      misc/ipc
      misc/klmmod
      misc/klmops
      misc/krtld
      misc/md5
      misc/nfs_dlboot
      misc/nfssrv
      misc/rpcsec
      misc/scsi
      misc/seg_drv
      misc/seg_mapdev
      misc/strplumb
      misc/swapgeneric
```

```
misc/tlimod
misc/ufs_log
strmod/bufmod
strmod/connld
strmod/dedump
strmod/ldterm
strmod/pckt
strmod/pfmod
strmod/pipemod
strmod/ptem
strmod/redirmod
strmod/rpcmod
        hard link:  sys/rpcmod
strmod/timod
strmod/tirdwr
strmod/ttcompat
*
* Loadable Object Path = /usr/kernel
*
exec/javaexec
fs/fdfs
fs/namefs
fs/pcfs
fs/s5fs
misc/diaudio
strmod/eucu8
strmod/u8euc
strmod/u8koi8
strmod/u8lat1
strmod/u8lat2
strmod/rlmod
strmod/telmod
sched/IA
sched/RT
sched/RT_DPTBL
sys/sysacct
drv/audiocs
drv/dump
drv/kstat
drv/ksyms
drv/lockstat
drv/logindmux
drv/ptm
drv/pts
drv/winlock
drv/pm
drv/tnf
drv/vol
*
* System Configuration
*
  swap files
swapfile            dev  swaplo blocks    free
```

```
/dev/dsk/c0d0s3     102,3       8 321288 321288
```

The key sections in the sysdef output are details of all devices, such as the PCI bus, and pseudo-devices for each loadable object path (including /kernel and /usr/kernel). Loadable objects are also identified, along with swap and virtual memory settings. Although the output may seem verbose, the information provided for each device can prove to be very useful in tracking down hardware errors or missing loadable objects.

Summary

In Solaris, devices are represented by files that are visible to all users, which makes it easier to understand how physical devices are mapped into logical devices by the operating system. The sophisticated methods that Solaris uses to refer to both physical and logical devices can seem daunting at first, especially if you are used to referring to disk drives as C: or D:, but the extra work is worth the effort when setting up server systems like the E450, which may have 20 or more internal disks, combined with fast, external storage in the form of an A1000 RAID system. Keeping track of the many different kinds of storage and devices can be made easier by learning the basics of device nomenclature as outlined in this chapter.

Questions

1. Which type of device is represented by /sbus@1f,0?
   A. Hard disk
   B. Tape drive
   C. CD-ROM
   D. SBUS

2. Which type of device is represented by /sbus@1f,0/SUNW,fas@2,8800000/ sd@1,0?
   A. Hard disk
   B. Tape drive
   C. CD-ROM
   D. SBUS

3. Where are logical device files stored?

A. /logical

B. /dev

C. /devices

D. /etc

4. Where are physical device names located?

    A. /logical

    B. /dev

    C. /devices

    D. /etc

5. What are /dev/tty1 and /dev/pty1?

    A. Terminal and pseudo-terminal devices

    B. Terminal and pseudo-terminal device drivers

    C. Login windows

    D. Terminal types

6. What is the command used to check all volumes managed by volume management?

    A. volumecheck

    B. volcheck

    C. format

    D. pmadm

7. Which command is used to check the validity of serial port settings?

    A. pmadm

    B. serialchk

    C. format

    D. linecheck

8. Which command is used to review system boot messages?

    A. revboot

    B. reboot

    C. bootmsg

    D. dmesg

Answers

1. D

2. A

3. B

4. C

5. A

6. B

7. A

8. D

The Service Access Facility (SAF)

In this chapter, you will learn the following:

- The primary Service Access Facility (SAF) process (sac)
- The SAF port monitor processes (ttymon and listen)
- Viewing SAF settings
- Managing port monitors

The SAF is a port management system that manages requests and responses for access to system ports. In this case, a port is defined as the physical connection between a peripheral device and the system. For example, most systems have one or more serial ports that enable sequential data transmission effectively down a single line. In contrast, a parallel port enables several lines of data to be transmitted bidirectionally. The SAF system is designed to enable requests to be made to the system from peripheral devices through ports and to ensure that these requests are appropriately serviced by the relevant port monitor.

The Primary SAF Process (sac)

The process that initiates the service access facility is known as the service access controller (/usr/lib/saf/sac). It is started when the system enters run level 2, 3, or 4, as shown in this /etc/inittab entry:

```
sc:234:respawn:/usr/lib/saf/sac -t 300
```

Here the respawn entry indicates that if a process is not running when it should be, then it should be respawned. For example, if a system changes from run level 2 to run level 3, sac should be running. If it is not present, it will be restarted.

When sac is started, it reads the script /etc/saf/_safconfig, which contains any local configurations tailored for the system. Next, the standard configuration file /etc/saf/_sactab is read, and sac spawns a separate child process for each of the port monitors it supports (ttymon and listen). A sample _sactab is shown here:

```
# VERSION=1
zsmon:ttymon::0:/usr/lib/saf/ttymon #
```

Each of these monitors also reads its own configuration file. The files /etc/saf/ttymon/_config and /etc/saf/listen/_config are used to configure the ttymon and listen port monitors, respectively. A sample _config file is shown here:

```
# VERSION=1
ttya:u:root:reserved:reserved:reserved:/dev/term/a:I::/usr/bin/
login::9600:ldterm,
ttcompat:ttya login\: ::tvi925:y:#
```

The point of this hierarchical configuration file structure is that values read from /etc/saf/_safconfig and /etc/saf/_sactab by sac are inherited by the spawned port monitor processes, which then have the capability to configure their own operations. This hierarchy is shown in Figure 25-1.

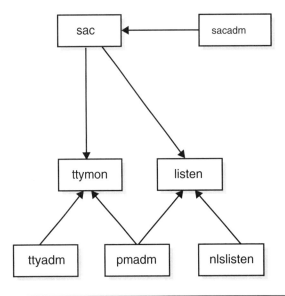

Figure 25-1   Command-set hierarchy for SAF

SAF Port Monitors

The SAF has two types of port monitors: the terminal port monitor (ttymon) and the network port monitor (listen). For example, the ttymon port monitor for the console is started in run levels 2, 3, and 4, through an /etc/inittab entry like the following:

```
co:234:respawn:/usr/lib/saf/ttymon -g -h -p "'uname -n' console
login: " -T vt100 -d /dev/console -l console -m ldterm,ttcompat
```

The port monitors are managed by the pmadm command. Port services can be managed by using the following commands:

- **pmadm -a**   Adding a port monitor service
- **pmadm -d**   Disarming a port monitor service
- **pmadm -e**   Enabling a port monitor service
- **pmadm -r**   Removing a port monitor service

ttymon

The ttymon port monitor is managed by the ttyadm command. ttymon is designed to monitor requests from ports to enable remote access to the system. The ttymon operates continually, spawning child processes when appropriate in order to service requests, which are sequentially numbered (ttymon1, ttymon2, and so on). The most common request for terminals is probably for an interactive login. Thus, /usr/bin/login is requested. The sacadm command can be used to list all current ttymon processes:

```
# sacadm -l
PMTAG       PMTYPE     FLGS    RCNT    STATUS    COMMAND
ttymon1     ttymon     -       2       ENABLED   /usr/lib/saf/ttymon #ttymon1
ttymon2     ttymon     -       2       ENABLED   /usr/lib/saf/ttymon #ttymon2
ttymon3     ttymon     -       2       ENABLED   /usr/lib/saf/ttymon #ttymon3
```

In order to view the services currently being provided through a particular monitor, you can use the pmadm command for each monitor process:

```
# pmadm -l -p ttymon2
PMTAG PMTYPE        SVCTAG       FLGS       ID       <PMSPECIFIC>
ttymon2     ttymon      11        u       root      /dev/term/11    -    -
      /usr/bin/login - 9600 - login:     -tvi925
ttymon2     ttymon      12        u       root      /dev/term/12    -    -
      /usr/bin/login - 9600 - login:     -tvi925
ttymon2     ttymon      13        u       root      /dev/term/13    -    -
      /usr/bin/login - 9600 - login:     -tvi925
ttymon2     ttymon      14        u       root      /dev/term/14    -    -
      /usr/bin/login - 9600 - login:     -tvi925
```

Here we can see that ports /dev/term/11 through /dev/term/14 are being serviced using the login service.

listen

The listen port monitor is managed by the nlslisten and nlsadmin commands. In contrast to ttymon, the listen port monitor manages network ports and connections by listening for requests to access services and daemons. The listen monitor uses the Transport Layer Interface (TLI) and STREAMS to implement OSI-compliant network-service layers. Specific network ports are assigned to the listen monitor, and child processes are spawned to handle each client request. One of the most important features of listen is that it can provide services that are not managed by inetd; all daemons can be accessed through a listen service.

The nlsadmin command is used to set up transport providers for STREAMS-compatible network services. In order to configure a TLI listener database, the nlsadmin command can be used to configure the listener. First, the TCP/IP database is created:

```
# nlsadmin -i tcp
```

Next, set the local hexadecimal address:

```
# nlsadmin -l \x11331223a11a58310000000000000000 tcp
```

All services that need to be run will then need to be entered into the TLI listener database.

Port Monitor Management

The sacadm command is used to manage port monitors. The following functions are available:

- **sacadm -a**   Attaching a new port monitor
- **sacadm -e**   Arming a port monitor
- **sacadm -d**   Disarming a port monitor
- **sacadm -s**   Initializing a port monitor
- **sacadm -k**   Killing a port monitor
- **sacadm -l**   Listing port monitor details
- **sacadm -r**   Deleting a port monitor

Summary

In this chapter, we have examined how the service access facility is configured. Although most of what the SAF does occurs automatically behind the scenes, it's important to understand the hierarchy of commands and administrative functions shown in Figure 25-1.

Questions

1. What is a port?
   A. A port is the physical connection between a peripheral device and the system.
   B. A port is the logical representation of a peripheral device on the system.
   C. A port is a number greater than 1,024.
   D. A port is the management process for the SAF.

2. Which process initiates the service access facility?
   A. saf
   B. sac
   C. sacadm
   D. init

3. In which run level is the service access facility started?
   A. 1
   B. 2
   C. 3
   D. 2, 3, and 4

4. Which file is read in when the service access starts?
   A. /etc/sac/_sacconfig
   B. /etc/sam/_samconfig
   C. /etc/saf/_safconfig
   D. /etc/san/_sanconfig

5. Which command is used to add a port monitor service?
   A. pmadm -a
   B. pmadm -d
   C. pmadm -e
   D. pmadm -r

6. Which command is used to enable a port monitor service?
   A. pmadm -a
   B. pmadm -d
   C. pmadm -e
   D. pmadm -r

7. Which command is used to disable a port monitor service?
   A. pmadm -a
   B. pmadm -d
   C. pmadm -e
   D. pmadm -r

8. Which command is used to remove a port monitor service?
   A. pmadm -a
   B. pmadm -d
   C. pmadm -e
   D. pmadm -r

Answers

1. A

2. B

3. D

4. C

5. A

6. B

7. C

8. D

Adding Terminals and Modems with Admintool

The following objectives will be met upon completing this chapter's material:

- Adding a serial port
- Adding a modem

Adding a Serial Port

Like any modern server system, Solaris supports the connection of simple external devices through both a serial (RS-232-C or RS-423) and a parallel port, as discussed in Chapter 24. The two most common uses of serial devices on a Scalable Processor Architecture (SPARC) system are connecting a VT-100 terminal or its equivalent in order to operate as the system console if no graphics device is installed, and as a modem, enabling dial-up Internet access using the Point-to-Point Protocol (PPP). The former is a common practice in many server rooms, where using a VT-100 terminal as the console can eliminate the expense of a monitor and video card, as many SPARC machines require a display device to boot at all.

On x86 systems, many more devices are available that often only have drivers available for other operating systems. Sun and other third-party hardware vendors are slowly making releases available for these devices through the Solaris Developer Connection. If you need to obtain an updated copy of the Solaris Device Configuration Assistant and any updated device drivers for supported external devices, these are currently available for download at **http://soldc.sun.com/support/drivers/boot.html**.

Unlike the other applications reviewed in this chapter for device configuration, Solaris has a graphical user interface (GUI) for serial device configuration, provided through the admintool program. admintool is generally used for system administration tasks, such as adding users and groups, but it also has facilities for configuring parallel devices like printers and serial devices like modems. It contains templates for configuring standard modem and terminal devices, and it supports multiple ports (see Figure 26-1).

Central to the idea of providing services through serial ports is the port monitor, which continuously monitors the serial ports for requests to login. The port monitor doesn't process the communication parameters directly, but accepts requests and passes them to the operating system. Newer releases of Solaris use the ttymon port monitor, which enables multiple concurrent getty requests from serial devices.

To configure the port for a terminal, start up admintool and enter the user mode, which can be either Basic, More, or Expert. In most cases, the Basic setup will be useful for most circumstances. admintool enables the configuration of most parameters for the port, including the baud rate for communications, the default terminal type, flow control, and carrier detection. The values entered here should match those on the

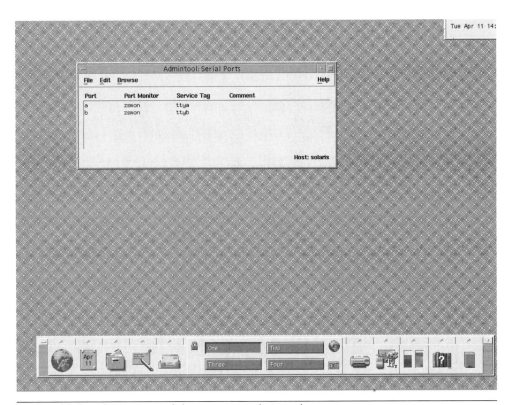

Figure 26-1   Managing serial devices using admintool

matching VT-100 terminal. Once the settings have been saved, it is possible to check the validity of the settings by using the pmadm command:

```
server# pmadm -l -s ttyb
```

tip

tip is a command that acts like a terminal. It can be used, for example, to access remote systems directly through a serial port, where one system acts as the console for the other. In this section, we'll use the tip command to connect a Solaris system to a modem. Before proceeding, however, we'll examine some of the key features of tip in its own right.

tip uses the /etc/remote file to enable it to make connections through the serial port. For example, if you have a profile setup in /etc/remote, it's possible to fire up a terminal session immediately by using the command

```
# tip -profile
```

where profile is the name of the profile that you've set up with all the settings that the port requires to operate. tip also uses initialization settings in the .tiprc file to specify its operational parameters. Table 26-1 shows the most commonly used tip commands.

Table 26-1   Commonly Used tip Commands

Command	Description
~.	Exit the session.
~c	Change the directory.
~!	Spawn a shell.
~>	Send a local file.
~<	Receive a remote file.
~p	Send a local file.
~t	Receive a remote file.
~C	Enable a local application to connect to a remote system.
~#	Issue a break command.
~s	Define a variable.
~^z	Suspend tip.

Adding a Modem

Solaris works best with external, Hayes-compatible modems, which are also supported by other operating systems such as Microsoft Windows. However, modems that require specific operating system support (such as so-called WinModems) will not work with Solaris. In addition, internal modem cards are generally not supported by Solaris. Although older modems tend to use external (but sometimes internal) Dual Inline Package (DIP) switches, modern modems can be soft-configured to set most of their key operational parameters.

Modem access can be configured to enable inbound-only, outbound-only, and bidirectional access, which enables traffic in both directions using a similar scheme. In the following example, we'll consider the common scenario of dial-out-only access. The modem should be connected to one of the system's serial ports (A or B) and switched on. The A and B serial ports map to the devices /dev/cua/a and /dev/cua/b, respectively.

To test the modem, use the tip command:

```
server# tip hardwire
```

where hardwire should be defined in /etc/remote. The hardwire entry should be similar to this entry:

```
hardwire:\
        :dv=/dev/cua/a:br#19200:el=^C^S^Q^U^D:ie=%$:oe=^D:
```

where 19200 bps is the connection speed between the modem and the serial port. In addition, /etc/remote should have a connection string associated with each modem that's connected to the system. For example, the following string

```
cua1:dv=/dev/cua/a:p8:br#19200
```

specifies that 19200 bps is the connection speed between the modem and the serial port, with eight-bit transmission and no parity enabled. To use this entry specifically, you would use the command:

```
# tip cua1
```

If the message

```
connected
```

appears on your terminal, then the system is able to communicate successfully with the modem. For Hayes-compatible modems, command strings can be entered directly such as

```
ATE1V1
```

If you see OK, then the modem is communicating as expected and can now be configured to run PPP. More information about PPP and Solaris can be found at **ftp://cs.anu.edu.au/pub/software/ppp**.

Summary

In this chapter, we've examined how to configure a serial port and add a modem to it. The modem can be configured using PPP. We also reviewed the possible commands that can be used with the tip command.

Questions

1. Which of the following is not a serial port property set by admintool?
    A. Baud rate
    B. Default terminal type
    C. Carrier detection
    D. Modem name

2. Which command can be used to check the status of a port?
    A. pmadm
    B. sacadm
    C. portmon
    D. portlisten

3. In which direction does Solaris support modem data transmission?
    A. Inbound-only
    B. Outbound-only
    C. Bidirectional access
    D. All of the above

4. Which command can be used to test a modem?
    A. tip hardwire
    B. modem
    C. modemchk
    D. modemtest

5. Name a valid serial port device.
   A. /dev/modem
   B. /dev/serial
   C. /dev/serial/a
   D. /dev/cua/b

Answers

1. D

2. A

3. D

4. A

5. D

Introduction to Disk Management

The following objectives will be met upon completing this chapter's material:

- Understanding the importance of the Redundant Array of Inexpensive Disks (RAID) technology
- Reviewing the features of virtual filesystems
- Setting up a striped disk using DiskSuite
- Setting up a mirrored disk using DiskSuite

What Is RAID?

Solaris servers are often set up to be "highly available," meaning that the databases, application servers, and distributed applications that they host must be accessible to clients at all times. Such applications and services are often deployed on Solaris because of the failover technologies provided by Sun's hardware offerings. For example, many high-end SPARC systems feature dual power supplies and enable the installation of many hard disks in a single cabinet. The E-450, for example, can house up to 20 high-speed, high-capacity disks (18GB at 10,000 RPM).

Production systems of this kind invariably experience two kinds of capacity problems: Firstly, even though the E-450 system discussed here may have a total capacity of 360GB, the largest file size that can be supported by the system is the size of an individual hard drive. This means that database servers, for example, will require multiple mount points to be located on a single filesystem for storing extremely large data files. Having 20 hard disks in this context is only as useful as having one. One solution is to wait until hard disks with higher capacities are manufactured; however, relying on future hardware updates is not feasible for systems that have immediate deployment requirements. What is required is some way of splitting physical data storage across several physical disk volumes while providing a single logical interface for access.

The second problem that arises is that hard disks and other physical media inevitably fail after periods of heavy use. Even if quality hard drives have mean time between failures (MTBFs) of several years, this is an average figure. Some drives last ten years; others only last one. Again, superior Sun hardware provides some relief here. It is possible to "hot swap" hard drives in an E-450, for example, without having to shut down the system and reboot. The faulty drive is simply removed and the new drive replaced. Once backups have been loaded, the system will be available once again.

However, the length of time it takes to restore disk contents from backups might take several hours, and customers often complain of downtime that lasts minutes. So, although restoring from backups is an excellent strategy for countering a catastrophic failure, it is simply not an option for production systems experiencing single-disk failures. What is required is some level of content redundancy that retains more than one copy of a system's data across different disks.

To solve the capacity and redundancy problem, Solaris provides support for the RAID standard. RAID defines a number of different levels that provide various types of striping and mirroring. In this context, striping means the process of spreading data across different physical disks while presenting a single logical interface for the logical volume. Thus, a striped disk set containing four 18GB drives would have a total logical capacity of 72GB. This configuration is shown in Figure 27-1.

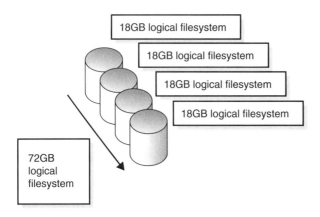

Figure 27-1   Striped disk configuration

A different approach is offered by mirroring. Here a logical volume's contents are copied in real time to more than one physical device. Thus, four 18GB drives could be mirrored to provide two completely redundant 18GB volumes. This means that if one disk fails, its mirror would automatically be used to continue to create, read, update, and delete operations on the filesystem while the disk was physically replaced (again, with no reboot required). This kind of seamless operation requires no downtime and is shown in Figure 27-2.

Alternatively, the four disks could be configured so that a 36GB striped volume could be created, combining the capacities of two disks, while the remaining two disks could be used to mirror this striped volume. Thus, the system is provided with a logical 36GB volume that also features complete redundancy. This configuration is shown in Figure 27-3.

Six major RAID levels are supported by DiskSuite, the tool that is used to set up mirrored and striped virtual filesystems on Solaris. RAID Level 0 is the primary striping level, which enables a virtual filesystem to be constructed of several physical disks. Their capacities are effectively combined to produce a single disk with a large capacity. In contrast, RAID Level 1 is the primary mirroring level. All data that is written to the virtual filesystem is also copied in real time to a separate physical disk that has the same capacity as the original. This level has the slowest performance because all data must be written twice to two different disks, and costs the most because each drive to be mirrored makes use of a second drive, which cannot be used for any other purpose. However, full redundancy can be achieved using RAID Level 1.

The remaining RAID levels are variations on these two themes. RAID Level 2 is a secondary mirroring level, which uses Hamming codes for error correction. RAID Levels 3

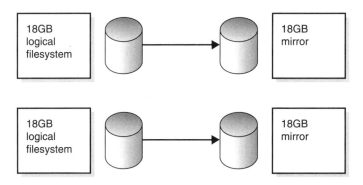

Figure 27-2   Mirrored disk configuration

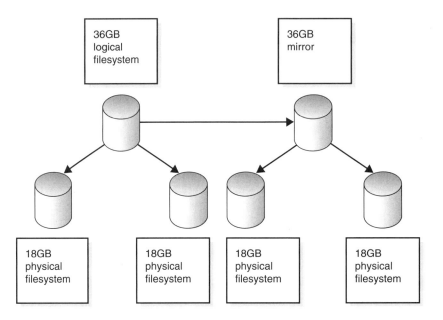

Figure 27-3   Striped and mirrored disk configuration

and 4 are secondary striping levels, writing parity information to a single drive, but writing all other data to multiple physical disks.

In contrast, RAID Level 5 is a striping and mirroring level that enables data to be written to different disks, including parity information. RAID 5 offers the best solution for systems that require both mirroring and striping. These levels are summarized in Table 27-1.

Setting up RAID

The first step in setting up any kind of RAID system is to install the DiskSuite packages and prepare the disks for mirroring or striping by formatting them. Primary disks and their mirrors must be set up with exactly the same partition structure to ensure that virtual filesystems can be created that are compatible with both the primary disk and the mirrors.

Once the DiskSuite packages have been installed, it is necessary to prepare disks that will be used with DiskSuite. This preparation includes creating state database replicas for virtual filesystems used on the system. Ideally, these state database replicas will be

Table 27-1   Commonly Used RAID Levels

Level	Description
0	Primary striping level enabling a single virtual filesystem to be constructed of multiple physical disks
1	Primary mirroring level where all data written to a virtual filesystem is copied in real time to a separate mirroring disk
2	A secondary mirroring level, which uses Hamming codes for error correction
3	A secondary striping level, which writes parity information to a single drive, but writes all other data to multiple drives
4	A secondary striping level, which writes parity information to a single drive, but writes all other data to multiple drives
5	A striping and mirroring level, which enables data to be written to different disks, including parity information

distributed across each controller and/or disk, so that maximum redundancy can be achieved. A small partition must be created on each disk that will contain the state database (typically around 5MB). For example, to create a state database replica on the filesystem /dev/dsk/c1t0d0s7, we would use the following command:

```
# metadb -c 3 -a -f /dev/dsk/c1t0d0s7 /dev/dsk/c0t0d0s7
```

This creates three replicas on each of the two disks specified (/dev/dsk/c1t0d0s7 and /dev/dsk/c0t0d0s7). Note that two controllers are used, rather than one.

If no state database replicas exist, the following message will be displayed:

```
metadb: There are no existing databases
```

Striping

Next, we need to create configurations for the virtual filesystems that we want to use. These can be permanently recorded in the DiskSuite configuration file (md.tab). For example, the striping configuration we mentioned previously involving four 18GB disks could have its configuration recorded with the following entry if the virtual filesystem (s5) had the path /dev/md/dsk/d5:

```
d5 4 1 c1t1d0s5 1 c1t2d0s5 1 c2t1d0s5 1 c2t2d0s5
```

Here the four physical disks involved are /dev/dsk/c1t1d0s5, /dev/dsk/c1t2d0s5, /dev/dsk/c2t1d0s5, and /dev/dsk/c2t2d0s5. To ensure that the virtual filesystem is mounted at boot time, it could be included in the /etc/vfstab file, just like a normal filesystem. Indeed, there should only be an entry for /dev/md/dsk/d5 in /etc/vfstab after striping is complete, and the entries for /dev/dsk/c1t1d0s5, /dev/dsk/c1t2d0s5, /dev/dsk/c2t1d0s5, and /dev/dsk/c2t2d0s5 should be commented out.

To initialize the d5 metadevice, we would use the command:

```
# metainit d5
```

If this commands succeeds, we simply treat the new metadevice as if it were a new filesystem and initialize a UFS filesystem on it:

```
# newfs /dev/md/rdsk/d5
```

Next, we need to create an appropriate mount point for the device (such as /staff) and mount the metadevice:

```
# mkdir /staff
# mount /dev/md/dsk/d5 /staff
```

The striped volume d5 is now ready for use.

Mirroring

In order to create a mirror between two filesystems, we follow a similar procedure of creating an entry in the md.tab file. For example, if we want to create a mirror of /dev/dsk/c1t1d0s5 with /dev/dsk/c0t1d0s5 (note the different controller), we would need to create a virtual filesystem (d50) that mirrored the primary filesystem (d52) to its mirror (d53). The following entries would need to be made in md.tab:

```
d50 -m /dev/md/dsk/d52 /dev/md/dsk/d53
d52 1 1 /dev/dsk/c1t1d0s5
d53 1 1 /dev/dsk/c0t1d0s5
```

To initialize the d5 metadevice, we would use the command:

```
# metainit d50
# metainit d52
# metainit d53
```

If this commands succeeds, we simply treat the new metadevice as if it were a new filesystem and initialize a UFS filesystem on it:

```
# newfs /dev/md/rdsk/d50
# newfs /dev/md/rdsk/d52
# newfs /dev/md/rdsk/d53
```

Next, we need to create an appropriate mount point for the device (such as /work) and mount the metadevice:

```
# mkdir /work
# mount /dev/md/dsk/d50 /work
```

The mirrored volume d50 is now ready for use.

Summary

In this chapter, we've examined the basics of creating striped and mirrored volumes using Solaris DiskSuite. RAID technology is critical to maintaining highly available Solaris systems, and although hardware-based RAID systems do exist, DiskSuite is a high performance tool that is available free of charge to implement software-based RAID.

Questions

1. What is the primary striping level enabling a single virtual filesystem to be constructed of multiple physical disks?
   A. 0
   B. 1
   C. 2
   D. 3

2. What is the primary mirroring level where all data written to a virtual filesystem is copied in real time to a separate mirroring disk?
   A. 0
   B. 1
   C. 2
   D. 3

3. What is the process of spreading data across different physical disks while presenting a single, logical interface for the logical volume?
   A. Backups
   B. Mirroring
   C. Striping
   D. Parity

4. What is the level of content redundancy that retains more than one copy of a system's data across different disks?
   A. Backups
   B. Mirroring
   C. Striping
   D. Parity

5. What is the command that creates state database replicas for virtual filesystems?
   A. metastat
   B. metaclear
   C. metainit
   D. metadb

6. What is the command that initializes metadevices?
   A. metastat
   B. metaclear
   C. metainit
   D. initmeta

Answers

1. A

2. B

3. C

4. B

5. D

6. C

Networks

The following objectives will be met upon completing this chapter's material:

- Subnet configurations
- Configuration network files (/etc/hosts and /etc/hostname)
- Checking logged-in users
- Login to a system remotely
- Understanding remote access security (/etc/hosts.equiv and .rhosts files)
- Checking if a host is up using ping and traceroute

Solaris networks and others are comprised of Class A, B, and C subnets interconnected by routers. The simplest Solaris network consists of two hosts connected using a hub or crossover cable to form a single Class C subnet. However, many larger Solaris networks are comprised of many Class C subnets that are connected to each other, perhaps as part of a large Class B network. In this chapter, we'll examine some networking basics that are essential for understanding more complex topics (such as routing).

Subnet Configurations

Subnets are visible to each other by means of a mask. Class A subnets use the mask 255.0.0.0, Class B networks use the mask 255.255.0.0, and Class C networks use the mask 255.255.255.0. These masks are used when broadcasts are made to specific subnets. A Class C subnet 134.132.23.0, for example, can have 255 hosts associated with it, starting with 134.132.23.1 and ending with 134.132.23.255. Class A and B subnets have their own distinctive enumeration schemes.

Configuration Network Files

The /etc/hostname file contains the fully qualified domain name of the local host. Thus, the system emu, in the DNS domain cassowary.net, has the fully qualified domain name emu.cassowary.net. Independent of the Domain Name System (DNS) is the local hosts file (/etc/hosts), which is used to list local hostnames and IP addresses. For a network with large numbers of hosts, using the /etc/hosts file is problematic, because its values must be updated on every host on the network each time a change is made. This is why DNS (or the Network Information Service [NIS/NIS+]) are better solutions for managing distributed host data.

However, the /etc/hosts file contains entries for some key services, such as logging, so it usually contains at least the following entries:

- The loopback address, 127.0.0.1, which is associated with the generic hostname localhost. This enables applications to be tested locally using the IP address 127.0.0.1 or the hostname localhost.

- The IP address, hostname, and fully qualified domain name of the localhost, because it requires this data before establishing a connection to a DNS server or NIS/NIS server when booting.

- An entry for a loghost, so that syslog data can be redirected to the appropriate host on the local network.

A sample /etc/hosts file is shown here:

```
127.0.0.1       localhost
192.68.16.1     emu        emu.cassowary.net
192.68.16.2     hawk       hawk.cassowary.net        loghost
192.68.16.3     eagle      eagle.cassowary.net
```

In this configuration, the localhost entry is defined, followed by the name and IP address of the localhost (hostname emu, with an IP address 192.68.16.1). In this case, emu redirects all of its syslog logging data to the host hawk (192.68.16.2), whereas another host eagle (192.68.16.3) is also defined.

Checking Logged-in Users

The command who displays who is currently logged into the system. The output of who displays the username, the connecting line, the date of login, the idle time, the process id, and a comment. An example output is as follows:

```
client% who
root console Nov 22 12:39
pwatters pts/0 Nov 19 21:05 (client.site.com)
```

This command can be automated to update the list of active users. An alternative to who is the w command, which displays a more detailed summary of the current activity on the system, including the current process name for each user. The header output from w shows the current time, the uptime of the current system, and the number of users actively logged into the system. The average system load is also displayed as a series of three numbers at the end of the w header, indicating the average number of jobs in the run queue for the previous 1, 5, and 15 minutes. In addition to the output generated by who, the w command displays the current foreground process for each user, which is usually a shell. For example, the output

```
root console Thu12pm 3days 6 6 /usr/openwin/bin/shelltool
pwatters pts/12 Thu11am 8:45 9 /usr/local/bin/tcsh
```

shows that the root user has an active shelltool running under Open Windows, while the user pwatters is running the Cornell shell. The w and who commands are useful tools for getting an overview of current and historical usage patterns on any Solaris system.

Login to a System Remotely

Telnet is the standard remote access tool for logging into a Solaris machine from a client using the original Defense Advanced Research Projects Agency (DARPA) Telnet protocol. A client can be executed on most operating systems that support TCP/IP. Alternatively, a Java telnet client is available at **http://srp.stanford.edu/~tjw/telnet.html** that is supported on any operating system that has a browser that runs Java natively or as a plug-in.

Telnet is a terminal-like program that gives users interactive access to a login shell of their choice (such as the C Shell or csh). Most Telnet clients support VT100 or VT220 terminal emulations. The login shell can be used to execute scripts, develop applications, and read e-mail and news—in short, everything a Solaris environment should provide to its users, with the exception of X11 graphics and Open Windows, or, more recently, the common desktop environment (CDE). A common arrangement in many organizations is for a Solaris server to be located in a secure area of a building, with Telnet-only access allowed. This arrangement is shown in Figure 28-1.

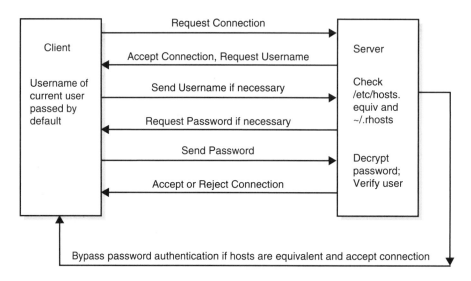

Figure 28-1   Identification and authentication sequence for rlogin

The sequence of events that occurs during a Telnet session begins with a request for a connection from the client to the server. The server either responds (or times out) with a connection being explicitly accepted or rejected. A rejection may occur because a packet filter, or firewall, has blocked the port that normally accepts Telnet client connections on the server. If the connection is accepted, the client is asked to enter a username followed by a password. If the username and password combination is valid, then a shell is spawned, and the user is logged in. This sequence of events is shown in Figure 28-2.

The standard port for Telnet connections is 23. Thus, a command like

```
client% telnet server
```

is expanded to give the effective command:

```
client% telnet server 25
```

Because a port number can be specified on the command line, Telnet clients can be used to connect to arbitrary ports on Solaris servers. This makes a Telnet client a very useful tool. For example, one can interactively issue commands to a FTP server on port 21:

```
client% telnet server 21
Trying 172.16.1.1...
```

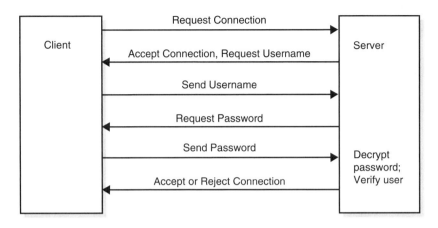

Figure 28-2 Identification and authentication of a Telnet session

```
Connected to server.
Escape character is '^]'.
220 server FTP server (UNIX(r) System V Release 4.0) ready.
```

and a sendmail server on port 25:

```
client% telnet server 25
Trying 172.16.1.1...
Connected to server.
Escape character is '^]'.
220 server ESMTP Sendmail 8.9.1a/8.9.1; Mon, 22 Nov 1999 14:31:36
+1100 (EST)
```

Interactive testing of this kind has many uses. For example, if we Telnet to port 80 on a server, we are usually connected to a Web server, where we can issue interactive commands using the Hypertext Transfer Protocol (HTTP). For example, to get the default index page on a server, we could type **get index.html**:

```
Trying 172.16.1.1...
Connected to server.
Escape character is '^]'.
GET index.html
<!DOCTYPE HTML PUBLIC "-//IETF//DTD HTML 2.0//EN">
<HTML><HEAD>
<TITLE>Server</TITLE></HEAD>
<h1>Welcome to server!</h1>
....
```

This technique is useful when testing proxy server configurations for new kinds of HTTP clients (such as HotJava browser) or during a script to check whether the Web server is active and serving expected content.

Telnet is controlled by the super Internet daemon inetd, which invokes the in.telnetd server. An entry is made in /etc/services that defines the port number for the Telnet service, which looks like the following:

```
telnet     23/tcp
```

The configuration file /etc/inetd.conf also contains important details of the services provided by inetd. The telnet daemon's location and properties are identified here:

```
telnet stream tcp nowait root /pkgs/tcpwrapper/bin/tcpd in.telnetd
```

In this case, we can see that in.telnetd is protected by the use of TCP wrappers, which facilitate the logging of Telnet access through the Solaris syslog facility. In addition, inetd has some significant historical security holes and performance issues that, although they have largely been fixed in recent years, have caused administrators to shy away from servers invoked by inetd. The Apache Web server (**http://www.apache.org**), supplied with Solaris 8, can run as a standalone daemon process.

Understanding Remote Access Security

inetd also controls many other standard remote access clients, such as the so-called r-commands, which include the remote login (rlogin) and remote shell (rsh) applications. The rlogin application is similar to Telnet in that it establishes a remote connection through TCP/IP to a server, spawning an interactive login shell. For example, the command

```
client% rlogin server
```

by default produces the response:

```
password:
```

after which the password is entered, authenticated by the server, and access is denied or granted. If the target user account has a different name to your current user account, you can try

```
client% rlogin server -1 user
```

Two main differences exist between Telnet and rlogin, however, which are significant. The first is that rlogin attempts to use the username on your current system as the account name to connect to on the remote service, whereas Telnet always prompts for a separate username. This makes remotely logging into machines on a single logical network much faster than Telnet.

Secondly, on a trusted, secure network, it is possible to set up a remote authentication mechanism by which the remote host enables a direct, no-username/no-password login from authorized clients. This automated authentication can be performed on a system-wide level by defining an equivalent host for authentication purposes on the server in /etc/hosts.equiv, or on a user-by-user basis with the file .rhosts. If the file /etc/hosts.equiv contains the client machine name and your user name, then you will be permitted to automatically execute a remote login.

For example, if the /etc/hosts.equiv file on server contains the line

```
client
```

then any user from the machine client may login to a corresponding account on the server without entering a username and password. Similarly, if your username and client machine name appear in the .rhosts file in the home directory of the user with the same name on the server, then you will also be permitted to remotely login without an identification/authentication challenge. The sequence of identification and authentication for rlogin is shown in Figure 28-3.

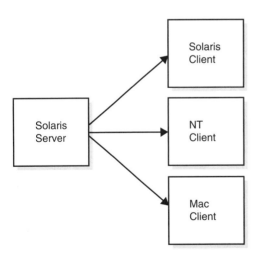

Figure 28-3   Typical remote access topology for client/server technology

Remote-shell (rsh) connects to a specified hostname and executes a command. rsh is equivalent to rlogin when no command arguments are specified. rsh copies its standard input to the remote command, the standard output of the remote command to its standard output, and the standard error of the remote command to its standard error. Interrupt, quit, and terminate signals are propagated to the remote command. In contrast to a command issued interactively through rlogin, rsh normally terminates when the remote command does.

As an example, the following command

```
client% rsh server df -k > server.df.txt
```

executes the command df -k on the server, returning information about disk slices and creating the local file server.df.txt, which contains the output of the command. Clearly, rsh has the potential to be very useful in scripts and automated command processing.

Although rlogin is the fastest kind of remote login possible, however, it can be easily exploited on systems that are not trusted and secure. Systems that are directly connected to the Internet or that form part of a subnet that is not firewalled should never be considered secure. This can be dangerous in some circumstances, even if it is convenient for remotely administering many different machines. The most dangerous use of /etc/hosts.equiv occurs when the file contains the single line:

```
=
```

This enables any users from any host that has equivalent usernames to remotely login. The .rhosts file is also considered dangerous in some situations. For example, it is common practice in some organizations to enable the root and privileged users to permit automatic logins by root users from other machines by creating a /.rhosts file. A more insidious problem can occur when users define their own .rhosts files, however, in their own home directories. These are not directly controlled by the system administrator and can be exploited by malicious remote users.

One way to remove this threat is to enforce a policy of disallowing user .rhosts files and activating a nightly cron job to search for and remove any files named .rhosts in the user directories. A cron entry for a root such as

```
0 2 * * * find /staff -name .rhosts -print -exec rm{} \;
```

should execute this simple find and remove command every morning at 2 A.M. for all user accounts with home directories that lie underneath the /staff filesystem.

Checking If a Host Is up

The easiest way to check if a remote host is accessible is to use the ping command. The following example checks whether the host emu is accessible from the host dingo:

```
dingo% ping emu
```

If emu is accessible, the following output will be generated:

```
emu is alive
```

However, if emu is not accessible, an error message similar to the following will be seen:

```
Request timed out
```

If you need to determine the point in the network where the connection is failing, the traceroute command can be used to display the path taken by packets between the two hosts as they travel across the network. For example, to observe the route of the path taken by packets from AT&T to Sun's Web server, we would use the following command:

```
client% traceroute www.sun.com
Tracing route to wwwwseast.usec.sun.com [192.9.49.30]
over a maximum of 30 hops:
 1 184 ms 142 ms 138 ms 202.10.4.131
 2 147 ms 144 ms 138 ms 202.10.4.129
 3 150 ms 142 ms 144 ms 202.10.1.73
 4 150 ms 144 ms 141 ms atm11-0-0-11.ia4.optus.net.au
[202.139.32.17]
 5 148 ms 143 ms 139 ms 202.139.1.197
 6 490 ms 489 ms 474 ms hssi9-0-0.sf1.optus.net.au [192.65.89.246]
 7 526 ms 480 ms 485 ms g-sfd-br-02-f12-0.gn.cwix.net
[207.124.109.57]
 8 494 ms 482 ms 485 ms core7-hssi6-0-0.SanFrancisco.cw.net
[204.70.10.9]
 9 483 ms 489 ms 484 ms corerouter2.SanFrancisco.cw.net
[204.70.9.132]
 10 557 ms 552 ms 561 ms xcore3.Boston.cw.net [204.70.150.81]
 11 566 ms 572 ms 554 ms sun-micro-system.Boston.cw.net
[204.70.179.102]
 12 577 ms 574 ms 558 ms wwwwseast.usec.sun.com [192.9.49.30]
Trace complete.
```

If the connection is broken at any point, then * or ! would be displayed in place of the average connection times displayed.

Summary

In this chapter, we've examined how to configure hosts and subnets for use with Solaris systems. In addition, we reviewed some standard methods for remote accessing, including Telnet and the r-commands. Finally, we learned about the traceroute and ping commands that can be used to determine whether a remote host is up.

Questions

1. What is the netmask of a Class A network?
   A. 255.255.255.255
   B. 255.255.255.0
   C. 255.255.0.0
   D. 255.0.0.0

2. What is the netmask of a Class B network?
   A. 255.255.255.255
   B. 255.255.255.0
   C. 255.255.0.0
   D. 255.0.0.0

3. What is the netmask of a Class C network?
   A. 255.255.255.255
   B. 255.255.255.0
   C. 255.255.0.0
   D. 255.0.0.0

4. What is the loopback address?
   A. 127.255.255.1
   B. 127.255.255.1
   C. 127.255.0.1
   D. 127.0.0.1

5. What does the who command display?
   A. Username, connecting line, netmask, idle time, process id, and a comment
   B. Username, remote host IP address, date of login, idle time, process id, and a comment

    C. Username, connecting line, date of login, idle time, process id, and a comment

    D. Username, process id, and a comment only

6. What is the rlogin command string for connecting to host emu as user pwatters?

    A. rlogin -host emu -user pwatters

    B. rlogin emu -l pwatters

    C. rlogin -h emu -l pwatters

    D. rlogin -h emu -u pwatters

7. What is the most dangerous entry that can be contained in /etc/hosts.equiv?

    A. *

    B. /

    C. +

    D. −

Answers

    1. D

    2. C

    3. B

    4. D

    5. C

    6. B

    7. C

Configuring the NFS Environment

The following objectives will be met upon completing this chapter's material:

- Understanding NFS client/server architecture
- Configuring a NFS server
- Configuring a NFS client
- Sharing filesystems
- Mounting remote filesystems

In this chapter, we examine Sun's Network File System (NFS), which is a distributed filesystem architecture based on the Remote Procedure Call (RPC) protocol. RPC is a standard method of allocating and managing shared resources between Solaris systems. Although NFS is similar to Samba in concept (transparent filesystem sharing between systems), NFS features high-data throughput because of dedicated support in the Solaris kernel and support for both NFS 2 and 3 (Linux, for example, only supports NFS 2).

NFS was one of the first distributed network applications to ever be successfully deployed on local area networks (LANs). It enables users to mount volumes of other systems connected to the network, with the same capability to change permissions, delete and create files, and apply security measures, as any other locally mounted filesystem. One of the great advantages of NFS is its efficient use of network bandwidth by using RPC calls. In Solaris 8, the NFS concept has been extended to the Internet, with the new WebNFS providing filesystem access through a URL similar to that used for Web pages (see Chapter 30 for details). In this section, we will examine the theory behind distributed filesystems and examine how they can best be established in practice.

Prior to Solaris 2.5, NFS 2 was deployed, which used the unreliable User Datagram Protocol (UDP) for data transfer, hence NFS 2's poor reputation for data integrity. However, the more modern NFS 3 protocol, based around TCP, is now implemented in all new Solaris releases. NFS 3 enables an NFS server to cache NFS client requests in RAM, speeding up disk-writing operations and the overall speed of NFS transactions.

In addition, Solaris 2.6 and onwards provides support for a new type of NFS called WebNFS. The WebNFS protocol enables filesystems to be shared across the Internet, as an alternative to traditional Internet file-sharing techniques, like the File Transfer Protocol (FTP). In addition, initial testing has shown that Sun's WebNFS server has greater bandwidth than a traditional Web server, meaning that it might one day replace the Hypertext Transfer Protocol (HTTP) as the Web standard for transferring data.

In this chapter, the reader will learn how to set up and install an NFS server, an NFS client, and how to export filesystems. In addition, we examine how to set up the automounter, so that a user's home directory across all machines on an intranet is automatically shared and available, irrespective of his or her login host.

NFS Architectures

Any Solaris system can share any of the filesystems with other systems, making them available for remote mounting. NFS considers the system that shares the filesystem to be a server, and the system that remotely mounts the filesystem as a client. When a NFS client mounts a remote filesystem, it is connected to a mount point on the local filesystem, which means it appears to local users as just another filesystem.

For example, a system called carolina could make its mail directory /var/mail available for remote mounting by NFS clients. This would enable users on machines like georgia, virginia, and fairfax to read their mail stored actually on carolina to be read locally from their own machines without their having to explicitly login to carolina. This means that a single mail server that acts as a NFS server can serve all NFS clients on a LAN with mail. Figure 29-1 shows this configuration.

However, one important aspect of NFS is the capability to export filesystems and mount them on a remote mount point that is different than the original shared directory. For example, the NFS server carolina can also export its Sun Answerbook files (from the directory /opt/answerbook) to the clients virginia, georgia, and fairfax. However, virginia mounts these files in the /usr/local/www/htdocs directory, as it publishes them via the Web, whereas georgia mounts them in /opt/doc/answerbook. The client

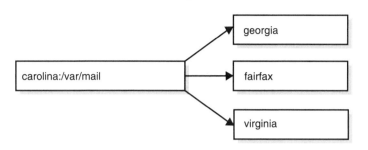

Figure 29-1   NFS server carolina exports its mail directory to NFS clients georgia, fairfax, and virginia, using the same mount point as the exported filesystem.

fairfax mounts them in /opt/answerbook, just like they are exported from carolina. The point is that the remote mount point can be completely different than the actual directory exported by an NFS server. This configuration is shown in Figure 29-2.

Configuring an NFS Server

If you installed the NFS server during installation, a startup script will have been created in /etc/init.d, called nfs.server. Thus, the NFS server can be started manually by typing the command

```
bash-2.03# /etc/init.d/nfs.server start
```

This command will start at least two daemons: the NFS server (/usr/lib/nfs/nfsd) and the mount daemon (/usr/lib/nfs/mountd). The nfsd is responsible for answering access

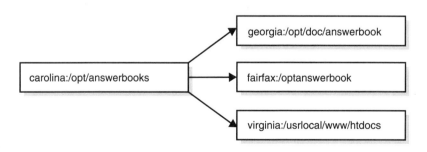

Figure 29-2   NFS server carolina exports its mail directory to NFS clients georgia, fairfax, and virginia, using their own mount points.

requests from clients for shared volumes on the server, whereas the mountd is responsible for providing information about mounted filesystems.

To check whether or not the NFS server has started correctly, it is possible to examine the process list for nfsd and mountd by using the following commands:

```
bash-2.03# ps -eaf | grep nfsd
    root 19961     1  0   Aug 31 ?         0:09 /usr/lib/nfs/nfsd -
    a 16
bash-2.03#  ps -eaf | grep mountd
    root   370     1  0   May 16 ?         2:49 /usr/lib/nfs/mountd
```

In this case, both the nfsd and mountd are operating correctly. In order to stop the NFS server, the following command may be used:

```
bash-2.03# /etc/init.d/nfs.server stop
```

Some optional services are started by the NFS server startup script, including daemons that support diskless booting (the Reverse Address Resolution Protocol [RARP] daemon, /usr/sbin/in.rarpd, and the boot parameter server, /usr/sbin/rpc.bootparamd). In addition, a separate daemon for x86 boot support (/usr/sbin/rpld), using the Network Booting Remote Program Load (RPL) protocol, can also be started. You only need to configure these services if you want to provide diskless booting for local clients; otherwise, they can be safely commented from the /etc/init.d/nfs.server script.

RPC

As we mentioned earlier, NFS makes use of RPC technology, which makes it easy for systems to make requests for the remote execution of procedures on server systems. RPC is currently supported across a number of different operating systems, including Solaris, Linux, and Microsoft Windows. The purpose of RPC is to abstract the connection details and methods required to access procedures across networks. That is, the client and server programs do not need to implement separate networking code, as a simple Application Programming Interface (API) is provided for finding services through a service called the portmapper (or rpcbind). The portmapper must be running on both the client and server for NFS to operate correctly. The portmapper is registered with both UDP and TCP 111, because requests may be generated for or received using NFS 2 or NFS 3 respectively.

rpcinfo

If you're having trouble starting the NFS daemon, it's often because of an RPC problem. In order to determine whether an RPC portmapper is running, use the rpcinfo command:

```
bash-2.03# rpcinfo -p
   program vers proto    port  service
    100000    4   tcp     111  rpcbind
    100000    3   tcp     111  rpcbind
    100000    2   tcp     111  rpcbind
    100000    4   udp     111  rpcbind
    100000    3   udp     111  rpcbind
    100000    2   udp     111  rpcbind
    100007    3   udp   32774  ypbind
    100007    2   udp   32774  ypbind
    100007    1   udp   32774  ypbind
    100007    3   tcp   32771  ypbind
    100007    2   tcp   32771  ypbind
    100007    1   tcp   32771  ypbind
    100011    1   udp   32785  rquotad
    100024    1   udp   32789  status
    100024    1   tcp   32775  status
    100021    1   udp    4045  nlockmgr
    100021    2   udp    4045  nlockmgr
    100021    3   udp    4045  nlockmgr
    100021    4   udp    4045  nlockmgr
    100068    2   udp   32809
    100068    3   udp   32809
    100068    4   udp   32809
    100068    5   udp   32809
    100083    1   tcp   32795
    100021    1   tcp    4045  nlockmgr
    100021    2   tcp    4045  nlockmgr
    100021    3   tcp    4045  nlockmgr
    100021    4   tcp    4045  nlockmgr
    100005    1   udp   32859  mountd
    100005    2   udp   32859  mountd
    100005    3   udp   32859  mountd
    100005    1   tcp   32813  mountd
    100005    2   tcp   32813  mountd
    100005    3   tcp   32813  mountd
    100026    1   udp   32866  bootparam
    100026    1   tcp   32815  bootparam
```

In this example, both the mountd and nfsd are running, along with several other services, so the NFS daemon should have no problems executing. However, the RPL service is not active, so x86 clients would not be able to use the local server as a boot server.

Sharing Filesystems

To actually share filesystems and directories, you can use the share command, with the options shown in Table 29-1. For example, if you want to share the /var/mail directory from carolina to georgia, you could use the command

```
carolina# share -F nfs -o rw=georgia /var/mail
```

Table 29-1   NFS Server Options

Parameter	Description
anon	Maps requests between users anonymously
nosuid	Prevents applications from executing as set-uid
ro	Prevents writing to an exported filesystem
root	Equates remote access by root to a local root access
rw	Permits reading and writing to an exported filesystem

In this example, -F nfs stands for a filesystem of type NFS. Of course, we really want to share the volume with virginia and fairfax as well, so we would probably use the command

```
carolina# share -F nfs -o rw=georgia,virginia,fairfax /var/mail
```

The /var/mail volume is shared with these clients because users on these systems need to read and write their e-mail. However, if we need to share a CD-ROM volume, we obviously need to share it read-only:

```
carolina# share -F nfs -o ro /cdrom
```

Normally, the volumes to be shared are identified in the /etc/dfs/dfstab file. One of the really innovative features of NFS is that a system that shares volumes to other systems can actually mount shared volumes remotely from its own clients. For example, carolina might share the volume /cdrom with georgia, fairfax, and virginia, while virginia might share the /staff directory, which contains home directories to carolina, georgia, and fairfax, using the command

```
virginia# share -F nfs -o rw=georgia,carolina,fairfax /staff
```

Filesystems can be unshared using the unshare command. For example, if we are going to change a CD-ROM on carolina, which is shared to clients using NFS, it might be wise to unmount it first:

```
carolina# unshare -F nfs /cdrom
```

The command dfmounts shows the local resources shared through the networked file system that are currently mounted by specific clients:

```
carolina# dfmounts
RESOURCE   SERVER PATHNAME                CLIENTS
   -           carolina /cdrom            virginia,georgia
   -           carolina /var/mail         fairfax,virginia,georgia
   -         carolina /opt/answerbook    fairfax
```

However, dfmounts does not provide information about the permissions that the directories and filesystems are shared with, nor does it show those shared resources that have no clients currently using them. To display this information, we need to use the share command with no arguments. On virginia, this looks like the following:

```
virginia# share
/staff rw=georgia,fairfax,carolina  "staff"
```

On carolina, the volumes are different:

```
carolina# share
-                 /cdrom   ro=georgia,fairfax,carolina "cdrom"
-                 /var/mail  rw=georgia,fairfax,carolina "mail"
```

Alternatively, the showmounts command can be used:

```
carolina# showmount -e
```

The output will be similar to the following:

```
export list for carolina:
/cdrom georgia.cassowary.net,fairfax.cassowary.net,carolina.
cassowary.net
```

Installing an NFS Client

In order to access filesystems being shared from an NFS server, a separate NFS client must be operating on the client system. Two main daemon processes must be running in order to use the mount command to access shared volumes: the NFS lock daemon (/usr/lib/nfs/lockd) and the NFS stat daemon (/usr/lib/nfs/statd). The lockd manages file sharing and locking at the user level, whereas the statd is used for file recovery after a connection outage.

If NFS was installed during the initial system setup, then a file called nfs.client should have been created in /etc/init.d. In order to run the NFS client, the following command needs to be executed:

```
bash-2.03# /etc/init.d/nfs.client start
```

Just like the NFS server, you can verify that the NFS daemons have started correctly by using the following commands:

```
bash-2.03# ps -eaf | grep statd
   daemon   211    1  0   May 16 ?        0:04 /usr/lib/nfs/statd
bash-2.03# ps -eaf | grep lockd
     root   213    1  0   May 16 ?        0:03 /usr/lib/nfs/lockd
```

If these two daemons are not active, then the NFS client will not run. The next step is for the client to consult the /etc/vfstab file, which lists both the UFS and NFS filesystems that need to be mounted, and the client attempts to mount the latter if they are available by using the mountall command.

In order to stop the NFS client once it is operating, the following command can be used:

```
bash-2.03# /etc/init.d/nfs.client stop
```

The NFS server is usually started automatically during run level 3.

Mounting Remote Filesystems

On the client side, if we want to mount a volume that has been shared from a NFS server, we would use the mount command. For example, if we want to mount the exported CD-ROM from carolina on the NFS client virginia, we would use the following command:

```
virginia# mount -F nfs -o ro carolina:/cdrom /cdrom
```

Like the /etc/dfs/dfstab files, which records a list of volumes to be exported, the /etc/vfstab file can contain entries for NFS volumes to be mounted from remote servers. For example, on the machine fairfax, if we wanted the /var/mail volume on carolina to be mounted locally as /var/mail, we would enter the following line in /etc/vfstab:

```
carolina:/var/mail   -   /var/mail   nfs   -   yes   rw
```

This line can be interpreted as a request to mount /var/mail from carolina's read/write on the local mount point /var/mail as an NFS volume, which should be mounted at boot time. If you make changes to the /etc/vfstab file on virginia, and you want to mount the /var/mail partition, you can use the following command:

```
virginia# mount /var/mail
```

This will attempt to mount the remote /var/mail directory from the server carolina. Alternatively, you can use this command:

```
virginia# mountall
```

which will mount all partitions that are listed in /etc/vfstab, but that have not yet been mounted. This should identify and mount all available partitions.

Filesystems can be unmounted using the umount command. For example, if the /cdrom filesystem on carolina is mounted on virginia as /cdrom, then the command

```
virginia# umount /cdrom
```

will unmount the mounted NFS volume. Alternatively, the unmountall command can be used, which unmounts all currently mounted NFS volumes. For example, the command

```
carolina# umountall -F nfs
```

unmounts all volumes that are currently mounted through NFS.

When a remote volume is mounted on a local client, it should be visible to the system just like a normal disk, and so commands like df display disk slice information:

```
fairfax# df -k
carolina:/cdrom     412456 341700   70756     83%   /cdrom
carolina:/var/mail       4194304 343234  3851070   8%   /var/mail
carolina:/opt/answerbook      2097152  1345634    750618  64%
/opt/answerbook
```

The main options available for mounting NFS filesystems are shown in Table 29-2.

Table 29-2 NFS Client Options

Option	Description
ro	Mounts a filesystem's read-only permissions.
rw	Mounts a filesystem's read/write permissions.
Hard	No timeouts permitted; the client will repeatedly attempt to make a connection.
Soft	Timeouts permitted; the client will attempt a connection and give an error message if a connection fails.
Bg	Attempts to mount a remote filesystem in the background if connection fails.

Summary

In this chapter, we have examined Sun's NFS as a method of sharing volumes across LANs. NFS is widely used to share mail folders, CD-ROMs, and home directories, although it can quickly exceed the capacity of many low-bandwidth networks when mounting and unmounting volumes. Although many heterogeneous networks will use Samba to serve PC clients, NFS has historically played an important part in sharing filesystems across networks.

Questions

1. An NFS volume shared from a server to a client can be accessed by which of the following?
   A. Mount point
   B. URL
   C. URI
   D. SMB client

2. Which daemons must be run to support a NFS server?
   A. inetd, sendmail
   B. nfsd, mountd
   C. pc.nfsd, in.rpld
   D. mountd, syslogd

3. Which of the following commands would share the volume /staff to the hosts georgia, carolina, and fairfax as read-only using NFS?
   A. share -F NFS -o rw=georgia,carolina,fairfax /staff
   B. share -protocol NFS -o rw=georgia,carolina,fairfax /staff
   C. share /staff -protocol nfs -o rw=georgia,carolina,fairfax
   D. share -F nfs -o ro=georgia,carolina,fairfax /staff

4. Which of the following commands would stop sharing the volume /data using NFS?
   A. shareoff /data
   B. umount /data
   C. unshare -F nfs /data
   D. unshare -protocol NFS /data

5. Which of the following commands would mount the shared volume /data using NFS from the server zemindar (read-write) on the mount point /zemindar?
   A. mount -protocol nfs -w ro zemindar:/data /data
   B. mount zemindar:/data -F NFS -rw zemindar:/data /data
   C. mount /zemindar -F nfs -rw zemindar:/data
   D. mount -F nfs -w rw zemindar:/data /zemindar

6. Which of the following commands would mount all partitions listed in /etc/vfstab that are not currently mounted?
   A. mount /etc/vfstab
   B. mountall -F nfs /etc/vfstab
   C. mountall
   D. vfsmount

7. Which of the following commands shows the local resources shared through the networked file system that are currently mounted by specific clients?
   A. dfmounts
   B. share
   C. showmounts
   D. nfsmounts

Answers

1. A

2. B

3. D

4. C

5. D

6. C

7. A

The CacheFS Filesystem

The following objectives will be met upon completing this chapter's material:

- Understanding the role of caches
- Configuring a CacheFS filesystem

Configure a CacheFS Filesystem

In general terms, a cache is a place where important material can be placed so that it can be quickly retrieved. The location of the cache can be quite different than the normal storage location for the specified material. For example, field commanders in the army store ammunitions in local caches, so that their forces can obtain their required materials quickly in case of war. These ammunitions would normally be stored securely well away from the battlefield, but must be highly available when required. The state of the battlefield may make it difficult to access outside sources of ammunition during live fire, so a sizable cache of arms is always wise.

This analogy can be easily extended to client-server scenarios, where an unreliable or slow data link may give rise to performance issues. A cache, in this case, can be created to locally store commonly used files, rather than retrieving them each time they are requested from a server. The cache approach has the advantage of speeding up client access to data. However, it has the disadvantage of data asynchronization, where a file is modified on the server after it has been stored in the cache. Thus, if a local file retrieved from the cache is modified before being sent back to the server, any modifications performed on the server's copy of the file would be overwritten. Conversely, cached data may be out of date by the time it is retrieved by the local client, meaning that important decisions could be taken on inaccurate information.

Many Internet client-server systems, involved in the exchange of data across an HTTP link, use a cache to store data. This data is never modified and sent back to the server, so overwriting server-side data is never an issue. Small ISPs with limited bandwidth often use caches to store files that are commonly retrieved from a server. For example, if the ISP has 1,000 customers who routinely download the front page of the *Sydney Morning Herald* each morning, it makes sense to download the file once from the *Sydney Morning Herald* Web site and store it locally for the other 999 users to retrieve. Because the front page only changes from day to day, the page will always be current, as long as the cache purges the front-page file at the end of each day. The daily amount of data to be downloaded from the *Sydney Morning Herald* Web site has been reduced by 99.9 percent, which can significantly boost the ISP's performance in downloading other non-cached files from the Internet as well as reduce the overall cost of data throughput.

Solaris provides a cache filesystem (CacheFS) that is designed to improve NFS client-server performance across slow or unreliable networks. The principles underlying CacheFS are exactly the same as the two previous examples: Locally stored files that are frequently requested can be retrieved by users on the client system without having to download them again from the server. This approach minimizes the number of connections required between an NFS client and a server to retrieve the same amount of data in a manner that is invisible to users on the client system. In fact, users will notice that their files are retrieved more quickly than before the cache was introduced.

CacheFS seamlessly integrates with existing NFS installations, with only simple modifications needed to mount command parameters and /etc/vfstab entries required to make use of the facility. The first task in configuring a cache is to create a mount point and a cache on a client system. If a number of NFS servers are to be used with the cache, it makes sense to create individual caches underneath the same top-level mount point. Many sites use the mount point /cache to store individual caches. In this example, we'll assume that a filesystem from the NFS server yorktown will be cached on the local client system midway, so the commands to create a cache on midway are as follows:

```
midway# mkdir /cache
midway # cfsadmin -c /cache/yorktown
```

Here we've used the cfsadmin command to create the cache once the mount point /cache has been created. Now let's examine how we would force the cache to be used for all access from midway to yorktown for the remote filesystem /staff, which is also mounted locally on /staff:

```
midway# mount -F cachefs -o
backfstype=nfs,cachedir=/cache/yorktown yorktown:/staff /staff
```

Once the yorktown:/staff filesystem has been mounted in this way, users on midway will not notice any difference in operation, except that file access to /staff will be much quicker.

It is possible to check the status of the cache by using the cachefsstat command. In order to verify that /cache/yorktown is operating correctly, the following command would be used:

```
midway# cachefsstat /cache/yorktown
```

Alternatively, the cfsadmin command can be used:

```
# cfsadmin -l /cache/yorktown
cfsadmin: list cache FS information
maxblocks 80%
minblocks 0%
threshblocks 75%
maxfiles 80%
minfiles 0%
threshfiles 75%
maxfilesize 12MB
yorktown:_staff:_staff
```

Note the last line, which is the current cache ID. You will need to remember the cache ID if you ever want to delete the cache. If a cache needs to be deleted, the cfsadmin command can be used with the -d option:

```
midway# umount /staff
midway# cfsadmin -d yorktown:_staff:_staff /cache/yorktown
```

Here we've unmounted the /staff volume on merlin locally before attempting to remove the cache by providing its ID along with its mount point.

Summary

In this chapter, we've examined how to configure and install an NFS cache, which can be used to significantly increase the speed of access to files on a remote NFS server. In addition, we examined how to review the performance of a cache and delete it if necessary.

Questions

1. What is the command used to create a cache?
   A. cfscreate
   B. cfsadmin
   C. cfsmake
   D. newfs

2. What is the command used to delete a cache?
   A. cfscreate
   B. cfsadmin
   C. cfsmake
   D. newfs

3. What is the command used to check cache status?
   A. cfscreate
   B. cfsadmin
   C. cfsmake
   D. newfs

4. What is the command used to check cache statistics?
   A. cachestat
   B. cachecheck
   C. checkcache
   D. cachefsstat

Answers

1. B

2. B

3. B

4. D

Using Automount

The following objectives will be met upon completing this chapter's material:

- Understanding the role of the automounter
- Using automounter maps
- Creating direct, indirect, and master maps

The automounter is a program that automatically mounts Network File System (NFS) filesystems when they are accessed and then unmounts them when they are no longer needed. It enables you to use special files, known as automounter maps, which contain information about the servers, the pathname to the NFS filesystem on the server, the local pathname, and the mount options. By using the automounter, you don't have to update the entries in /etc/vfstab on every client by hand every time you make a change to the NFS servers.

Normally, only root can mount filesystems, so when users need to mount an NFS filesystem, they need to find the system administrator. The main problem is that once users are finished with a filesystem, they rarely tell the system administrator. If the NFS server containing that filesystem ever crashes, you will be left with one or more hanging processes. This can easily increase your workload if you are responsible for maintaining an NFS server. The automounter can solve both of these problems because it automatically mounts an NFS filesystem when a user references a file in that filesystem, and it will automatically unmount the NFS filesystem if it is not referenced for more than five minutes.

The automounter is a Remote Procedure Call (RPC) daemon that services request from clients to mount and unmount remote volumes using NFS. During installation, a set of server-side maps is created that lists the filesystems to be automatically mounted.

Typically, these filesystems include shared user home directories (under /home) and network-wide mail directories (/var/mail).

Enabling the Automounter

The automount command installs automount points and associates an automount map with each mount point. This requires that the automount daemon be running (automountd). When the automount daemon is initialized on the server, no exported directories are mounted by the clients. These are only mounted when a remote user attempts to access a file on the directory from a client. The connection eventually times out, in which case the exported directory is unmounted by the client. Automounter maps usually use a network information service, such as NIS+, to manage shared volumes, meaning that a single home directory for individual users can be provided on request from a single server, no matter which client machine they login to. Connection and reconnection is handled by the automount daemon. If automount starts up and has nothing to mount or unmount, this is reported and is quite normal:

```
burbank# automount
automount: no mounts
automount: no unmounts
```

Automounter Maps

The behavior of the automounter is determined by a set of files called automounter maps. Two main types of maps exist: indirect and direct. An indirect map is useful when you are mounting several filesystems that will share a common pathname prefix. As we will see shortly, an indirect map can be used to manage the directory tree in /home. A direct map is used to mount filesystems where each mount point does not share a common prefix with other mount points in the map. In this section, we will look at examples of each of these types of maps. An additional map, called the master map, is used by the automounter to determine the names of the files corresponding to the direct and indirect maps.

Indirect Maps

The most common type of automounter map is an indirect map, which corresponds to regularly named filesystems like /home or /usr directory trees. Regularly named filesystems share the same directory prefix. For example, the directories /home/jdoe and /home/sdoe are regularly named directories in the /home directory tree.

Normally, indirect maps are stored in the /etc directory and are named with the convention auto_directory, where directory is the name of the directory prefix (without slashes) that the indirect map is responsible for. As an example, the indirect map responsible for the /home directory is usually named auto_home. An indirect map is made up of a series of entries in the following format:

```
directory      options      host:filesystem
```

Here, directory is the relative pathname of a directory that will be appended to the name of the directory that is corresponding to this indirect map as specified in the master map file. (The master map is covered later in this section.) For options, you can use any of the mount options covered earlier in this chapter. To specify options, you will need to prefix the first option with a dash (-). If you do not need any extra options, you can omit the options entirely. The final entry in the map contains the location of the NFS filesystem.

Here is an example of the indirect map that is responsible for the directories in /home:

```
# /etc/auto_home - home directory map for automounter
jdoe          orem:/store/home/jdoe
sdoe          orem:/store/home/sdoe
kdoe -bg srv-ss10:/home/kdoe
```

Here, the entries for jdoe, sdoe, and kdoe correspond to the directories /home/jdoe, /home/sdoe, and /home/kdoe respectively. The first two entries indicate that the automounter should mount the directories /home/jdoe and /home/sdoe from the NFS server orem, while the last one specifies that the directory /home/kdoe should be mounted from the NFS server srv-ss10. The last entry also demonstrates the use of options.

Now that we have taken a look at an indirect map, let's walk through what happens when you access a file on an NFS filesystem that is handled by the automounter. For example, consider the following command that accesses the file /home/jdoe/docs/book/ch17.doc:

```
bash-2.03$ more /home/jdoe/docs/book/ch17.doc
```

Because the directory /home/jdoe is automounted, the following steps are used by the automounter to enable you to access the file:

1. The automounter looks at the pathname and determines that the directory /home is controlled by the indirect map auto_home.

2. The automounter looks at the rest of the pathname for a corresponding entry in the auto_home map. In this case, it finds the matching entry, jdoe.

3. Once a matching entry has been found, the automounter checks to see if the directory /home/jdoe is already mounted. If the directory is already mounted, you can directly access the file; otherwise, the automounter mounts this directory and then enables you to access the file.

Direct Maps

When you use an indirect map, the automounter takes complete control of the directory corresponding to the indirect map. This means that no user, not even root, can create entries in a directory corresponding to an indirect map. For this reason, directories specified in an indirect map cannot be automounted on top of an existing directory. In this case, you need a special type of map known as a direct map. A direct map enables you to mix automounter mount points and normal directories in the same directory tree. The directories specified in a direct map have non-regular mount points, which simply means that they do not share a common prefix. A common use for direct maps is to enable directories in the /usr directory tree to be automounted.

The direct map is normally stored in the file /etc/auto_direct. The format of this file is similar to the format of the indirect maps:

```
directory      options      host:filesystem
```

Here, directory is the absolute pathname of the directory. For options, you can use any of the mount options covered earlier in this chapter. To specify options, you will need to prefix the first option with a dash (-). If you do not need any extra options, you can omit the options entirely. The final entry in the map contains the location of the NFS filesystem. Here is an example of the direct map that is responsible for some of the directories in /usr:

```
# /etc/auto_direct - Direct Automount map
/usr/pubsw/man  orem:/internal/opt/man
/usr/doc        orem:/internal/httpd/htdocs
```

When any files in the directories /usr/pubsw/man or /usr/doc are accessed, the automounter will automatically handle the mounting of these directories.

Master Maps

When the automounter first starts, it reads the file /etc/auto_master to determine where to find the direct and indirect map files. The auto_master file is known as the master map. Its consists of lines with the following format:

```
directory      map
```

Here, directory is the name of the directory that corresponds to the indirect map. For a direct map, this entry is /-. The map is the name of the map file in the /etc directory corresponding to the directory given in the first column. The following example shows a master map file for the direct and indirect maps given earlier in this section:

```
# Master map for automounter
/home           auto_home
/-                auto_direct
```

Other entries can also be made in the master map. For example, to share a common directory for mail between a number of clients and a mail server, we would enter the definition:

```
/-                      /etc/auto_mail
```

This creates a share called auto_mail that makes mail on a single server accessible to all client machines upon request. Automounter permits two kinds of shares that can be defined by direct and indirect maps; a direct map is a set of arbitrary mount points that are listed together, while an indirect map mounts everything under a specific directory. For example, auto_home mounts user directories and all subdirectories underneath them. If an automounted share is available on the server, then you should see its details being displayed in the /etc/mnttab file:

```
burbank:/var/mail   /var/mail   nfs      nosuid,dev=2bc0012
951071258
```

Continuing with the example of auto_mail, as defined in the master map, a file /etc/auto_mail would have to contain the following entry:

```
denver# cat /etc/auto_mail
  /var/mail burbank:/var/mail
```

This ensures that the burbank server knows where to find the /var/mail directory physically, and that automount can mount the shared volume at will. Sometimes the network load caused by mounting and unmounting home directories can lead to an increase in input/output (I/O) load and reduce the effective bandwidth of a network. For this reason, only volumes that need to be shared should be shared. Alternatively, the timeout parameter for automount can be modified to extend its latency for mounting and unmounting directories.

Automount and NIS+

A common problem with auto_home is that systems in a NIS+ environment may create user accounts on a filesystem mounted as /home. This means that if auto_home is active, as defined by /etc/auto_master, then after rebooting, the shared home directories are mounted on /home, and when the local /home attempts to mount the same point, it fails. This is one of the most frequently asked questions about Solaris 8, as the convention was different for earlier Solaris systems, which used local /home directories. The recommended practice is now to create home directories under /export/home on the local filesystem if required or to use auto_home in a NIS+ environment. However, if you want to disable this feature altogether and stick with a local /home, then simply remove +auto_master from the master map (/etc/auto_master).

Starting and Stopping the Automounter

Starting and stopping the automounter is normally handled by your system at boot and shutdown time, but you will have to start and stop the automounter manually if you make changes to any of its map files.

The automount daemon is typically started from /etc/init.d/autofs during the multi-user startup with a command such as

```
bash-2.03# /etc/init.d/autofs start
```

This should start the automounter. You can confirm that it started correctly by using the following command:

```
bash-2.03# /bin/ps -ef | grep automountd
```

The output should look like the following:

```
root 21642    1  0 11:27:29 ?        0:00 /usr/lib/autofs/automountd
```

If you receive no output, then the automounter has not started correctly. In that case, you should run the startup script again.

Stopping the NFS client is similar to starting it:

```
bash-2.03# /etc/init.d/autofs stop
```

The stop script usually stops the automounter, but you can confirm this using the following command:

```
bash-2.03# /bin/ps -ef | grep automountd
```

This is the same command that is used to check to see if the automounter is running, except that once you stop it, this command should not produce any output. If you do see some output and it contains a grep command, you can ignore those lines. Any other output indicates that the automounter has not stopped, in which case you should execute the NFS client stop command again.

If you receive a message similar to the following

```
/home: busy
```

you will need to determine if anyone is logged on to the system and is using files from /home. If you cannot determine this, you can use the following command to get a list of all of the mounted directories in the directory that caused the error message (in this case /home):

```
$ df -k -F nfs
/home/jdoe
```

Just replace /home with the name of the directory that produced the error message. In this case, only one directory, /home/jdoe, is automounted. Once you have a list of these directories, try unmounting each one with the umount command. When you receive an error message, you will know which directory contains the files that are in use. You can ask the user to finish with those files and then proceed to stop the automounter.

Summary

In this chapter, we have examined how to use the automounter to automatically mount commonly used remote drives, such as /home, to provide centralized file-sharing services on Solaris. We explored the uses of master, direct, and indirect maps, and reviewed some issues between NIS+ and the automounter.

Questions

1. Which of the following programs must be running to support automount?
    A. automountd, in.rpld
    B. automountd, rpcbind
    C. nfsd, rpcbind
    D. rpcbind, in.rpld

2. Which of the following is an example of the indirect map that is responsible for the directories in /home for the use pwatters on server toga?
    A. pwatters   auto   toga:/home/pwatters
    B. toga:/ home/pwatters   pwatters   auto

      C. ALL   toga:/home/pwatters

      D. pwatters   toga:/home/pwatters

3. Which of the following is an example of the direct map that is responsible for mapping the directory /games/adventure/misc on toga to /usr/local/games?

      A. /usr/local/games toga:/games/adventure/misc

      B. /usr/local/* ALL toga:/games/adventure/misc

      C. /usr/local/games ALL toga:/games/*

      D. /usr/local/games -rw toga:/games/adventure/misc

Answers

1. B

2. D

3. A

Naming Services Overview

The following objectives will be met upon completing this chapter's material:

- Understanding the concept of a name service
- Exploring which name services are available under Solaris (NIS, NIS+, and DNS)
- Investigating DNS
- Comprehending NIS
- Examining NIS+
- Discussing the role of the name service switch

Every computer that is connected to the Internet must have an IP address, which identifies it uniquely within the network. For example, 192.18.97.241 is the IP address of the Web server at Sun. IP addresses are hard for humans to remember and don't adequately describe the network on which a host resides. Thus, by examining the Fully Qualified Domain Name (FQDN) of 192.18.97.241, **www.sun.com**, it's immediately obvious that the host www lies within the sun.com domain. The mapping between human-friendly domain names and machine-friendly IP addresses is performed by a distributed naming service, known as the Domain Name Service (DNS). DNS is the standard protocol used by Unix systems (and other operating systems) for mapping IP addresses to hostnames and vice versa.

Although Solaris provides complete support for DNS, it does have its own domain management and naming system, known as the Network Information Service (NIS). NIS is not only responsible for host naming and management, but it is a comprehensive resource management solution that can be used to structure and administer groups of local and remote users. NIS uses a series of maps to create namespace structures.

Sometimes administrators ask why this extra effort is required to manage hosts and naming, because DNS already provides this for Internet hosts by converting computer-friendly IP addresses to human-friendly "names." However, NIS does not just provide naming services; an NIS server also acts as a central repository of all information about users, hosts, Ethernet addresses, mail aliases, and supported Remote Procedure Call (RPC) services within a network. This information is physically stored in a set of maps that are intended to replace the network configuration files usually stored in a server's /etc directory, ensuring that configuration data within the local area network (LAN) is always synchronized. Many large organizations use NIS alongside DNS to manage both their Internet and LAN spaces effectively. Linux also supports NIS.

In recent years, Sun has introduced an enhanced version of NIS known as NIS+. Instead of a simple mapping system, it uses a complex series of tables to store configuration information and hierarchical naming data for all networks within an organization. Individual namespaces may contain up to 10,000 hosts, with individual NIS+ servers working together to support a completely distributed service. NIS+ also includes greater capabilities in the area of authentication, security (using Data Encryption Standard [DES] encryption), and resource access control.

DNS Defined

DNS is a distributed database that maps human-friendly hostnames, like paulwatters.com, to a numeric IP address like 209.67.50.203. In the early days of the Internet, a single file was distributed to various hosts (called the HOSTS.TXT file), which contained an address to hostname mapping for known hosts. Administrators would periodically upload a list of any new hosts added to their networks, after which they would download the latest version of the file. However, as the Internet grew, maintaining this text database became impossible. A new system for mapping addresses to names was proposed in RFC 882 and 883, based around information about local networks being sourced from designated servers for each network.

It should be noted that Solaris retains a variant of the HOSTS.TXT file in the form of the /etc/hosts file, which is typically used to map IP addresses to domain names for the localhost as well as to key network servers, such as the local domain name server. This is very useful in situations where the DNS server is not responding while the system is being booted. The /etc/hosts file is consulted by some applications, such as the syslog daemon (syslogd) to determine which host (the loghost) should be used for system logging. A typical /etc/hosts file looks like the following:

```
127.0.0.1       localhost
204.168.14.23   leura         leura.paulwatters.com      loghost
204.168.14.24   katoomba      katoomba.paulwatters.com
```

Of course, only key servers and the localhost should be defined in the /etc/hosts file. Otherwise, any change in the IP address for that server will not be reflected in the value resolved from /etc/hosts.

DNS works on a simple client-server principle. If you know the name of a DNS server for a particular network, you will be able to retrieve the IP address of any host within that network. For example, if I know that the name server for the domain paulwatters.com is dns20.register.com, I can contact dns20.register.com to retrieve the address for any host within the paulwatters.com domain (including **www.paulwatters.com**, or 209.67.50.203). Of course, this leads to a classic chicken-and-egg problem. How would we know, in the first instance, that the DNS server dns20.register.com is authoritative for paulwatters.com? The answer is that, in the same way that the DNS server manages the addresses of all the hosts under paulwatters.com, the next server along the chain manages the address of the DNS server; in this case, it is the DNS server for the .com domain.

Many such top-level domains are now in existence, including the traditional .edu (educational organizations), .com (commercial organizations), and .net (network) top-level domains. Most countries now have their own top-level domains, including .au (Australia), .ck (Cook Islands), and .ph (Philippines). Underneath each top-level domain are a number of second-level domains. For example, Australia has .com.au (Australian commercial organizations), .edu.au (Australian educational organizations), and .asn.au (Australian non-profit associations). The organizations that manage each top-level and second-level domain can also be quite different. Although Network Solutions Inc. (**www.nsi.com**) is responsible for the wholesale allocation of domain names for the .com top-level domain, Melbourne IT (**www.melbourneit.com.au**) manages the .com.au second-level domain.

As an example, let's look at how the hostname **www.finance.bigbank.com** is resolved. The client resolver needs to determine which DNS server is authoritative for .com domains, followed by the DNS server that is authoritative for bigbank.com domains. This DNS server is potentially followed by the DNS server that is authoritative for the finance.bigbank.com domain if all mappings for bigbank.com are not stored on a single server. The .com resolution is taken care of by the list of root servers provided by the WHOIS database (**ftp://ftp.rs.internic.net/domain/named.root**):

```
>>> Last update of whois database: Mon, 9 Oct 2000 09:43:11 EDT <<<

The Registry database contains ONLY .COM, .NET, .ORG, .EDU domains and
Registrars.

ftp://ftp.rs.internic.net/domain/named.root
;       This file holds the information on root name servers needed to
;       initialize cache of Internet domain name servers
;       (e.g. reference this file in the "cache  .  <file>"
;       configuration file of BIND domain name servers).
;
;       This file is made available by InterNIC registration services
;       under anonymous FTP as
;           file                    /domain/named.root
;           on server              FTP.RS.INTERNIC.NET
;       -OR- under Gopher at       RS.INTERNIC.NET
;           under menu             InterNIC Registration Services (NSI)
;              submenu             InterNIC Registration Archives
;           file                   named.root
;
;       last update:    Aug 22, 1997
;       related version of root zone:   1997082200
;
;
; formerly NS.INTERNIC.NET
;
.                           3600000  IN  NS    A.ROOT-SERVERS.NET.
A.ROOT-SERVERS.NET.         3600000      A     198.41.0.4
;
; formerly NS1.ISI.EDU
;
.                           3600000      NS    B.ROOT-SERVERS.NET.
B.ROOT-SERVERS.NET.         3600000      A     128.9.0.107
;
; formerly C.PSI.NET
;
.                           3600000      NS    C.ROOT-SERVERS.NET.
C.ROOT-SERVERS.NET.         3600000      A     192.33.4.12
;
; formerly TERP.UMD.EDU
;
.                           3600000      NS    D.ROOT-SERVERS.NET.
D.ROOT-SERVERS.NET.         3600000      A     128.8.10.90
;
; formerly NS.NASA.GOV
;
.                           3600000      NS    E.ROOT-SERVERS.NET.
E.ROOT-SERVERS.NET.         3600000      A     192.203.230.10
;
; formerly NS.ISC.ORG
```

```
;
.                               3600000    NS    F.ROOT-SERVERS.NET.
F.ROOT-SERVERS.NET.             3600000    A     192.5.5.241
;
; formerly NS.NIC.DDN.MIL
;
.                               3600000    NS    G.ROOT-SERVERS.NET.
G.ROOT-SERVERS.NET.             3600000    A     192.112.36.4
;
; formerly AOS.ARL.ARMY.MIL
;
.                               3600000    NS    H.ROOT-SERVERS.NET.
H.ROOT-SERVERS.NET.             3600000    A     128.63.2.53
;
; formerly NIC.NORDU.NET
;
.                               3600000    NS    I.ROOT-SERVERS.NET.
I.ROOT-SERVERS.NET.             3600000    A     192.36.148.17
;
; temporarily housed at NSI (InterNIC)
;
.                               3600000    NS    J.ROOT-SERVERS.NET.
J.ROOT-SERVERS.NET.             3600000    A     198.41.0.10
;
; housed in LINX, operated by RIPE NCC
;
.                               3600000    NS    K.ROOT-SERVERS.NET.
K.ROOT-SERVERS.NET.             3600000    A     193.0.14.129
;
; temporarily housed at ISI (IANA)
;
.                               3600000    NS    L.ROOT-SERVERS.NET.
L.ROOT-SERVERS.NET.             3600000    A     198.32.64.12
;
; housed in Japan, operated by WIDE
;
.                               3600000    NS    M.ROOT-SERVERS.NET.
M.ROOT-SERVERS.NET.             3600000    A     202.12.27.33
; End of File
```

The named.root file shown previously can be used by servers to resolve IP addresses for root DNS servers if they do not run a local DNS server. After obtaining an IP address for a root server for the .com domain, a query is then made to bigbank.com for the address **www.finance.bigbank.com**. Two possible scenarios can occur at this point: Either the DNS server, which is authoritative for the entire bigbank.com domain, can resolve the address, or the query is passed to a DNS server for the finance.bigbank.com domain if the root server has delegated authority to another server. In the latter situation, the bigbank.com DNS server does not know the IP address for any hosts within the finance.bigbank.com domain, except for the address of the DNS server. DNS is therefore a very flexible system for managing the mapping of domain names to IP addresses.

The software that carries out the client request for and the server resolution of IP addresses is the Berkeley Internet Daemon (BIND). Although most vendors, including Sun, ship their own customized version of BIND, it is possible to download, compile, configure, and install your own version of BIND (available for download from **www.isc.org**).

Configuring a DNS client in Solaris is very easy and can be accomplished in a few easy steps. First, you must have installed the BIND package during system installation to use the DNS client tools. Secondly, you must configure the name service switch (/etc/nsswitch.conf) to consult DNS for domain name resolution, in addition to checking the /etc/hosts file and/or NIS/NIS+ maps or tables for hostnames. The following line must appear in /etc/nsswitch.conf for DNS to work correctly:

```
/etc/nsswitch.conf hosts:        dns [NOTFOUND=return] files
```

If you have NIS+ running, the line would look like this:

```
/etc/nsswitch.conf hosts:        dns nisplus nis [NOTFOUND=return]
files
```

Next, the name of the local domain should be entered into the file /etc/defaultdomain. For example, the /etc/defaultdomain file for the host **www.paulwatters.com** should have the following entry:

```
paulwatters.com
```

Finally, the /etc/resolv.conf file needs to contain the name of the local domain, the IP addresses of the local primary DNS server, and a secondary (offsite) DNS server. This means that even if your local DNS server goes down, you can rely on the secondary one to provide up-to-date information about external hosts, relying on data within the /etc/hosts file to resolve local addresses. In the following example, we demonstrate how the /etc/resolv.conf file might look for the host **www.finance.bigbank.com**:

```
domain finance.bigbank.com
domain bigbank.com
nameserver 204.168.12.1
nameserver 204.168.12.16
nameserver 64.58.24.1
```

Here the host belongs to two domains: the subdomain finance.bigbank.com and the domain bigbank.com. Thus, two primary DNS servers are listed within the local domain (204.168.12.1 and 204.168.12.16). In addition, an external secondary is also listed, corresponding to ns.bigisp.com, or 64.58.24.1.

Once the client resolver is configured in this way, a number of tools can test whether DNS is working and also further examine how IP addresses are resolved. The most important tool for performing DNS resolutions is nslookup, which can be used in a simple command-line mode to look up fully qualified domain names from IP addresses, and vice versa. However, nslookup also features an interactive mode that is very useful for retrieving name server characteristics for a particular domain, and it can also determine which DNS servers are authoritative for a specific host or network.

Let's look at a simple example. If we wanted to determine the IP address of the host **www.paulwatters.com** using a client on the host gamera.cassowary.net, we would use the following command:

```
godzilla:~:60 % nslookup www.paulwatters.com
```

The following response would be returned:

```
Server:   gamera.cassowary.net
Address:  206.68.216.16

Name:     paulwatters.com
Address:  209.67.50.203
Aliases:  www.paulwatters.com
```

This means that the primary DNS server for the local (cassowary.net) domain is gamera.cassowary.net (206.68.216.16). This server then makes a connection to the DNS server that is authoritative for the domain paulwatters.com (dns19.hostsave.com). This server then returns the canonical (actual) name for the host (paulwatters.com), the alias name (**www.paulwatters.com**), and the desired IP address. If we reversed the process and instead supplied the IP address 209.67.50.203 on the command line, we would be able to perform a reverse lookup on that address, which would resolve to the domain name paulwatters.com.

If you want to verify that your DNS server is returning the correct IP address, or if you want to verify an address directly yourself, then running nslookup in interactive mode enables you to set the name of the DNS server to use for all lookups. For example, if you wanted to resolve the domain name for the Web server of the University of Sydney, you could use the following command:

```
godzilla:~:61 % nslookup www.usyd.edu.au
```

The following response would then be returned:

```
Server:   gamera.cassowary.net
Address:  206.68.216.16
```

```
Name: solo.ucc.usyd.edu.au
Address:  129.78.64.2
Aliases:  www.usyd.edu.au
```

However, you could verify that this IP address is indeed correct by setting your DNS server to be the DNS server that is authoritative for the ucc.usyd.edu.au domain:

```
> godzilla:~:62 % nslookup
Default Server:  gamera.cassowary.net
Address:  206.68.216.16
```

Here you enter the name of the DNS server that is authoritative for the target domain:

```
> server metro.ucc.su.oz.au
Default Server:  metro.ucc.su.oz.au
Address:  129.78.64.2
```

Next, you enter the name of the host to resolve:

```
> www.usyd.edu.au
Server:  metro.ucc.su.oz.au
Address:  129.78.64.2
```

And the IP address is returned correctly:

```
Name:     solo.ucc.usyd.edu.au
Address:  129.78.64.24
Aliases:  www.usyd.edu.au
```

If you wanted to determine some of the key characteristics of the DNS entry for **www.usyd.edu.au**, such as the DNS server that is authoritative for the host, and the mail address of the administrator who is responsible for the host, it is possible to retrieve the Start of Authority (SOA) record through nslookup:

```
> godzilla:~:63 % nslookup
Default Server:  gamera.cassowary.net
Address:  206.68.216.16

> server metro.ucc.su.oz.au
Default Server:  metro.ucc.su.oz.au
Address:  129.78.64.2
> set q=soa
> www.usyd.edu.au
Server:  metro.ucc.su.oz.au
Address:  129.78.64.2

www.usyd.edu.au canonical name = solo.ucc.usyd.edu.au
ucc.usyd.edu.au
```

```
origin = metro.ucc.usyd.edu.au
mail addr = root.metro.ucc.usyd.edu.au
serial = 316
refresh = 3600 (1 hour)
retry   = 1800 (30 mins)
expire  = 36000 (10 hours)
minimum ttl = 43200 (12 hours)
```

This SOA record indicates the following:

- The canonical name of **www.usyd.edu.au** is solo.ucc.usyd.edu.au.

- The origin of the DNS record is metro.ucc.usyd.edu.au (and this server is authoritative for the host solo.ucc.usyd.edu.au).

- The serial number for the current record is 316. Next time a change is made to the record, the serial number should be incremented.

- The refresh rate is one hour.

- The retry rate is 30 minutes.

- The expiry rate is 10 hours.

- The time to live (TTL) is 12 hours.

We further examine the meaning of each field later in the chapter when we discuss how to create DNS records for the server.

The use of nslookup to determine which servers are authoritative for a particular query is not limited to individual hosts. In fact, the authoritative servers for entire networks can be determined by using nslookup. For example, if we wanted to determine which servers are authoritative for the Cook Islands' top-level domain (.ck), we would use the following command:

```
godzilla:~:64 % nslookup
> set type=ns
> ck.
Server:  gamera.cassowary.net
Address:  206.68.216.16

Non-authoritative answer:
ck      nameserver = DOWNSTAGE.MCS.VUW.AC.NZ
ck      nameserver = NS1.WAIKATO.AC.NZ
ck      nameserver = PARAU.OYSTER.NET.ck
ck      nameserver = POIPARAU.OYSTER.NET.ck
ck      nameserver = CIRCA.MCS.VUW.AC.NZ

Authoritative answers can be found from:
DOWNSTAGE.MCS.VUW.AC.NZ internet address = 130.195.6.10
NS1.WAIKATO.AC.NZ       internet address = 140.200.128.13
```

```
PARAU.OYSTER.NET.ck       internet address = 202.65.32.128
POIPARAU.OYSTER.NET.ck    internet address = 202.65.32.127
CIRCA.MCS.VUW.AC.NZ       internet address = 130.195.5.12
```

Some servers that are authoritative for the Cook Islands' top-level domains are located in New Zealand. This geographic separation may seem strange, but it makes sense if you've ever lived through a tropical storm in Rarotonga. If the power to the OYSTER.NET.ck network is disrupted, hostnames could still be resolved through the backup servers at WAIKATO.AC.NZ.

It's also possible to obtain a list of all the networks and hosts within a particular top-level domain by using the ls command, but be warned. The output can be verbose:

```
godzilla:~:65 % nslookup
> set type=ns
> ls ck.
[DOWNSTAGE.MCS.VUW.AC.NZ]
 ck.                                   server = parau.oyster.net.ck
 parau.oyster.net                      202.65.32.128
 ck.                                   server = poiparau.oyster.net.ck
 poiparau.oyster.net                   202.65.32.127
 ck.                                   server = downstage.mcs.vuw.ac.nz
 ck.                                   server = circa.mcs.vuw.ac.nz
 sda.org                               server = parau.oyster.net.ck
 parau.oyster.net                      202.65.32.128
 sda.org                               server = poiparau.oyster.net.ck
```

The final tool that is often useful for resolving hostnames is the whois command. This uses Internet Network Information Center (InterNIC) servers to perform all of the resolutions for you, and it includes useful information, such as the registrar of the domain name (helpful when making complaints about SPAM or harassment on the net!). Here's the whois entry for paulwatters.com:

```
godzilla:~:66 % whois paulwatters

Whois Server Version 1.3

Domain names in the .com, .net, and .org domains can now be
registered with many different competing registrars. Go to
http://www.internic.net for detailed information.

   Domain Name: PAULWATTERS.COM
   Registrar: REGISTER.COM, INC.
   Whois Server: whois.register.com
   Referral URL: www.register.com
   Name Server: DNS19.REGISTER.COM
   Name Server: DNS20.REGISTER.COM
   Updated Date: 30-may-2000
```

Understanding NIS and NIS+

NIS+ is a Solaris network information service and its primary focus is the management of users, hosts, networks, services, and protocols. NIS+ does not replace DNS, which is still required for host addressing and identification with respect, but NIS+ namespaces can be constructed to parallel the host designations assigned through DNS, to simplify operations, and to make the integration of both services more seamless.

NIS+ gives networks more than just DNS. Namespaces are used as centralized repositories of shared network information that can be used to more effectively manage large networks. However, many organizations choose not to use NIS+ because it has some overlap with DNS, and because of the extra administrative burden involved in installing and configuring NIS+ primary and slave servers. Yet if you use the NIS+ scripts to install and configure namespaces, instead of using NIS+ commands directly, NIS+ can be much easier to configure.

NIS revolves around the idea of maps. A map is generally a database with two columns, of which one is a primary key that is used to retrieve an associated value. This associative nature makes the storage and retrieval of group, mail, passwords, and Ethernet information fast for small networks, but it can rapidly become difficult to manage (not to mention very slow!) for large networks. NIS+, in contrast, uses tables, of which 16 are defined by the system. Tables store information like server addresses, timezones, and networks services. In this section, we review the most commonly used types of NIS maps and NIS+ tables.

Firstly, however, we present a conceptual overview of how NIS+ could be used to better manage an organization's network data. Let's imagine that we're setting up a Solaris network for an imaginary college called Dover College, which has a DNS domain of dover.edu. Dover has two teaching divisions: an undergraduate school (undergrad. dover.edu) and a graduate school (graduate.dover.edu). dover.edu has a Class C network (192.12.1.0), as do each of the undergraduate (192.12.2.0) and graduate schools (192.12.3.0). Each of these networks can have up to 255 hosts each, which more than adequately covers the staff members in both teaching divisions. To support DNS, a campus-wide DNS server ns.dover.edu at 192.12.1.16 may be needed, while the undergrad.dover.edu network has its own DNS server at ns.undergrad.dover.edu (192.12.1.16) and at ns.graduate.dover.edu (192.12.2.16). This is a fairly standard setup for a medium-sized network like a college campus and is demonstrated in Figure 32-1.

The NIS+ domains for Dover College can exactly mirror the DNS configuration, as shown in Figure 32-2. However, some differences in naming are immediately apparent. Although DNS uses lower-case names by convention, which does not terminate in a period, the NIS+ convention is to name write elements in a domain beginning with capital letters and terminating with a period.

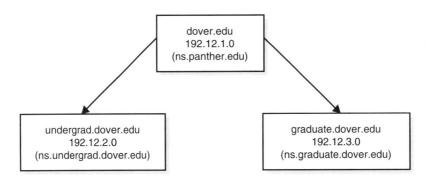

Figure 32-1 DNS configuration for a fictional college with two divisions: graduate and undergraduate, both of which have their own nameserver

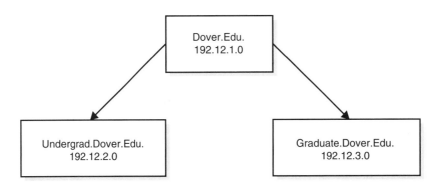

Figure 32-2 NIS+ domains for Dover College

In addition, the second-level domain identified in DNS as dover.edu would be the root domain in an NIS+ network, and the third-level domains, undergrad.dover.edu and graduate.dover.edu, would be described as nonroot domains. Each of these domains would be associated with a server, in which case the existing DNS servers would double-up as NIS+ servers. In fact, in normal NIS+ usage, each of the three domains at Dover College would require two servers: a master server and at least one replica or slave server. This ensures that if the master server is disrupted or experiences hardware failure, then the replica server holds copies of network service information. The expanded NIS+ domains for Dover College, with a master and slave server each (called Master and Replica), are shown in Figure 32-3.

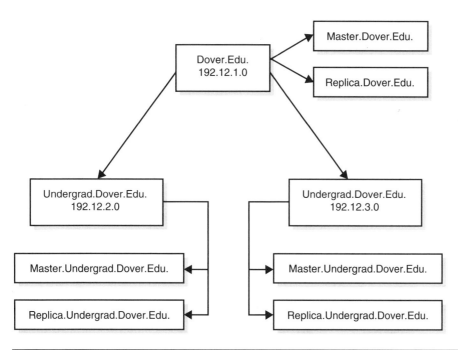

Figure 32-3 NIS+ domains with a master and a slave server each

In addition to domains and servers, NIS+ also caters for clients. Each client is associated with a specific server and domain. For example, a client in the chemistry lab in the graduate school (Curie.Graduate.Dover.Edu.) would be served by Master.Graduate. Dover.Edu. and would be part of the Graduate.Dover.Edu. domain. Alternatively, a history professor in the undergraduate school with a computer named FDR.Undergrad. Dover.Edu would be served by Master.Undergrad.Dover.Edu. and would be part of the Undergrad.Dover.Edu. domain. Figure 32-4 shows the hierarchy of control for the FDR.Undergrad.Dover.Edu. client. When each client is installed, a directory cache is created, which enables the client to locate other hosts and services via the appropriate server.

So far, we have mentioned only one of the many kinds of namespace components: the domain. However, many other components exist in the namespace, including group objects, directory objects, and table objects. We will examine these important features of the namespace in the following sections. In addition, we review the specific configuration of NIS maps and NIS+ tables.

It is worth mentioning at this point that one of the main reasons that organizations choose to implement NIS+ is the improved security that accompanies the system. For example, NIS+ tables are not directly editable, unlike their normal Solaris counterparts

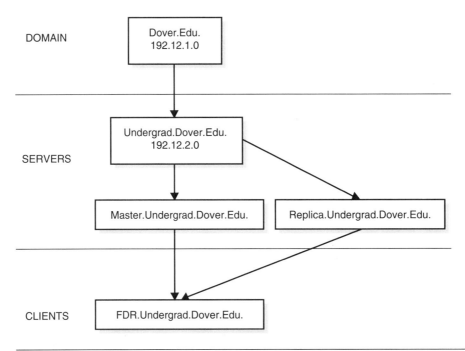

Figure 32-4   Hierarchy of control for a specific domain client (FDR.Undergrad.Dover.Edu.)

in the /etc directory. Requests to change or even access information in the namespace can only take place once a user has been authenticated. In addition to authentication, each user must be authorized to access a particular resource. This doubly protects sensitive and organizational data in a networked environment.

The main authentication exchange takes place when either a user presents his or her credentials or a host presents its credentials in the form of an unencrypted LOCAL form or a more secure, DES-encrypted exchange. The former is used for testing, while the latter is always used for deployment. After authentication, authorization for the requested resource is checked. Access rights can always be examined by using the niscat command, which is discussed later in this chapter.

NIS Maps

NIS uses a series of maps to encode data about the network structure. Many of these are in a form that can be accessed through an address key (having a byaddr suffix) or through a name (with a byname suffix). Whenever a client needs to find information about a particular host, service, group, network, or netgroup, it can be retrieved by consulting the appropriate map as defined in the namespace. The main system maps are as follows:

- **bootparams** contains a list of diskless clients for a domain.

- **ethers.byaddr** contains a list of the Ethernet addresses of all hosts in the domain and their hostnames.

- **ethers.byname** contains a list of the hostnames of all hosts in the domain and their Ethernet addresses.

- **group.bygid** contains a list of groups that are indexed by group ID (gid).

- **group.byname** contains a list of groups that are indexed by group name.

- **hosts.byaddr** contains a list of the addresses of all hosts in the domain and their hostnames.

- **hosts.byname** contains a list of the hostnames of all hosts in the domain and their addresses.

- **mail.aliases** contains a list of mail aliases within the namespace, indexed by name.

- **mail.byaddr** contains a list of mail aliases within the namespace, indexed by address.

- **netgroup** contains netgroup information, indexed by group name.

- **netgroup.byhost** contains netgroup information, indexed by hostname.

- **netgroup.byuser** contains netgroup information, indexed by username.

- **netid.byname** contains the netnames of hosts and users.

- **netmasks.byaddr** defines the netmasks defined in the domain namespace.

- **networks.byaddr** defines the networks in the domain namespace, sorted by address.

- **networks:byname** defines the networks in the domain namespace, sorted by name.

- **passwd.byname** defines the password database, sorted by username.

- **passwd.byuid** defines the password database, sorted by user ID.

- **protocols.byname** defines the network protocols used in the domain, sorted by name.

- **protocols.bynumber** defines the network protocols used in the domain, sorted by number.

- **publickey.byname** contains public keys for RPC.

- **rpc.bynumber** contains RPC details indexed by number.

- **services.byname** defines all available Internet services by name.

- **ypservers** contains a list of all NIS servers available.

As we can see, many similarities in name and function exist between the NIS maps and the /etc system files they are intended to replace. However, both the /etc files and NIS maps perform poorly under heavy loads when the number of hosts defined in a specific namespace exceeds the hundreds. In this case, it is much more appropriate to bypass NIS and /etc, and move directly to a NIS+ installation where a single table (such as Ethers) replaces the dual lookup system used by NIS (such as ethers.byname and ethers.byaddr).

Name Service Switch

You might be wondering how, in a mixed network information service environment comprised of NIS maps, NIS+ tables, and DNS servers, name services are selected to resolve particular requests. The answer is the name service switch, which is very useful because it enables the administrator to configure which name service handles specific kinds of requests. It is also possible to specify more than one kind of service for every kind of request. Thus, if a request fails on the default service, it can be applied to a different service.

For example, to resolve hostnames, many sites will have at least some local hostnames statically hardwired into the /etc/hosts database. In addition, many sites connected to the Internet will use the DNS for resolving hostnames. Where does this leave the relative sophistication of NIS+ namespaces or the legacy of NIS maps? The answer is that DNS, NIS, and NIS+ files can be configured to be selected as the first, second, third, and fourth choices for the default name service that resolves hosts in /etc/nsswitch.conf.

For instance, the line

```
hosts: files dns nisplus nis
```

indicates that the /etc/hosts file should be consulted first and, if a match cannot be found for a hostname, try DNS second. If DNS fails to resolve, then NIS+ should be tried. As a last resort, NIS map resolution can be attempted. This is a useful setup for a network that makes great use of the Internet and relies less on NIS+ and NIS.

Of course, many NIS+ advocates would suggest using the line

```
hosts: nisplus nis files dns
```

because this ensures that NIS+ is always selected over the /etc/hosts database or DNS.

In addition to host resolution, nsswitch.conf also enables the configuration of 14 other options, which roughly correspond to the contents of the NIS+ tables and/or the NIS maps. A NIS+-oriented nsswitch.conf file would look like the following:

```
passwd:      files nisplus
group:       files nisplus
hosts:       nisplus dns [NOTFOUND=return] files
services:    nisplus [NOTFOUND=return] files
networks:    nisplus [NOTFOUND=return] files
protocols:   nisplus [NOTFOUND=return] files
rpc:         nisplus [NOTFOUND=return] files
ethers:      nisplus [NOTFOUND=return] files
netmasks:    nisplus [NOTFOUND=return] files
bootparams:  nisplus [NOTFOUND=return] files
publickey:   nisplus
netgroup:    nisplus
automount: nisplus files
aliases: nisplus files
sendmailvars: nisplus files
```

In most of these situations, NIS+ is consulted before the files, except for the password and group information. In addition, DNS is listed as a host resolution method after NIS+. However, it would also be possible to implement a bare-bones system that only relies on files for most resource information and DNS for name resolution:

```
passwd:      files
group:       files
hosts:       dns [NOTFOUND=return] files
networks:    files
protocols:   files
rpc:         files
ethers:      files
netmasks:    files
bootparams:  files
publickey:   files
netgroup:    files
automount:   files
aliases:     files
services:    files
sendmailvars:   files
```

Summary

In this chapter, we have explored the concept of a name service and examined the name services that are available under Solaris, such as NIS, NIS+, and DNS. In addition to investigating DNS and its uses, we have also investigated the structure and content of NIS maps. After discussing how NIS+ domains are typically structured, we discussed how the name service switch can be used to select an appropriate naming service for each type of name resolution required by Solaris clients and servers.

Questions

1. Which of the following is a fully qualified domain name?
   A. savannah
   B. 255.0.0.0
   C. savannah.georgia.com
   D. 192.23.34.255

2. Which of the following is a valid /etc/hosts entry?

A. 204.168.14.23	leura	10.168.14.23
B. 204.168.14.23	leura	leura.paulwatters.com loghost
C. leura	204.168.14.23	leura.paulwatters.com loghost
D. leura	leura.paulwatters.com	204.168.14.23

3. Which of the following is defined in named.root?
   A. Root name server data required to initialize the DNS server cache
   B. Authorization for the root user to set up DNS services
   C. Access permissions for nonroot users to access DNS data installed by root
   D. Zone data for hosts within the local root NIS1 domain

4. Which of the following is defined in /etc/defaultdomain?
   A. The fully qualified domain name of the localhost
   B. The default Web site domain to connect through using Netscape
   C. The name of the local NIS1 domain
   D. The name of the local DNS domain

5. What is the purpose of nslookup?
   A. To resolve IP addresses using hostnames only
   B. To resolve hostnames using IP addresses only

    C. To resolve both hostnames or IP addresses given an IP address or hostname

    D. To look up a list of users who can edit zone files

6. Which fields can be found in the SOA record?

    A. origin, mail addr, serial, refresh, retry, expire, minimum ttl

    B. original serial, mail refresh, ttl retry, expiry date

    C. original serial, mail addr, ttl retry, ttl expire, minimum refresh

    D. origin, serial date, refresh time, retry, expire, minimum ttl

7. Which of the following data is not found in NIS maps?

    A. group

    B. mail

    C. ethernet

    D. boot device

8. What is the minimal recommended configuration for an NIS+ network?

    A. A root domain with a master server

    B. A root domain with a master and a slave server

    C. A root domain with at least one nonroot domain

    D. A root domain with at least two nonroot domains

9. Authentication credentials are exchanged using DES with which name service?

    A. DNS

    B. NIS

    C. NIS+

    D. None of the above

10. The bootparams map contains what kind of data?

    A. The name of the boot device

    B. The physical path to the boot device

    C. A list of all bootable devices

    D. A list of diskless clients

Answers

1. C

2. B

3. A

4. D

5. C

6. A

7. D

8. B

9. C

10. D

NIS

The following objectives will be met upon completing this chapter's material:

- Installing a root domain
- Creating NIS+ tables
- Non-root domain installation
- Populating tables
- Using NIS+

Root Domain Installation

Before any other services can be installed, the Network Information Service (NIS+) requires that the master server for the root domain be created. The master server will primarily be responsible for the management of the NIS+ namespace. For example, in the Cassowary.Net. domain, the Domain Name Service (DNS) server, ns.cassowary.net, will also be used for NIS+. This means that the nisserver script can be executed on the DNS server system, ns.cassowary.net, in order to initialize the master server for the root domain:

```
ns.cassowary.net# nisserver -r -d Cassowary.Net.
This script sets up this machine "ns" as an NIS+
root master server for domain Cassowary.Net..

Domain name             : Cassowary.Net.
NIS+ group              : admin.Cassowary.Net.
NIS (YP) compatibility  : OFF
Security level          : 2=DES

Is this information correct? (type 'y' to accept, 'n' to change) y
This script will set up your machine as a root master server for
domain Cassowary.Net. without NIS compatibility at security level 2.
```

Use "nisclient -r" to restore your current network service
environment.

Do you want to continue? (type 'y' to continue, 'n' to exit this
script)

setting up domain information "Cassowary.Net." ...

setting up switch information ...

running nisinit ...
This machine is in the "Cassowary.Net." NIS+ domain.
Setting up root server .

starting root server at security level 0 to create credentials...

running nissetup to create standard directories and tables ...

running nissetup to create standard directories and tables ...
org_dir.Cassowary.Net. created
groups_dir.Cassowary.Net. created
passwd.org_dir.Cassowary.Net. created
group.org_dir.Cassowary.Net. created
auto_master.org_dir.Cassowary.Net. created
auto_home.org_dir.Cassowary.Net. created
bootparams.org_dir.Cassowary.Net. created
cred.org_dir.Cassowary.Net. created
ethers.org_dir.Cassowary.Net. created
hosts.org_dir.Cassowary.Net. created
ipnodes.org_dir.Cassowary.Net. created
mail_aliases.org_dir.Cassowary.Net. created
sendmailvars.org_dir.Cassowary.Net. created
netmasks.org_dir.Cassowary.Net. created
netgroup.org_dir.Cassowary.Net. created
networks.org_dir.Cassowary.Net. created
protocols.org_dir.Cassowary.Net. created
rpc.org_dir.Cassowary.Net. created
services.org_dir.Cassowary.Net. created
timezone.org_dir.Cassowary.Net. created
client_info.org_dir.Cassowary.Net. created
auth_attr.org_dir.Cassowary.Net. created
exec_attr.org_dir.Cassowary.Net. created
prof_attr.org_dir.Cassowary.Net. created
user_attr.org_dir.Cassowary.Net. created
audit_user.org_dir.Cassowary.Net. created

adding credential for ns.Cassowary.Net...
Enter login password:
creating NIS+ administration group: admin.Cassowary.Net. ...
adding principal ns.Cassowary.Net. to admin.Cassowary.Net. ...

restarting NIS+ root master server at security level 2 ...
starting NIS+ password daemon ...
starting NIS+ cache manager ...

```
This system is now configured as a root server for domain
Cassowary.Net.
You can now populate the standard NIS+ tables by using the
nispopulate script or /usr/lib/nis/nisaddent command.
```

That's all that's required for NIS+ support. However, in order to enable support for NIS clients within the domain, you would need to use the following command instead:

```
ns.cassowary.net# nisserver -Y -r -d Cassowary.Net.
```

Creating Tables

As we mentioned earlier, NIS+ operates by creating a centralized set of tables that act as replacements for the localized configuration files in the /etc directory. In order to begin the process of creating these tables on the master server for the root domain, we need to use the nispopulate command to insert initial values into the tables:

```
ns.cassowary.net# nispopulate -F -p /etc -d Cassowary.Net.
```

The nispopulate command is responsible for storing all the appropriate information in the NIS+ tables. If your master server for root domain needs to support NIS clients, then you would need to use the following command instead:

```
ns.cassowary.net# nispopulate -Y -F -p /etc -d Cassowary.Net.
```

Next, we need to determine which users on the master server for the root domain should have administrative access to the NIS+ namespace. This gives the users named as administrators the ability to modify all of the data that NIS+ clients can look up; thus, it is a role of considerable responsibility. Changes made to the NIS+ tables do not just affect the local machine; they are reflected network-wide. If we had two network administrators, moppet and miki, they could be added to the administrator's group by using the nisgrpadm command:

```
ns.cassowary.net# nisgrpadm -a Cassowary.Net.
moppet.Cassowary.Net. miki.Cassowary.Net.
```

In order to check the configuration and create a checkpoint, you can use the nisping command on the domain:

```
ns.cassowary.net# nisping -C Cassowary.Net.
```

This concludes the configuration required to install the root domain. In the next section, we examine how to set up master and replica servers for the two nonroot domains that lie underneath the Cassowary.Net. domain: Develop.Cassowary.Net. and Sales. Cassowary.Net.

Nonroot Domain Installation

The first step in installing the nonroot domains Develop.Cassowary.Net. and Sales. Cassowary.Net. is to configure a master server for each nonroot domain by using the nisclient command. These master servers are effectively clients of the Cassowary.Net. root domain, which is why the nisclient command is used to initialize their settings. In this case, the server moorea.cassowary.net is assigned to be the root server of the nonroot domain Sales.Cassowary.Net., while the host borabora.cassowary.net is assigned to be the root server of the nonroot domain Develop.Cassowary.Net. To create the master servers, we would execute the following commands on each of these hosts respectively:

```
moorea.cassowary.net# nisclient -i -d Cassowary.Net. -h
Ns.Cassowary.Net
borabora.cassowary.net# nisclient -i -d Cassowary.Net. -h
Ns.Cassowary.Net
```

After the master servers have been initialized, clients for that domain can actually set up from individual user accounts. For example, for the user maya in the domain Sales.Cassowary.Net, we would use the following command to allow client access to the local namespace:

```
maya@moorea.cassowary.net$ nisclient -u
```

Alternatively, for the user natashia in the domain Develop.Cassowary.Net, we would use the following to initialize client access:

```
natashia@borabora.cassowary.net$ nisclient -u
```

Now that the servers that act as master servers for the nonroot domains have been set up as clients of the server that manages the root domain, these systems must themselves be set up as master servers for their own domains. In addition, replica servers may be installed at this time. In the previous example, we allocated moorea.cassowary.net the role of being master server for the nonroot domain Sales.Cassowary.Net. Imagine that we now allocated tahiti.cassowary.net the role of replica server for the nonroot domain Sales.Cassowary.Net. The first step is to ensure that the NIS+ service is running via RPC:

```
moorea.cassowary.net# rpc.nisd
```

Next, we utilize a command similar to that used for setting up the master server of the root domain:

```
ns.cassowary.net# nisserver -R -d Cassowary.Net. -h
moorea.cassowary.net
```

The authority to begin serving is then set by using the following command:

```
ns.cassowary.net# nisserver -M -d Sales.Cassowary.Net. -h
moorea.cassowary.net
```

The tables for the domain Sales.Cassowary.Net must then be populated by using the same procedure as for the master server:

```
moorea.cassowary.net# nispopulate -F -p /etc -d
Sales.Cassowary.Net.
```

The final step is assigning the role of replica server to the host tahiti.cassowary.net by using the nisclient command:

```
moorea.cassowary.net# nisclient -R -d Sales.Cassowary.Net. -h
tahiti.cassowary.net
```

We now repeat these commands for the non-root domain Develop.Cassowary.Net., which has been assigned the server orana.cassowary.net as a replica server:

```
borabora.cassowary.net# rpc.nisd
orana.cassowary.net# rpc.nisd
ns.cassowary.net# nisserver -R -d Cassowary.Net. -h
borabora.cassowary.net
ns.cassowary.net# nisserver -M -d Develop.Cassowary.Net. -h
borabora.cassowary.net
borabora.cassowary.net# nispopulate -F -p /etc -d
Develop.Cassowary.Net.
borabora.cassowary.net# nisclient -R -d Develop.Cassowary.Net. -h
orana.cassowary.net
```

NIS+ Tables

All data within NIS+ is stored in tables, which are loosely based on several configuration files that are located in the /etc directory on a standard host. The major difference between file-centric and NIS+ administration is security and the centralization of administration. On a network with 100 hosts, around 1,500 individual configuration files need to be managed using a files approach, whereas an NIS+ approach requires the maintenance of only 15 files. Any modifications to the NIS+ tables are automatically distributed to clients requesting namespace data. This applies equally to hostname resolution as it does to accessing authorization credentials, such as usernames and passwords.

Trying to update a password file on 100 hosts takes a long time if that user needs access to any particular host on the network. For example, students may work on any workstation within a computer lab, or stock traders may be rotated regularly throughout an office for security reasons. To gain access to any workstation at any time, a single set of credentials is required. NIS+ is particularly suited to this environment.

If you are worried about redundancy and backups, the master/replica server model used by NIS+ ensures that even if the master server for a root or nonroot domain goes down, its replica server will be able to provide authoritative data until normal service is resumed.

Auto_Home

The Auto_Home table enables all users within a domain to access a single home directory, irrespective of which system they login to. The capability to centrally support this kind of distributed filesystem is one of the best features of NIS+. One of the main issues that arises when using the automounter is that local partitions called /home cannot be mounted by the local system; this mount point is reserved for the automounter, which can cause some consternation for administrators who are unfamiliar with the automounter.

The Auto_Home table contains two columns: a username column, which identifies the user on a network, and a column for the hostname and path to the user's home directory. Once an entry is created in the Auto_Home table, the home directory for that user will be available for mounting on any host within the network that is part of the NIS+ domain. Let's look at an example:

```
avarua:/users/export/julian
```

Here the user julian's home directory is always mounted from the host avarua, with the mount point /users/export/julian.

Auto_Master

The Auto_Master table is used in conjunction with the Network File System (NFS) to create maps that relate specific mount points to use the automounter. For example, if we wanted to map home directories from /staff and /students using Auto_Home, then we'd need to insert the following entries into the Auto_Master table:

```
/staff auto_home
/students    auto_home
```

Bootparams

Solaris supports the booting of diskless clients, such as X-terminals, by using the Bootparams table. Every diskless client within the domain will have an entry in the Bootparams table, which defines the root directory and the swap and dump partitions for the client. For example, the diskless client cardiff has its root directory on the server macquarie, but actually accesses its swap and dump partitions from the server tuggerah. The following entry would need to be inserted into the Bootparams table to support this functionality:

```
cardiff     root=macquarie:/export/root/cardiff \
            swap=tuggerah:/export/swap/cardiff \
            dump=tuggerah:/export/dump/cardiff
```

Ethers

All network interface cards (NICs) have a low-level hardware address associated with them called an Ethernet (media access control [MAC]) address. NIS+ associates each host's Ethernet address with a specific hostname within the domain. For example, if the host charleston has a single network interface with the Ethernet address 01:ab:b1:c3:d2:c3, then the following entry would be inserted into the Ethers table:

```
01:ab:b1:c3:d2:c3 charlestown
```

All entries in the ethers table are statically stored as arp entries and are typically used by diskless X-terminals or for jumpstart configurations.

Group

The Group table stores information about user groups that have been defined within the domain. The NIS+ Group table stores details of the group name, a group password (if applicable), the group ID (GID), and a list of all users who are members of the group. For example, the group staff may have the members paul, maya, moppet, and miki, as shown in the following entry:

```
staff::10:paul,maya,moppet,miki
```

Hosts

The Hosts table associates an Internet Protocol (IP) address with a specific hostname and/or a number of optional hostname aliases. For example, if the host speers has an

IP address of 10.36.12.54 and an alias of cockle, then the following entry would be inserted into the Hosts table:

```
192.34.54.3    speers cockle
```

Mail Aliases

Mail Transport Agents (MTAs) under Solaris typically make use of the mail aliases database (/etc/aliases) to define mailing lists or aliases for specific users. In an NIS+ domain, the /etc/aliases file is replaced by the Mail Aliases table, which can map a specific username to an alias name or a single alias to a list of valid usernames (that is, a mailing list). For example, the alias postmaster is typically used to identify the mail administrator within a domain. To associate this alias with a specific user account (such as maya), we would insert the following alias into the Mail Aliases table:

```
postmaster:maya
```

Aliases can also be matched with other aliases that have already been defined. For example, many sites forward all e-mail for the root user to the alias postmaster. In combination with our existing rule that forwards all e-mail for postmaster to maya, the following entry would have the net result of forwarding all e-mail for root to the user maya:

```
root:postmaster
```

Finally, imagine that a restaurant chain has an e-mail distribution list to managers at all local restaurants. A mail alias called managers could be set up so that the managers at the different restaurants would all receive a copy of e-mail sent to the user managers. In this example, the accounts hamilton, swansea, barbeach, and belmont would all receive a copy of any messages sent to the alias managers:

```
managers: hamilton,swansea,barbeach,belmont
```

Netgroups

Netgroups are authorization lists that can be used to govern access to resources within a network and to determine which groups of users can perform specific operations. For example, a group called admins within the Cassowary.Net. domain might be authorized to add or delete clients to the domain. A netgroups entry that defines the admins netgroup would look like this:

```
admins cassowary.net
```

Netmasks

The Netmasks table defines all of the netmasks required for the local network. For a Class A network, the netmask is 255.0.0.0, whereas the netmask for a Class B network is 255.255.0.0. The most common netmask is 255.255.255.0, which is for a Class C network (204.128.64.0), as shown in the following example:

```
204.128.64.0255.255.255.0
```

Networks

Individual networks can be defined within an NIS+ domain by inserting entries into the Networks table. In addition, aliases for entire networks can also be entered into the Networks table. For example, if the network broadmeadow (203.48.16.0) acted as a backup network for a primary network, it may have the following alias backup:

```
broadmeadow   203.48.16.0   backup
```

Passwd

The Passwd table replaces the /etc/passwd file, which is typically used by non-NIS+ systems for user identification and authentication. The Passwd table contains one row for each user, containing a number of fields. These fields include the username, the encrypted password field (now replaced by the shadow password file), a user ID, the primary group ID, the user's real name, and their home directory default login shell. In addition, some extra fields are shown, including the number of days before which a password can be changed and/or how often a password must be changed. A sample row inserted into the Passwd table for the user pwatters would look like this:

```
pwatters:x:1024:20:Paul Watters:/home/pwatters:/bin/csh:10923:-1:-
1:-1:-1:0
```

Protocols

The Protocols table lists all protocols that are supported on the network. For example, to support the Transmission Control Protocol (TCP) and User Datagram Protocol (UDP) transport layers, the IP must be supported, which is typically listed as protocol zero:

```
ip    0
```

RPC

The RPC table lists all the available RPC services on the local network. The first program that must be supported is the rpcbind program, which is also known as the portmap program, and it runs on port 100000:

```
rpcbind    100000    portmap
```

In addition, to support services like NFS, the rquotad and mountd services will also need to be supported:

```
rquotad 100011  quotad
mountd 100005
```

Services

The Services table contains entries that define all of the services that are available on the NIS+ network under both UDP and TCP. For example, the sendmail service typically runs on TCP port 25; thus, the following entry would have to be inserted into the Services table to be supported in the network:

```
sendmail    25/tcp
```

Timezone

The Timezone table sets the appropriate timezone for hosts within the NIS+ domain. For example, the following entry sets the timezone for the host borabora to be Australia/NSW:

```
borabora Australia/NSW
```

However, the server tahiti might well be located in a different timezone, particularly if the NIS+ extends beyond the local area:

```
tahiti Australia/QLD
```

The Timezone entries affect all applications that need to process dates and times, such as mail transport agents, and the cron process scheduling application.

Using NIS+

Having reviewed the configuration of NIS+ and the main tables that are used to define an NIS+ domain, we now examine how to use NIS+ effectively to manage hosts and resources within a domain. As we have seen, many different objects can be managed and identified within an NIS+ domain, and several commands are used to access them. In this section, we examine commands, such as nisdefault, which displays the NIS+ settings for the local client system, as well as nischmod, which is used to set access rights on NIS+ objects. In addition, the nisls command is reviewed, which can be used for object lookups and queries. Finally, we will examine the niscat command, which displays the contents of table entries and can be used to examine NIS+ objects in detail.

Displaying Default Settings

The current settings for a local client system and the active user can be displayed by using the nisdefaults command. The nisdefaults command is commonly used when attempting to troubleshoot an error, such as a user's credentials not being correctly authenticated from the Passwd table. As an example, let's examine the nisdefaults for the host comorin when executed by the user sukhdev:

```
comorin$ nisdefaults
Principal Name : simon.develop.cassowary.net.
Domain Name    : develop.cassowary.net.
Host Name      : comorin.develop.cassowary.net.
Group Name     : develop
Access Rights  : ----rmcdr---r---
Time to live   : 11:00:00
Search Path    : develop.cassowary.net. cassowary.net.
```

The output of the nisdefaults command can be interpreted in the following way:

- The principal user is sukhdev, who belongs to the NIS+ domain develop. cassowary.net.

- The primary domain name is develop.cassowary.net.

- The hostname of the local system is comorin.develop.cassowary.net.

- The user sukhdev's primary group is develop.

- The time-to-live setting is 11 hours.

- The client's access rights within the domain are stated.

- The search path starts with the current nonroot domain (develop.cassowary.net), followed by the root domain (cassowary.net).

The access rights stated for the user in this example are outlined in more detail in the next section.

Understanding Object Permissions

Every user has a set of access rights for accessing objects within the network. The notation for setting and accessing object permissions is very similar to that used for Solaris filesystems. The following permissions can be set on any object or can be defined as the default settings for a particular client:

- **c**   Sets the create permission
- **d**   Sets the delete permission
- **m**   Sets the modify permission
- **r**   Sets the read permission

This nischmod command is used to set permissions on objects within the domain. The following operands are used to specify access rights for specific classes of users:

- **a**   all (all authenticated and unauthenticated users)
- **g**   group
- **n**   nobody (all unauthenticated users)
- **o**   object owner
- **w**   world (all authenticated users)

Two operators can be used to set and remove permissions:

- **+**   Sets a permission
- **−**   Removes a permission

Some examples of how permissions strings are constructed will clarify how these operators and operands are combined for use with the nichmod command. The following command removes all modify (m) and create (c) access rights on the password table for all unauthenticated (n) users:

```
moorea# nischmod n-cm passwd.org_dir
```

Even unauthenticated users require read (r) access to the password table for authentication, which can be granted with the following command:

```
moorea# nischmod n+r passwd.org_dir
```

To grant, modify, and create access rights to the current user (in this case root) and his or her primary group on the same table, we would use the following command:

```
moorea# nischmod og+cm passwd.org_dir
```

NIS+ permission strings are easy to remember, but hard to combine into single commands where some permissions are granted while others are removed, unlike the octal codes used to specify absolute permissions on Solaris filesystems. However, it is possible to combine permissions strings by using a comma to separate individual strings. The following complex string is an example of how it is possible to set permissions within a single string, but it equally shows how challenging it is to interpret:

```
moorea# nischmod o=rmcd,g=rmc,w=rm,n=r hosts.org_dir
```

This command grants the following permissions to four different categories of users:

- **owner**   read, modify, create and delete
- **group**   read, modify and create
- **world**   read and modify
- **nobody**   read-only

Listing Objects

The nisls command is used as a lookup and query command that can provide views on NIS+ directories and tables. For example, to view all of the NIS+ directories that have been populated within the local namespace, we can use the *nisls* command:

```
moorea# nisls
develop.cassowary.net.:
org_dir
groups_dir
```

Two directory object types are listed here: the org_dir, which lists all of the tables that have been set up within the namespace, while the groups_dir stores details of all the NIS+ groups. We can view a list of tables by using the nisls command once again on the org_dir directory:

```
moorea# nisls org_dir
org_dir.sales.cassowary.net.:
auto_home
auto_master
bootparams
client_info
cred
ethers
group
hosts
```

```
mail_aliases
netgroup
netmasks
networks
passwd
protocols
rpc
sendmailvars
services
timezone
```

A large number of tables have been populated for this domain. The groups directory contains the admin group we created earlier, which lists all of the administrators as well as several other groups that are based on distinct organizational units within the current domain:

```
moorea# nisls groups_dir
groups_dir.sales.cassowary.net.:
admin
adverts
legal
media
```

Displaying Objects

The niscat command is used to retrieve the contents of objects within the domain, primarily the data contained within NIS+ tables. For example, all hosts listed within the domain can be listed by using the following command:

```
moorea$ niscat -h hosts.org_dir
moorea.cassowary.net moorea 10.58.64.16
borabora.cassowary.net borabora 10.58.64.17
tahiti.cassowary.net tahiti 10.58.64.18
orana.cassowary.net orana 10.58.64.19
```

Alternatively, we can use the niscat command to examine the contents of the Password table:

```
moorea$ niscat passwd.org_dir
moppet:*LK*:1001:1:moppet:/staff/moppet:/bin/tcsh:10910:-1:-1:-1:-1:0
miki:*LK*:1002:1:miki:/staff/miki:/bin/bash:10920:-1:-1:-1:-1:0
maya:*LK*:1003:1:maya:/staff/maya:/bin/sh:10930:-1:-1:-1:-1:0
paul:*LK*:1004:1:paul:/staff/paul:/bin/csh:10940:-1:-1:-1:-1:0
```

Next, we can examine which groups these users belong to by using the niscat command once again:

```
moorea$ niscat group.org_dir
root::0:root
```

```
staff::1:moppet,miki,maya,paul
bin::2:root,bin,daemon
sys:*:3:root,bin,sys,adm
adm::4:root,adm,daemon
uucp::5:root,uucp
mail::6:root
```

All of the hosts that form part of the local domain can be examined based on their Ethernet address, which is extracted from the ethers table, as shown in the following example:

```
moorea$ niscat ethers.org_dir
1:4a:16:2f:13:b2 moorea.cassowary.net.
1:02:1e:f4:61:2e borabora.cassowary.net.
f4:61:2e:1:4a:16 tahiti.cassowary.net.
2f:13:b2:1:02:1e orana.cassowary.net.
```

In order to determine which services are offered within the local domain, we can also examine the services table:

```
moorea$ niscat services.org_dir
tcpmux tcpmux tcp 1
echo echo tcp 7
echo echo udp 7
discard discard tcp 9
discard sink tcp 9
discard null tcp 9
discard discard udp 9
discard sink udp 9
discard null udp 9
systat systat tcp 11
systat users tcp 11
daytime daytime tcp 13
daytime daytime udp 13
```

Every other table that is defined within the domain can be viewed by using the niscat command in this way.

Summary

In this chapter, we have examined how NIS+ is actually used to manage domains and which tables are commonly used to store domain data. We have walked through the process of installing both root and nonroot domains, as well as populating and creating key NIS+ tables.

Questions

1. What does the nisserver command do?
   A. Sets up a root NIS+ domain
   B. Sets up a nonroot NIS+ domain
   C. Starts the NIS+ daemon
   D. None of the above

2. What does the nispopulate command do?
   A. Adds clients to an NIS+ table
   B. Adds clients to an NIS map
   C. Extracts data from existing /etc files and inserts it into NIS+ tables
   D. None of the above

3. What does the nisgrpadm command do?
   A. Adds users to an NIS+ group
   B. Adds users to an NIS map
   C. Extracts data from existing /etc files and inserts it into NIS+ tables
   D. None of the above

4. What does the nisclient command do?
   A. Adds clients to an NIS+ table
   B. Adds clients to an NIS map
   C. Extracts data from existing /etc files and inserts it into NIS+ tables
   D. Assigns the role of a replica server

5. Which command would you use to create an NIS+ configuration checkpoint?
   A. nisclient
   B. nisping
   C. nischeck
   D. nisgrpadm

6. What does the Auto_Home table do?
   A. Enables some groups within a domain to access a single home directory
   B. Enables all groups within a domain to access multiple home directories
   C. Enables all users within a domain to access a single home directory
   D. Enables all users to have an account on each system in the domain

7. What does the netgroups table do?
   A. Enables some groups within a domain to access a single home directory
   B. Enables all groups within a domain to access multiple home directories

C. Enables all users within a domain to access a single home directory

D. Contains authorization lists that can be used to govern access to resources within a network

8. What are valid object permissions?
    A. c, d, m, r
    B. x, d, m, r
    C. r, w, x, S
    D. r, w, x, C

9. Which operands are used to specify access rights for specific classes of users?
    A. a, d, S, x
    B. S, g, m, x
    C. A, g, x, S
    D. a, g, n, o, w

10. What does the niscat command do?
    A. It is used to retrieve the contents of objects within the domain.
    B. It is used to displays user lists.
    C. It is used to grant/deny access to network resources.
    D. It is used to display lists of current access permissions.

Answers

1. A

2. C

3. A

4. D

5. B

6. C

7. D

8. A

9. D

10. A

Admintool

The following objectives will be met upon completing this chapter's material:

- Understanding the role of admintool
- Using admintool to add a user
- Using admintool to modify a user's details
- Using admintool to manage groups

So far, we have only examined user and group administration by using command-line tools, such as useradd and groupadd. This will suit administrators who have experience with Linux, because many of the commands have the same name as Solaris. However, Microsoft Windows administrators may find it difficult to remember command and option names, after using the NT User Manager, shown in Figure 34-1, which is a graphic user interface (GUI)-based administration tool. This application enables the easy management of users and groups by pointing and clicking.

Managing Users

Fortunately, Solaris also provides an easy-to-use administrative interface for adding users and groups to the admintool system. The admintool interface is shown in Figure 34-2. The interface shown is for user management and displays the username, user ID (UID), and user comment. In addition to managing users and groups, admintool is also useful for managing hosts, printers, serial ports, and software. Each management option has its own interface, which is accessible from the Browse menu. When an interface is selected, such as the printer's interface, administrators can then add, modify, or

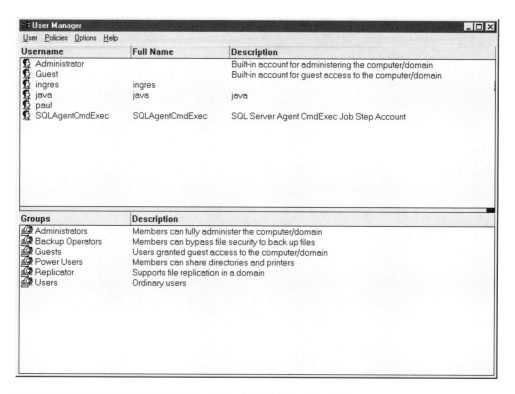

Figure 34-1   The Windows NT User Manager

delete the entries in the current database (in this case, administrators can add, delete, or modify the entries for printers).

A number of other user characteristics are associated with each user, in addition to a username and password. These features include the following:

- The UID, which is a unique integer that begins with the root user (UID = 1), with other UIDs typically (but not necessarily) being allocated sequentially. Some systems will reserve all UIDs below 1023 for system accounts (such as the Apache' user for managing the Apache Web server), whereas those UIDs 1024 and above are designated for ordinary users. The UID of 0 designates the super-user account that is typically called root. This is equivalent to the Administrator account in Windows NT. The maximum UID is 2147483647.

- A flexible mechanism for distinguishing different classes of users, known as groups. Groups are not just sets of related users. The Solaris filesystem enables group-designated read, write, and execute file access for groups, in addition to per-

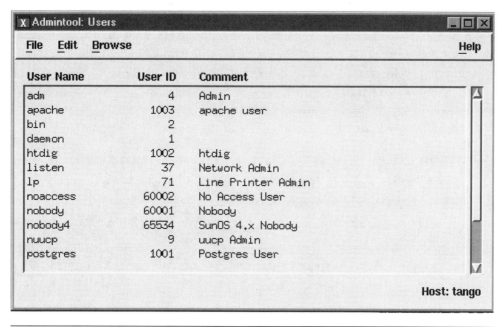

Figure 34-2   The Solaris admintool

missions granted to the individual user and to all users. Every UID is associated with a primary group ID (GID); however, UIDs can also be associated with more than one secondary group.

- A home directory, which is the default file storage location for all files created by a particular user. If the automounter is used, then home directories can be exported using NFS on /home. When a user spawns a login shell, the current working directory will always be the home directory.

- A login shell, which can be used to issue commands interactively or to write simple programs, as reviewed in Chapters 5 and 6. A number of different shells are available under Solaris, including the Bourne shell (sh), C shell (csh), the Bourne again shell (bash), and the Cornell shell (tcsh). The choice of shell depends largely on personal preference, user experience with C-like programming constructs, and terminal handling.

- A comment, which is typically the user's full name, such as Paul Watters. However, system accounts may use names that describe their purpose (for example, the command Web Server might be associated with the Apache user).

Adding a user to a Solaris system is easy, but this operation can only be performed by the root user. Two options are available: the first option is to edit the /etc/passwd file directly, increment the UID, add the appropriate GID, add a home directory (remembering to physically create it on the filesystem), insert a comment, and choose a login name. In addition, a passwd for the user must be set using the passwd command. The second option is to use the admintool add user feature.

The admintool add user feature can fail under the following conditions:

- The UID that you specified has already been taken by another user. Unlike Windows NT, UIDs can be recycled, as long as precautions are taken to ensure that a previous owner of the UID no longer owns files on the filesystem.

- The GID that you specified does not exist. Verify its entry in the groups database (/etc/group).

- The comment contains special characters, like double quotes (""), exclamation marks (!), or slashes (/).

- The shell that you specified does not exist. Check that the shell actually exists in the path specified, and that the shell has an entry in the shells database (/etc/shells).

Let's examine how to modify existing user information using the admintool, as shown in Figure 34-3. Firstly, select the user whose data you want to modify (such as the adm user, one of the preconfigured system accounts that is created during Solaris installation). Next, select the Modify . . . option from the admintool Edit menu. The User Entry Modification window is shown in Figure 34-3 for the adm user. Here it is possible to modify the following options:

- The username

- The primary group

- All secondary groups

- The user comment

- The login shell, which be selected from a drop-down menu containing all the valid shells defined in the shells database (/etc/shells)

- The minimum and maximum days required before a password change

- The maximum number of inactive days for an account

- An expiry date for the user's account

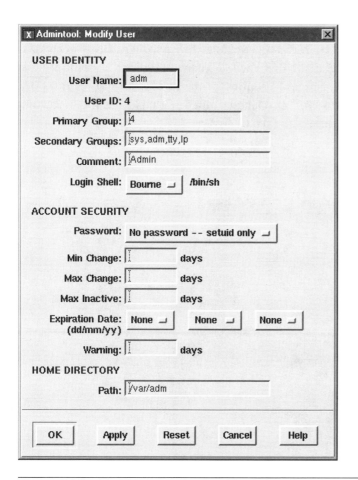

Figure 34-3 Modifying user details with admintool

- The number of days' warning to give a user before his or her password must be changed

- The path to the user's home directory

Of course, all of this information can be set on the command line by using the passwd command. However, the admintool interface is easier to use and provides some additional functionality. For example, it is impossible to enter an invalid expiration date, because the day, month, and year are selected from drop-down boxes. In addition, if any problems are encountered during modification, no changes will be recorded.

Adding a user to the system involves entering data into the same interface used for modifying user details, as shown in Figure 34-4. The UID is sequentially generated, as it contains a default primary group, a user shell, a password option (not set until first login), and the option to create a new directory for the user as their home directory. Again, admintool has advanced error-checking facilities that make it difficult to damage or overwrite system files with invalid data.

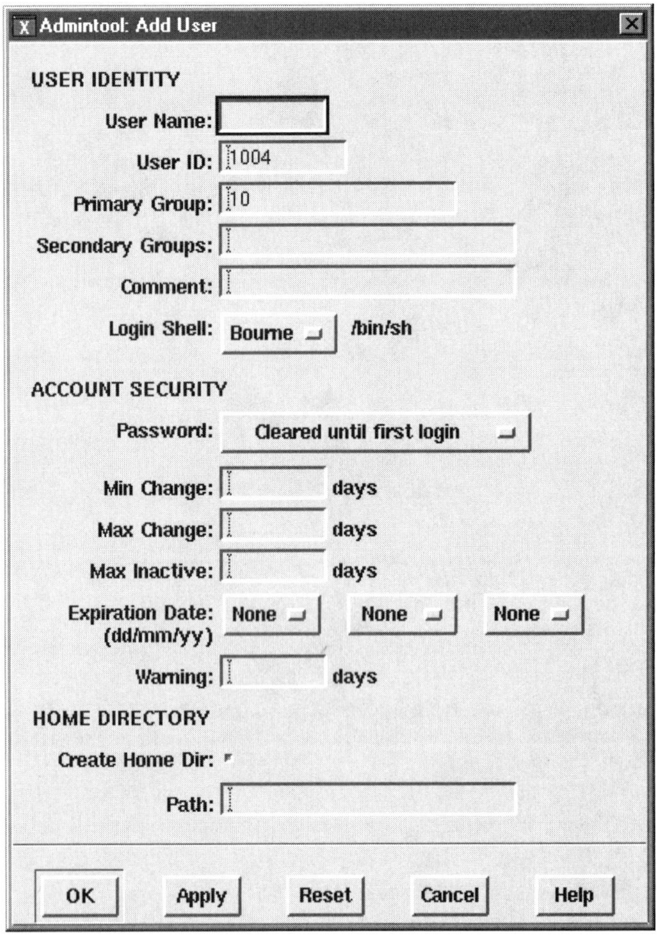

Figure 34-4   Adding user details with admintool

Managing Groups

Admintool can also be used as a group administration tool. Solaris provides a facility for identifying sets of related users into groups. Each user is associated with a primary GID, which is associated with a name. The group name and GID can be used interchangeably. In addition, users can also be associated with one or more secondary groups. This flexibility means that although a user might have a primary group membership based on their employment or organizational status (such as staff or managers), they can actively share data and system privileges with other groups based on their workgroup needs (such as sales or engineer).

Groups can be created and users can be added or removed from groups using admintool. In addition, groups can also be deleted using admintool. The group administration interface is shown in Figure 34-5. Here five groups are shown. The adm group (GID 4) has three members: root, adm, and daemon. To add a user to the group, simply select the adm group, and click on the Add . . . entry in the Edit menu. A comma-delimited list of users in the group would then be displayed. The bin user could be added to the adm group by inserting a comma after the last entry and adding the name "bin" to the list.

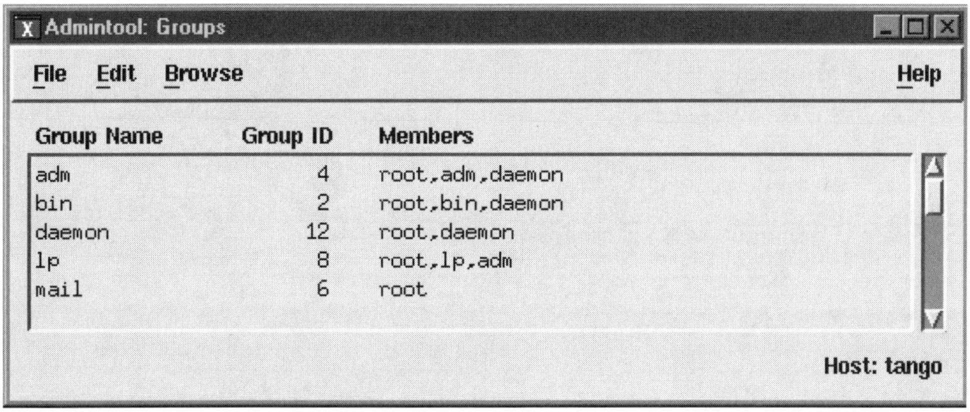

Figure 34-5 Adding groups with admintool

Summary

In this chapter, we've examined how to use the admintool to manage users and system resources. Admintool is a convenient GUI-based interface that provides an alternative to the common command-line tools used to administer Solaris systems.

Questions

1. What is the maximum UID that can be set through admintool?
   A. 1024
   B. 2048
   C. 8192
   D. 2147483647

2. Which of the following items does admintool *not* administer?
   A. Users and groups
   B. Hosts and printers
   C. Public keys
   D. Serial ports

3. In each admintool interface, which of the following operations *cannot* be performed?
   A. Add entries
   B. Modify entries
   C. Copy entries
   D. Delete entries

Answers

1. D

2. C

3. C

JumpStart—Automatic Installation

The following objectives will be met upon completing this chapter's material:

- Understanding the purpose of JumpStart
- Reviewing the process for setting up JumpStart
- Setting up a network to use JumpStart
- Setting up boot and install servers
- Initializing install clients
- Booting install clients
- The role of the sysidcfg file

Introducing JumpStart

JumpStart is a client/server system for installing Solaris systems on a local area network (LAN) using a Standard Operating Environment (SOE). This removes the need to individually configure each installation on every host on a subnet. This greatly reduces the administrative burden on sysadmins, as most client systems use exactly the same settings, particularly within the same organizational unit.

JumpStart has three roles that are filled by different systems on the network:

- An install server, which provides all of the data and services required to install the system.
- A boot server, which the Reverse Address Resolution Protocol (RARP) daemon uses to boot client systems that have not been installed.
- An install client, which is the target system for installation.

Boot Servers

A boot server provides a copy of the operating system to be installed on a target host. Once the target host has been booted using the network and install options (discussed in the following section), a kernel is downloaded to the target host from an install server and booted locally. Once the system has been loaded, the operating system is then downloaded from the boot server. The rules for downloading and installing specific files are located in the rules.ok file. Individual systems can have their own entries in the rules file, or generic rules can be inserted. After loading the system from the boot server, the install client then executes a post-installation script and will then be ready for use.

Install Servers

The install server uses RARP to listen for requests to install the system from target hosts. Once such a request is received, a mini-root system is downloaded from the install server to the target host.

To set up an install server, you need to perform the following tasks:

```
# mkdir -p /export/install /export/config
# cp -r /cdrom/sol_8_sparc/s0/Solaris_2.8/Misc/jumpstart_sample/
* /export/config
# /cdrom/sol_8_sparc/s0/Solaris_2.8/Tools ./setup_install_server
/export/install
```

This assumes that /export/install has sufficient space to store the installation files, and that the JumpStart configuration data, such as the rules file, will be stored in /export/config. Here is a sample host_class file, which is referred to in rules, that specifies the UNIX filesystem (UFS) disk layout for all boot clients:

```
install_type initial_install
system_type standalone
partitioning explicit
filesys c1t2d0s0 512 /
filesys c1t2d0s3 2048 /usr
filesys c1t2d0s4 256 /var
filesys c0t3d1s0 1024 swap
filesys c0t3d1s1 free /export
cluster SUNWCall
```

Here we can see that the standard layout allocated 512M to /, 2048M to /usr, 256M to /var, 1024M to swap, and all free space to /export. In addition, the cluster SUNWCall is to be installed.

Once the rules file has been customized, its contents must be verified by using the check command. Once the check command parses the rules file and validates its contents, a rules.ok file is created.

Boot Clients

In order to set up a boot client, the target system must be shut down to init level 0 by using the init 0 command or the equivalent. Next, the system needs to be booted by using the following command from the ok prompt:

```
boot net - install
```

At this point, a broadcast is made on the local subnet to locate an install server. Once an install server is located, a mini-root system is downloaded to the target system. Once the kernel is loaded from the mini-root system, the operating system in then downloaded from the boot server:

```
Resetting ...
SPARCstation 20 MP (2 X SuperSPARC-II)
ROM Rev. 2.28, 256 MB memory installed, Serial #345665.
Ethernet address 8:0:19:6b:22:a2, Host ID: 49348a3.
Initializing Memory |
Boot device: /iommu/sbus/ledma@f,400010/le@f,c00000 File and args: -
hostname: paul.cassowary.net
domainname: cassowary.net
root server: installserv
root directory: /solaris_2.8/export/exec/kvm/sparc.sun
Copyright (c) 1983-2000, Sun Microsystems, Inc.
The system is coming up. Please wait.
```

Once the system has started, you'll see individual clusters being installed:

```
Selecting cluster: SUNWCXall
Total software size: 324.55 MB
Preparing system to install Solaris. Please wait.
Setting up disk c1t2d0:
- Creating Solaris disk label (VTOC)
Creating and checking UFS file systems:
- Creating / (c1t2d0)
- Creating /var (c1t2d0)
- Creating /scratch (c1t2d0)
- Creating /opt (c1t2d0)
- Creating /usr (c1t2d0)
- Creating /staff (c1t2d0)
Beginning Solaris package installation...
SUNWcsu.....done. 321.23 MB remaining.
SUNWcsr.....done. 277.34 MB remaining.
SUNWcsd.....done. 312.23 MB remaining.
```

sysidcfg

When installing JumpStart on a large number of clients, installation can be expedited by using a sysidcfg file, which defines a number of standard parameters for installation. The sysidcfg file can contain configuration entries for the following properties:

- Date and time
- Dynamic Host Configuration Protocol (DHCP)
- Domain name
- Graphics card
- Hostname
- IP address
- IPv6
- Language
- Locale
- Monitor type
- Name server
- Name service
- Netmask
- Network interface
- Pointing device
- Power management
- Root password
- Security policy
- Terminal type
- Timezone

The following is a sample sysidcfg file:

```
system_locale=en_US
timezone=US/Eastern
timeserver=localhost
network_interface=le0 {netmask=255.255.255.0 protocol_ipv6=yes}
security_policy=NONE
terminal=dtterm
name_service=NONE
root_password=
```

Summary

In this chapter, we've examined how to set up boot and install servers for JumpStart, and how to boot an install client to retrieve data from both servers. JumpStart is often used when a number of different clients must be installed on the same subnet and when their configuration is common.

Questions

1. Which of the following *cannot* be specified in the sysidcfg file?
   A. Terminal type
   B. Timezone
   C. Terminal width
   D. Security policy

2. Which type of server provides all the data and services required to install a client using JumpStart?
   A. Boot server
   B. Install server
   C. DNS server
   D. Install client

3. Which type of server uses the RARP daemon to boot client systems that have not been installed?
   A. Boot server
   B. Install server
   C. DNS server
   D. Install client

4. Which command parses the rules file and validates its contents?
   A. lex
   B. yacc
   C. perl
   D. check

5. Which command is used to boot an install client?
   A. boot net - jumpstart
   B. boot net
   C. boot net - install
   D. boot jumpstart

Answers

1. C

2. B

3. A

4. D

5. C

## CHAPTER 36

Configuring and Using the CDE

The following objectives will be met upon completing this chapter's material:

- Using the CDE
- Accessing the CDE with dtlogin
- Configuring the CDE workspace
- Launching applications
- Reviewing available CDE applications

When Solaris is installed, the Common Desktop Environment (CDE) will be installed as the default window manager running under X11. The CDE supersedes Sun's own OpenWindows platform and is commonly found on HP-UX, Linux, and other Unix systems. CDE is an initiative of the Common Open Software Environment (COSE), which aims to standardize Unix operations across platforms. Before learning about Solaris, it's important to master the CDE, particularly if Microsoft Windows administrators want to avoid using the command line as much as possible.

Using CDE

The CDE is best learned by experience. You will quickly become competent at logging in, running applications, configuring your own workspace, and customizing applications. In the following sections, we examine how to run the most popular applications, navigate around the workspace, and run the CDE terminal application (dtterm) to spawn a user's default shell.

dtlogin

After your system has been installed, you will be presented with the graphical login screen shown in Figure 36-1. You must enter your username and click OK. A new screen will then appear, asking for the correct password for the login that you entered on the previous screen. If the username and password are authenticated by using the password database (/etc/passwd), then the CDE workspace will be launched, as shown in Figure 36-2. Typically, the Front Panel will appear, which consists of a toolbar that contains a set of hierarchical menus, from which various CDE applications can be launched.

One of the nice features of the CDE login screen, which is provided by the dtscreen application and managed by the dtlogin application, is that you can elect to use either the CDE workspace or the old OpenWindows desktop if you prefer. This can be done by selecting CDE or OpenWindows from the Session menu. Prior to the adoption of CDE by Sun, OpenWindows was the standard desktop for all Solaris systems, and some users may prefer OpenWindows to CDE.

In addition, it is possible to configure a language to be used from the CDE login screen by selecting a language from one of the menus. Users can choose from all of the languages that are currently supported by Solaris or use the standard POSIX environment.

Two more menus are available on the login screen: the remote login menu, where it is possible to login directly to another host on the local area network (LAN) using CDE, or to login using the command line. In a LAN, it is useful to be able to launch a CDE session on any host using the same terminal, rather than having to physically sit at another console. Alternatively, when performing system maintenance, it is often preferable to login to a single user session from the CDE login screen and boot into single

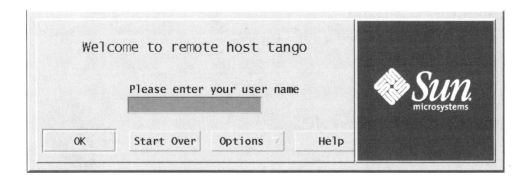

Figure 36-1   The CDE login screen

Figure 36-2   The CDE workspace

user mode. The dtlogin screen should disappear, and you should see the following message:

```
*************************************************************
* Suspending Desktop Login
* If currently logged out, press [ENTER] for a console prompt.
* Desktop Login will resume shortly after you exit console session
*************************************************************
```

If you press Enter, you should see a login prompt:

```
cassowary console login:
```

You can then proceed with performing system maintenance or rebooting the system.

CDE Workspace

The CDE workspace looks very similar to Gnome (for Linux users) and the Windows desktop (for Microsoft users). The main difference for Windows users is that CDE supports a middle mouse button, whereas only left- and right-hand buttons are generally supported under Windows.

When an application is launched from either a menu on the Front Panel or from the Workspace menu (accessed by right-clicking anywhere in the workspace), it appears in its own separate window. For example, the Terminal application (dtterm) can be launched by right-clicking the workspace, selecting the Programs menu, and selecting the Terminal . . . option. A new CDE Terminal window will then appear in the workspace and will be active (that is, it will have the focus). The terminal window activated is shown in Figure 36-3. The user's default login shell will be spawned, and commands will be entered interactively on the command line.

The CDE Terminal window has three menus:

- The Window menu has two options: New window, which spawns another CDE Terminal window, and Close, which closes the current CDE Terminal window. The Close window option also has a keyboard shortcut equivalent (Alt+F4).

- The Edit menu enables the user to copy and paste data to and from any CDE application, including other terminal windows, text editors, and so on.

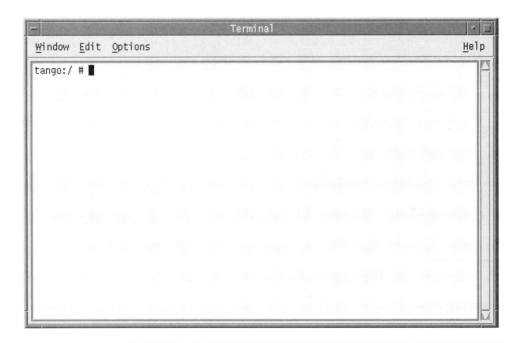

Figure 36-3   CDE Terminal window

- The Options menu is used to set the many different options supported by the CDE Terminal window, including whether or not to display the menu and scroll bar, and the width of the terminal window (80 or 132 characters). In addition, a number of dialog boxes can be used to set global options, such as the cursor style, the cursor blink rate, colors, sounds, and the font size and display.

The dtterm can be started with a number of command lines that can set some of these properties automatically. The benefit of this approach is that these parameters can be embedded in a script or startup file, so that your favorite settings will automatically be used every time dtterm is started. Table 36-1 shows the most commonly used dtterm command-line parameters.

CDE windows can be layered, one on top of the other, and be activated by left-clicking any part of an inactive window. All CDE windows have a drop-down menu at their top left-hand corner. This menu has similar functions in both Gnome and Microsoft Windows. It contains items that enable the user to restore the window size, change the window size, lower the window, expand the window to occupy the entire workspace, toggle the display of the window menus, and close the window. In addition, windows can be minimized from the window drop-down menu or be maximized again by double-clicking their icons on the desktop. Figure 36-4 shows a series of minimized CDE windows in the workspace, including the style manager, terminal, process viewer, application manager, and mail.

In addition to a point-and-click interface, the CDE workspace supports a number of different keystroke options. This is particularly useful for users who have traditionally used the command line. Table 36-2 summarizes the main keystroke shortcuts used to shift the focus within a window, if that window is active, or within a dialog box that has popped up. These keystrokes can also be used to navigate the different menus on the Front Panel.

Table 36-1 Commonly Used dtterm Options

Parameter	Purpose
-background	Sets the default background color of the terminal.
-foreground	Sets the default text color of the terminal.
-font	Sets the font size for the terminal.
-geometry	Sets the width and height of the terminal window.
-title	Sets the title of the window to the specified string.

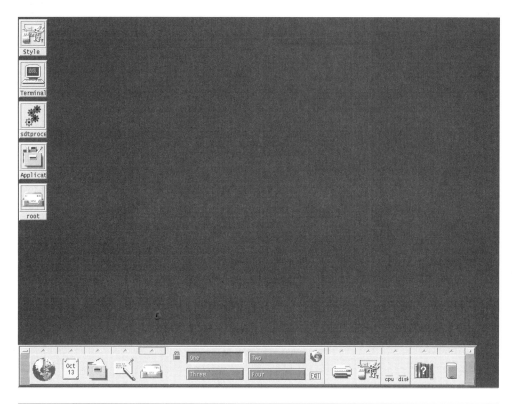

Figure 36-4   Minimizing CDE windows

Table 36-2   Keystrokes and Actions Within Windows, Dialog Boxes, and the Front Panel

Keystroke	Action
Tab	Moves to the next tab group.
Shift+Tab	Moves to the previous tab group.
Down Arrow	Moves to the next control in the tab group.
Up Arrow	Moves to the previous control in the tab group.

Keyboard navigation is slightly different within a workspace because more actions are available than within a single window. Table 36-3 summarizes the main keystroke shortcuts used to shift the focus within a CDE workspace.

Within a menu, the arrow keys can be used to navigate between items, rather than the Tab key.

Table 36-3 Keystrokes and Actions Within the Workspace

Keystroke	Action
Alt+Tab	Moves to the next window or icon.
Shift+Alt+Tab	Moves to the previous window or icon.
Alt+Up Arrow	Moves to the bottom window in a stack of windows (bringing it forward).
Alt+Down Arrow	Moves to the bottom of the window stack.
Alt+F6	Moves to the next window belonging to an application, or between the Front Panel and a subpanel.
Shift+Alt+F6	Moves to the previous window belonging to an application, or between the Front Panel and a subpanel.

Launching Applications

Applications can be launched within CDE in two different ways: either a command is issued through a shell from within a CDE terminal window, or it is selected from the Workspace menu or the Front Panel. For example, if we wanted to execute the clock application, we could run the following command from a shell:

```
bash-2.03% clock&
[1] 8836
bash-2.03%
```

By sending the clock process to the background, it is possible to continue to issue commands using the same shell. Alternatively, to run the Clock application from the Workspace menu, simply right-click anywhere on the workspace, select the Programs menu, and select the Clock . . . item. Finally, you could select the Application Manager from the Applications menu, and open the OpenWindows collection of applications. After double-clicking the OW Clock icon, the clock will be executed, as shown in Figure 36-5.

The Workspace menu is the fastest way to get an application running and to perform CDE administrative tasks, such as adding new items to a menu. From the Workspace menu, it is possible to launch applications, manage workspace windows, customize the menu options displayed, lock the system display, and logout of the CDE desktop.

The Front Panel is more comprehensive than the Workspace menu because it contains ten menus, instead of one. In addition, the CDE desktop enables four different workspaces to be maintained. By simply clicking the One, Two, Three, or Four panels in the center of the Front Panel, users can maintain completely separate workspaces (one

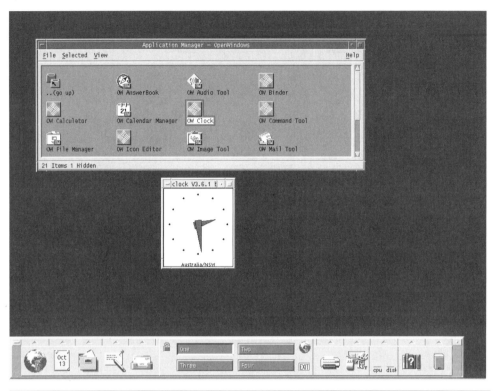

Figure 36-5 Executing the OW Clock application from the Application Manager

for development, one for system administration, one for playing games, and so on). Although Linux users will be familiar with multiple workspaces, Microsoft Windows users will find this a refreshing innovation. The menus included on the Front Panel are as follows:

- **Links**, including Clock, Web Browser, Personal Bookmarks, and Find Web Page.
- **Cards**, including Today's Card and Find Card.
- **Files**, including the Home Folder, Open Floppy, Open CD-ROM, Properties, Encryption, Compress File, Archive, and Find File.
- **Applications**, including Text Note, Text Editor, Voice Note, and the Application Manager.
- **Mail**, including the mailer and the Suggestion Box.
- **Personal Printers**, including the default printer and the Print Manager.

- **Tools**, including Desktop Style, CDE Error Log, the Customize Workspace menu, the Add Item to menu, and the Find Process.

- **Hosts**, including the Performance Meter, This Host, System Info, the Console, and Find Host.

- **Help**, including Help Manager, SunSolve Online, Solaris Support, Information, Desktop Introduction, Front Panel Help, On Item Help, and Answer Book 2.

The Application Manager is the encyclopedic directory of most CDE applications on a Solaris system, as shown in Figure 36-6. The applications are divided into six categories:

- **Desktop applications**, including Address Manager, Application Builder, Audio, Calculator, Calendar, Create Action, File Manager, and the Help Viewer.

- **Desktop controls**, including AccessX, Add Item to menu, Customize Workspace menu, Edit Dtwmrc, Reload Actions, Reload Applications, Reload Resources, and Restore the Front Panel.

- **Desktop tools**, including Archive, Archive List Contents, Archive Unpack, Check Spelling, Clipboard Contents, Compare Files, Compress File, and Count Words.

- **Information**, including documentation for Solaris 8, the Answerbook, and sample bookmarks.

- **OpenWindows applications**, including the old OpenWindows AnswerBook, the Audio Tool, the OW Binder, the OW Calculator, the OW Calendar Manager, the OW Clock, the OW Command Tool, and the OW File Manager.

Figure 36-6   CDE Application Manager

- **System Admin**, including Admintool, AnswerBook Admin, Disk Usage, Eject CD-ROM, Eject Floppy, Format Floppy, Open CD-ROM, and Open Floppy.

The main CDE applications that are available from the Workspace menu are discussed in the following section.

File Manager

The main panel for the File Manager is shown in Figure 36-7, with a view of the devices directory (/dev). The File Manager shares many of the same features with those found in Microsoft Windows and Linux (in KDE and Gnome). The contents of folders on different filesystems can be viewed by double-clicking the appropriate icon. For example, if we click the pcmcia directory, we would see all of the PCMCIA card entries for the system. In addition, new files and folders can be created at any time by selecting the appropriate item from the File menu. Files can be located by using the Find facility, and

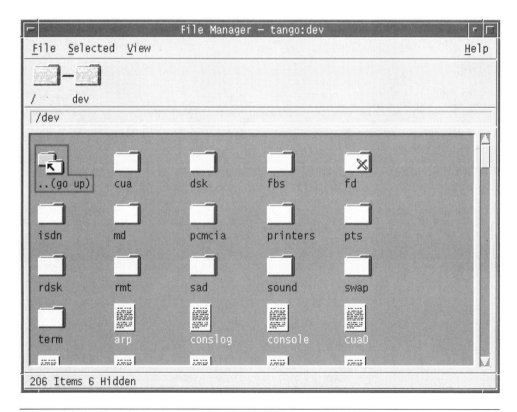

Figure 36-7 The CDE File Manager

individual file properties can be viewed by selecting the target file's icon and selecting the Properties item from the Selected menu.

Text Editor

In order to write shell scripts, you must use a Solaris editor, such as the vi visual editor program, which can be executed within a CDE terminal window. The visual editor is not as easy to use as some other editors available for Solaris, such as the pico editor bundled with the Pine mail-reading program. vi requires users to master separate controls as well as editing and data entry modes, and it requires the user to remember key commands for navigation, data insertion, and text deletion. In contrast, pico enables use of WordStar-style control commands for copying and pasting text, saving files, and highlighting text. However, pico does not enable users to perform the complex search and replace utilities available to vi users. In this section, we examine how to use the vi editor to create shell scripts and any other text files that need to be created or modified (such as application configuration files).

An easier alternative to vi is the text editor program that operates directly under CDE (dtpad), shown in Figure 36-8. This looks much more like Notepad, Write, and other

```
#
#pragma ident    "@(#)format.dat 1.21    98/01/24 SMI"
#
# Copyright (c) 1991,1998 by Sun Microsystems, Inc.
# All rights reserved.
#
# Data file for the 'format' program.  This file defines the known
# disks, disk types, and partition maps.
#

#
# This is the list of supported disks for the Emulex MD21 controller.
#
disk_type = "Micropolis 1355" \
        : ctlr = MD21 \
        : ncyl = 1018 : acyl = 2 : pcyl = 1024 : nhead = 8 : nsect = 34 \
        : rpm = 3600 : bpt = 20832

disk_type = "Toshiba MK 156F" \
        : ctlr = MD21 \
        : ncyl = 815 : acyl = 2 : pcyl = 830 : nhead = 10 : nsect = 34 \
        : rpm = 3600 : bpt = 20832

disk_type = "Micropolis 1558" \
```

Figure 36-8   The dtpad Editor

editing programs that will be more familiar to users of Microsoft Windows. The dtpad application has a number of features that distinguish it from Graphic User Interface (GUI) editors in other operating systems. For example, it is possible to drag and drop data from other CDE applications.

In addition, dtpad offers standard file and formatting options, including saving data to an existing file, saving data to a new file, opening an existing file for editing, and a handy undo facility, which reverses the last change performed on the text. Users can perform a global search and replace on specific text strings, and it even includes a spell-checking facility, which is almost unique in a text-editing facility. Formatting options include the capability to insert text with overstriking as well as line wrapping to 60 characters. A status bar, which is continuously updated, displays the total number of lines in the current document, as well as the line in which the cursor is currently located.

In the example shown in Figure 36-8, we have opened the /etc/format.dat system configuration file, which defines formatting data for all supported hard disks.

Mailer

Electronic mail (e-mail) has long been supported on Solaris for both local and remote users. CDE provides an easy-to-use e-mail client known as dtmail. The interface for the dtmail program is shown in Figure 36-9. The inbox for the root user is shown in the top panel. The user has 19 messages, the first of which is being displayed in the bottom window (the message shows an error generated by the cron scheduling facility).

The dtmail program can either be controlled through a menu system or by clicking one of the icons found on the middle panel between the list of inbox messages and the text of the current message. The icons perform several different functions:

- Send the currently selected message to the trash.
- Read the next message down the list.
- Read the previous message in the list.
- Forward the current message to another user.
- Reply to the current message.
- Create a new message.
- Print the current message.

Using a mail client is only one side of the e-mail equation. It's also necessary to set up a mail server, which is covered in Chapter 11.

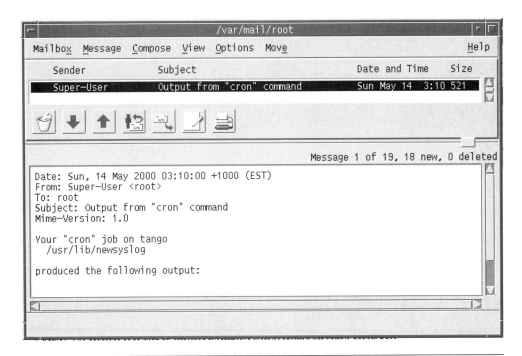

Figure 36-9 Using the dtmail e-mail client

Calendar

The Calendar tool is a daily organizer that enables users to view past and current calendars month by month, but also to enter events for particular days. The calendar is shown in Figure 36-10 and is operated by either icons on a control panel at the top of the screen or by using one of the menus, which contain options for file management, editing, and viewing entries.

Web Browser

Most Solaris systems will be connected to the Internet and will require a method of browsing the Web using a Hypertext Transfer Protocol (HTTP)-compliant client. Solaris includes the HotJava client, which is a 100-percent Java implementation. Although HotJava has few features compared with other Web browsers (such as Netscape Navigator), it is part of the Solaris environment and doesn't require any software or licenses from third parties to operate. It can be used in conjunction with the Answer Book and any documentation set that is created using the Hypertext Markup Language (HTML).

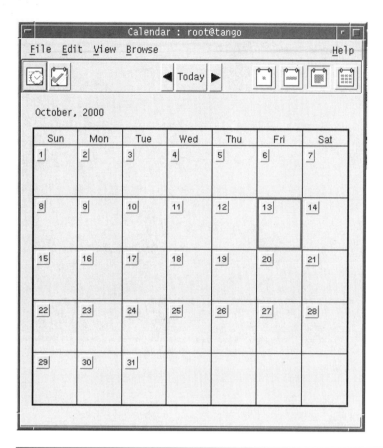

Figure 36-10 The Calendar tool

Figure 36-11 shows the HotJava client displaying the default page for the Apache Web server, which is now included in the Solaris operating environment.

HotJava is operated by using the icon bar located at the top of the screen. The icons displayed perform the following functions:

- Navigate backward to the last accessed document.
- Navigate forward to the last accessed document.
- Go to the home page.
- Refresh the page contents.
- Stop loading the current page.

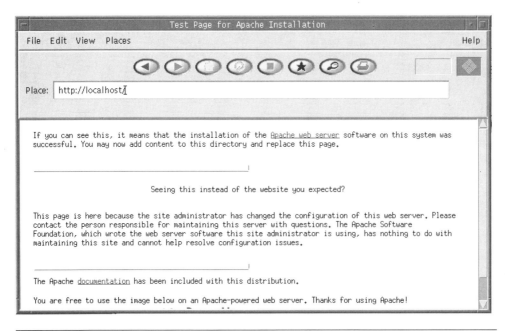

Figure 36-11   HotJava Web browser

- Search for a page on the Internet.
- Print the current page.

Console

The console is similar to the dtterm. When executed, the user's default shell is spawned, and commands can be executed interactively. The difference between dtterm and the console is that the latter displays informative messages about the system status that are normally sent to the screen of the physical console of a Solaris system. However, if the physical console is actually running CDE, then such messages would be lost. The console provides a facility to view these messages as they are generated. A sample CDE console is shown in Figure 36-12.

The kinds of messages displayed on the console are controlled by the syslog facility. Thus, the file /etc/syslog.conf would need to be edited to either increase or decrease the number of messages piped to the console, and the content of these messages would also need to be changed. For example, a typical console message might warn the superuser that someone attempted to login to an account, but typed the wrong password. You probably don't need to see the same message every time someone fumbles their

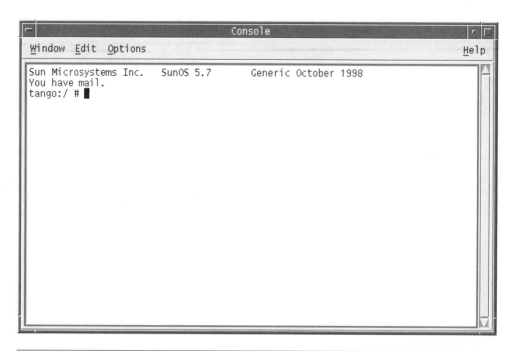

Figure 36-12 CDE Console

login. However, another kind of message might warn that the filesystem is full, and that applications can no longer write to the disk. This is a critical message, and further action should be taken immediately.

Calculator

The CDE Calculator is a fully featured scientific calculator, which is capable of computing all trigonometric functions and the most commonly used exponential and factorial functions. The supported functions include the sine, cosine, and tangent, as well as computing e^x, where x is the desired exponent. Memory facilities are available for storing the results of computations as well as for creating expressions by enclosing individual operations within brackets. A number of different base numbering systems are available, in addition to the decimal system, and the results of trigonometric functions can be displayed in either degrees or radians. Figure 36-13 shows the interface for the CDE Calculator.

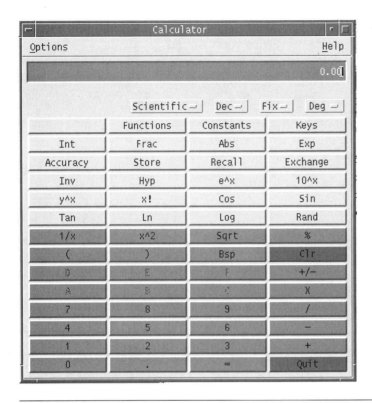

Figure 36-13 CDE Calculator

Performance Meter

One of the most common questions a Solaris administrator is asked is, "Why is the system slow?" Usually, a Solaris system becomes slow for one of the following reasons:

- Too many processes are being spawned for the central processing unit (CPU) to maintain the concurrent executions of the applications being run by all users.

- Too many lightweight processes are being created.

- Disk input/output (I/O) is being challenged by the needs of applications, such as databases, which are disk-intensive.

- The amount of disk space allocated to supporting virtual memory operations is insufficient to support all current applications.

If your system appears to be running more slowly than usual, the first place to look for trouble is the Performance Meter, which continuously prints the current system load, as shown in Figure 36-14. The Performance Meter often looks like a stockmarket chart. It contains peaks and troughs, as more or less processes are executed. This activity is quite normal. However, if you begin to notice a sustained increase in the system load, well above the normal level of 1.0 for a system operating at capacity, then it may be time to begin examining which processes are hogging all of the system resources. The system load will be reduced if these processes have their nice value set to a lower priority.

Print Manager

Solaris supports a wide variety of printers, whether attached to a local parallel port or accessed through a LAN by using Network File System (NFS) or Samba. One way to examine jobs that have been issued to various printers from a Solaris system is to use the Print Manager, which is similar to the print management facilities found in Linux and Microsoft Windows. Figure 36-15 shows the Find Print Jobs window from the Print Manager. To locate a print job in order to view its status or cancel it, the job name can be entered into the Job Name field, and searching initiated by clicking the Start Find button.

Image Viewer

Solaris has multimedia support, including sound, movies, and images. Although many seasoned Linux users will be familiar with the xv program, which is available under both Solaris and Linux, CDE actually has its own image-viewing and manipulation program.

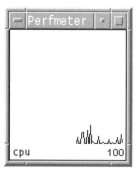

Figure 36-14 CDE Performance Meter

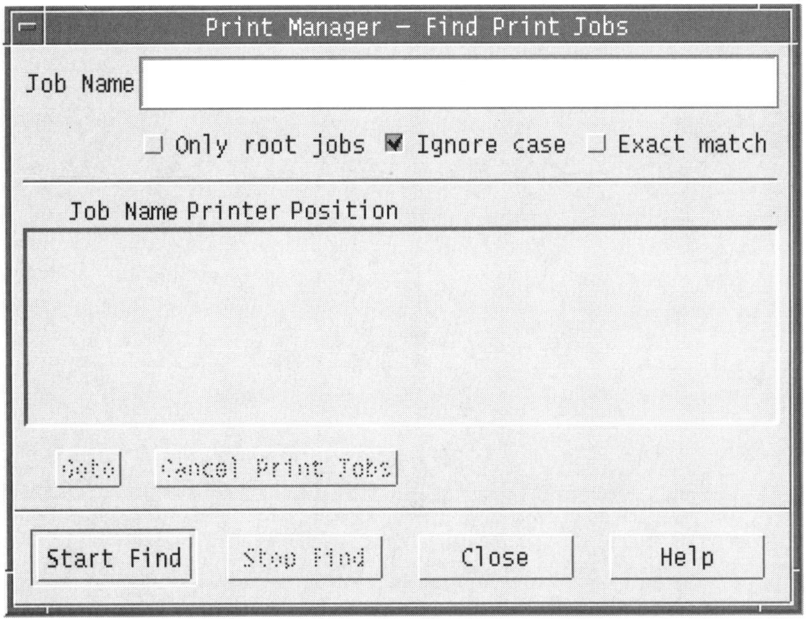

Figure 36-15   CDE Print Manager

The image viewer has the capability to load and save images in a wide variety of popular formats, including GIF, JPEG, TIF, and output from the snapshot program reviewed in the next section. It has cropping, cutting, copying, and pasting functions, as well as capabilities for supporting image rotation, image mirroring, and image reduction and enlargement. These functions are supported by the palette shown in Figure 36-16.

Snapshot

The Snapshot program is a screen capture utility that can be used to capture the entire CDE workspace or the contents of individual windows. The screenshot utility has its own special file format (.rs files), which can be easily converted to PC-friendly file formats using the Image Convertor program. Fortunately, the Snapshot interface actually has a button that enables the current snapshot to be launched with the Image Convertor program, making it easy to take a screenshot, edit its contents, and save it in your favorite file format. Many of the images contained in this book were captured using Snapshot.

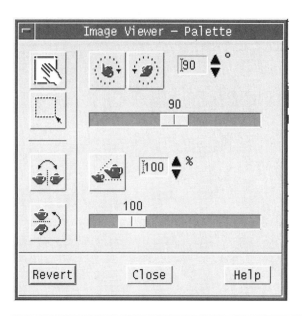

Figure 36-16   CDE Image Viewer

Icon Editor

As you will have realized after reading this chapter, the CDE uses icons extensively to represent files, applications, folders, and many other display objects within the work-space. However, you are not limited to using the icons supplied with Solaris to repre-sent your own applications. CDE is supplied with an icon editor that enables you to create your own bitmapped images, as shown in Figure 36-17. These images can be used as icons to represent applications or actions within the CDE workspace. The images are 32×32 pixels (1,024 pixels), with a choice of eight different colors or shades of gray. In addition, it is possible to specify dynamic colors for the foreground and background. Standard image editing tools are also included, with cropping, filling, and several geometric shapes (circles, lines, and rectangles) available from the Tools palette.

Style Manager

The Style Manager is similar to the Desktop Themes or Display Settings options avail-able under Microsoft Windows. It is responsible for all aspects of presentation for the CDE workspace, and you can use different styles for the different workspaces available under the CDE desktop. The Style Manager has several different control panels that are

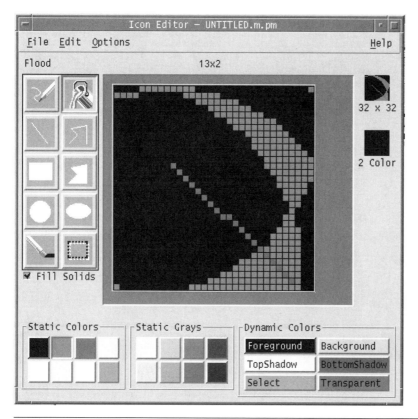

Figure 36-17   CDE Icon Editor

available by clicking one of the icons displayed in Figure 36-18. These panels are used to set the following options:

- Available color schemes for the workspace
- Default fonts for all text in CDE applications
- Backdrop patterns for the workspace
- Keyboard options, including the key repeat rate
- Mouse configurations, including speed
- Beep settings for warnings
- Screen settings, including the screen saver

Figure 36-18   CDE Style Manager

- Window options, including whether the focus is set by clicking the mouse or hovering over a window

- Startup configuration, including session saving and loading

Help

On most of the CDE screens we have seen, the most important menu is located at the top right-hand corner, the Help menu. The Help facility provides information and assistance on using and managing most of the applications that are supplied with the Solaris operating environment, including the File Manager, Style Manager, and Print Manager. Users can browse available help topics or search by keyword for topics relevant to the current application. For CDE applications that are developed in-house, it is possible to provide customized help in the CDE Help format.

Answer Book 2

Help is usually only applicable for the standard CDE applications. However, because the vast majority of the applications supplied with Solaris do not require CDE to operate, Solaris provides the Answer Book facility. The Answer Book has two components: the HotJava browser, which acts as the Answer Book client, and the Answer Book server, which is a Web server that only provides access to HTML versions of the man pages and the various reference manuals that accompany Solaris.

However, one of the best features of the Answer Book is that it is available over the Internet, from **http://docs.sun.com/**. This means that any Solaris user, without local access to an Answer Book, can freely download PDF versions of the reference manuals or search interactively across books in all Answer Book collections.

Summary

In this chapter, we have examined how to use and configure the CDE workspace. For users who prefer GUI-based tools to command-line interfaces, CDE provides easy access to the facilities provided by Solaris. In addition, CDE tools such as the HotJava browser can be used to access external services, such as the Answer Book. We should point out that CDE is not the only desktop system available for use with X11 under Solaris. It is now possible to use Gnome and Enlightenment on Solaris, which may be useful if you come from a Linux background. However, CDE is now the standard Unix desktop platform, and learning CDE will make your skills more transferable to other platforms.

Questions

1. What is the default window manager for Solaris 8?
   A. Gnome
   B. X11
   C. CDE
   D. OpenWindows

2. What is the name of the default CDE terminal?
   A. xterm
   B. term
   C. cdeterm
   D. dtterm

3. Which options can be configured on the default CDE terminal?
   A. The cursor style and the cursor blink rate
   B. The font size and display, and the background image
   C. The terminal width and the number of menus
   D. The menu and scroll bar display, and the keypress delay

4. What is the recommended way to launch CDE applications in CDE?
   A. Start menu
   B. Workspace menu
   C. Command line
   D. Hotkeys

5. Which administrative tools are available under CDE?
   A. Admintool and Usertool
   B. Disk Usage and Eject CD-ROM
   C. AnswerBook Admin and Unformat Floppy
   D. Open CD-ROM and Write CD-ROM

6. Which properties can be set using the Style Manager?
   A. The available color schemes for the workspace
   B. The optional fonts for all text in CDE applications
   C. The background images for the workspace
   D. The keyboard options, including the keyboard type

Answers

1. C

2. D

3. A

4. B

5. B

6. A

Solaris Administration Quick Reference

The following reference provides important file size and security information for the key system administration applications provided with Solaris. Most of these programs are located in the /usr/bin and /usr/sbin directories. You can refer to these listings if you need to compare the checksum of an installed binary which you suspect has been modified by a trojan horse, since both the expected file size and checksum are shown for each application. In addition, it's wise to check that the ownership and file permission data shown here matches your own system.

/usr/bin Commands

```
Pathname: /usr/bin/alias
Type: regular file
Expected mode: 0555
Expected owner: root
Expected group: bin
Expected file size (bytes): 131
Expected sum(1) of contents: 9284
Expected last modification: Jan 06 10:56:53 2000
Referenced by the following packages:
     SUNWcsu
Current status: installed

Pathname: /usr/bin/arch
Type: regular file
Expected mode: 0555
Expected owner: root
Expected group: bin
Expected file size (bytes): 944
Expected sum(1) of contents: 3574
```

```
Expected last modification: Jan 06 10:51:22 2000
Referenced by the following packages:
     SUNWcsu
Current status: installed

Pathname: /usr/bin/at
Type: regular file
Expected mode: 4755
Expected owner: root
Expected group: sys
Expected file size (bytes): 37876
Expected sum(1) of contents: 42912
Expected last modification: Jul 10 21:22:23 2000
Referenced by the following packages:
     SUNWcsu
Current status: installed

Pathname: /usr/bin/atq
Type: regular file
Expected mode: 4755
Expected owner: root
Expected group: sys
Expected file size (bytes): 13796
Expected sum(1) of contents: 39936
Expected last modification: Jan 06 10:54:30 2000
Referenced by the following packages:
     SUNWcsu
Current status: installed

Pathname: /usr/bin/atrm
Type: regular file
Expected mode: 4755
Expected owner: root
Expected group: sys
Expected file size (bytes): 12792
Expected sum(1) of contents: 33448
Expected last modification: Jul 10 21:22:24 2000
Referenced by the following packages:
     SUNWcsu
Current status: installed

Pathname: /usr/bin/auths
Type: regular file
Expected mode: 0555
Expected owner: root
Expected group: bin
Expected file size (bytes): 7416
Expected sum(1) of contents: 131
Expected last modification: Jan 06 10:51:29 2000
```

Referenced by the following packages:
     SUNWcsu
Current status: installed

Pathname: /usr/bin/basename
Type: regular file
Expected mode: 0555
Expected owner: root
Expected group: bin
Expected file size (bytes): 901
Expected sum(1) of contents: 3031
Expected last modification: Jan 06 10:51:27 2000
Referenced by the following packages:
     SUNWcsu
Current status: installed

Pathname: /usr/bin/busstat
Type: regular file
Expected mode: 0555
Expected owner: root
Expected group: bin
Expected file size (bytes): 16884
Expected sum(1) of contents: 47273
Expected last modification: Jan 06 10:51:44 2000
Referenced by the following packages:
     SUNWcsu
Current status: installed

Pathname: /usr/bin/captoinfo
Type: regular file
Expected mode: 0555
Expected owner: root
Expected group: bin
Expected file size (bytes): 28068
Expected sum(1) of contents: 26302
Expected last modification: Jan 06 10:52:14 2000
Referenced by the following packages:
     SUNWcsu
Current status: installed

Pathname: /usr/bin/cat
Type: regular file
Expected mode: 0555
Expected owner: root
Expected group: bin
Expected file size (bytes): 10092
Expected sum(1) of contents: 1282
Expected last modification: Jul 10 21:23:34 2000
Referenced by the following packages:
     SUNWcsu
Current status: installed

```
Pathname: /usr/bin/chgrp
Type: regular file
Expected mode: 0555
Expected owner: root
Expected group: bin
Expected file size (bytes): 7728
Expected sum(1) of contents: 24857
Expected last modification: Jan 06 10:51:40 2000
Referenced by the following packages:
     SUNWcsu
Current status: installed

Pathname: /usr/bin/chmod
Type: regular file
Expected mode: 0555
Expected owner: root
Expected group: bin
Expected file size (bytes): 18236
Expected sum(1) of contents: 27295
Expected last modification: Jan 06 10:51:44 2000
Referenced by the following packages:
     SUNWcsu
Current status: installed

Pathname: /usr/bin/chown
Type: regular file
Expected mode: 0555
Expected owner: root
Expected group: bin
Expected file size (bytes): 6884
Expected sum(1) of contents: 38217
Expected last modification: Jan 06 10:51:41 2000
Referenced by the following packages:
     SUNWcsu
Current status: installed

Pathname: /usr/bin/ckdate
Type: regular file
Expected mode: 0555
Expected owner: root
Expected group: bin
Expected file size (bytes): 9216
Expected sum(1) of contents: 64378
Expected last modification: Jan 06 11:25:40 2000
Referenced by the following packages:
     SUNWcsu
Current status: installed

Pathname: /usr/bin/ckgid
Type: regular file
```

```
Expected mode: 0555
Expected owner: root
Expected group: bin
Expected file size (bytes): 7872
Expected sum(1) of contents: 27521
Expected last modification: Jan 06 11:25:48 2000
Referenced by the following packages:
     SUNWcsu
Current status: installed

Pathname: /usr/bin/ckint
Type: regular file
Expected mode: 0555
Expected owner: root
Expected group: bin
Expected file size (bytes): 7560
Expected sum(1) of contents: 20701
Expected last modification: Jan 06 11:25:41 2000
Referenced by the following packages:
     SUNWcsu
Current status: installed

Pathname: /usr/bin/ckitem
Type: regular file
Expected mode: 0555
Expected owner: root
Expected group: bin
Expected file size (bytes): 9900
Expected sum(1) of contents: 28949
Expected last modification: Jan 06 11:26:00 2000
Referenced by the following packages:
     SUNWcsu
Current status: installed

Pathname: /usr/bin/ckkeywd
Type: regular file
Expected mode: 0555
Expected owner: root
Expected group: bin
Expected file size (bytes): 6788
Expected sum(1) of contents: 32831
Expected last modification: Jan 06 11:25:42 2000
Referenced by the following packages:
     SUNWcsu
Current status: installed

Pathname: /usr/bin/ckpath
Type: regular file
Expected mode: 0555
Expected owner: root
```

```
Expected group: bin
Expected file size (bytes): 9856
Expected sum(1) of contents: 64975
Expected last modification: Jan 06 11:25:58 2000
Referenced by the following packages:
     SUNWcsu
Current status: installed

Pathname: /usr/bin/ckrange
Type: regular file
Expected mode: 0555
Expected owner: root
Expected group: bin
Expected file size (bytes): 8196
Expected sum(1) of contents: 8743
Expected last modification: Jan 06 11:25:43 2000
Referenced by the following packages:
     SUNWcsu
Current status: installed

Pathname: /usr/bin/ckstr
Type: regular file
Expected mode: 0555
Expected owner: root
Expected group: bin
Expected file size (bytes): 8572
Expected sum(1) of contents: 15264
Expected last modification: Jan 06 11:25:56 2000
Referenced by the following packages:
     SUNWcsu
Current status: installed

Pathname: /usr/bin/cksum
Type: regular file
Expected mode: 0555
Expected owner: root
Expected group: bin
Expected file size (bytes): 6980
Expected sum(1) of contents: 60794
Expected last modification: Jan 06 10:51:41 2000
Referenced by the following packages:
     SUNWcsu
Current status: installed

Pathname: /usr/bin/cktime
Type: regular file
Expected mode: 0555
Expected owner: root
Expected group: bin
Expected file size (bytes): 9040
Expected sum(1) of contents: 49490
Expected last modification: Jan 06 11:25:50 2000
```

```
Referenced by the following packages:
     SUNWcsu
Current status: installed

Pathname: /usr/bin/ckuid
Type: regular file
Expected mode: 0555
Expected owner: root
Expected group: bin
Expected file size (bytes): 7880
Expected sum(1) of contents: 27260
Expected last modification: Jan 06 11:25:51 2000
Referenced by the following packages:
     SUNWcsu
Current status: installed

Pathname: /usr/bin/ckyorn
Type: regular file
Expected mode: 0555
Expected owner: root
Expected group: bin
Expected file size (bytes): 7752
Expected sum(1) of contents: 26219
Expected last modification: Jan 06 11:25:44 2000
Referenced by the following packages:
     SUNWcsu
Current status: installed

Pathname: /usr/bin/clear
Type: regular file
Expected mode: 0555
Expected owner: root
Expected group: bin
Expected file size (bytes): 647
Expected sum(1) of contents: 52049
Expected last modification: Jan 06 10:51:33 2000
Referenced by the following packages:
     SUNWcsu
Current status: installed

Pathname: /usr/bin/cmp
Type: regular file
Expected mode: 0555
Expected owner: root
Expected group: bin
Expected file size (bytes): 6440
Expected sum(1) of contents: 25415
Expected last modification: Jan 06 10:51:43 2000
Referenced by the following packages:
     SUNWcsu
Current status: installed
```

```
Pathname: /usr/bin/coreadm
Type: regular file
Expected mode: 0555
Expected owner: root
Expected group: bin
Expected file size (bytes): 12052
Expected sum(1) of contents: 807
Expected last modification: Jan 06 10:51:58 2000
Referenced by the following packages:
     SUNWcsu
Current status: installed

Pathname: /usr/bin/cp
Type: regular file
Expected mode: 0555
Expected owner: root
Expected group: bin
Expected file size (bytes): 18652
Expected sum(1) of contents: 48668
Expected last modification: Jan 09 13:05:31 2000
Referenced by the following packages:
     SUNWcsu
Current status: installed

Pathname: /usr/bin/cpio
Type: regular file
Expected mode: 0555
Expected owner: root
Expected group: bin
Expected file size (bytes): 59564
Expected sum(1) of contents: 52519
Expected last modification: Jan 06 10:53:47 2000
Referenced by the following packages:
     SUNWcsu
Current status: installed

Pathname: /usr/bin/crle
Type: regular file
Expected mode: 0555
Expected owner: root
Expected group: bin
Expected file size (bytes): 27040
Expected sum(1) of contents: 41382
Expected last modification: Aug 03 06:44:11 2000
Referenced by the following packages:
     SUNWcsu
Current status: installed

Pathname: /usr/bin/crontab
Type: regular file
Expected mode: 4555
```

```
Expected owner: root
Expected group: bin
Expected file size (bytes): 17136
Expected sum(1) of contents: 40921
Expected last modification: Jan 06 10:54:30 2000
Referenced by the following packages:
     SUNWcsu
Current status: installed

Pathname: /usr/bin/crypt
Type: regular file
Expected mode: 0555
Expected owner: root
Expected group: bin
Expected file size (bytes): 6628
Expected sum(1) of contents: 35493
Expected last modification: Jan 06 10:52:01 2000
Referenced by the following packages:
     SUNWcsu
Current status: installed

Pathname: /usr/bin/csh
Type: regular file
Expected mode: 0555
Expected owner: root
Expected group: bin
Expected file size (bytes): 159216
Expected sum(1) of contents: 55509
Expected last modification: Jan 22 03:22:47 2001
Referenced by the following packages:
     SUNWcsu
Current status: installed

Pathname: /usr/bin/cut
Type: regular file
Expected mode: 0555
Expected owner: root
Expected group: bin
Expected file size (bytes): 10288
Expected sum(1) of contents: 24074
Expected last modification: Jan 06 10:52:24 2000
Referenced by the following packages:
     SUNWcsu
Current status: installed

Pathname: /usr/bin/date
Type: regular file
Expected mode: 0555
Expected owner: root
Expected group: bin
Expected file size (bytes): 8552
```

```
Expected sum(1) of contents: 23536
Expected last modification: Jan 06 10:52:32 2000
Referenced by the following packages:
     SUNWcsu
Current status: installed

Pathname: /usr/bin/dd
Type: regular file
Expected mode: 0555
Expected owner: root
Expected group: bin
Expected file size (bytes): 16948
Expected sum(1) of contents: 47980
Expected last modification: Jan 06 10:53:00 2000
Referenced by the following packages:
     SUNWcsu
Current status: installed

Pathname: /usr/bin/devattr
Type: regular file
Expected mode: 0555
Expected owner: root
Expected group: bin
Expected file size (bytes): 6076
Expected sum(1) of contents: 58780
Expected last modification: Jan 06 10:52:43 2000
Referenced by the following packages:
     SUNWcsu
Current status: installed

Pathname: /usr/bin/devfree
Type: regular file
Expected mode: 0555
Expected owner: root
Expected group: bin
Expected file size (bytes): 6496
Expected sum(1) of contents: 24258
Expected last modification: Jan 06 10:53:31 2000
Referenced by the following packages:
     SUNWcsu
Current status: installed

Pathname: /usr/bin/devreserv
Type: regular file
Expected mode: 0555
Expected owner: root
Expected group: bin
Expected file size (bytes): 7528
Expected sum(1) of contents: 9114
Expected last modification: Jan 06 10:52:54 2000
```

Referenced by the following packages:
     SUNWcsu
Current status: installed

Pathname: /usr/bin/dirname
Type: regular file
Expected mode: 0555
Expected owner: root
Expected group: bin
Expected file size (bytes): 784
Expected sum(1) of contents: 58012
Expected last modification: Jan 06 10:52:51 2000
Referenced by the following packages:
     SUNWcsu
Current status: installed

Pathname: /usr/bin/domainname
Type: regular file
Expected mode: 0555
Expected owner: root
Expected group: bin
Expected file size (bytes): 4160
Expected sum(1) of contents: 11860
Expected last modification: Jan 06 10:58:06 2000
Referenced by the following packages:
     SUNWcsu
Current status: installed

Pathname: /usr/bin/du
Type: regular file
Expected mode: 0555
Expected owner: root
Expected group: bin
Expected file size (bytes): 9336
Expected sum(1) of contents: 12346
Expected last modification: Jul 10 21:24:08 2000
Referenced by the following packages:
     SUNWcsu
Current status: installed

Pathname: /usr/bin/dumpcs
Type: regular file
Expected mode: 0555
Expected owner: root
Expected group: bin
Expected file size (bytes): 6540
Expected sum(1) of contents: 44280
Expected last modification: Jan 06 10:53:15 2000
Referenced by the following packages:
     SUNWcsu
Current status: installed

```
Pathname: /usr/bin/dumpkeys
Type: regular file
Expected mode: 0555
Expected owner: root
Expected group: bin
Expected file size (bytes): 7288
Expected sum(1) of contents: 8999
Expected last modification: Jan 06 10:56:55 2000
Referenced by the following packages:
     SUNWcsu
Current status: installed

Pathname: /usr/bin/echo
Type: regular file
Expected mode: 0555
Expected owner: root
Expected group: bin
Expected file size (bytes): 5488
Expected sum(1) of contents: 56761
Expected last modification: Jan 06 10:53:18 2000
Referenced by the following packages:
     SUNWcsu
Current status: installed

Pathname: /usr/bin/ed
Type: regular file
Expected mode: 0555
Expected owner: root
Expected group: bin
Expected file size (bytes): 43812
Expected sum(1) of contents: 10200
Expected last modification: Jan 06 10:54:08 2000
Referenced by the following packages:
     SUNWcsu
Current status: installed

Pathname: /usr/bin/edit
Type: regular file
Expected mode: 0555
Expected owner: root
Expected group: bin
Expected file size (bytes): 206948
Expected sum(1) of contents: 42453
Expected last modification: Jan 06 11:27:07 2000
Referenced by the following packages:
     SUNWcsu
Current status: installed
```

```
Pathname: /usr/bin/egrep
Type: regular file
Expected mode: 0555
Expected owner: root
Expected group: bin
Expected file size (bytes): 26940
Expected sum(1) of contents: 28166
Expected last modification: Jan 06 10:53:50 2000
Referenced by the following packages:
     SUNWcsu
Current status: installed

Pathname: /usr/bin/eject
Type: regular file
Expected mode: 4555
Expected owner: root
Expected group: bin
Expected file size (bytes): 13808
Expected sum(1) of contents: 15887
Expected last modification: Jan 06 11:26:40 2000
Referenced by the following packages:
     SUNWcsu
Current status: installed

Pathname: /usr/bin/env
Type: regular file
Expected mode: 0555
Expected owner: root
Expected group: bin
Expected file size (bytes): 5116
Expected sum(1) of contents: 61664
Expected last modification: Jan 06 10:53:34 2000
Referenced by the following packages:
     SUNWcsu
Current status: installed

Pathname: /usr/bin/expr
Type: regular file
Expected mode: 0555
Expected owner: root
Expected group: bin
Expected file size (bytes): 11660
Expected sum(1) of contents: 59487
Expected last modification: Jan 06 10:54:03 2000
Referenced by the following packages:
     SUNWcsu
Current status: installed
```

```
Pathname: /usr/bin/false
Type: regular file
Expected mode: 0555
Expected owner: root
Expected group: bin
Expected file size (bytes): 314
Expected sum(1) of contents: 23085
Expected last modification: Jan 06 10:53:46 2000
Referenced by the following packages:
     SUNWcsu
Current status: installed

Pathname: /usr/bin/fdetach
Type: regular file
Expected mode: 0555
Expected owner: root
Expected group: bin
Expected file size (bytes): 3840
Expected sum(1) of contents: 58111
Expected last modification: Jan 06 10:53:52 2000
Referenced by the following packages:
     SUNWcsu
Current status: installed

Pathname: /usr/bin/fdformat
Type: regular file
Expected mode: 4555
Expected owner: root
Expected group: bin
Expected file size (bytes): 26372
Expected sum(1) of contents: 49041
Expected last modification: Jan 06 10:54:12 2000
Referenced by the following packages:
     SUNWcsu
Current status: installed

Pathname: /usr/bin/fgrep
Type: regular file
Expected mode: 0555
Expected owner: root
Expected group: bin
Expected file size (bytes): 11460
Expected sum(1) of contents: 54355
Expected last modification: Jan 06 10:54:03 2000
Referenced by the following packages:
     SUNWcsu
Current status: installed

Pathname: /usr/bin/file
Type: regular file
```

Expected mode: 0555
Expected owner: root
Expected group: bin
Expected file size (bytes): 20804
Expected sum(1) of contents: 53654
Expected last modification: Mar 16 21:53:37 2000
Referenced by the following packages:
     SUNWcsu
Current status: installed

Pathname: /usr/bin/find
Type: regular file
Expected mode: 0555
Expected owner: root
Expected group: bin
Expected file size (bytes): 20064
Expected sum(1) of contents: 59784
Expected last modification: Jan 22 07:19:24 2001
Referenced by the following packages:
     SUNWcsu
Current status: installed

Pathname: /usr/bin/finger
Type: regular file
Expected mode: 0555
Expected owner: root
Expected group: bin
Expected file size (bytes): 19644
Expected sum(1) of contents: 12954
Expected last modification: Jan 06 11:00:43 2000
Referenced by the following packages:
     SUNWcsu
Current status: installed

Pathname: /usr/bin/fmli
Type: regular file
Expected mode: 0755
Expected owner: root
Expected group: bin
Expected file size (bytes): 314004
Expected sum(1) of contents: 14304
Expected last modification: Jan 06 10:56:23 2000
Referenced by the following packages:
     SUNWcsu
Current status: installed

Pathname: /usr/bin/fmt
Type: regular file
Expected mode: 0555
Expected owner: root

```
Expected group: bin
Expected file size (bytes): 13524
Expected sum(1) of contents: 38718
Expected last modification: Jan 06 10:54:13 2000
Referenced by the following packages:
     SUNWcsu
Current status: installed

Pathname: /usr/bin/fmtmsg
Type: regular file
Expected mode: 0555
Expected owner: root
Expected group: bin
Expected file size (bytes): 7868
Expected sum(1) of contents: 55313
Expected last modification: Jan 06 10:54:12 2000
Referenced by the following packages:
     SUNWcsu
Current status: installed

Pathname: /usr/bin/fold
Type: regular file
Expected mode: 0555
Expected owner: root
Expected group: bin
Expected file size (bytes): 7420
Expected sum(1) of contents: 24491
Expected last modification: Jan 06 10:54:12 2000
Referenced by the following packages:
     SUNWcsu
Current status: installed

Pathname: /usr/bin/ftp
Type: regular file
Expected mode: 0555
Expected owner: root
Expected group: bin
Expected file size (bytes): 75440
Expected sum(1) of contents: 48582
Expected last modification: Mar 16 21:46:31 2000
Referenced by the following packages:
     SUNWcsu
Current status: installed

Pathname: /usr/bin/geniconvtbl
Type: regular file
Expected mode: 0555
Expected owner: root
Expected group: bin
```

```
Expected file size (bytes): 123520
Expected sum(1) of contents: 27123
Expected last modification: Jan 06 10:55:26 2000
Referenced by the following packages:
     SUNWcsu
Current status: installed

Pathname: /usr/bin/getconf
Type: regular file
Expected mode: 0555
Expected owner: root
Expected group: bin
Expected file size (bytes): 13592
Expected sum(1) of contents: 16151
Expected last modification: Jan 06 10:54:26 2000
Referenced by the following packages:
     SUNWcsu
Current status: installed

Pathname: /usr/bin/getdev
Type: regular file
Expected mode: 0555
Expected owner: root
Expected group: bin
Expected file size (bytes): 5792
Expected sum(1) of contents: 39325
Expected last modification: Jan 06 10:53:40 2000
Referenced by the following packages:
     SUNWcsu
Current status: installed

Pathname: /usr/bin/getdgrp
Type: regular file
Expected mode: 0555
Expected owner: root
Expected group: bin
Expected file size (bytes): 6164
Expected sum(1) of contents: 56458
Expected last modification: Jan 06 10:53:54 2000
Referenced by the following packages:
     SUNWcsu
Current status: installed

Pathname: /usr/bin/getfacl
Type: regular file
Expected mode: 0555
Expected owner: root
Expected group: bin
Expected file size (bytes): 7224
```

```
Expected sum(1) of contents: 7727
Expected last modification: Jan 06 10:54:28 2000
Referenced by the following packages:
     SUNWcsu
Current status: installed

Pathname: /usr/bin/getopt
Type: regular file
Expected mode: 0555
Expected owner: root
Expected group: bin
Expected file size (bytes): 5504
Expected sum(1) of contents: 22510
Expected last modification: Jan 06 10:54:34 2000
Referenced by the following packages:
     SUNWcsu
Current status: installed

Pathname: /usr/bin/gettext
Type: regular file
Expected mode: 0555
Expected owner: root
Expected group: bin
Expected file size (bytes): 4872
Expected sum(1) of contents: 44476
Expected last modification: Jan 06 10:54:36 2000
Referenced by the following packages:
     SUNWcsu
Current status: installed

Pathname: /usr/bin/getvol
Type: regular file
Expected mode: 0555
Expected owner: root
Expected group: bin
Expected file size (bytes): 6616
Expected sum(1) of contents: 18819
Expected last modification: Jan 06 10:53:07 2000
Referenced by the following packages:
     SUNWcsu
Current status: installed

Pathname: /usr/bin/grep
Type: regular file
Expected mode: 0555
Expected owner: root
Expected group: bin
Expected file size (bytes): 10032
Expected sum(1) of contents: 47345
Expected last modification: Jan 06 10:54:47 2000
```

```
Referenced by the following packages:
     SUNWcsu
Current status: installed

Pathname: /usr/bin/groups
Type: regular file
Expected mode: 0555
Expected owner: root
Expected group: bin
Expected file size (bytes): 5092
Expected sum(1) of contents: 64332
Expected last modification: Jan 06 10:54:46 2000
Referenced by the following packages:
     SUNWcsu
Current status: installed

Pathname: /usr/bin/head
Type: regular file
Expected mode: 0555
Expected owner: root
Expected group: bin
Expected file size (bytes): 6000
Expected sum(1) of contents: 49192
Expected last modification: Jan 06 10:55:10 2000
Referenced by the following packages:
     SUNWcsu
Current status: installed

Pathname: /usr/bin/hostid
Type: regular file
Expected mode: 0555
Expected owner: root
Expected group: bin
Expected file size (bytes): 3944
Expected sum(1) of contents: 63383
Expected last modification: Jan 06 10:55:10 2000
Referenced by the following packages:
     SUNWcsu
Current status: installed

Pathname: /usr/bin/hostname
Type: regular file
Expected mode: 0555
Expected owner: root
Expected group: bin
Expected file size (bytes): 525
Expected sum(1) of contents: 39271
Expected last modification: Jan 06 10:55:11 2000
Referenced by the following packages:
     SUNWcsu
Current status: installed
```

```
Pathname: /usr/bin/i286
Type: regular file
Expected mode: 0555
Expected owner: root
Expected group: bin
Expected file size (bytes): 4432
Expected sum(1) of contents: 36365
Expected last modification: Jan 06 10:57:26 2000
Referenced by the following packages:
     SUNWcsu
Current status: installed

Pathname: /usr/bin/iconv
Type: regular file
Expected mode: 0555
Expected owner: root
Expected group: bin
Expected file size (bytes): 11996
Expected sum(1) of contents: 42547
Expected last modification: Jan 06 10:55:34 2000
Referenced by the following packages:
     SUNWcsu
Current status: installed

Pathname: /usr/bin/id
Type: regular file
Expected mode: 0555
Expected owner: root
Expected group: bin
Expected file size (bytes): 8044
Expected sum(1) of contents: 51256
Expected last modification: Mar 16 21:53:38 2000
Referenced by the following packages:
     SUNWcsu
Current status: installed

Pathname: /usr/bin/infocmp
Type: regular file
Expected mode: 0555
Expected owner: root
Expected group: bin
Expected file size (bytes): 19576
Expected sum(1) of contents: 35536
Expected last modification: Jan 06 10:55:41 2000
Referenced by the following packages:
     SUNWcsu
Current status: installed

Pathname: /usr/bin/iostat
Type: regular file
```

Expected mode: 0555
Expected owner: root
Expected group: bin
Expected file size (bytes): 34088
Expected sum(1) of contents: 61248
Expected last modification: Apr 13 21:17:15 2000
Referenced by the following packages:
        SUNWcsu
Current status: installed

Pathname: /usr/bin/isainfo
Type: regular file
Expected mode: 0555
Expected owner: root
Expected group: bin
Expected file size (bytes): 7508
Expected sum(1) of contents: 16796
Expected last modification: Jan 06 10:55:57 2000
Referenced by the following packages:
        SUNWcsu
Current status: installed

Pathname: /usr/bin/isalist
Type: regular file
Expected mode: 0555
Expected owner: root
Expected group: bin
Expected file size (bytes): 4016
Expected sum(1) of contents: 2366
Expected last modification: Jan 06 10:55:57 2000
Referenced by the following packages:
        SUNWcsu
Current status: installed

Pathname: /usr/bin/join
Type: regular file
Expected mode: 0555
Expected owner: root
Expected group: bin
Expected file size (bytes): 12288
Expected sum(1) of contents: 18853
Expected last modification: Jan 06 10:56:13 2000
Referenced by the following packages:
        SUNWcsu
Current status: installed

Pathname: /usr/bin/jsh
Type: regular file
Expected mode: 0555
Expected owner: root

```
Expected group: root
Expected file size (bytes): 95316
Expected sum(1) of contents: 57321
Expected last modification: May 26 21:32:29 2000
Referenced by the following packages:
     SUNWcsu
Current status: installed

Pathname: /usr/bin/kbd
Type: regular file
Expected mode: 0555
Expected owner: root
Expected group: bin
Expected file size (bytes): 7072
Expected sum(1) of contents: 6406
Expected last modification: Jan 06 10:56:17 2000
Referenced by the following packages:
     SUNWcsu
Current status: installed

Pathname: /usr/bin/kdestroy
Type: regular file
Expected mode: 0555
Expected owner: root
Expected group: bin
Expected file size (bytes): 8944
Expected sum(1) of contents: 49467
Expected last modification: Jan 09 13:04:40 2000
Referenced by the following packages:
     SUNWcsu
Current status: installed

Pathname: /usr/bin/keylogin
Type: regular file
Expected mode: 0555
Expected owner: root
Expected group: bin
Expected file size (bytes): 10044
Expected sum(1) of contents: 56339
Expected last modification: Jan 06 10:58:05 2000
Referenced by the following packages:
     SUNWcsu
Current status: installed

Pathname: /usr/bin/keylogout
Type: regular file
Expected mode: 0555
Expected owner: root
Expected group: bin
Expected file size (bytes): 5188
```

```
Expected sum(1) of contents: 1984
Expected last modification: Jan 06 10:58:05 2000
Referenced by the following packages:
     SUNWcsu
Current status: installed

Pathname: /usr/bin/kinit
Type: regular file
Expected mode: 0555
Expected owner: root
Expected group: bin
Expected file size (bytes): 15520
Expected sum(1) of contents: 41809
Expected last modification: Jan 09 13:04:41 2000
Referenced by the following packages:
     SUNWcsu
Current status: installed

Pathname: /usr/bin/klist
Type: regular file
Expected mode: 0555
Expected owner: root
Expected group: bin
Expected file size (bytes): 13428
Expected sum(1) of contents: 46476
Expected last modification: Jan 09 13:04:40 2000
Referenced by the following packages:
     SUNWcsu
Current status: installed

Pathname: /usr/bin/kpasswd
Type: regular file
Expected mode: 0555
Expected owner: root
Expected group: bin
Expected file size (bytes): 8420
Expected sum(1) of contents: 25490
Expected last modification: Jan 09 13:04:43 2000
Referenced by the following packages:
     SUNWcsu
Current status: installed

Pathname: /usr/bin/ksh
Type: regular file
Expected mode: 0555
Expected owner: root
Expected group: bin
Expected file size (bytes): 200944
Expected sum(1) of contents: 10677
Expected last modification: Jan 26 16:35:02 2001
```

```
Referenced by the following packages:
     SUNWcsu
Current status: installed

Pathname: /usr/bin/ktutil
Type: regular file
Expected mode: 0555
Expected owner: root
Expected group: bin
Expected file size (bytes): 10752
Expected sum(1) of contents: 28413
Expected last modification: Jan 09 13:04:41 2000
Referenced by the following packages:
     SUNWcsu
Current status: installed

Pathname: /usr/bin/line
Type: regular file
Expected mode: 0555
Expected owner: root
Expected group: bin
Expected file size (bytes): 3936
Expected sum(1) of contents: 3542
Expected last modification: Jan 06 10:56:31 2000
Referenced by the following packages:
     SUNWcsu
Current status: installed

Pathname: /usr/bin/listdgrp
Type: regular file
Expected mode: 0555
Expected owner: root
Expected group: bin
Expected file size (bytes): 5400
Expected sum(1) of contents: 9318
Expected last modification: Jan 06 10:53:47 2000
Referenced by the following packages:
     SUNWcsu
Current status: installed

Pathname: /usr/bin/listusers
Type: regular file
Expected mode: 0555
Expected owner: root
Expected group: bin
Expected file size (bytes): 7932
Expected sum(1) of contents: 13782
Expected last modification: Jan 06 11:06:10 2000
```

```
Referenced by the following packages:
    SUNWcsu
Current status: installed

Pathname: /usr/bin/loadkeys
Type: regular file
Expected mode: 0555
Expected owner: root
Expected group: bin
Expected file size (bytes): 17360
Expected sum(1) of contents: 48391
Expected last modification: Jan 06 10:56:55 2000
Referenced by the following packages:
    SUNWcsu
Current status: installed

Pathname: /usr/bin/localedef
Type: regular file
Expected mode: 0555
Expected owner: root
Expected group: bin
Expected file size (bytes): 172768
Expected sum(1) of contents: 31236
Expected last modification: Jan 06 10:57:26 2000
Referenced by the following packages:
    SUNWcsu
Current status: installed

Pathname: /usr/bin/logger
Type: regular file
Expected mode: 0555
Expected owner: root
Expected group: bin
Expected file size (bytes): 7204
Expected sum(1) of contents: 49121
Expected last modification: Jan 06 10:57:09 2000
Referenced by the following packages:
    SUNWcsu
Current status: installed

Pathname: /usr/bin/login
Type: regular file
Expected mode: 4555
Expected owner: root
Expected group: bin
Expected file size (bytes): 29292
Expected sum(1) of contents: 59075
Expected last modification: Jan 06 10:57:23 2000
```

```
Referenced by the following packages:
    SUNWcsu
Current status: installed

Pathname: /usr/bin/logins
Type: regular file
Expected mode: 0750
Expected owner: root
Expected group: bin
Expected file size (bytes): 12924
Expected sum(1) of contents: 94
Expected last modification: Jan 06 10:57:18 2000
Referenced by the following packages:
    SUNWcsu
Current status: installed

Pathname: /usr/bin/ls
Type: regular file
Expected mode: 0555
Expected owner: root
Expected group: bin
Expected file size (bytes): 18844
Expected sum(1) of contents: 34850
Expected last modification: Jan 06 10:57:54 2000
Referenced by the following packages:
    SUNWcsu
Current status: installed

Pathname: /usr/bin/mach
Type: regular file
Expected mode: 0555
Expected owner: root
Expected group: bin
Expected file size (bytes): 145
Expected sum(1) of contents: 10872
Expected last modification: Jan 06 10:57:22 2000
Referenced by the following packages:
    SUNWcsu
Current status: installed

Pathname: /usr/bin/mail
Type: regular file
Expected mode: 2511
Expected owner: root
Expected group: mail
Expected file size (bytes): 61288
Expected sum(1) of contents: 50965
Expected last modification: Jan 06 10:57:54 2000
Referenced by the following packages:
    SUNWcsu
Current status: installed
```

```
Pathname: /usr/bin/mailx
Type: regular file
Expected mode: 2511
Expected owner: root
Expected group: mail
Expected file size (bytes): 126808
Expected sum(1) of contents: 30865
Expected last modification: Jan 06 11:00:48 2000
Referenced by the following packages:
     SUNWcsu
Current status: installed

Pathname: /usr/bin/makedev
Type: regular file
Expected mode: 0555
Expected owner: root
Expected group: bin
Expected file size (bytes): 9488
Expected sum(1) of contents: 61025
Expected last modification: Jan 06 11:06:35 2000
Referenced by the following packages:
     SUNWcsu
Current status: installed

Pathname: /usr/bin/mesg
Type: regular file
Expected mode: 0555
Expected owner: root
Expected group: bin
Expected file size (bytes): 5248
Expected sum(1) of contents: 2397
Expected last modification: Jan 06 10:57:54 2000
Referenced by the following packages:
     SUNWcsu
Current status: installed

Pathname: /usr/bin/mkdir
Type: regular file
Expected mode: 0555
Expected owner: root
Expected group: bin
Expected file size (bytes): 18168
Expected sum(1) of contents: 25919
Expected last modification: Jan 06 10:58:12 2000
Referenced by the following packages:
     SUNWcsu
Current status: installed

Pathname: /usr/bin/more
Type: regular file
Expected mode: 0555
```

```
Expected owner: root
Expected group: bin
Expected file size (bytes): 28472
Expected sum(1) of contents: 7439
Expected last modification: Jan 06 10:58:38 2000
Referenced by the following packages:
     SUNWcsu
Current status: installed

Pathname: /usr/bin/mpstat
Type: regular file
Expected mode: 0555
Expected owner: root
Expected group: bin
Expected file size (bytes): 8576
Expected sum(1) of contents: 30798
Expected last modification: Jan 06 10:58:26 2000
Referenced by the following packages:
     SUNWcsu
Current status: installed

Pathname: /usr/bin/mt
Type: regular file
Expected mode: 0555
Expected owner: root
Expected group: bin
Expected file size (bytes): 9000
Expected sum(1) of contents: 46018
Expected last modification: Jan 06 10:58:35 2000
Referenced by the following packages:
     SUNWcsu
Current status: installed

Pathname: /usr/bin/netstat
Type: regular file
Expected mode: 2555
Expected owner: root
Expected group: sys
Expected file size (bytes): 55168
Expected sum(1) of contents: 21029
Expected last modification: Jan 06 11:01:00 2000
Referenced by the following packages:
     SUNWcsu
Current status: installed

Pathname: /usr/bin/newgrp
Type: regular file
Expected mode: 4755
Expected owner: root
Expected group: sys
```

```
Expected file size (bytes): 7328
Expected sum(1) of contents: 37117
Expected last modification: Jan 06 10:58:45 2000
Referenced by the following packages:
     SUNWcsu
Current status: installed

Pathname: /usr/bin/newtask
Type: regular file
Expected mode: 4755
Expected owner: root
Expected group: sys
Expected file size (bytes): 7764
Expected sum(1) of contents: 17821
Expected last modification: Mar 16 21:53:43 2000
Referenced by the following packages:
     SUNWcsu
Current status: installed

Pathname: /usr/bin/nfsstat
Type: regular file
Expected mode: 0555
Expected owner: root
Expected group: bin
Expected file size (bytes): 22372
Expected sum(1) of contents: 15246
Expected last modification: Jan 06 10:56:00 2000
Referenced by the following packages:
     SUNWcsu
Current status: installed

Pathname: /usr/bin/nice
Type: regular file
Expected mode: 0555
Expected owner: root
Expected group: bin
Expected file size (bytes): 5008
Expected sum(1) of contents: 56461
Expected last modification: Jan 06 10:58:55 2000
Referenced by the following packages:
     SUNWcsu
Current status: installed

Pathname: /usr/bin/nohup
Type: regular file
Expected mode: 0555
Expected owner: root
Expected group: bin
Expected file size (bytes): 6576
Expected sum(1) of contents: 13222
```

```
Expected last modification: Jan 06 10:59:11 2000
Referenced by the following packages:
     SUNWcsu
Current status: installed

Pathname: /usr/bin/on
Type: regular file
Expected mode: 0555
Expected owner: root
Expected group: bin
Expected file size (bytes): 21140
Expected sum(1) of contents: 56982
Expected last modification: Jan 06 11:01:48 2000
Referenced by the following packages:
     SUNWcsu
Current status: installed

Pathname: /usr/bin/optisa
Type: regular file
Expected mode: 0555
Expected owner: root
Expected group: bin
Expected file size (bytes): 478
Expected sum(1) of contents: 29597
Expected last modification: Jan 06 10:55:57 2000
Referenced by the following packages:
     SUNWcsu
Current status: installed

Pathname: /usr/bin/pagesize
Type: regular file
Expected mode: 0555
Expected owner: root
Expected group: bin
Expected file size (bytes): 3696
Expected sum(1) of contents: 49772
Expected last modification: Jan 06 10:59:28 2000
Referenced by the following packages:
     SUNWcsu
Current status: installed

Pathname: /usr/bin/passwd
Type: regular file
Expected mode: 6555
Expected owner: root
Expected group: sys
Expected file size (bytes): 101744
Expected sum(1) of contents: 17766
Expected last modification: Jan 06 10:59:44 2000
```

```
Referenced by the following packages:
     SUNWcsu
Current status: installed

Pathname: /usr/bin/patch
Type: regular file
Expected mode: 0555
Expected owner: root
Expected group: bin
Expected file size (bytes): 37548
Expected sum(1) of contents: 39365
Expected last modification: Jan 06 10:59:54 2000
Referenced by the following packages:
     SUNWcsu
Current status: installed

Pathname: /usr/bin/pathchk
Type: regular file
Expected mode: 0555
Expected owner: root
Expected group: bin
Expected file size (bytes): 6484
Expected sum(1) of contents: 38945
Expected last modification: Jan 06 10:59:48 2000
Referenced by the following packages:
     SUNWcsu
Current status: installed

Pathname: /usr/bin/pax
Type: regular file
Expected mode: 0555
Expected owner: root
Expected group: bin
Expected file size (bytes): 71864
Expected sum(1) of contents: 6870
Expected last modification: Jan 06 10:59:57 2000
Referenced by the following packages:
     SUNWcsu
Current status: installed

Pathname: /usr/bin/pfexec
Type: regular file
Expected mode: 4555
Expected owner: root
Expected group: bin
Expected file size (bytes): 6508
Expected sum(1) of contents: 15149
Expected last modification: Jan 06 10:59:56 2000
```

```
Referenced by the following packages:
     SUNWcsu
Current status: installed

Pathname: /usr/bin/pg
Type: regular file
Expected mode: 0555
Expected owner: root
Expected group: bin
Expected file size (bytes): 26852
Expected sum(1) of contents: 59592
Expected last modification: Jan 06 11:00:16 2000
Referenced by the following packages:
     SUNWcsu
Current status: installed

Pathname: /usr/bin/pgrep
Type: regular file
Expected mode: 0555
Expected owner: root
Expected group: bin
Expected file size (bytes): 14688
Expected sum(1) of contents: 63968
Expected last modification: Mar 16 21:53:45 2000
Referenced by the following packages:
     SUNWcsu
Current status: installed

Pathname: /usr/bin/pkginfo
Type: regular file
Expected mode: 0555
Expected owner: root
Expected group: sys
Expected file size (bytes): 98980
Expected sum(1) of contents: 2737
Expected last modification: Jan 06 11:01:42 2000
Referenced by the following packages:
     SUNWcsu
Current status: installed

Pathname: /usr/bin/pkgmk
Type: regular file
Expected mode: 0555
Expected owner: root
Expected group: bin
Expected file size (bytes): 125796
Expected sum(1) of contents: 60401
Expected last modification: Jan 06 11:02:58 2000
```

```
Referenced by the following packages:
     SUNWcsu
Current status: installed

Pathname: /usr/bin/pkgparam
Type: regular file
Expected mode: 0555
Expected owner: root
Expected group: sys
Expected file size (bytes): 86128
Expected sum(1) of contents: 5063
Expected last modification: Jan 06 11:03:48 2000
Referenced by the following packages:
     SUNWcsu
Current status: installed

Pathname: /usr/bin/pkgproto
Type: regular file
Expected mode: 0555
Expected owner: root
Expected group: bin
Expected file size (bytes): 31100
Expected sum(1) of contents: 31181
Expected last modification: Jan 06 11:01:48 2000
Referenced by the following packages:
     SUNWcsu
Current status: installed

Pathname: /usr/bin/pkgtrans
Type: regular file
Expected mode: 0555
Expected owner: root
Expected group: bin
Expected file size (bytes): 69620
Expected sum(1) of contents: 51235
Expected last modification: Jan 06 11:03:25 2000
Referenced by the following packages:
     SUNWcsu
Current status: installed

Pathname: /usr/bin/pr
Type: regular file
Expected mode: 0555
Expected owner: root
Expected group: bin
Expected file size (bytes): 21328
Expected sum(1) of contents: 57810
Expected last modification: Jan 06 11:00:36 2000
```

```
Referenced by the following packages:
     SUNWcsu
Current status: installed

Pathname: /usr/bin/priocntl
Type: regular file
Expected mode: 0555
Expected owner: root
Expected group: bin
Expected file size (bytes): 17480
Expected sum(1) of contents: 11762
Expected last modification: Mar 16 21:53:46 2000
Referenced by the following packages:
     SUNWcsu
Current status: installed

Pathname: /usr/bin/profiles
Type: regular file
Expected mode: 0555
Expected owner: root
Expected group: bin
Expected file size (bytes): 6764
Expected sum(1) of contents: 24071
Expected last modification: Jan 06 11:00:24 2000
Referenced by the following packages:
     SUNWcsu
Current status: installed

Pathname: /usr/bin/projects
Type: regular file
Expected mode: 0555
Expected owner: root
Expected group: bin
Expected file size (bytes): 6352
Expected sum(1) of contents: 1460
Expected last modification: Mar 16 21:53:47 2000
Referenced by the following packages:
     SUNWcsu
Current status: installed

Pathname: /usr/bin/putdev
Type: regular file
Expected mode: 0555
Expected owner: root
Expected group: bin
Expected file size (bytes): 9420
Expected sum(1) of contents: 22965
Expected last modification: Jan 06 10:54:02 2000
Referenced by the following packages:
     SUNWcsu
Current status: installed
```

```
Pathname: /usr/bin/putdgrp
Type: regular file
Expected mode: 0555
Expected owner: root
Expected group: bin
Expected file size (bytes): 6940
Expected sum(1) of contents: 43345
Expected last modification: Jan 06 10:53:21 2000
Referenced by the following packages:
     SUNWcsu
Current status: installed

Pathname: /usr/bin/pwd
Type: regular file
Expected mode: 0555
Expected owner: root
Expected group: bin
Expected file size (bytes): 4360
Expected sum(1) of contents: 11342
Expected last modification: Jan 06 11:01:00 2000
Referenced by the following packages:
     SUNWcsu
Current status: installed

Pathname: /usr/bin/rcp
Type: regular file
Expected mode: 4555
Expected owner: root
Expected group: bin
Expected file size (bytes): 21008
Expected sum(1) of contents: 46516
Expected last modification: Jan 06 11:00:47 2000
Referenced by the following packages:
     SUNWcsu
Current status: installed

Pathname: /usr/bin/rdate
Type: regular file
Expected mode: 0555
Expected owner: root
Expected group: bin
Expected file size (bytes): 6240
Expected sum(1) of contents: 11264
Expected last modification: Jan 06 11:00:43 2000
Referenced by the following packages:
     SUNWcsu
Current status: installed

Pathname: /usr/bin/rdist
Type: regular file
Expected mode: 4555
```

```
Expected owner: root
Expected group: bin
Expected file size (bytes): 55480
Expected sum(1) of contents: 2951
Expected last modification: Jan 06 11:01:02 2000
Referenced by the following packages:
     SUNWcsu
Current status: installed

Pathname: /usr/bin/renice
Type: regular file
Expected mode: 0555
Expected owner: root
Expected group: bin
Expected file size (bytes): 6824
Expected sum(1) of contents: 48846
Expected last modification: Jan 06 11:01:09 2000
Referenced by the following packages:
     SUNWcsu
Current status: installed

Pathname: /usr/bin/rlogin
Type: regular file
Expected mode: 4555
Expected owner: root
Expected group: bin
Expected file size (bytes): 16012
Expected sum(1) of contents: 22907
Expected last modification: Jan 06 11:00:48 2000
Referenced by the following packages:
     SUNWcsu
Current status: installed

Pathname: /usr/bin/rm
Type: regular file
Expected mode: 0555
Expected owner: root
Expected group: bin
Expected file size (bytes): 18384
Expected sum(1) of contents: 17205
Expected last modification: Jan 06 11:01:22 2000
Referenced by the following packages:
     SUNWcsu
Current status: installed

Pathname: /usr/bin/rmdir
Type: regular file
Expected mode: 0555
Expected owner: root
Expected group: bin
```

```
Expected file size (bytes): 6360
Expected sum(1) of contents: 64026
Expected last modification: Jan 06 11:01:14 2000
Referenced by the following packages:
     SUNWcsu
Current status: installed

Pathname: /usr/bin/roles
Type: regular file
Expected mode: 0555
Expected owner: root
Expected group: bin
Expected file size (bytes): 5304
Expected sum(1) of contents: 5539
Expected last modification: Jan 06 11:01:19 2000
Referenced by the following packages:
     SUNWcsu
Current status: installed

Pathname: /usr/bin/rpcinfo
Type: regular file
Expected mode: 0555
Expected owner: root
Expected group: bin
Expected file size (bytes): 23680
Expected sum(1) of contents: 27837
Expected last modification: Jan 06 11:01:30 2000
Referenced by the following packages:
     SUNWcsu
Current status: installed

Pathname: /usr/bin/rsh
Type: regular file
Expected mode: 4555
Expected owner: root
Expected group: bin
Expected file size (bytes): 8964
Expected sum(1) of contents: 44609
Expected last modification: Jan 06 11:00:49 2000
Referenced by the following packages:
     SUNWcsu
Current status: installed

Pathname: /usr/bin/ruptime
Type: regular file
Expected mode: 0555
Expected owner: root
Expected group: bin
Expected file size (bytes): 7312
Expected sum(1) of contents: 14559
```

```
Expected last modification: Jan 06 11:00:43 2000
Referenced by the following packages:
     SUNWcsu
Current status: installed

Pathname: /usr/bin/rwho
Type: regular file
Expected mode: 0555
Expected owner: root
Expected group: bin
Expected file size (bytes): 6280
Expected sum(1) of contents: 2694
Expected last modification: Jan 06 11:00:45 2000
Referenced by the following packages:
     SUNWcsu
Current status: installed

Pathname: /usr/bin/script
Type: regular file
Expected mode: 0555
Expected owner: root
Expected group: bin
Expected file size (bytes): 8328
Expected sum(1) of contents: 35750
Expected last modification: Jan 06 11:01:45 2000
Referenced by the following packages:
     SUNWcsu
Current status: installed

Pathname: /usr/bin/sed
Type: regular file
Expected mode: 0555
Expected owner: root
Expected group: bin
Expected file size (bytes): 26704
Expected sum(1) of contents: 875
Expected last modification: Jan 06 11:02:07 2000
Referenced by the following packages:
     SUNWcsu
Current status: installed

Pathname: /usr/bin/setfacl
Type: regular file
Expected mode: 0555
Expected owner: root
Expected group: bin
Expected file size (bytes): 13144
Expected sum(1) of contents: 62746
Expected last modification: Jan 06 11:02:05 2000
```

```
Referenced by the following packages:
     SUNWcsu
Current status: installed

Pathname: /usr/bin/setpgrp
Type: regular file
Expected mode: 0555
Expected owner: root
Expected group: sys
Expected file size (bytes): 4064
Expected sum(1) of contents: 818
Expected last modification: Jan 06 11:02:03 2000
Referenced by the following packages:
     SUNWcsu
Current status: installed

Pathname: /usr/bin/settime
Type: regular file
Expected mode: 0555
Expected owner: root
Expected group: bin
Expected file size (bytes): 7720
Expected sum(1) of contents: 52217
Expected last modification: Jan 06 11:05:19 2000
Referenced by the following packages:
     SUNWcsu
Current status: installed

Pathname: /usr/bin/sleep
Type: regular file
Expected mode: 0555
Expected owner: root
Expected group: bin
Expected file size (bytes): 4696
Expected sum(1) of contents: 38646
Expected last modification: Jan 06 11:02:19 2000
Referenced by the following packages:
     SUNWcsu
Current status: installed

Pathname: /usr/bin/sparcv7
Type: directory
Expected mode: 0755
Expected owner: root
Expected group: bin
Referenced by the following packages:
     SUNWcsu        SUNWesu        SUNWipc        SUNWtoo
SUNWcpcu
     SUNWmdb        SUNWtnfc
Current status: installed
```

```
Pathname: /usr/bin/sparcv7/adb
Type: regular file
Expected mode: 0555
Expected owner: root
Expected group: bin
Expected file size (bytes): 131124
Expected sum(1) of contents: 43913
Expected last modification: Jul 20 23:41:56 2000
Referenced by the following packages:
        SUNWcsu
Current status: installed

Pathname: /usr/bin/sparcv7/prstat
Type: regular file
Expected mode: 0555
Expected owner: root
Expected group: bin
Expected file size (bytes): 37080
Expected sum(1) of contents: 35827
Expected last modification: Mar 16 21:54:06 2000
Referenced by the following packages:
        SUNWcsu
Current status: installed

Pathname: /usr/bin/sparcv7/ps
Type: regular file
Expected mode: 4555
Expected owner: root
Expected group: sys
Expected file size (bytes): 28196
Expected sum(1) of contents: 23827
Expected last modification: Mar 16 21:53:49 2000
Referenced by the following packages:
        SUNWcsu
Current status: installed

Pathname: /usr/bin/sparcv7/savecore
Type: regular file
Expected mode: 0555
Expected owner: root
Expected group: bin
Expected file size (bytes): 12340
Expected sum(1) of contents: 25299
Expected last modification: Jan 06 11:01:46 2000
Referenced by the following packages:
        SUNWcsu
Current status: installed

Pathname: /usr/bin/sparcv7/setuname
Type: regular file
Expected mode: 0555
```

```
Expected owner: root
Expected group: bin
Expected file size (bytes): 8316
Expected sum(1) of contents: 4365
Expected last modification: Jan 06 11:02:16 2000
Referenced by the following packages:
    SUNWcsu
Current status: installed

Pathname: /usr/bin/sparcv7/uptime
Type: regular file
Expected mode: 4555
Expected owner: root
Expected group: bin
Expected file size (bytes): 11368
Expected sum(1) of contents: 18254
Expected last modification: Jan 06 11:25:47 2000
Referenced by the following packages:
    SUNWcsu
Current status: installed

Pathname: /usr/bin/strchg
Type: regular file
Expected mode: 0555
Expected owner: root
Expected group: root
Expected file size (bytes): 8304
Expected sum(1) of contents: 49588
Expected last modification: Jan 06 11:03:14 2000
Referenced by the following packages:
    SUNWcsu
Current status: installed

Pathname: /usr/bin/strconf
Type: regular file
Expected mode: 0555
Expected owner: root
Expected group: root
Expected file size (bytes): 5600
Expected sum(1) of contents: 37954
Expected last modification: Jan 06 11:03:14 2000
Referenced by the following packages:
    SUNWcsu
Current status: installed

Pathname: /usr/bin/stty
Type: regular file
Expected mode: 0555
Expected owner: root
Expected group: bin
Expected file size (bytes): 33572
```

```
Expected sum(1) of contents: 23087
Expected last modification: Jan 06 11:07:25 2000
Referenced by the following packages:
     SUNWcsu
Current status: installed

Pathname: /usr/bin/su
Type: regular file
Expected mode: 4555
Expected owner: root
Expected group: sys
Expected file size (bytes): 17564
Expected sum(1) of contents: 50905
Expected last modification: Mar 16 21:53:31 2000
Referenced by the following packages:
     SUNWcsu
Current status: installed

Pathname: /usr/bin/tabs
Type: regular file
Expected mode: 0555
Expected owner: root
Expected group: bin
Expected file size (bytes): 11872
Expected sum(1) of contents: 52902
Expected last modification: Jan 06 11:03:56 2000
Referenced by the following packages:
     SUNWcsu
Current status: installed

Pathname: /usr/bin/tail
Type: regular file
Expected mode: 0555
Expected owner: root
Expected group: bin
Expected file size (bytes): 9456
Expected sum(1) of contents: 36405
Expected last modification: Jan 06 11:04:04 2000
Referenced by the following packages:
     SUNWcsu
Current status: installed

Pathname: /usr/bin/talk
Type: regular file
Expected mode: 0555
Expected owner: root
Expected group: bin
Expected file size (bytes): 18372
Expected sum(1) of contents: 36048
Expected last modification: Jan 06 11:01:05 2000
```

Referenced by the following packages:
    SUNWcsu
Current status: installed

Pathname: /usr/bin/tee
Type: regular file
Expected mode: 0555
Expected owner: root
Expected group: bin
Expected file size (bytes): 5556
Expected sum(1) of contents: 27374
Expected last modification: Jan 06 11:04:11 2000
Referenced by the following packages:
    SUNWcsu
Current status: installed

Pathname: /usr/bin/telnet
Type: regular file
Expected mode: 0555
Expected owner: root
Expected group: bin
Expected file size (bytes): 85612
Expected sum(1) of contents: 54732
Expected last modification: Jan 06 11:01:10 2000
Referenced by the following packages:
    SUNWcsu
Current status: installed

Pathname: /usr/bin/tftp
Type: regular file
Expected mode: 0555
Expected owner: root
Expected group: bin
Expected file size (bytes): 20848
Expected sum(1) of contents: 26051
Expected last modification: Jun 09 02:08:34 2000
Referenced by the following packages:
    SUNWcsu
Current status: installed

Pathname: /usr/bin/tic
Type: regular file
Expected mode: 0555
Expected owner: root
Expected group: bin
Expected file size (bytes): 23900
Expected sum(1) of contents: 3185
Expected last modification: Jan 06 11:05:02 2000
Referenced by the following packages:
    SUNWcsu
Current status: installed

```
Pathname: /usr/bin/time
Type: regular file
Expected mode: 0555
Expected owner: root
Expected group: bin
Expected file size (bytes): 6160
Expected sum(1) of contents: 65229
Expected last modification: Jan 06 11:04:52 2000
Referenced by the following packages:
     SUNWcsu
Current status: installed

Pathname: /usr/bin/tip
Type: regular file
Expected mode: 4511
Expected owner: uucp
Expected group: bin
Expected file size (bytes): 55228
Expected sum(1) of contents: 34692
Expected last modification: Jan 06 11:05:16 2000
Referenced by the following packages:
     SUNWcsu
Current status: installed

Pathname: /usr/bin/tplot
Type: regular file
Expected mode: 0555
Expected owner: root
Expected group: bin
Expected file size (bytes): 574
Expected sum(1) of contents: 42169
Expected last modification: Jan 06 11:05:35 2000
Referenced by the following packages:
     SUNWcsu
Current status: installed

Pathname: /usr/bin/tput
Type: regular file
Expected mode: 0555
Expected owner: root
Expected group: bin
Expected file size (bytes): 10608
Expected sum(1) of contents: 27738
Expected last modification: Jan 06 11:05:23 2000
Referenced by the following packages:
     SUNWcsu
Current status: installed

Pathname: /usr/bin/tr
Type: regular file
```

```
Expected mode: 0555
Expected owner: root
Expected group: bin
Expected file size (bytes): 15508
Expected sum(1) of contents: 58343
Expected last modification: Jan 06 11:05:27 2000
Referenced by the following packages:
     SUNWcsu
Current status: installed

Pathname: /usr/bin/true
Type: regular file
Expected mode: 0555
Expected owner: root
Expected group: bin
Expected file size (bytes): 304
Expected sum(1) of contents: 22371
Expected last modification: Jan 06 11:05:29 2000
Referenced by the following packages:
     SUNWcsu
Current status: installed

Pathname: /usr/bin/tty
Type: regular file
Expected mode: 0555
Expected owner: root
Expected group: bin
Expected file size (bytes): 4392
Expected sum(1) of contents: 27227
Expected last modification: Jan 06 11:05:40 2000
Referenced by the following packages:
     SUNWcsu
Current status: installed

Pathname: /usr/bin/uname
Type: regular file
Expected mode: 0555
Expected owner: root
Expected group: bin
Expected file size (bytes): 6772
Expected sum(1) of contents: 53666
Expected last modification: Jan 06 11:06:01 2000
Referenced by the following packages:
     SUNWcsu
Current status: installed

Pathname: /usr/bin/vmstat
Type: regular file
Expected mode: 0555
Expected owner: root
```

```
Expected group: bin
Expected file size (bytes): 17996
Expected sum(1) of contents: 48477
Expected last modification: Jan 06 11:25:52 2000
Referenced by the following packages:
     SUNWcsu
Current status: installed

Pathname: /usr/bin/wc
Type: regular file
Expected mode: 0555
Expected owner: root
Expected group: bin
Expected file size (bytes): 7160
Expected sum(1) of contents: 63496
Expected last modification: Jan 06 11:25:35 2000
Referenced by the following packages:
     SUNWcsu
Current status: installed

Pathname: /usr/bin/which
Type: regular file
Expected mode: 0555
Expected owner: root
Expected group: bin
Expected file size (bytes): 1287
Expected sum(1) of contents: 25204
Expected last modification: Jan 06 11:25:26 2000
Referenced by the following packages:
     SUNWcsu
Current status: installed

Pathname: /usr/bin/who
Type: regular file
Expected mode: 0555
Expected owner: root
Expected group: bin
Expected file size (bytes): 13080
Expected sum(1) of contents: 31735
Expected last modification: Jan 06 11:25:57 2000
Referenced by the following packages:
     SUNWcsu
Current status: installed

Pathname: /usr/bin/whois
Type: regular file
Expected mode: 0555
Expected owner: root
Expected group: bin
Expected file size (bytes): 5576
Expected sum(1) of contents: 24691
Expected last modification: Jan 06 11:00:46 2000
```

```
Referenced by the following packages:
     SUNWcsu
Current status: installed

Pathname: /usr/bin/wracct
Type: regular file
Expected mode: 0555
Expected owner: root
Expected group: bin
Expected file size (bytes): 5732
Expected sum(1) of contents: 41134
Expected last modification: Mar 16 21:53:58 2000
Referenced by the following packages:
     SUNWcsu
Current status: installed

Pathname: /usr/bin/write
Type: regular file
Expected mode: 2555
Expected owner: root
Expected group: tty
Expected file size (bytes): 11344
Expected sum(1) of contents: 52327
Expected last modification: Jan 06 11:25:43 2000
Referenced by the following packages:
     SUNWcsu
Current status: installed

Pathname: /usr/bin/xargs
Type: regular file
Expected mode: 0555
Expected owner: root
Expected group: bin
Expected file size (bytes): 14868
Expected sum(1) of contents: 14413
Expected last modification: Jan 06 11:25:47 2000
Referenced by the following packages:
     SUNWcsu
Current status: installed

Pathname: /usr/bin/xstr
Type: regular file
Expected mode: 0555
Expected owner: root
Expected group: bin
Expected file size (bytes): 10100
Expected sum(1) of contents: 58789
Expected last modification: Jan 06 11:25:41 2000
Referenced by the following packages:
     SUNWcsu
Current status: installed
```

/usr/sbin Commands

```
Pathname: /usr/sbin/acctadm
Type: regular file
Expected mode: 0555
Expected owner: root
Expected group: bin
Expected file size (bytes): 17336
Expected sum(1) of contents: 13192
Expected last modification: Mar 16 21:53:28 2000
Referenced by the following packages:
     SUNWcsu
Current status: installed

Pathname: /usr/sbin/audit
Type: regular file
Expected mode: 0555
Expected owner: root
Expected group: bin
Expected file size (bytes): 5460
Expected sum(1) of contents: 18640
Expected last modification: Jan 06 11:25:40 2000
Referenced by the following packages:
     SUNWcsu
Current status: installed

Pathname: /usr/sbin/auditconfig
Type: regular file
Expected mode: 0555
Expected owner: root
Expected group: bin
Expected file size (bytes): 27928
Expected sum(1) of contents: 21152
Expected last modification: Jan 06 11:26:05 2000
Referenced by the following packages:
     SUNWcsu
Current status: installed

Pathname: /usr/sbin/auditd
Type: regular file
Expected mode: 0555
Expected owner: root
Expected group: bin
Expected file size (bytes): 13372
Expected sum(1) of contents: 60907
Expected last modification: Jul 12 21:33:28 2000
Referenced by the following packages:
     SUNWcsu
Current status: installed
```

Pathname: /usr/sbin/auditreduce
Type: regular file
Expected mode: 0555
Expected owner: root
Expected group: bin
Expected file size (bytes): 53288
Expected sum(1) of contents: 8428
Expected last modification: Jan 06 11:27:04 2000
Referenced by the following packages:
      SUNWcsu
Current status: installed

Pathname: /usr/sbin/auditstat
Type: regular file
Expected mode: 0555
Expected owner: root
Expected group: bin
Expected file size (bytes): 6852
Expected sum(1) of contents: 63671
Expected last modification: Jan 06 11:25:50 2000
Referenced by the following packages:
      SUNWcsu
Current status: installed

Pathname: /usr/sbin/autopush
Type: regular file
Expected mode: 0555
Expected owner: root
Expected group: bin
Expected file size (bytes): 11448
Expected sum(1) of contents: 4973
Expected last modification: Jan 06 10:51:47 2000
Referenced by the following packages:
      SUNWcsu
Current status: installed

Pathname: /usr/sbin/cfgadm
Type: regular file
Expected mode: 0555
Expected owner: root
Expected group: bin
Expected file size (bytes): 21132
Expected sum(1) of contents: 61997
Expected last modification: Jan 06 10:51:59 2000
Referenced by the following packages:
      SUNWcsu
Current status: installed

Pathname: /usr/sbin/chroot
Type: regular file

```
Expected mode: 0555
Expected owner: root
Expected group: bin
Expected file size (bytes): 4640
Expected sum(1) of contents: 34386
Expected last modification: Jan 06 10:51:38 2000
Referenced by the following packages:
     SUNWcsu
Current status: installed

Pathname: /usr/sbin/clear_locks
Type: regular file
Expected mode: 0555
Expected owner: root
Expected group: bin
Expected file size (bytes): 5368
Expected sum(1) of contents: 16557
Expected last modification: Jan 06 10:55:29 2000
Referenced by the following packages:
     SUNWcsu
Current status: installed

Pathname: /usr/sbin/clinfo
Type: regular file
Expected mode: 0555
Expected owner: root
Expected group: bin
Expected file size (bytes): 5036
Expected sum(1) of contents: 55559
Expected last modification: Jan 06 10:51:40 2000
Referenced by the following packages:
     SUNWcsu
Current status: installed

Pathname: /usr/sbin/clri
Type: regular file
Expected mode: 0555
Expected owner: root
Expected group: bin
Expected file size (bytes): 9492
Expected sum(1) of contents: 29385
Expected last modification: Jan 09 13:06:49 2000
Referenced by the following packages:
     SUNWcsu
Current status: installed

Pathname: /usr/sbin/consadm
Type: regular file
Expected mode: 0555
Expected owner: root
Expected group: sys
```

```
Expected file size (bytes): 15504
Expected sum(1) of contents: 55454
Expected last modification: Jan 06 10:52:30 2000
Referenced by the following packages:
     SUNWcsu
Current status: installed

Pathname: /usr/sbin/cron
Type: regular file
Expected mode: 0555
Expected owner: root
Expected group: sys
Expected file size (bytes): 56772
Expected sum(1) of contents: 46133
Expected last modification: Jul 10 21:22:24 2000
Referenced by the following packages:
     SUNWcsu
Current status: installed

Pathname: /usr/sbin/devfsadm
Type: regular file
Expected mode: 0755
Expected owner: root
Expected group: sys
Expected file size (bytes): 65832
Expected sum(1) of contents: 38389
Expected last modification: Dec 15 13:46:53 2000
Referenced by the following packages:
     SUNWcsu
Current status: installed

Pathname: /usr/sbin/devinfo
Type: regular file
Expected mode: 0555
Expected owner: root
Expected group: bin
Expected file size (bytes): 6040
Expected sum(1) of contents: 52905
Expected last modification: Jan 06 10:52:43 2000
Referenced by the following packages:
     SUNWcsu
Current status: installed

Pathname: /usr/sbin/df
Type: regular file
Expected mode: 0555
Expected owner: root
Expected group: bin
Expected file size (bytes): 23924
Expected sum(1) of contents: 41753
Expected last modification: Jan 09 13:06:47 2000
```

```
Referenced by the following packages:
     SUNWcsu
Current status: installed

Pathname: /usr/sbin/dfmounts
Type: regular file
Expected mode: 0555
Expected owner: root
Expected group: bin
Expected file size (bytes): 6456
Expected sum(1) of contents: 20420
Expected last modification: Jan 06 10:52:55 2000
Referenced by the following packages:
     SUNWcsu
Current status: installed

Pathname: /usr/sbin/dispadmin
Type: regular file
Expected mode: 0555
Expected owner: root
Expected group: bin
Expected file size (bytes): 6840
Expected sum(1) of contents: 49772
Expected last modification: Jan 06 10:53:47 2000
Referenced by the following packages:
     SUNWcsu
Current status: installed

Pathname: /usr/sbin/dminfo
Type: regular file
Expected mode: 0755
Expected owner: root
Expected group: bin
Expected file size (bytes): 9292
Expected sum(1) of contents: 8456
Expected last modification: Jan 06 11:25:51 2000
Referenced by the following packages:
     SUNWcsu
Current status: installed

Pathname: /usr/sbin/dumpadm
Type: regular file
Expected mode: 0555
Expected owner: root
Expected group: bin
Expected file size (bytes): 16136
Expected sum(1) of contents: 31108
Expected last modification: Jul 20 23:38:19 2000
Referenced by the following packages:
     SUNWcsu
Current status: installed
```

```
Pathname: /usr/sbin/eeprom
Type: regular file
Expected mode: 0555
Expected owner: root
Expected group: sys
Expected file size (bytes): 532
Expected sum(1) of contents: 42223
Expected last modification: Jan 06 10:53:58 2000
Referenced by the following packages:
     SUNWcsu
Current status: installed

Pathname: /usr/sbin/exportfs
Type: regular file
Expected mode: 0555
Expected owner: root
Expected group: bin
Expected file size (bytes): 2367
Expected sum(1) of contents: 41920
Expected last modification: Jan 06 10:55:16 2000
Referenced by the following packages:
     SUNWcsu
Current status: installed

Pathname: /usr/sbin/ff
Type: regular file
Expected mode: 0555
Expected owner: root
Expected group: bin
Expected file size (bytes): 9724
Expected sum(1) of contents: 58945
Expected last modification: Jan 09 13:06:51 2000
Referenced by the following packages:
     SUNWcsu
Current status: installed

Pathname: /usr/sbin/fmthard
Type: regular file
Expected mode: 0555
Expected owner: root
Expected group: sys
Expected file size (bytes): 9876
Expected sum(1) of contents: 29163
Expected last modification: Jan 06 10:54:11 2000
Referenced by the following packages:
     SUNWcsu
Current status: installed

Pathname: /usr/sbin/format
Type: regular file
Expected mode: 0555
```

```
Expected owner: root
Expected group: bin
Expected file size (bytes): 173040
Expected sum(1) of contents: 20709
Expected last modification: Jan 22 04:04:18 2001
Referenced by the following packages:
     SUNWcsu
Current status: installed

Pathname: /usr/sbin/fsck
Type: regular file
Expected mode: 0555
Expected owner: root
Expected group: bin
Expected file size (bytes): 20304
Expected sum(1) of contents: 42283
Expected last modification: Jan 09 13:06:50 2000
Referenced by the following packages:
     SUNWcsu
Current status: installed

Pathname: /usr/sbin/fstyp
Type: regular file
Expected mode: 0555
Expected owner: root
Expected group: sys
Expected file size (bytes): 1607
Expected sum(1) of contents: 53640
Expected last modification: Jan 06 10:54:14 2000
Referenced by the following packages:
     SUNWcsu
Current status: installed

Pathname: /usr/sbin/fuser
Type: regular file
Expected mode: 0555
Expected owner: root
Expected group: bin
Expected file size (bytes): 6912
Expected sum(1) of contents: 48384
Expected last modification: Jan 06 10:54:20 2000
Referenced by the following packages:
     SUNWcsu
Current status: installed

Pathname: /usr/sbin/getmajor
Type: regular file
Expected mode: 0755
Expected owner: root
Expected group: sys
```

```
Expected file size (bytes): 299
Expected sum(1) of contents: 21857
Expected last modification: Jan 06 10:54:23 2000
Referenced by the following packages:
     SUNWcsu
Current status: installed

Pathname: /usr/sbin/groupadd
Type: regular file
Expected mode: 0555
Expected owner: root
Expected group: sys
Expected file size (bytes): 9148
Expected sum(1) of contents: 48303
Expected last modification: Jan 06 10:59:36 2000
Referenced by the following packages:
     SUNWcsu
Current status: installed

Pathname: /usr/sbin/groupdel
Type: regular file
Expected mode: 0555
Expected owner: root
Expected group: sys
Expected file size (bytes): 7216
Expected sum(1) of contents: 3105
Expected last modification: Jan 06 10:59:37 2000
Referenced by the following packages:
     SUNWcsu
Current status: installed

Pathname: /usr/sbin/groupmod
Type: regular file
Expected mode: 0555
Expected owner: root
Expected group: sys
Expected file size (bytes): 8724
Expected sum(1) of contents: 33069
Expected last modification: Jan 06 10:59:37 2000
Referenced by the following packages:
     SUNWcsu
Current status: installed

Pathname: /usr/sbin/grpck
Type: regular file
Expected mode: 0555
Expected owner: root
Expected group: bin
Expected file size (bytes): 8656
Expected sum(1) of contents: 39888
```

```
Expected last modification: Jan 06 10:54:52 2000
Referenced by the following packages:
     SUNWcsu
Current status: installed

Pathname: /usr/sbin/halt
Type: regular file
Expected mode: 0755
Expected owner: root
Expected group: bin
Expected file size (bytes): 7556
Expected sum(1) of contents: 58884
Expected last modification: Jan 06 10:55:07 2000
Referenced by the following packages:
     SUNWcsu
Current status: installed

Pathname: /usr/sbin/hostconfig
Type: regular file
Expected mode: 0555
Expected owner: root
Expected group: bin
Expected file size (bytes): 9740
Expected sum(1) of contents: 50730
Expected last modification: Jan 06 11:02:01 2000
Referenced by the following packages:
     SUNWcsu
Current status: installed

Pathname: /usr/sbin/ifconfig
Type: regular file
Expected mode: 0555
Expected owner: root
Expected group: bin
Expected file size (bytes): 65252
Expected sum(1) of contents: 15108
Expected last modification: Jul 10 21:27:13 2000
Referenced by the following packages:
     SUNWcsu
Current status: installed

Pathname: /usr/sbin/in.comsat
Type: regular file
Expected mode: 0555
Expected owner: root
Expected group: bin
Expected file size (bytes): 11012
Expected sum(1) of contents: 29347
Expected last modification: Jan 06 11:01:58 2000
```

```
Referenced by the following packages:
     SUNWcsu
Current status: installed

Pathname: /usr/sbin/in.fingerd
Type: regular file
Expected mode: 0555
Expected owner: root
Expected group: bin
Expected file size (bytes): 5892
Expected sum(1) of contents: 50443
Expected last modification: Jan 06 11:01:58 2000
Referenced by the following packages:
     SUNWcsu
Current status: installed

Pathname: /usr/sbin/in.named
Type: regular file
Expected mode: 0555
Expected owner: root
Expected group: bin
Expected file size (bytes): 265768
Expected sum(1) of contents: 63034
Expected last modification: Jan 06 11:00:50 2000
Referenced by the following packages:
     SUNWcsu
Current status: installed

Pathname: /usr/sbin/in.rarpd
Type: regular file
Expected mode: 0555
Expected owner: root
Expected group: bin
Expected file size (bytes): 17132
Expected sum(1) of contents: 57459
Expected last modification: Jan 06 11:01:58 2000
Referenced by the following packages:
     SUNWcsu
Current status: installed

Pathname: /usr/sbin/in.rdisc
Type: regular file
Expected mode: 0555
Expected owner: root
Expected group: bin
Expected file size (bytes): 25576
Expected sum(1) of contents: 18876
Expected last modification: Jan 06 11:01:58 2000
```

```
Referenced by the following packages:
      SUNWcsu
Current status: installed

Pathname: /usr/sbin/in.rexecd
Type: regular file
Expected mode: 0555
Expected owner: root
Expected group: bin
Expected file size (bytes): 11672
Expected sum(1) of contents: 55587
Expected last modification: Jan 06 11:01:58 2000
Referenced by the following packages:
      SUNWcsu
Current status: installed

Pathname: /usr/sbin/in.rlogind
Type: regular file
Expected mode: 0555
Expected owner: root
Expected group: bin
Expected file size (bytes): 19324
Expected sum(1) of contents: 5743
Expected last modification: Jan 06 11:01:58 2000
Referenced by the following packages:
      SUNWcsu
Current status: installed

Pathname: /usr/sbin/in.routed
Type: regular file
Expected mode: 0555
Expected owner: root
Expected group: bin
Expected file size (bytes): 36728
Expected sum(1) of contents: 10239
Expected last modification: Apr 13 21:11:19 2000
Referenced by the following packages:
      SUNWcsu
Current status: installed

Pathname: /usr/sbin/in.rshd
Type: regular file
Expected mode: 0555
Expected owner: root
Expected group: bin
Expected file size (bytes): 19512
Expected sum(1) of contents: 5399
Expected last modification: Jul 10 21:22:22 2000
Referenced by the following packages:
      SUNWcsu
Current status: installed
```

```
Pathname: /usr/sbin/in.rwhod
Type: regular file
Expected mode: 0555
Expected owner: root
Expected group: bin
Expected file size (bytes): 12324
Expected sum(1) of contents: 5354
Expected last modification: Jan 06 11:01:58 2000
Referenced by the following packages:
     SUNWcsu
Current status: installed

Pathname: /usr/sbin/in.talkd
Type: regular file
Expected mode: 0555
Expected owner: root
Expected group: bin
Expected file size (bytes): 12092
Expected sum(1) of contents: 56350
Expected last modification: Jan 06 10:52:27 2000
Referenced by the following packages:
     SUNWcsu
Current status: installed

Pathname: /usr/sbin/in.telnetd
Type: regular file
Expected mode: 0555
Expected owner: root
Expected group: bin
Expected file size (bytes): 28100
Expected sum(1) of contents: 57182
Expected last modification: Jan 06 11:01:59 2000
Referenced by the following packages:
     SUNWcsu
Current status: installed

Pathname: /usr/sbin/in.tftpd
Type: regular file
Expected mode: 0555
Expected owner: root
Expected group: bin
Expected file size (bytes): 27248
Expected sum(1) of contents: 57342
Expected last modification: Jun 09 02:08:34 2000
Referenced by the following packages:
     SUNWcsu
Current status: installed

Pathname: /usr/sbin/in.tnamed
Type: regular file
Expected mode: 0555
```

```
Expected owner: root
Expected group: bin
Expected file size (bytes): 6504
Expected sum(1) of contents: 34296
Expected last modification: Jan 06 11:01:59 2000
Referenced by the following packages:
     SUNWcsu
Current status: installed

Pathname: /usr/sbin/inetd
Type: regular file
Expected mode: 0555
Expected owner: root
Expected group: bin
Expected file size (bytes): 36100
Expected sum(1) of contents: 40293
Expected last modification: Jan 06 11:01:59 2000
Referenced by the following packages:
     SUNWcsu
Current status: installed

Pathname: /usr/sbin/init
Type: regular file
Expected mode: 0555
Expected owner: root
Expected group: sys
Expected file size (bytes): 37128
Expected sum(1) of contents: 18312
Expected last modification: Jan 06 10:56:19 2000
Referenced by the following packages:
     SUNWcsu
Current status: installed

Pathname: /usr/sbin/install
Type: regular file
Expected mode: 0555
Expected owner: root
Expected group: bin
Expected file size (bytes): 7129
Expected sum(1) of contents: 22283
Expected last modification: Jan 09 13:04:35 2000
Referenced by the following packages:
     SUNWcsu
Current status: installed

Pathname: /usr/sbin/installboot
Type: regular file
Expected mode: 0555
Expected owner: root
Expected group: sys
```

```
Expected file size (bytes): 630
Expected sum(1) of contents: 46770
Expected last modification: Jan 06 10:44:24 2000
Referenced by the following packages:
     SUNWcsu
Current status: installed

Pathname: /usr/sbin/installf
Type: regular file
Expected mode: 0555
Expected owner: root
Expected group: sys
Expected file size (bytes): 100628
Expected sum(1) of contents: 45809
Expected last modification: Jan 06 11:03:18 2000
Referenced by the following packages:
     SUNWcsu
Current status: installed

Pathname: /usr/sbin/ipsecconf
Type: regular file
Expected mode: 0555
Expected owner: root
Expected group: bin
Expected file size (bytes): 27404
Expected sum(1) of contents: 824
Expected last modification: Jan 06 11:01:59 2000
Referenced by the following packages:
     SUNWcsu
Current status: installed

Pathname: /usr/sbin/ipseckey
Type: regular file
Expected mode: 0555
Expected owner: root
Expected group: bin
Expected file size (bytes): 43984
Expected sum(1) of contents: 42658
Expected last modification: Jan 06 11:01:59 2000
Referenced by the following packages:
     SUNWcsu
Current status: installed

Pathname: /usr/sbin/keyserv
Type: regular file
Expected mode: 0555
Expected owner: root
Expected group: sys
Expected file size (bytes): 45064
Expected sum(1) of contents: 62745
Expected last modification: Jan 06 10:58:07 2000
```

```
Referenced by the following packages:
     SUNWcsu
Current status: installed

Pathname: /usr/sbin/killall
Type: regular file
Expected mode: 0555
Expected owner: root
Expected group: bin
Expected file size (bytes): 4100
Expected sum(1) of contents: 16783
Expected last modification: Jan 06 10:56:16 2000
Referenced by the following packages:
     SUNWcsu
Current status: installed

Pathname: /usr/sbin/link
Type: regular file
Expected mode: 0555
Expected owner: root
Expected group: bin
Expected file size (bytes): 4180
Expected sum(1) of contents: 9870
Expected last modification: Jan 06 10:56:42 2000
Referenced by the following packages:
     SUNWcsu
Current status: installed

Pathname: /usr/sbin/lofiadm
Type: regular file
Expected mode: 0555
Expected owner: root
Expected group: bin
Expected file size (bytes): 8796
Expected sum(1) of contents: 62422
Expected last modification: Jan 06 10:57:11 2000
Referenced by the following packages:
     SUNWcsu
Current status: installed

Pathname: /usr/sbin/makedbm
Type: regular file
Expected mode: 0555
Expected owner: root
Expected group: bin
Expected file size (bytes): 12132
Expected sum(1) of contents: 48157
Expected last modification: Jan 06 11:28:27 2000
Referenced by the following packages:
     SUNWcsu
Current status: installed
```

```
Pathname: /usr/sbin/mkdevalloc
Type: regular file
Expected mode: 4755
Expected owner: root
Expected group: bin
Expected file size (bytes): 9800
Expected sum(1) of contents: 55620
Expected last modification: Jan 06 11:26:29 2000
Referenced by the following packages:
     SUNWcsu
Current status: installed

Pathname: /usr/sbin/mkdevmaps
Type: regular file
Expected mode: 4755
Expected owner: root
Expected group: bin
Expected file size (bytes): 10032
Expected sum(1) of contents: 62005
Expected last modification: Apr 13 21:11:26 2000
Referenced by the following packages:
     SUNWcsu
Current status: installed

Pathname: /usr/sbin/mkfile
Type: regular file
Expected mode: 0555
Expected owner: root
Expected group: bin
Expected file size (bytes): 6304
Expected sum(1) of contents: 13923
Expected last modification: Jan 06 10:58:07 2000
Referenced by the following packages:
     SUNWcsu
Current status: installed

Pathname: /usr/sbin/mknod
Type: regular file
Expected mode: 0555
Expected owner: root
Expected group: bin
Expected file size (bytes): 5104
Expected sum(1) of contents: 64643
Expected last modification: Jan 06 10:58:12 2000
Referenced by the following packages:
     SUNWcsu
Current status: installed

Pathname: /usr/sbin/modinfo
Type: regular file
Expected mode: 0555
```

```
Expected owner: root
Expected group: bin
Expected file size (bytes): 13884
Expected sum(1) of contents: 15276
Expected last modification: Jan 06 10:59:21 2000
Referenced by the following packages:
     SUNWcsu
Current status: installed

Pathname: /usr/sbin/modload
Type: regular file
Expected mode: 0555
Expected owner: root
Expected group: bin
Expected file size (bytes): 14128
Expected sum(1) of contents: 19173
Expected last modification: Jan 06 10:59:22 2000
Referenced by the following packages:
     SUNWcsu
Current status: installed

Pathname: /usr/sbin/modunload
Type: regular file
Expected mode: 0555
Expected owner: root
Expected group: bin
Expected file size (bytes): 13660
Expected sum(1) of contents: 59244
Expected last modification: Jan 06 10:59:22 2000
Referenced by the following packages:
     SUNWcsu
Current status: installed

Pathname: /usr/sbin/mount
Type: regular file
Expected mode: 0555
Expected owner: root
Expected group: bin
Expected file size (bytes): 27208
Expected sum(1) of contents: 47232
Expected last modification: Jan 09 13:06:42 2000
Referenced by the following packages:
     SUNWcsu
Current status: installed

Pathname: /usr/sbin/mountall
Type: regular file
Expected mode: 0555
Expected owner: root
Expected group: sys
```

Expected file size (bytes): 8258
Expected sum(1) of contents: 51535
Expected last modification: May 26 21:35:27 2000
Referenced by the following packages:
     SUNWcsu
Current status: installed

Pathname: /usr/sbin/msgid
Type: regular file
Expected mode: 0555
Expected owner: root
Expected group: bin
Expected file size (bytes): 4064
Expected sum(1) of contents: 2118
Expected last modification: Jan 06 10:58:25 2000
Referenced by the following packages:
     SUNWcsu
Current status: installed

Pathname: /usr/sbin/mvdir
Type: regular file
Expected mode: 0555
Expected owner: root
Expected group: bin
Expected file size (bytes): 1095
Expected sum(1) of contents: 13823
Expected last modification: Jan 06 10:58:30 2000
Referenced by the following packages:
     SUNWcsu
Current status: installed

Pathname: /usr/sbin/named-bootconf
Type: regular file
Expected mode: 0555
Expected owner: root
Expected group: bin
Expected file size (bytes): 6730
Expected sum(1) of contents: 18339
Expected last modification: Jan 06 11:01:15 2000
Referenced by the following packages:
     SUNWcsu
Current status: installed

Pathname: /usr/sbin/named-xfer
Type: regular file
Expected mode: 0555
Expected owner: root
Expected group: bin
Expected file size (bytes): 45000
Expected sum(1) of contents: 34115
Expected last modification: Jan 06 11:00:56 2000

```
Referenced by the following packages:
    SUNWcsu
Current status: installed

Pathname: /usr/sbin/ndd
Type: regular file
Expected mode: 0555
Expected owner: root
Expected group: bin
Expected file size (bytes): 8404
Expected sum(1) of contents: 34540
Expected last modification: Jan 06 11:01:59 2000
Referenced by the following packages:
    SUNWcsu
Current status: installed

Pathname: /usr/sbin/nlsadmin
Type: regular file
Expected mode: 0755
Expected owner: root
Expected group: adm
Expected file size (bytes): 19396
Expected sum(1) of contents: 59712
Expected last modification: Jan 06 10:59:14 2000
Referenced by the following packages:
    SUNWcsu
Current status: installed

Pathname: /usr/sbin/nscd
Type: regular file
Expected mode: 0555
Expected owner: root
Expected group: bin
Expected file size (bytes): 56868
Expected sum(1) of contents: 44815
Expected last modification: Jan 06 11:00:29 2000
Referenced by the following packages:
    SUNWcsu
Current status: installed

Pathname: /usr/sbin/nslookup
Type: regular file
Expected mode: 0555
Expected owner: root
Expected group: bin
Expected file size (bytes): 50464
Expected sum(1) of contents: 16787
Expected last modification: Jan 06 11:01:07 2000
Referenced by the following packages:
    SUNWcsu
Current status: installed
```

```
Pathname: /usr/sbin/nstest
Type: regular file
Expected mode: 0555
Expected owner: root
Expected group: bin
Expected file size (bytes): 9260
Expected sum(1) of contents: 56363
Expected last modification: Jan 06 11:01:14 2000
Referenced by the following packages:
     SUNWcsu
Current status: installed

Pathname: /usr/sbin/nsupdate
Type: regular file
Expected mode: 0555
Expected owner: root
Expected group: bin
Expected file size (bytes): 9500
Expected sum(1) of contents: 47695
Expected last modification: Jan 06 11:01:11 2000
Referenced by the following packages:
     SUNWcsu
Current status: installed

Pathname: /usr/sbin/passmgmt
Type: regular file
Expected mode: 0555
Expected owner: root
Expected group: sys
Expected file size (bytes): 20212
Expected sum(1) of contents: 2484
Expected last modification: Jan 06 10:59:42 2000
Referenced by the following packages:
     SUNWcsu
Current status: installed

Pathname: /usr/sbin/pbind
Type: regular file
Expected mode: 0555
Expected owner: root
Expected group: sys
Expected file size (bytes): 6856
Expected sum(1) of contents: 54076
Expected last modification: Jan 06 10:59:52 2000
Referenced by the following packages:
     SUNWcsu
Current status: installed

Pathname: /usr/sbin/ping
Type: regular file
Expected mode: 4555
```

```
Expected owner: root
Expected group: bin
Expected file size (bytes): 48028
Expected sum(1) of contents: 22774
Expected last modification: Jan 06 10:53:52 2000
Referenced by the following packages:
      SUNWcsu
Current status: installed

Pathname: /usr/sbin/pkgadd
Type: regular file
Expected mode: 0555
Expected owner: root
Expected group: sys
Expected file size (bytes): 105196
Expected sum(1) of contents: 52501
Expected last modification: Jan 06 10:59:42 2000
Referenced by the following packages:
      SUNWcsu
Current status: installed

Pathname: /usr/sbin/pkgchk
Type: regular file
Expected mode: 0555
Expected owner: root
Expected group: sys
Expected file size (bytes): 164904
Expected sum(1) of contents: 38135
Expected last modification: Jan 06 11:02:03 2000
Referenced by the following packages:
      SUNWcsu
Current status: installed

Pathname: /usr/sbin/pkgmv
Type: regular file
Expected mode: 0555
Expected owner: root
Expected group: sys
Expected file size (bytes): 52140
Expected sum(1) of contents: 16437
Expected last modification: Jan 06 11:03:31 2000
Referenced by the following packages:
      SUNWcsu
Current status: installed

Pathname: /usr/sbin/pkgrm
Type: regular file
Expected mode: 0555
Expected owner: root
Expected group: sys
```

```
Expected file size (bytes): 82980
Expected sum(1) of contents: 35355
Expected last modification: Jan 06 11:01:16 2000
Referenced by the following packages:
     SUNWcsu
Current status: installed

Pathname: /usr/sbin/pmadm
Type: regular file
Expected mode: 0555
Expected owner: root
Expected group: sys
Expected file size (bytes): 23132
Expected sum(1) of contents: 51919
Expected last modification: Jan 06 11:01:41 2000
Referenced by the following packages:
     SUNWcsu
Current status: installed

Pathname: /usr/sbin/praudit
Type: regular file
Expected mode: 0555
Expected owner: root
Expected group: bin
Expected file size (bytes): 29828
Expected sum(1) of contents: 15242
Expected last modification: Jan 06 11:26:35 2000
Referenced by the following packages:
     SUNWcsu
Current status: installed

Pathname: /usr/sbin/projadd
Type: regular file
Expected mode: 0555
Expected owner: root
Expected group: sys
Expected file size (bytes): 6153
Expected sum(1) of contents: 23892
Expected last modification: Mar 16 21:54:05 2000
Referenced by the following packages:
     SUNWcsu
Current status: installed

Pathname: /usr/sbin/projdel
Type: regular file
Expected mode: 0555
Expected owner: root
Expected group: sys
Expected file size (bytes): 1764
Expected sum(1) of contents: 11450
Expected last modification: Mar 16 21:54:05 2000
```

```
Referenced by the following packages:
     SUNWcsu
Current status: installed

Pathname: /usr/sbin/projmod
Type: regular file
Expected mode: 0555
Expected owner: root
Expected group: sys
Expected file size (bytes): 6721
Expected sum(1) of contents: 5208
Expected last modification: Mar 16 21:54:05 2000
Referenced by the following packages:
     SUNWcsu
Current status: installed

Pathname: /usr/sbin/prtvtoc
Type: regular file
Expected mode: 0555
Expected owner: root
Expected group: sys
Expected file size (bytes): 12260
Expected sum(1) of contents: 19313
Expected last modification: Jan 06 11:00:36 2000
Referenced by the following packages:
     SUNWcsu
Current status: installed

Pathname: /usr/sbin/psradm
Type: regular file
Expected mode: 0555
Expected owner: root
Expected group: sys
Expected file size (bytes): 7180
Expected sum(1) of contents: 9550
Expected last modification: Jan 06 11:00:48 2000
Referenced by the following packages:
     SUNWcsu
Current status: installed

Pathname: /usr/sbin/psrinfo
Type: regular file
Expected mode: 0555
Expected owner: root
Expected group: sys
Expected file size (bytes): 7204
Expected sum(1) of contents: 10960
Expected last modification: Jan 06 11:00:49 2000
Referenced by the following packages:
     SUNWcsu
Current status: installed
```

Pathname: /usr/sbin/psrset
Type: regular file
Expected mode: 0555
Expected owner: root
Expected group: sys
Expected file size (bytes): 12400
Expected sum(1) of contents: 11040
Expected last modification: Jan 06 11:00:56 2000
Referenced by the following packages:
     SUNWcsu
Current status: installed

Pathname: /usr/sbin/pwck
Type: regular file
Expected mode: 0555
Expected owner: root
Expected group: bin
Expected file size (bytes): 6596
Expected sum(1) of contents: 46407
Expected last modification: Jan 06 11:00:56 2000
Referenced by the following packages:
     SUNWcsu
Current status: installed

Pathname: /usr/sbin/pwconv
Type: regular file
Expected mode: 0555
Expected owner: root
Expected group: sys
Expected file size (bytes): 9596
Expected sum(1) of contents: 15510
Expected last modification: Jan 06 11:01:06 2000
Referenced by the following packages:
     SUNWcsu
Current status: installed

Pathname: /usr/sbin/rem_drv
Type: regular file
Expected mode: 0555
Expected owner: root
Expected group: bin
Expected file size (bytes): 15064
Expected sum(1) of contents: 12302
Expected last modification: Jan 06 10:59:22 2000
Referenced by the following packages:
     SUNWcsu
Current status: installed

Pathname: /usr/sbin/rmt
Type: regular file
Expected mode: 0555

```
Expected owner: root
Expected group: bin
Expected file size (bytes): 9996
Expected sum(1) of contents: 58870
Expected last modification: Jan 06 11:01:20 2000
Referenced by the following packages:
     SUNWcsu
Current status: installed

Pathname: /usr/sbin/route
Type: regular file
Expected mode: 0555
Expected owner: root
Expected group: bin
Expected file size (bytes): 37196
Expected sum(1) of contents: 44016
Expected last modification: Jan 06 11:02:00 2000
Referenced by the following packages:
     SUNWcsu
Current status: installed

Pathname: /usr/sbin/rpc.bootparamd
Type: regular file
Expected mode: 0555
Expected owner: root
Expected group: bin
Expected file size (bytes): 14516
Expected sum(1) of contents: 49544
Expected last modification: Jan 06 11:03:25 2000
Referenced by the following packages:
     SUNWcsu
Current status: installed

Pathname: /usr/sbin/rpcbind
Type: regular file
Expected mode: 0555
Expected owner: root
Expected group: bin
Expected file size (bytes): 45976
Expected sum(1) of contents: 14301
Expected last modification: Jan 06 11:02:00 2000
Referenced by the following packages:
     SUNWcsu
Current status: installed

Pathname: /usr/sbin/rpld
Type: regular file
Expected mode: 0555
Expected owner: root
Expected group: bin
Expected file size (bytes): 38348
Expected sum(1) of contents: 24316
```

```
Expected last modification: Jan 06 11:02:21 2000
Referenced by the following packages:
     SUNWcsu
Current status: installed


Pathname: /usr/sbin/rwall
Type: regular file
Expected mode: 0555
Expected owner: root
Expected group: bin
Expected file size (bytes): 7388
Expected sum(1) of contents: 60513
Expected last modification: Jan 06 11:03:07 2000
Referenced by the following packages:
     SUNWcsu
Current status: installed


Pathname: /usr/sbin/sacadm
Type: regular file
Expected mode: 4755
Expected owner: root
Expected group: sys
Expected file size (bytes): 22640
Expected sum(1) of contents: 34467
Expected last modification: Jan 06 11:01:41 2000
Referenced by the following packages:
     SUNWcsu
Current status: installed


Pathname: /usr/sbin/setmnt
Type: regular file
Expected mode: 0555
Expected owner: root
Expected group: bin
Expected file size (bytes): 153
Expected sum(1) of contents: 11450
Expected last modification: Jan 06 11:01:58 2000
Referenced by the following packages:
     SUNWcsu
Current status: installed


Pathname: /usr/sbin/share
Type: regular file
Expected mode: 0555
Expected owner: root
Expected group: bin
Expected file size (bytes): 7388
Expected sum(1) of contents: 19604
Expected last modification: Jan 06 10:53:12 2000
Referenced by the following packages:
     SUNWcsu
Current status: installed
```

```
Pathname: /usr/sbin/shareall
Type: regular file
Expected mode: 0555
Expected owner: root
Expected group: bin
Expected file size (bytes): 1545
Expected sum(1) of contents: 49757
Expected last modification: Jan 06 10:53:16 2000
Referenced by the following packages:
     SUNWcsu
Current status: installed

Pathname: /usr/sbin/shutdown
Type: regular file
Expected mode: 0755
Expected owner: root
Expected group: sys
Expected file size (bytes): 4094
Expected sum(1) of contents: 51916
Expected last modification: Jan 06 10:55:25 2000
Referenced by the following packages:
     SUNWcsu
Current status: installed

Pathname: /usr/sbin/snoop
Type: regular file
Expected mode: 0555
Expected owner: root
Expected group: bin
Expected file size (bytes): 312612
Expected sum(1) of contents: 17831
Expected last modification: Jun 09 02:08:35 2000
Referenced by the following packages:
     SUNWcsu
Current status: installed

Pathname: /usr/sbin/sparcv7
Type: directory
Expected mode: 0755
Expected owner: root
Expected group: bin
Referenced by the following packages:
     SUNWcsu
Current status: installed

Pathname: /usr/sbin/sparcv7/crash
Type: regular file
Expected mode: 0755
Expected owner: root
Expected group: sys
Expected file size (bytes): 136412
Expected sum(1) of contents: 42108
```

```
Expected last modification: Apr 13 21:10:29 2000
Referenced by the following packages:
     SUNWcsu
Current status: installed


Pathname: /usr/sbin/sparcv7/lockstat
Type: regular file
Expected mode: 0555
Expected owner: root
Expected group: bin
Expected file size (bytes): 30720
Expected sum(1) of contents: 14918
Expected last modification: Jan 06 10:57:16 2000
Referenced by the following packages:
     SUNWcsu
Current status: installed


Pathname: /usr/sbin/sparcv7/prtconf
Type: regular file
Expected mode: 2555
Expected owner: root
Expected group: sys
Expected file size (bytes): 19544
Expected sum(1) of contents: 58600
Expected last modification: Jan 06 11:00:40 2000
Referenced by the following packages:
     SUNWcsu
Current status: installed


Pathname: /usr/sbin/sparcv7/swap
Type: regular file
Expected mode: 2555
Expected owner: root
Expected group: sys
Expected file size (bytes): 10316
Expected sum(1) of contents: 41822
Expected last modification: Jan 06 11:03:18 2000
Referenced by the following packages:
     SUNWcsu
Current status: installed


Pathname: /usr/sbin/sparcv7/sysdef
Type: regular file
Expected mode: 2555
Expected owner: root
Expected group: sys
Expected file size (bytes): 22656
Expected sum(1) of contents: 30408
Expected last modification: Jan 06 11:03:33 2000
Referenced by the following packages:
     SUNWcsu
Current status: installed
```

```
Pathname: /usr/sbin/sparcv7/whodo
Type: regular file
Expected mode: 4555
Expected owner: root
Expected group: bin
Expected file size (bytes): 12916
Expected sum(1) of contents: 13815
Expected last modification: Jan 06 11:25:47 2000
Referenced by the following packages:
     SUNWcsu
Current status: installed

Pathname: /usr/sbin/spray
Type: regular file
Expected mode: 0555
Expected owner: root
Expected group: bin
Expected file size (bytes): 7224
Expected sum(1) of contents: 6360
Expected last modification: Jan 06 11:03:07 2000
Referenced by the following packages:
     SUNWcsu
Current status: installed

Pathname: /usr/sbin/strace
Type: regular file
Expected mode: 0555
Expected owner: root
Expected group: sys
Expected file size (bytes): 6040
Expected sum(1) of contents: 17767
Expected last modification: Jan 06 11:03:12 2000
Referenced by the following packages:
     SUNWcsu
Current status: installed

Pathname: /usr/sbin/strclean
Type: regular file
Expected mode: 0555
Expected owner: root
Expected group: sys
Expected file size (bytes): 5784
Expected sum(1) of contents: 40659
Expected last modification: Jan 06 11:03:12 2000
Referenced by the following packages:
     SUNWcsu
Current status: installed

Pathname: /usr/sbin/strerr
Type: regular file
Expected mode: 0555
```

Expected owner: root
Expected group: sys
Expected file size (bytes): 6312
Expected sum(1) of contents: 6569
Expected last modification: Jan 06 11:03:12 2000
Referenced by the following packages:
       SUNWcsu
Current status: installed

Pathname: /usr/sbin/sttydefs
Type: regular file
Expected mode: 0755
Expected owner: root
Expected group: sys
Expected file size (bytes): 25844
Expected sum(1) of contents: 23929
Expected last modification: Jan 06 11:07:24 2000
Referenced by the following packages:
       SUNWcsu
Current status: installed

Pathname: /usr/sbin/sync
Type: regular file
Expected mode: 0555
Expected owner: root
Expected group: bin
Expected file size (bytes): 3548
Expected sum(1) of contents: 46534
Expected last modification: Jan 06 11:03:17 2000
Referenced by the following packages:
       SUNWcsu
Current status: installed

Pathname: /usr/sbin/syncinit
Type: regular file
Expected mode: 0555
Expected owner: root
Expected group: bin
Expected file size (bytes): 23492
Expected sum(1) of contents: 817
Expected last modification: Jan 06 11:02:02 2000
Referenced by the following packages:
       SUNWcsu
Current status: installed

Pathname: /usr/sbin/syncloop
Type: regular file
Expected mode: 0555
Expected owner: root
Expected group: bin
Expected file size (bytes): 28060

```
Expected sum(1) of contents: 22526
Expected last modification: Jan 06 11:01:58 2000
Referenced by the following packages:
     SUNWcsu
Current status: installed

Pathname: /usr/sbin/syncstat
Type: regular file
Expected mode: 0555
Expected owner: root
Expected group: bin
Expected file size (bytes): 22856
Expected sum(1) of contents: 18076
Expected last modification: Jan 06 11:02:02 2000
Referenced by the following packages:
     SUNWcsu
Current status: installed

Pathname: /usr/sbin/syslogd
Type: regular file
Expected mode: 0555
Expected owner: root
Expected group: sys
Expected file size (bytes): 46308
Expected sum(1) of contents: 16900
Expected last modification: Jan 06 11:03:54 2000
Referenced by the following packages:
     SUNWcsu
Current status: installed

Pathname: /usr/sbin/tar
Type: regular file
Expected mode: 0555
Expected owner: root
Expected group: bin
Expected file size (bytes): 64008
Expected sum(1) of contents: 35163
Expected last modification: Jan 27 02:22:16 2001
Referenced by the following packages:
     SUNWcsu
Current status: installed

Pathname: /usr/sbin/traceroute
Type: regular file
Expected mode: 4555
Expected owner: root
Expected group: bin
Expected file size (bytes): 35652
Expected sum(1) of contents: 19177
Expected last modification: Jan 06 10:53:35 2000
```

```
Referenced by the following packages:
     SUNWcsu
Current status: installed

Pathname: /usr/sbin/ttyadm
Type: regular file
Expected mode: 0755
Expected owner: root
Expected group: sys
Expected file size (bytes): 10204
Expected sum(1) of contents: 10385
Expected last modification: Jan 06 11:07:24 2000
Referenced by the following packages:
     SUNWcsu
Current status: installed

Pathname: /usr/sbin/uadmin
Type: regular file
Expected mode: 0555
Expected owner: root
Expected group: sys
Expected file size (bytes): 4860
Expected sum(1) of contents: 41738
Expected last modification: Jan 06 11:05:54 2000
Referenced by the following packages:
     SUNWcsu
Current status: installed

Pathname: /usr/sbin/umount
Type: regular file
Expected mode: 0555
Expected owner: root
Expected group: bin
Expected file size (bytes): 16476
Expected sum(1) of contents: 19126
Expected last modification: Jan 09 13:06:41 2000
Referenced by the following packages:
     SUNWcsu
Current status: installed

Pathname: /usr/sbin/umountall
Type: regular file
Expected mode: 0555
Expected owner: root
Expected group: sys
Expected file size (bytes): 3321
Expected sum(1) of contents: 46464
Expected last modification: Jan 06 10:55:25 2000
Referenced by the following packages:
     SUNWcsu
Current status: installed
```

```
Pathname: /usr/sbin/unlink
Type: regular file
Expected mode: 0555
Expected owner: root
Expected group: bin
Expected file size (bytes): 4188
Expected sum(1) of contents: 10844
Expected last modification: Jan 06 11:06:04 2000
Referenced by the following packages:
     SUNWcsu
Current status: installed

Pathname: /usr/sbin/unshare
Type: regular file
Expected mode: 0555
Expected owner: root
Expected group: bin
Expected file size (bytes): 5776
Expected sum(1) of contents: 42721
Expected last modification: Jan 06 10:52:46 2000
Referenced by the following packages:
     SUNWcsu
Current status: installed

Pathname: /usr/sbin/unshareall
Type: regular file
Expected mode: 0555
Expected owner: root
Expected group: bin
Expected file size (bytes): 976
Expected sum(1) of contents: 7590
Expected last modification: Jan 06 10:53:18 2000
Referenced by the following packages:
     SUNWcsu
Current status: installed

Pathname: /usr/sbin/useradd
Type: regular file
Expected mode: 0555
Expected owner: root
Expected group: sys
Expected file size (bytes): 32256
Expected sum(1) of contents: 45521
Expected last modification: Mar 16 21:54:09 2000
Referenced by the following packages:
     SUNWcsu
Current status: installed

Pathname: /usr/sbin/userdel
Type: regular file
Expected mode: 0555
Expected owner: root
```

```
Expected group: sys
Expected file size (bytes): 17080
Expected sum(1) of contents: 45044
Expected last modification: Mar 16 21:54:09 2000
Referenced by the following packages:
     SUNWcsu
Current status: installed

Pathname: /usr/sbin/usermod
Type: regular file
Expected mode: 0555
Expected owner: root
Expected group: sys
Expected file size (bytes): 30908
Expected sum(1) of contents: 62167
Expected last modification: Mar 16 21:54:09 2000
Referenced by the following packages:
     SUNWcsu
Current status: installed

Pathname: /usr/sbin/volcopy
Type: regular file
Expected mode: 0555
Expected owner: root
Expected group: bin
Expected file size (bytes): 9668
Expected sum(1) of contents: 15002
Expected last modification: Jan 09 13:06:51 2000
Referenced by the following packages:
     SUNWcsu
Current status: installed

Pathname: /usr/sbin/wall
Type: regular file
Expected mode: 2555
Expected owner: root
Expected group: tty
Expected file size (bytes): 9872
Expected sum(1) of contents: 39608
Expected last modification: Jan 06 11:25:41 2000
Referenced by the following packages:
     SUNWcsu
Current status: installed

Pathname: /usr/sbin/zdump
Type: regular file
Expected mode: 0555
Expected owner: root
Expected group: bin
Expected file size (bytes): 7816
Expected sum(1) of contents: 61543
Expected last modification: Jan 06 11:25:39 2000
```

```
Referenced by the following packages:
     SUNWcsu
Current status: installed

Pathname: /usr/sbin/zic
Type: regular file
Expected mode: 0555
Expected owner: root
Expected group: bin
Expected file size (bytes): 27484
Expected sum(1) of contents: 34574
Expected last modification: Jan 06 11:26:48 2000
Referenced by the following packages:
     SUNWcsu
Current status: installed
```

INDEX

M

INTERNATIONAL CONTACT INFORMATION

AUSTRALIA
McGraw-Hill Book Company Australia Pty. Ltd.
TEL +61-2-9417-9899
FAX +61-2-9417-5687
http://www.mcgraw-hill.com.au
books-it_sydney@mcgraw-hill.com

CANADA
McGraw-Hill Ryerson Ltd.
TEL +905-430-5000
FAX +905-430-5020
http://www.mcgrawhill.ca

GREECE, MIDDLE EAST,
NORTHERN AFRICA
McGraw-Hill Hellas
TEL +30-1-656-0990-3-4
FAX +30-1-654-5525

MEXICO (Also serving Latin America)
McGraw-Hill Interamericana Editores S.A. de C.V.
TEL +525-117-1583
FAX +525-117-1589
http://www.mcgraw-hill.com.mx
fernando_castellanos@mcgraw-hill.com

SINGAPORE (Serving Asia)
McGraw-Hill Book Company
TEL +65-863-1580
FAX +65-862-3354
http://www.mcgraw-hill.com.sg
mghasia@mcgraw-hill.com

SOUTH AFRICA
McGraw-Hill South Africa
TEL +27-11-622-7512
FAX +27-11-622-9045
robyn_swanepoel@mcgraw-hill.com

UNITED KINGDOM & EUROPE
(Excluding Southern Europe)
McGraw-Hill Education Europe
TEL +44-1-628-502500
FAX +44-1-628-770224
http://www.mcgraw-hill.co.uk
computing_neurope@mcgraw-hill.com

ALL OTHER INQUIRIES Contact:
Osborne/McGraw-Hill
TEL +1-510-549-6600
FAX +1-510-883-7600
http://www.osborne.com
omg_international@mcgraw-hill.com

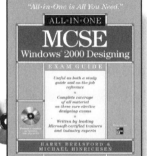

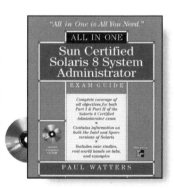

LICENSE AGREEMENT

THIS PRODUCT (THE "PRODUCT") CONTAINS PROPRIETARY SOFTWARE, DATA AND INFORMATION (INCLUDING DOCUMENTATION) OWNED BY THE McGRAW-HILL COMPANIES, INC. ("McGRAW-HILL") AND ITS LICENSORS. YOUR RIGHT TO USE THE PRODUCT IS GOVERNED BY THE TERMS AND CONDITIONS OF THIS AGREEMENT.

LICENSE: Throughout this License Agreement, "you" shall mean either the individual or the entity whose agent opens this package. You are granted a non-exclusive and non-transferable license to use the Product subject to the following terms:

(i) If you have licensed a single user version of the Product, the Product may only be used on a single computer (i.e., a single CPU). If you licensed and paid the fee applicable to a local area network or wide area network version of the Product, you are subject to the terms of the following subparagraph (ii).

(ii) If you have licensed a local area network version, you may use the Product on unlimited workstations located in one single building selected by you that is served by such local area network. If you have licensed a wide area network version, you may use the Product on unlimited workstations located in multiple buildings on the same site selected by you that is served by such wide area network; provided, however, that any building will not be considered located in the same site if it is more than five (5) miles away from any building included in such site. In addition, you may only use a local area or wide area network version of the Product on one single server. If you wish to use the Product on more than one server, you must obtain written authorization from McGraw-Hill and pay additional fees.

(iii) You may make one copy of the Product for back-up purposes only and you must maintain an accurate record as to the location of the back-up at all times.

COPYRIGHT; RESTRICTIONS ON USE AND TRANSFER: All rights (including copyright) in and to the Product are owned by McGraw-Hill and its licensors. You are the owner of the enclosed disc on which the Product is recorded. You may not use, copy, decompile, disassemble, reverse engineer, modify, reproduce, create derivative works, transmit, distribute, sublicense, store in a database or retrieval system of any kind, rent or transfer the Product, or any portion thereof, in any form or by any means (including electronically or otherwise) except as expressly provided for in this License Agreement. You must reproduce the copyright notices, trademark notices, legends and logos of McGraw-Hill and its licensors that appear on the Product on the back-up copy of the Product which you are permitted to make hereunder. All rights in the Product not expressly granted herein are reserved by McGraw-Hill and its licensors.

TERM: This License Agreement is effective until terminated. It will terminate if you fail to comply with any term or condition of this License Agreement. Upon termination, you are obligated to return to McGraw-Hill the Product together with all copies thereof and to purge all copies of the Product included in any and all servers and computer facilities.

DISCLAIMER OF WARRANTY: THE PRODUCT AND THE BACK-UP COPY ARE LICENSED "AS IS." McGRAW-HILL, ITS LICENSORS AND THE AUTHORS MAKE NO WARRANTIES, EXPRESS OR IMPLIED, AS TO THE RESULTS TO BE OBTAINED BY ANY PERSON OR ENTITY FROM USE OF THE PRODUCT, ANY INFORMATION OR DATA INCLUDED THEREIN AND/OR ANY TECHNICAL SUPPORT SERVICES PROVIDED HEREUNDER, IF ANY ("TECHNICAL SUPPORT SERVICES"). McGRAW-HILL, ITS LICENSORS AND THE AUTHORS MAKE NO EXPRESS OR IMPLIED WARRANTIES OF MERCHANTABILITY OR FITNESS FOR A PARTICULAR PURPOSE OR USE WITH RESPECT TO THE PRODUCT. McGRAW-HILL, ITS LICENSORS, AND THE AUTHORS MAKE NO GUARANTEE THAT YOU WILL PASS ANY CERTIFICATION EXAM WHATSOEVER BY USING THIS PRODUCT. NEITHER McGRAW-HILL, ANY OF ITS LICENSORS NOR THE AUTHORS WARRANT THAT THE FUNCTIONS CONTAINED IN THE PRODUCT WILL MEET YOUR REQUIREMENTS OR THAT THE OPERATION OF THE PRODUCT WILL BE UNINTERRUPTED OR ERROR FREE. YOU ASSUME THE ENTIRE RISK WITH RESPECT TO THE QUALITY AND PERFORMANCE OF THE PRODUCT.

LIMITED WARRANTY FOR DISC: To the original licensee only, McGraw-Hill warrants that the enclosed disc on which the Product is recorded is free from defects in materials and workmanship under normal use and service for a period of ninety (90) days from the date of purchase. In the event of a defect in the disc covered by the foregoing warranty, McGraw-Hill will replace the disc.

LIMITATION OF LIABILITY: NEITHER McGRAW-HILL, ITS LICENSORS NOR THE AUTHORS SHALL BE LIABLE FOR ANY INDIRECT, SPECIAL OR CONSEQUENTIAL DAMAGES, SUCH AS BUT NOT LIMITED TO, LOSS OF ANTICIPATED PROFITS OR BENEFITS, RESULTING FROM THE USE OR INABILITY TO USE THE PRODUCT EVEN IF ANY OF THEM HAS BEEN ADVISED OF THE POSSIBILITY OF SUCH DAMAGES. THIS LIMITATION OF LIABILITY SHALL APPLY TO ANY CLAIM OR CAUSE WHATSOEVER WHETHER SUCH CLAIM OR CAUSE ARISES IN CONTRACT, TORT, OR OTHERWISE. Some states do not allow the exclusion or limitation of indirect, special or consequential damages, so the above limitation may not apply to you.

U.S. GOVERNMENT RESTRICTED RIGHTS: Any software included in the Product is provided with restricted rights subject to subparagraphs (c), (1) and (2) of the Commercial Computer Software-Restricted Rights clause at 48 C.F.R. 52.227-19. The terms of this Agreement applicable to the use of the data in the Product are those under which the data are generally made available to the general public by McGraw-Hill. Except as provided herein, no reproduction, use, or disclosure rights are granted with respect to the data included in the Product and no right to modify or create derivative works from any such data is hereby granted.

GENERAL: This License Agreement constitutes the entire agreement between the parties relating to the Product. The terms of any Purchase Order shall have no effect on the terms of this License Agreement. Failure of McGraw-Hill to insist at any time on strict compliance with this License Agreement shall not constitute a waiver of any rights under this License Agreement. This License Agreement shall be construed and governed in accordance with the laws of the State of New York. If any provision of this License Agreement is held to be contrary to law, that provision will be enforced to the maximum extent permissible and the remaining provisions will remain in full force and effect.